The New Lion of Damascus

The New Lion of Damascus
Bashar al-Asad and Modern Syria

David W. Lesch

Yale University Press
New Haven and London

For information about this and other Yale University Press publications, please contact:
   U.S. Office: sales.press@yale.edu   yalebooks.com
   Europe Office: sales@yaleup.co.uk   www.yaleup.co.uk

Set in Minion by J&L Composition, Filey, North Yorkshire
Printed in Great Britain by St Edmundsbury Press Ltd, Bury St Edmunds

Library of Congress Cataloging-in-Publication Data

Lesch, David W.
  The new Lion of Damascus: Bashar al-Asad and modern Syria/
David W. Lesch.—1st ed.
    p. cm.
  Includes bibliographical references and index.
  ISBN 0–300–10991–1 (cl.: alk. paper)
  1. Syria—Politics and government—2000–2. Assad, Bashar, 1965–
I. Title.
  DS98.6.L47 2005
  956.9104′2—dc22

                                    2005011804

A catalogue record for this book is available from the British Library.

10 9 8 7 6 5 4 3 2 1

Contents

Illustrations

Plates

1. Bashar al-Asad, aged three.
2. The Asad family with President and Mrs. Nixon, 1974.
3. Bashar and Basil al-Asad with their parents.
4. Bashar assisting with eye surgery, 1992.
5. President Bashar in Homs, June 2003.
6. President Bashar with his wife, Asma, and children, January 2004.
7. President Bashar with family, summer 2003.
8. Popular portrait of President Bashar.
9. President Bashar with José Maria Aznar, 2001.
10. President Bashar with Colin Powell, May 2003.
11. Pope John Paul II visiting Damascus, May 2001.
12. President Bashar with Tony Blair, 2002.
13. President Bashar with King Abdullah of Saudi Arabia, 2005.
14. President Bashar with Husni Mubarek, 2005.
15. President Bashar with Muammar al-Qadhdhafi, March 2005.
16. President Bashar with Emile Lahhoud.
17. President Bashar with Vladimir Putin, 2005.
18. The author with President Bashar, June 2004.
19. President Bashar at a military occasion.

All photographs are reproduced here courtesy of the Photo Archives of the Office of President Bashar al-Asad.

Preface

The population of Syria is a little over eighteen million, 38 percent of which is below the age of fourteen. Approximately 90.3 percent of the population is Arab, including some four hundred thousand Palestinian refugees, with Kurds, Armenians, and a smattering of other ethnicities comprising the remaining 9.7 percent. Sunni Muslims account for 74 percent of the population, with the Alawites at 12 percent, Christians 10 percent, Druze 3 percent, and Jews and some other obscure Muslim sects about 1 percent. Geographically, Syria measures 71,504 square miles (185,170 square kilometers), including the Israeli-occupied Golan Heights—all in all about the size of North Dakota. The capital and largest city in Syria, Damascus, has a population of approximately five million, Aleppo has 4.5 million, Homs (Hims) 1.8 million, Hama 1.6 million, and Latakia one million.[1]

Syria is a country that has been called a crossroads of civilization for the history it has experienced, witnessed, and contributed to over the millennia. Of late, however, it is probably a nation that feels as if it is more in the cross hairs than the crossroads. From the U.S. point of view, Syria has been on the wrong side of history with respect to the current situation in Iraq, Lebanon, and Israel, the global war on terrorism, and the growth of democracy in the Middle East. Syria is an important country in each of these areas. It is also a country in transition after the death of long-time Syrian ruler Hafiz al-Asad in 2000.

His son Bashar succeeded him. He inherited a worn-down dictatorship, and soon he encountered momentous regional and international events that to date have enveloped Syria as they have much of the rest of the Middle East. In the face of this change, Syria has been accused of being stuck in the past, and in many ways it is. Bashar wants the country to be seamlessly integrated into this changing environment rather than coerced. There are many in Syria who do not want to make the adjustment for fear of losing the political and economic positions they enjoyed during the reign of Hafiz al-Asad. These are the multi-dimensional complexities that have confronted the young Syrian president. He has waded through these domestic, regional, and international challenges with some success and some failure. The question remains, however, whether Bashar will still be in power when the waters settle down, and if so, what type of ruler will he be and what type of country will he rule over? Will he become just another Middle Eastern dictator who muddles his country along through the torment from year to year, or will he lead Syria in a new direction that is more at the crest of the wave rather than being washed away in its wake? Will the dictatorship created by his father mold Bashar into the reluctant dictator, or will he become a new type of Syrian leader? The fate of Syria will say much about what type of Middle East will emerge in the near future, and that fate is very much tied to the person of Bashar al-Asad.

At an individual level, Bashar al-Asad is interesting to me for two reasons in particular. First, I find the story of his rise to power as president of Syria a compelling one, particularly as he was not earmarked for the presidency nor was it the career path he originally chose. It is not as though he went from being a provincial governor or city mayor to being president, or even from being a corporate icon to holding the highest position in the land. He essentially went from being an ophthalmologist to becoming the president of a country—not quite the segue one expects. I can relate to some extent with and am sympathetic toward the adjustment in his life. I, too, had a sudden career change, although it was not quite as dramatic as Bashar's. I was the number one draft pick of the Los Angeles Dodgers baseball club in the 1980 winter draft (when there was both a winter and summer draft). I played for two years in the Dodger minor league system, incurring more injuries than victories as a pitcher, my brief baseball career mercifully coming to an end with a rotator cuff injury. I then somehow went in to what seemed be the completely polar opposite direction of academia, or as one person put it, from the "pitching mound to the podium." As such, I have an intrinsic interest in those who have gone through a similar transformation, analyzing the traits that one brings from one career to the other, the smoothness or difficulty of the transition, etc.

More important, though, I was interested in finding out first hand who Bashar really was. Even to someone who specializes on Syria, he was something of an enigma—as he was to most of the world outside of Syria. The question making the rounds regarding Bashar had to do with whether or not he was really in control, whether there were leftovers from his father's regime in the government that were running the show, with Bashar as a compliant front man whose only appreciable asset was the fact that his last name was Asad. Was he a closet tyrant or a closet reformer as different groups at different times have made him out to be? What better way to explore the answers to these questions than to go to the horse's mouth. It is easy to throw darts from afar based on second-hand reports and rumors often constructed with a tendentious slant. I am fully aware of the critique of Bashar and Syria. I, myself, have in a small way contributed to it; indeed, I authored the chapter on Syria in the most recent annual Freedom House survey of democratic governance. In it I gave Syria low scores in the areas of civil liberties, rule of law, anti-corruption and transparency, and accountability and public voice, and I recommended dramatic new measures to improve the overall political, juridical, and business environments in the country.[2] But I wanted to fill in the other side of the equation first before I totaled the sum of its parts. Whether you agree or disagree with Syria's stance on a variety of issues, it is important to learn more about how the Syrian leadership views the world and its country's position in the region. A better understanding of this is necessary in order to construct cogent and sagacious policies toward Damascus. It is an exercise in which many Syrians need to engage as well, *vis-à-vis* the United States and Israel.

I started this project about three years ago, when my interest in and curiosity about the new president of Syria really began. I contacted my colleague and good friend Dr. Ghias Barakat, who had been at the University of Aleppo and was intimately involved in the Syrian Computer Society, of which Bashar was chair before he became president. Soon after assuming office, Bashar brought Ghias, as well as a number of others from the Syrian Computer Society and university settings, into the government. Ghias became a member of the Baath party's Regional Command, the highest body in the party and one of the more powerful organs in the state. In this position and because of his past relationship with him, Ghias could contact Bashar directly. So in early 2002 I brought my idea of writing a book about Bashar and modern Syria to Ghias' attention. He very much liked the idea, and himself brought it to Bashar's attention. I knew that, in typical Syrian fashion, it may take a couple of years before I'd even receive a response, and lo and behold, almost two years to the day after I originally proposed the idea, I received word from one of Ghias' friends, Dr. Imad Moustapha, who happened to become the Syrian ambassador to the United States in February 2004, that Bashar had approved the project and agreed to meet with me.

I spent about three weeks in Syria in May to June 2004 conducting most of my interviews for the book, during which time I met extensively with Bashar on a number of occasions in different settings. I again met with Bashar in May 2005, this time to gather his thoughts on the situation following the withdrawal of Syrian forces from Lebanon in late April. Throughout this roughly year-long period I also maintained an e-mail correspondence with Bashar when necessary, primarily for the purpose of follow-up questions and clarifications. I felt I really got to know the man as well as the head of a country, and this is in no small measure due to Bashar's own unpretentious and extremely personable demeanor. He was very welcoming. I think being close in age also helped, as we could discuss socio-cultural affairs from a similar generational perspective and background. He was also very cooperative in setting up meetings with other leading Syrian figures as well as some of his lifelong friends, childhood teachers, and family members.

No questions were off-limits, and I believe he tried to answer every question in as straightforward a way as he possibly could. There were obviously some questions that were particularly sensitive, to which he could only respond so much, and there were some responses that conformed to the rote lines that have been expressed through the media over the years—this was to be expected, especially on issues relating to Israel and Lebanon. But overall I was immensely pleased with his forthrightness and the extemporaneous way in which he responded to my queries.

I told Bashar that I was not an apologist for Syria, and he said he already knew that, having read some of my works that had been critical of Syria, especially during his father's tenure. He understood that I would call it as I see it; however, I think he correctly understood as well that I am someone who would treat him—and Syria in general—fairly, having visited the country on numerous occasions and developed a large number of friends and contacts. Often when writing about a particular individual, an author can get too close to his subject in a way that may affect his or her objectivity. I certainly grew to like the man at a personal level—almost everyone who meets him has a similar experience. Maybe at some subconscious level it is easier or more comforting to write about someone you like and respect rather than the obverse. But I also believe I maintained my objectivity; in fact, what has drawn me to Bashar on a personal level is all part of a package that I believe bodes well for Syria in the long run, if he is able to survive the multitude of problems and difficulties he is currently confronting. In that sense, yes, I would like to see him succeed. If I am reading him correctly, his own personal success would be good for Syria, good for the region, and ultimately good for U.S.-Syrian relations.

This is not a book engineered from the beginning as an attempt to redefine the image of Syria in general or Bashar al-Asad in particular. I went into this fully prepared—and in some ways expecting—to reveal the "evil truth," thus confirming at least elements of the largely negative image of the country and the man that prevails today in the United States. By early 2005 Bashar's image had deteriorated so much in the United States that he was frequently referred to in print and on television as the "evil eye doctor," an unfortunate and gross mischaracterization that consciously or unconsciously even contains undertones suggesting equivalence with Nazis who engaged in inhuman medical experiments in World War Two. But that is not what I found. There are some elements who, no matter what the evidence to the contrary, do not want to read or hear anything good about Syria or Bashar, a subject I tackle later in the book; indeed, they may contend that the Syrians really pulled off a "con-job" on me—I like to think I am more perspicacious than that. But for those people who cast Syria in a negative light, a view that is sometimes richly deserved, yet still remain open-minded to the possibilities of learning about the other perspective and understanding context, I hope this book will compel them to think twice about this country and about this young Syrian president. If at the end of the book you come to the conclusion that, "yes, maybe we should give this man a chance," then you would be coming to the same conclusion that I did at the end of my journey. It is a most worthy change of heart—I know, because it happened to me.

The book begins by introducing the reader to Bashar and his family, particularly the emergence of his father as a leading figure in Syria. The reader then goes on to learn about many of the important events in the Middle East over the last forty years or so that have had a direct bearing upon Syria. This provides historical context for much of what Syria encounters presently. Following this, we turn to Bashar's adulthood, from his time spent studying ophthalmology in London to his return to Syria as the putative heir apparent to his father. The primary domestic and foreign policy issues with which Bashar is faced are then examined one by one: the United States and Lebanon; Israel; Iraq; and internal reform. Each chapter provides additional historical context in more specific terms. The reader will notice that some events and occurrences are referenced more than once, each time from a different viewpoint. This reveals the interrelatedness of all of the issues, how events in one arena affect progress in another and how the pertinent leaders need to contemplate their actions and policies in a multidimensional fashion.

As in any research project, this book represents the collective efforts of many more people than just the author. First and foremost, I would like to thank Dr. Ghias Barakat and Dr. Imad Moustapha for their efforts to facilitate this project. They are good friends and represent the best of what Syria has to offer. I would also like to thank Dr. Robert O. Freedman, one of the leading lights in the field for years. Bob has been supportive of this project from the very beginning, and his comments on drafts of the manuscript have, as usual, made the final product infinitely better. Former U.S. ambassador to Syria, Theodore (Ted) Kattouf, and a leading Syria reformer and critic of the regime,

Ammar Abd al-Hamid, have provided me with crucial and valuable insights into the country and the regime that they were uniquely placed to provide, one from serving there, one from living there—both from having an intimate and nuanced understanding of the complexities of what is Syria.

Heather McCallum, a senior editor at Yale University Press, has been someone with whom it has been an absolute joy to work. She recognized the value and utility of this project the second she heard about it and worked assiduously to make it happen. I wish all publishers—and authors—were fortunate enough to have someone like her. Trinity University in San Antonio, Texas, has been supportive of my efforts, having generously funded most of the research, thus allowing me to complete the project in the timely fashion that I had envisioned and wanted. The outgoing and incoming chairs of the Department of History at Trinity, Char Miller and John Martin, respectively, have also been most helpful in facilitating my efforts. I would also like to thank Peter Coveney, a (now former) senior editor at Oxford University Press, who graciously allowed me to delay the delivery of my manuscript on a history of the Arab-Israeli conflict I am writing for Oxford in order to complete this book— he is a true professional. Others who have assisted in one way or another—by commenting on my various writings on Syria, providing suggestions regarding sources, suggesting questions for my interviews, giving administrative assistance, etc., for all of which I am no less grateful—are the following: Nayef al-Yasin, Joshua Landis, Bassam al-Kahouaji, JCLS, Eunice Herrington, Adeeb al-Ashkar, Mazen Daud, Naji Saba, Naji al-Rashan, and Yasser Hourieh. Finally, I could not complete a project of any appreciable length and investment of time without the extraordinary support of my wife, Suzanne, and son Michael, to whom this book is so appropriately dedicated.

Note on the Text

The transliteration of Arabic words into English varies quite a bit depending upon whom or what publication is doing the translating. More often than not I selected the more recognizable version rather than a strict transliteration: for example, "Hussein" rather than "Husayn"; "Nasser" rather than "Nasir"; and "Faisal" rather than "Faysal." Sometimes the transliteration I utilize is different from that which is employed in quotes from other sources in the text: for instance, I write "Hizbollah" whereas in newspapers it often appears as "Hezbollah." In addition, I have eliminated the diacritical marks for Arabic sounds and consonants to facilitate reading and recognition: for example, I write "Baath" instead of the more accurate transliteration of "Ba`th" that includes a diacritical mark for the Arabic consonant "`ayn" for which there is no English-language consonant equivalent.

In addition, I have given a more neutral appellation to some of the Arab-Israeli wars over the years. The Arab-Israeli conflict has been and still is such a politically charged dynamic that oftentimes how a person designates a particular event says more about where they stand on the issue rather than being a reference to the event itself. As such, for the seminal conflict in this arena in 1967, I simply refer to it as the "1967 Arab-Israeli war" rather than the "June war" or the "Six-Day War." Similarly, I refer to the 1973 conflict as the "1973 Arab-Israeli war" rather than the "Ramadan war," "Yom Kippur war," or "October war." And even though Israel did not come into being officially until May 1948, I refer to the 1947 to 1949 conflagration simply as the "1947–1949 Arab-Israeli war" rather than the "Israeli War of Independence" or the "Palestine war." Along these lines, since the international community, including the United States, still recognizes Tel Aviv as the official capital of Israel, I use this rather than Jerusalem in some references to Israeli policy even though the seat of government in Israel is clearly located in Jerusalem. The various sides to the conflict also give different names to bodies of water or tracts of land. I have attempted to be as neutral and objective in this regard as possible.

Syria

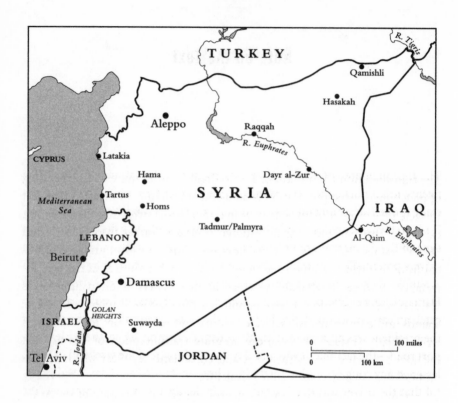

Chapter 1

Two Phone Calls

The thoroughfare connecting Damascus with its international airport some twenty miles outside the city is one of the easiest rides in the country, especially if one is traveling on it early in the morning to catch an a.m. flight out. It is a well-manicured, smooth four-lane highway with very little traffic at this time of the day. If you are in a hurry you can stay in the fast lane, and Syrian drivers potentially impeding your progress typically shift to the slow lane on a simple flicking of your lights or tapping of your horn. When exiting Damascus upon one of my recent trips to Syria, I was, indeed, in a rush to catch an early morning flight. The driver I had assigned to me by the office of the president was approaching eighty miles an hour on the virtually clear airport road—the fact that it was a Friday, the beginning of the weekend in Syria, lessened any congestion that might have been there on a workday. I was grateful that the driver was driving fast and efficiently, but as we approached the airport I began to entertain some unnerving feelings and thoughts. It was not that I felt I was in any danger, but I began to remember what it must have been like on a day back in January 1994 under somewhat similar circumstances.

That day was a Friday as well—January 21, 1994. It was on this day that Basil al-Asad, the eldest son of Syrian President Hafiz al-Asad, was killed in a car accident just outside Damascus International Airport. He, too, was leaving Syria, in his case traveling on a tourist visit to Germany. He was driving his own car, and he was driving it very fast, as one is apt to do on this road. It was very early in the morning, about 7:00 a.m., and there was virtually no traffic. Yet there was one significant difference between my Friday drive to the airport and the one Basil encountered over a decade ago. On January 21, 1994, it was a very foggy morning, which is not unusual in Syria in the winter months as the days and evenings can be quite climatically disparate at times, often resulting in fog in the early hours. There is a roundabout that is wide in circumference lying just at the end of the airport road and at the entrance into the airport itself. If one is driving fast, even on a clear day, it kind of sneaks up on you—even my driver had to apply the brakes heavily in order to negotiate the turns. Basil had made this drive on many occasions, but on this one morning he did not see the roundabout amid the dense fog. Instead of going right, he went straight ahead at high speed and the car rolled over several times. Basil apparently hit his head on the corner where the front window and the door meet, in between the airbags—he died immediately from the severe head injury. He was thirty-two years old. He was also generally considered to be the heir apparent to his father, as the next president of Syria.

London, England, is two hours behind Damascus. Basil's brother Bashar was there as an ophthalmologist continuing his studies at the Western Eye Hospital, part of the St. Mary's Hospital system. The phone in his flat rang at about 7:00 a.m. local time, as he was typically getting ready for another day of ophthalmological study and clinical work. He was told the news that his brother had died. He probably did not fully digest it at the time, but his world had just changed dramatically. His first thoughts, of course, were ones of shock and sadness. This was viewed, and rightly so, as such a tragedy for the family and, indeed, for the country. A charismatic, outgoing, and popular leading figure in the country had been struck down in his prime in an almost inexplicable and certainly unexpected fashion. Bashar was very close to Basil. They shared the same room when they were children, and although they were different in various ways, Bashar looked up to Basil as any younger brother does to his elder sibling. As the eldest son, Basil undertook a number of responsibilities on behalf of his father, which was very typical in Arab families. He seemed to be following in his father's footsteps in terms of accumulating leadership positions in the country, which is why it was widely viewed, especially from outside Syria, that he was being groomed to succeed his father.

After the initial shock wore off, Bashar began to wonder if he would be able to continue his studies in London. Now he was the eldest son, and that entails certain responsibilities that Bashar knew might alter his career plans. Interestingly, his father wanted him to return to London to complete his studies and not immediately become involved in the "family business," so to speak. In terms of expectations and unexpected career paths, Bashar's story reminds me very much of that of Michael Corleone in the Godfather movies. Michael was the one son who had seemingly shunned the family business, setting out a course for himself that was much different than that of his siblings, particularly his own elder brother, Sonny. Only after Sonny was killed and his father was in ill health did he feel compelled to engage in the family business in an active and intimate manner. In a way, Michael was the reluctant "godfather," yet he would become as cunning and powerful as his father ever was. It still remains to be seen what type of leader Bashar will emerge as in the long run, but it is clear to me that he also was something of the reluctant president, at least at first, yet he has immersed himself into the office with gusto, and his career as an ophthalmologist seems like a distant memory. He tried not to be emotional after his brother died, as is his demeanor, and Bashar was a rock in the traumatic immediate aftermath of Basil's death not only for the Asad clan members but also for Basil's closest friends, who leaned on the younger brother in a way that foreshadowed the respect a younger man would garner from his peers and elders throughout the country as president. Bashar quickly thought about the future for himself and his family—he did not have time to be emotional.

It was Saturday, June 10, 2000. Saturday is the second day of the weekend in Syria, Friday being the day when most Muslims attend the communal mosque, so it was supposed to be a fairly quiet morning before the workweek geared up again on Sunday. It was early, and Bashar was cycling and lifting weights at one of his frequent workouts at a gym near his family home in the Malki district of Damascus, which is not that far from the American embassy.

He received a phone call.

Hafiz al-Asad, the president of Syria since coming to power in an intra-Baath party coup in November 1970, the inveterate, taciturn, and implacable leader who had reached iconic status for a host of different reasons depending on one's perspective in the region, had died. In many ways, when you visit Syria today, five years after his death, you could be excused for thinking that Hafiz is still alive and in power. While his portraits are not nearly as omnipresent as they were in the past, when he was alive, since Bashar has generally eschewed the cult-like tendencies Syrians accorded his father, Hafiz al-Asad's images still leave an impressionable imprint on the country; indeed, about halfway along the two-hour drive north from Damascus to Homs there is a huge statue of the former president perched atop a hill overlooking the road, as if even in death he is still at least in spirit guiding and overseeing the country, and by implication, his son.

Bashar was aware the end was near, and his father had told him that he would not be around much longer. The son was often by his ailing father's side at home, but even though it was somewhat expected, it is still an emotional moment when a parent passes on. Bashar believed he needed to forgo emotion, at least outwardly—it was not a time to be emotional; that could happen later. Of more immediate concern was what would happen to the country— would there be instability? Most believe he was being groomed for succession, but according to Bashar, his father never mentioned or pushed the notion of his son succeeding him. Even if the latter is true, the possibility certainly raised its head in a very real and serious fashion almost the second after

Hafiz al-Asad died. On June 11, Bashar was promoted to lieutenant-general and named Supreme Commander of the Armed Forces; the same day he was also nominated by the Baath party, the ruling instrument in Syria since 1963, for the presidency (there were no other nominees). On June 24, at a previously scheduled annual meeting of the Baath party Regional Command, Bashar was elected secretary-general of the Arab Socialist Resurrection (Baath) Party, or ASRP. Three days later the Syrian parliament voted in agreement with the Baath nomination, and in a subsequent general referendum, the Syrian public concurred with 97.29% of the vote. On July 17, 2000, Bashar took the constitutional oath, and he delivered his inauguration speech.

The combination computer nerd, ophthalmologist, devoted family man, westernized pop-culturist, outgoing and caring friend, humble and reluctant leader, avid photographer, health and fitness advocate, and lurking reformer had all of a sudden become a Middle Eastern dictator. He entered upon a region, and soon a world, in turmoil. The change of president alone would have been enough to make his task a complicated one in Syria, but he soon had to deal with the regional and international repercussions of the Palestinian al-Aqsa intifada (uprising) that erupted in September 2000, the attacks on the World Trade Center in New York and the Pentagon in Washington, DC, a year later, and the shattering American response first in Afghanistan in late 2001 and then in Iraq in 2003. It was and continues to be anything but a stable and benevolent neighborhood for what most outside of Syria believe was and is a young and untested leader. What is Syria's future? Is Bashar up to the job? Will the dictatorship continue?

Chapter 2

The Asads of Syria

The family name Asad, meaning "lion" in Arabic, had in 1927 been given to Hafiz al-Asad's father, Ali Sulayman, whose family name had been "Wahhish" (beast). According to Patrick Seale's magnificent biography of Hafiz al-Asad, the commonly accepted story behind the change of name was that it reflected Ali's having "so distinguished himself as a pillar of village society" in Qurdaha that the other leading families acclaimed him as a "lion" and no longer a "wahhish."[1] Qurdaha was a traditionally poor and neglected Alawite village in the mountains marking off the coastal plain to the east of the port city of Latakia, a locale that has become something of a beach resort and getaway for many in Syria and from across the Arab world. It is also where the Asads have had a summer vacation villa for about 30 years. The Alawites are an obsure offshoot of Twelver Shiite Islam. They venerate Ali ibn Abi Talib as the "bearer of divine essence," second only to the Prophet Muhammad himself. Ali was the son-in-law and cousin of Muhammad, the fourth caliph or successor to the Prophet as leader of the Islamic community, and one of the seminal figures in Islamic history. The name "Alawite" or "Alawi" translates into "those who follow Ali." Also known as Nusayris, a name derived from a ninth-century Muslim prophet, Muhammad ibn Nusayr al-Namiri, the Alawites integrate some Christian and even Persian Zoroastrian rituals and holidays into their faith. For this reason, Sunni Muslims and even most Shiite Muslims have considered Alawite Islam to be heretical. The great thirteenth- to fourteenth-century Sunni Islamic scholar Ibn Taymiyya issued a fatwa, or legal ruling, calling the Alawites greater infidels than Christians, Jews, or idolaters, and he authorized a jihad (struggle or holy war) against them. As such, the Alawites have been a persecuted minority over the centuries in what is today the northern reaches of Syria and Lebanon. It would, therefore, be a struggle for any Alawite to advance to a leadership position in an unwelcoming environment.

Because of his family name, Hafiz al-Asad became known in the Middle East as the "lion of Damascus." It is a nickname he probably liked very much, connoting strength, power, and even ruthlessness. Sometimes his sons were affectionately called his "cubs," implying that one or all of his four sons could become the next "lions" of Damascus. This was certainly the case with his eldest son, Basil, who seemed to fit the mold, but Bashar appeared to be altogether different.

The Emergence of Hafiz

Hafiz was the first of the Asad clan to receive formal education. He was born in 1930, when Syria was under the control of France as a mandate awarded to Paris after the defeat of the Ottoman empire in World War I. France had a millennium-long historic connection with Syria going back to the time of the Crusades. As it had been in its other colonial or pseudo-colonial (since "mandate" was really just a more palatable term for colonial rule) territories, France was reluctant to shed the influence it had gained during the days of empire and was eager to keep up with the British in the postwar reconfigurations in the Middle East and elsewhere. It bequeathed to Syria a political, legal, and educational system that still affects the way things operate (or are intended to operate) today.

It was this educational tradition that Hafiz al-Asad was able to take advantage of in order to improve his chances for successful upward social mobility, an opportunity that was generally not available to the minority Alawite Muslim sect to which he—and his village—belonged; indeed, connections to the French in any capacity were frowned upon by the majority Sunni Muslim population for nationalistic reasons, and Syria had been the birthplace of a more mature form of Arab nationalism that frowned upon if not castigated those who associated with the French. But the lowly Alawites were desperate to latch themselves to any ladder that could improve their collective lot, deprived and discriminated against as they had been for centuries. More widespread access to education was only seen as a benefit, and, eventually, enrolling in the military, looked down upon by most Syrians as an exercise in colonial appeasement, would become a bastion of Alawite participation. It would soon provide an opening to gain influence in the post-World War II environment, when the military symbiotically converged with party politics to climb to power by the early 1960s, bringing people such as Hafiz al-Asad along for the ride. So, as many other Alawites had done before him, Hafiz joined the military air academy in 1952, graduating as a pilot at the rank equivalent to lieutenant in 1955.

Hafiz al-Asad joined the Baath party in 1946, the same year that Syria received its formal independence from a bedraggled France after World War II.

The last contingent of French troops departed in April. The country was now in the hands of a group of politicians who had gained popularity from their long struggle against Ottoman and French suzerainty; however, these politicians also had very little experience in the everyday operations of running a government and, in some cases, had become disreputable in the eyes of many Syrians for having cooperated with and/or been too conciliatory toward the French mandate regime in the interest of obtaining and maintaining their political and economic status.[2] The 1947 parliamentary elections gave visible indications of the growing fragmentation of the Syrian polity as well as the increasing public disenchantment with the mandate-era politicians. The elections of 1947 also introduced interested observers to the Baath or Resurrection party, an ardently nationalistic group operating under a pan-Arab socialist doctrine. It would systematically improve its power position in Syria to the point of virtually dictating by 1955 the government's neutralist and largely anti-West foreign policy.[3]

The Baath party was primarily the product of the ideological meeting-of-the-minds of three Syrian men, Michel Aflaq, a Christian Arab, Salah al-Din Bitar, a Sunni Arab, and Zaki al-Arzuzi, an Alawite. At first flirting with communism while studying together in Paris from 1929 to 1934, Aflaq and Bitar ultimately rejected communist doctrine and promoted the "trinity of indissolubly fused" ideas: Arab unity, freedom, and socialism.[4] The Baath became the foremost proponent of Arab neutralism a decade before Egyptian President Gamal Abd al-Nasser made the term famous. The communists, small in number though they were, were also opposed to the so-called capitalist reactionaries and imperialists, but they were under suspicion from the Baath because their ideology was anything but home-grown, and their actions were dictated by another outside power, the Soviet Union. They did, however, share the objective of ridding the country of malevolent outside interference and maintaining Syrian independence. As such, the two groups cooperated from time to time against identical external threats, but as would become apparent into the late 1950s and early 1960s, their latent differences typically manifested themselves in an open breach.

The Baath party might have remained an ideological party on the periphery if it were not for its association with the parliamentary deputy from Hama, Akram al-Hawrani. He ultimately provided the muscle for the Baath through his close ties with various elements of the Syrian military, which would soon become the final political arbiter in the country. The relationship would prove to be symbiotic, for Hawrani's Arab Socialist party was in need of an ideological foundation, which the Baath was amply qualified to provide. The formal merger occurred in late 1952 while Hawrani, Aflaq, and Bitar were all in exile in Lebanon. This was a propitious occurrence that had a lasting effect upon the future of Syria, for the new Arab Socialist Resurrection Party (ASRP, or still simply referred to as the Baath party) was now endowed with the political wherewithal to seriously contend for power in Syria and thereafter force upon whatever regime that was formally in power the increasingly popular foreign policy edicts of anti-Zionism and neutralist Arab nationalism. The Baath became the voice of opposition to Western imperialism and Israel, and to anyone in the government who was seen as collaborating with either one of these.

The seminal event during this period, however, was the first Arab-Israeli war of 1947 to 1949 (also known as the First Palestine War or the Israeli War of Independence), during which time, in May 1948, Israel declared itself a state. The Syrian regime at the time, composed of many of the so-called nationalists of the mandate period, was utterly discredited by its corrupt and inept mishandling of a war that resulted in a humiliating defeat for all the Arab combatants, most of whom, including Syria, were more concerned about the strategic designs of rival Arab states than focused on coordinating military strategy against Israel.[5] The discontent among the populace and in the military following the war created an opening for the entrance of the army into Syrian politics with the overthrow of the regime in March 1949 by a military junta led by General Husni al-Zaim, a position from which the military has yet to retreat. The coup signaled an end to Syria's brief and immature encounter with parliamentary democracy and created the foundation for the important alliance between the Baath party and the military.

Hafiz was a rising star in the Baath party, which formally came to power in Syria in March 1963, less than a month after the party had risen to power for the first time in the Arab world when a combination of Baathists and other Arab nationalist groups toppled the regime of Abd al-Karim Qassim in Iraq in a bloody coup. In the relatively quiescent year of 1965, while Hafiz al-Asad was assiduously establishing himself as a leading figure in the party, he would have his third child, Bashar, in Damascus on September 11. A year later Hafiz would be promoted to commander of the Air Defense Forces as well as minister of defense. It would be in these two capacities that he would have a front-row seat a year after that, in 1967, in the most dramatic and earth-shattering of all the Arab-Israeli wars.

Father and Son

Bashar was the third of five children. As he fondly recalls, since he was the middle child he *had* to get along with all of his siblings. Bushra, the only daughter, was Hafiz and Anisa al-Asad's first-born. Basil was the eldest son, born in 1962. Bashar describes his childhood as "very normal." "We had a very normal family life. We had two very caring parents, and our happiness derived from these two caring parents." He played with his friends in the neighborhood, they came over often to play at his house, and other parents also visited his home to chat with his mother and cook meals. It seemed like a very open household, something that Bashar and his wife, Asma, have tried to replicate today with their home. Bashar still keeps in touch with many of his friends from his childhood years. He says that they always treated him as "one of the guys" when they were in elementary school together, i.e. not the son of the president. This is also a reflection of Bashar, since he himself eschews the trappings of presidency and power—he obviously wants to be seen as being as "normal" as possible, with family, friends, and a life outside the spotlight. This is the family environment in which he was raised, as opposed to many of his friends, classmates, and colleagues from powerful families in Syria who did everything they could to acquire the trappings of power and wealth. This did not appeal to Bashar; indeed, he viewed it as unnecessarily ostentatious and wasteful. He has always been and continues to be uncomfortable with his inherited family legacy and his position.

Bashar's family's house when he was a child was quite modest considering the fact that his father was a very powerful man in Syria in the first five years of his life, as minister of defense and commander of the air force, and of course from 1970 on as the leader of the country. It was a typical middle-class Damascene home at best, located in a residential area downtown near Seven Lakes Square, just north of the old city of Damascus. They lived on the third floor of the three-story building, which had the look of a condominium, with neighbors across the hall and below, although the Asad's had a prime location on the corner of the building at the intersection of two streets. The neighborhood has the air of the French mandate in architecture, with narrow streets and houses with terraces. The Asad family purchased the home in 1964, bought with a loan taken from a financial institution in the military—in essence, a military loan. They moved to a new home in 1973, three years after Hafiz had risen to power. The new home was almost as modest as the old one, although it was be located in the more upscale Malki district of Damascus, the location of a number of embassies and consulates (including the U.S. embassy) as well as the abodes of many leading Syrian officials. It is in this home, again on the third floor of a three-story typical middle-class Damascene building, that Bashar and his family still live today.

Bashar told me that when he was young, the children in the neighborhood played soccer and other games in and around the home near Seven Lakes

Square, often in the streets just outside. Interestingly, when I visited near his home in June 2004 I could see children playing soccer and rollerblading in the street outside his family compound. The only difference is that the entrance to the street is blocked off by security, as at least one nod to the fact that he is president, which, I am sure, the neighborhood children must love, because they never have to worry about traffic interrupting their activities. The sense of normalcy in family life attempted by Hafiz and Anisa al-Asad is immensely strong in Bashar and his wife, Asma al-Asad; indeed, Asma told me that she even has to make sure her blinds and curtains at her bedroom window are closed or else the neighbors next door would be able to peer inside! Not exactly the distance between rulers and ruled that we have come to expect from many kings, princes, emirs, presidents, and prime ministers in the Middle East.

The old home has a special place in the heart of Bashar, as it had also in his father's. The third floor was a library from 1973 until 1995, comprising mostly history and archeology books, reflecting Hafiz's voracious appetite for reading works in those two disciplines. Hafiz very much wanted his old home to become a library, and he refused repeated offers to turn it into a museum. The Department of Antiquities within the Ministry of Culture has maintained the home since his death. Today, the neighborhood has become a commercial center, and the rents are very high compared to what they were in the 1960s. It is fitting, however, that the occupant of the first floor of the building is an Internet service provider (called Cham Net). This mirrors the interests of the current president of Syria in technological progress. It also reflects the change that has occurred over the last 30 to 40 years. That the same building houses an ISP as well as an office of the Department of Antiquities serves as a metaphor for the duality of Syria and the struggle to adapt to the new without abandoning the old.

Bashar was very fond of sports and physical fitness as a youngster, and he continues to be today. So was his family, including, foremost, his father, with whom he used to play ping-pong periodically when he was a child, especially before Hafiz became president and was consumed for the most part with work. When I asked Bashar what would be good for Americans to see and learn about him if they were able to follow him around for a typical day in the life of the Syrian president, he responded:

> One of the most important things for me is sports. If you do not work out, you won't have the energy. Every other day I work out for a couple of hours in the morning, particularly on a stationary bike. I also make sure I see my family in the morning every day, and then I do my work . . . and

I make sure I see my family in the evening. If I have to work late, I go home early to see my children before they go to bed and then I go back to my office.

The attitudes, relationships, and discipline of sports and family are very much intertwined in his outlook toward life in general. One of Bashar's and Basil's friends recounted to me a story from their childhood. They were all playing soccer in the garage area of the residential building in which they lived when President Hafiz al-Asad appeared, heading to his car to go to work. He saw the children and came toward them. The children thought they might be in trouble, but all of a sudden Hafiz rolled up the legs of his pants and entered the game. This friend happened to be playing goalie, and he said that whenever Hafiz kicked the ball toward the goal, he would not try to stop it, allowing the president to score! Bashar played not only soccer, but also volleyball, badminton, and a host of water sports, such as water-skiing in the Mediterranean when the family would spend a good portion of the summer, as most well-to-do and powerful Syrian officials did, in the resort city of Latakia along the coast. Not only was this close to the ancestral origins of the Asads, but it also allowed them to escape the stifling heat of the Damascus summer. As the years went on, Bashar got into cycling and even boxing for a time. Today, he still enjoys water sports, and he tries to cycle regularly in order to stay in shape.[6]

The Importance of Education

For those who could gain entry and pay a slight fee, as opposed to taking advantage of the free education available to Syrians under the socialist welfare compact the Baath party established, schooling started quite early. This was the case with all of the Asad children. Bashar attended a well-known semi-private school called Laique, located on Baghdad Street just past Seven Lakes Square, near Bashar's first home. The school was built by the French in 1912, and by the 1960s it had attained a reputation as one of the best schools in the country. The word *laïque* in French means "lay," as in non-clerical, and refers to the secular nature of the French educational system; indeed, *laïcité* is at the heart of the separation of Church and State in the French constitution. The school itself is a prime example of the influence of France upon the educational system in Syria as well as the secular societal trends reinforced by Baathist ideology. The school had not only quality teachers, but also classrooms with high ceilings, which made them a bit cooler than those in most other schools. Today, the school is formally called the Institute of the Martyr

Basil al-Asad, named after Bashar's brother, although most in Damascus still refer to it simply as Laique. When Bashar first attended in 1968 at the age of three, the school had approximately 545 students, about two-thirds boys and the rest girls—today the school has about 2,300 students, with the same male-female ratio. A very high percentage of the students go on to the university, and although the school offers an all-around curriculum, it has acquired a reputation for special proficiency in math and the sciences. One could attend Laique from the age of three to the age of 18 and then go on to college. During Bashar's day, sub-elementary was from age three to five, elementary school from six to ten, preparatory from 11 to 13, and then secondary school from 14 to 18.[7]

Bashar described himself as being an average student; in some years he had good grades, and in some years he did not—his teachers at Laique described him as not an outstanding student in terms of grades, but better than average. He admitted to me that he actually attended another school, called Le Frère, in the last two years before attending the University of Damascus, i.e. the last two years of secondary school. His parents made the change because his grades in his last year at Laique in 1981 were not very good—he himself apparently did not care about his grades much at the time. One must remember that this was in the midst of the Muslim Brotherhood (Ikhwan al-Muslimun) uprising in Syria that severely tested the regime and the stability of the country. Hundreds of Syrian officials, soldiers, and civilians were killed by Islamic extremists, and there were a number of assassination attempts against Hafiz al-Asad, and certainly the president's family was fair game. Although Bashar says he was just spending too much time with his friends, under these conditions one might expect him not to be concerned with grades; however, his parents were, and they moved him to a school that was much smaller in size. Laique had grown considerably by the late 1970s, with almost 3,000 students and class sizes reaching 50 per section, with five sections per grade. By contrast, at Le Frère each grade had only one class, and it was an all-male school. His grades improved accordingly over the next year, especially in math, in which he had become somewhat deficient in his final year at Laique.

After speaking with two of Bashar's teachers at Laique—Lorraine Douna, who began there in 1973 and was Bashar's teacher in the fifth elementary grade in 1975, and Muwaffaq Rajab, who taught Bashar in his third preparatory year or ninth grade, both of whom are still there today—as well as interviewing one of the president's childhood friends at Laique from fourth to ninth grades, I find that one observation stands out: Bashar generally did not act like a privileged son of the president. He rarely took advantage of his position for gain. The implication, of course, is that a number of other sons and daughters of the Syrian elite, most of whom also attended Laique, did act as privileged members of society and attempted to take advantage of their parents' position in government or in the military.

There was almost amazement in the faces of the two teachers as they recalled that Bashar not only acted like one of the boys, but also desperately sought to be treated as any everyday student. He did not have the hordes of bodyguards that other children of the elite had.[8] He went on field trips with the students and traveled in the bus unlike some other privileged children who often arrived at such events in separate, chauffeur-driven cars. He very much enjoyed being with his friends, and he seemed to be genuinely popular in his classes for reasons other than that he was the son of the president. Bashar takes friendship very, very seriously, something that is not unusual in the Arab world. He has kept in touch with his closest friends from his years in school to this day, and he greatly enjoys just hanging out with them, something he is less able to do since he has become president, which is one of his biggest regrets. This also characterized the other members of the Asad brood, all of whom attended Laique, but one gets the sense that Bashar was more humble and unassuming than any of his siblings.

Knowing the purpose of my visit to Laique, the teachers were not going to offer up any terribly negative stories about Bashar, but I could see the sincerity with which they spoke when describing his politeness, a characteristic that was mentioned to me over and over by his teachers as well as his friends from throughout his lifetime, and something that struck me in my own observations of him. Even when he helped a teacher with a matter outside the school that only a member of the Asad family could deal with, Bashar would forget about it immediately and not lord it over the teacher for extra favors. He was hard working and a very inquisitive student. He was quiet, yet very calm, especially in situations where other students did not possess the same level of equanimity. Madame Lorraine and Mr. Muwaffaq described him as being very shy, almost to the point where he would blush when the teachers spoke to him or called on him in class. But one of his childhood friends described it as less shy and more self-effacing, because Bashar was a very outgoing individual with his friends, never shying away from a social event. In fact, Bashar himself is quick to say that he got into his share of trouble, especially when he was a rebellious teenager. He recounted to me a story that when he was 11 or 12 years old he invited all his friends from school to his house, about 20 in all. Once in the Asad household, they gathered all of the mattresses and laid them side-by-side in what is the equivalent of the family room. The object of the endeavor: to make a wrestling ring. They proceeded to wrestle vigorously, having a great time, exerting adolescent angst and energy—and also breaking several items in the room. He did not have to say another word to me—his look clearly revealed that he was soon on the receiving end of a mother's wrath!

Bashar is also described by all those with whom I spoke as having a strong character even as an adolescent, although he was very modest, which is not surprising considering the fact that the whole family followed the father's example of a relatively austere, modest lifestyle. The contrast with Saddam Hussein and his children, particularly Uday and Qusay, could not be more starkly apparent. For instance, the following was written about Uday and Qusay Hussein in a report appearing out of London in the *Weekly Telegraph*:

> Uday's classmates recall that, although he rarely did any work, he always came first in class. When Uday demanded extra time to finish a test, the teachers had to obey him, as he was always accompanied by half a dozen burly bodyguards, most of them ex-wrestlers. Both brothers frequently violated the dress code and broke school rules, driving their limousines on to the school campus. In 1984 ... Uday graduated from the University of Baghdad College of Engineering with an average grade of 98.5 per cent. Tutors who failed to give him full marks were tortured and lost their jobs.[9]

This type of behavior would be abhorrent to the Asads, and this is one of the reasons the Syrian people by and large over the years had genuine respect, if not affection, for the Asads, because they did not squander the national wealth for personal use. Quite to the contrary, Bashar and his siblings received less than stellar grades on many an occasion, indicating that the teachers were not pressured and did not feel intimidated—the children were compelled to succeed on their own merits for the most part.

Again in contrast to other members of the Syrian elite, Bashar's parents were actively involved in their children's schooling and activities. Bashar's progress reports every month were personally signed by Hafiz al-Asad. His parents would call the homes of Bashar's friends to inquire as to his whereabouts if he was late coming home. His mother would come to the school personally on Teacher's Day to speak with Bashar's instructors. Even with this parental attention, Bashar did not like to distinguish himself from the other students; indeed, Madame Lorraine still has Bashar's 1975 class picture that was taken on a class picnic just outside Damascus. Bashar had long, bushy, curly hair, was not at the center of the picture, and he was dressed like all the other students; indeed, the class has a typical 1970s mod look that could have been seen anywhere in the United States. As an indication of the importance to him of his time at Laique, Bashar drove himself to the school to cast his vote in the July 2000 referendum on whether or not he should be president. He inquired about his teachers who were still at the school and asked them if they needed anything in particular. It is clear that at least in Bashar's mind, the school was a very positive influence on his life, and his presence there for the referendum immediately showed the importance Bashar places on education.

One childhood friend of Bashar's recollected to me that even as a young boy the Syrian president had a very strong character—the strong, silent type is the picture that emerged over and over again; however, there was also a firm desire in Bashar to please people in the sense of trying to help them with specific problems. He was always polite in trying to meet various requests, a trait that continues to be associated with him. As such, Bashar has had a tendency during his lifetime to be non-confrontational. This view of the president has come from a variety of perspectives among those who are close to him, but it emerges not from a sense that this is because he is weak, but rather because of his strong character—he tries always to take the high road if possible. There are others, however, inside and outside Syria, who believe that Bashar is a relatively weak leader, especially when compared with his father. Certainly today there are fervent supporters of Bashar who wish he would be more overtly confrontational, particularly when it comes to pushing aside some of the deadwood in the government held over from his father's tenure in power. I tend to agree. As will be discussed in chapter nine, Bashar has taken some positive steps in this direction—he needs to do more.

A high-level Syrian official, let's call him Ali, recounted to me a story of when he was a teenager. He and his fiancée went to a disco one evening in Damascus, certainly one of the typical things that teens did—and continue to do—for nighttime entertainment in Syria. At the disco, one either dances on the floor or sits to the side of the dance floor and is content to watch the others express themselves to the music. Ali and his fiancée garnered a table next to the dance floor. Two young men, a bit younger than Ali, as well as a young woman entered the disco and proceeded to watch those who were dancing, but they had plopped themselves right in front of Ali and blocked his view of the dance floor. Ali was incensed, and sensing his manhood at risk in front of his fiancée, he started shouting at the three, employing some very choice words not fit to print. The older of the two young men apologized and moved off to the side to get out of Ali's line of vision. Suddenly, the manager of the disco along with several waiters frantically gathered a table and some chairs and set up a place for the three to sit near the dance floor. A bit bewildered and increasingly tense, Ali asked one of the waiters who the three were to warrant such special attention. The waiter said they were Bashar al-Asad, his younger brother Maher, and his sister, Bushra, three of President Hafiz al-Asad's five children. Ali had committed an affront of the highest order. A dramatic pall immediately overcame him as he thought the worst was about to happen. It didn't. No one said anything to Ali for the rest of the evening—there were never any negative repercussions. Ali obviously did not know Bashar at the time, and he probably jokes to himself that the president has now gotten him back by appointing him to such a difficult job! But Ali told me that in retrospect he is so grateful that all this occurred with Bashar and not some spoiled son of a high-level Syrian official; indeed, he is sure that many of these other pampered, corrupted sons would simply have taken out a gun and shot him on the spot, something, again, you might have expected from a Qusay or Uday Hussein.

A friend of Bashar's from his medical-school days told me of another story along the same lines. In their second year of medical school, there was a celebration of sorts at the University of Damascus held in the main auditorium. There was a progression of "very boring" speakers commenting on nationalistic themes. Every time Hafiz al-Asad's name was mentioned the audience erupted in applause. Bashar hated this. He felt that applauding just at the mere mention of a name was totally unnecessary, unless it was attached to some specific deed worthy of such accolade. So Bashar did not applaud as everyone else did. All of a sudden, a man from behind, who obviously did not know that it was Bashar al-Asad, hit him fairly hard on the back of the neck and berated him for not applauding. Bashar did not say a word; he just started to applaud politely when his father's name was mentioned from then on. His friends were very nervous because they thought Bashar would react negatively and that this man would have been at the very least roughed up and taken away. But Bashar did not want to make a scene, and he did not want to lord his inherited status over anyone else. Three months later the man came up to Bashar to apologize for the incident—one can only speculate the horror he must have felt when he found out who he had slapped on the back of the neck! Bashar simply responded that he should not worry about it—he recognized that he was just doing his job.

Brothers

Bashar's older brother, Basil, was not so reserved, although he was not known as one to fly off the handle. Basil was a dominant personality; one could not help but notice him in a group setting. Whereas Bashar tends to shy away from the limelight, Basil, while not desperately seeking it, was certainly more comfortable with the usual attention accorded a son of the president. A very close friend of Basil's since childhood, who became equally close to Bashar after

Basil's car accident in 1994, described the eldest son of Hafiz in the following manner:

> He [Basil] was a very enthusiastic person. He had a vision, and personally I think it was very similar to his father's vision. He had a very strong character and a very strong personality—you knew he was going to be a very influential person. He was like this since he was young because he used to be the "commander" in the family and would give orders to the rest of his siblings. He had the character of a leader. He was definitely ambitious, but primarily to serve his country. He felt strongly about building a modern Syria, and he used to be hands on in everything—he wanted to know all of the details and at the same time wanted to be very close to the people; he wanted to be a people person, and at the same time he wanted to be a leader. He was adamantly against everything that was wrong in the country. He used to get very upset, very upset when he saw something wrong. He convinced me to return to Syria [after studying in the United States], that it was important to serve your country—he would tell me that Syria cannot afford to lose good people; it needs them.[10]

This individual is one of the few people outside of the family who knew both Bashar and Basil extremely well. I asked him in what ways the two brothers were different, and he responded:

> They had the same parents so they had the same values. Maybe they approached problems in different ways, but they had the same intention of doing good, but they looked at things from different angles. The difference is that Basil was the type of person who was a bit more energetic—he used to take matters into his own hands in an energetic fashion. Bashar, on the other hand, is more of a cool person, maybe because of his medical background—he is very calm. In ten years I have never seen him lose his temper—I have seen him upset but he would never lose his temper. He has a very solid personality. He has a very solid mood and is not the kind of person who shows his ups and downs. He might be in a very serious matter but you cannot tell—he handles these situations in a very calm fashion— lots of equanimity.[11]

Bashar and Basil were very close. They shared the same bedroom in their old house near Seven Lakes Square. They often studied together, although being three years apart, they had different sets of friends while growing up. There does not seem to have been any overt rivalry between the two, other than what is normal among brothers. Bashar seemed to be settled on a different career path from Basil and satisfied with his choices. They seemed to have personalities that are quite common with first- and second-born sons: the elder one tends to be more outgoing and forceful, while the younger one tends to be more calm, reflective, and introspective. A question that many Syrians discuss is who would be the better president. Oftentimes the answer to this question reflects the type of Syria envisioned by the person responding. If it is a Syria that reflects more of what the father built and established during his long reign, based on enforced stability, steadfastness, independence, and strength, then Basil is usually the choice. If it is a Syria that is seen to require systemic change in order to move forward economically and politically, one that needs to better integrate itself in the global community through modernization, and a country that will emphasize diplomacy over force, and toleration over dictatorship, then Bashar is usually the choice. They even looked different: Basil was shorter and ruggedly handsome, while Bashar is tall like his father, with a gentle, erudite look. Even though most Syrians are ready for more pluralism and democratization, the one brother who is more favorably predisposed to this is also the perceived weaker leader, therefore possibly less able to implement such change. Basil, who was certainly a stronger personality, a military figure loved by his comrades-in-arms, could have possibly been in a better position to bring about such change, but his personality type and the base of support engendered by him might also have cemented another type of dictatorship. This is the fundamental dilemma in Syria today. One senses that many Syrians wish Bashar had some more Basil in him and that Basil had had more Bashar. But Bashar alone is now president.

The family of Hafiz al-Asad seems to have been very close, or, at least, close as one could be when the father is a workaholic, and for this a great deal of credit goes to Bashar's mother, Anisa al-Asad, who lives in the same compound with Bashar and Asma to this day—she still plays a very important role in his life. He eats dinner with her frequently, calls her three or four times a week, and every Friday evening if possible Bashar gathers the immediate family members with their spouses and children—and often his closest friends as well—for a dinner at his home. Anisa provides both Bashar and Asma with sage advice, because, as Asma indicates, she has already been through it all and can give the presidential couple a great deal of insight as to what to expect and how to react to the triumphs, trials, and tribulations of being the president and first lady of the country.[12] It is clear that family life, at least having a recognizable one, is very important to Bashar and his wife.

Bashar describes the atmosphere in his home—despite the concerted attempts to live a typical life—as being that of a "political family." In other words, despite attempts to insulate the family, various moments such as political crises, war, internal and external turbulence do, indeed, find their way into the home at least to some extent. He and Basil used to fight over newspapers to see who could read them first. They were very interested in public issues, sometimes at the expense of homework. The children were aware that their father was a very important man in the country, and they would soon accept the fact that he was not only Dad but also the president. Certainly one gets the sense that the children felt a responsibility to be knowledgeable about the country and the world, an unceasing curiosity to learn that they no doubt acquired from their parents.

One cannot be a member of a leading family in the Middle East without being directly and indirectly affected by the plethora of events that have befallen the region in its modern history. Before Bashar was even two years old, the Middle East had been torn asunder in a way that would define his father's presidency and, to date, his own.

Chapter 3

Syria in the Middle East

The Golan (Jawlan in Arabic) Heights is one of the most hotly contested areas in the world; in this case, the claimants are Syria and Israel. Geologically the Golan is part of a plateau formed during the Holocene epoch, i.e. within the last ten thousand years. It is a volcanic field that extends to the east and north-east of the Syrian-Israeli border almost to Damascus—all in all some 1,750 square kilometers in southern Syria. The Golan Heights, or at least that which was captured by Israel in 1967, covers approximately 1,250 square kilometers, including Mount Hermon at its northernmost point, making up about one percent of the total area of Syria.[1] The Golan Heights runs north–south along the Syrian and Israeli extant, bordered on the north by Lebanon and in the south by Jordan. The length of the territory is about sixty-five kilometers, while the width varies between twelve and twenty-five kilometers, the thickest portion almost smack in the middle of the traverse. The average height of the Golan is about 1,000 meters, rising up from 400 meters to 1,700 meters along the western escarpment overlooking the Huleh Valley in northern Israel, the most fertile agricultural land in the Jewish state. The tallest single point is Mt. Hermon (Jabal al-Shaykh in Syria), rising 2,224 meters above sea level. It is of great strategic value to whomever holds it (currently Israel) since it peers over much of southern Lebanon, northern Israel, southern Syria, and, of course, the Golan Heights itself.

The Golan Heights is geo-strategically important for two reasons primarily: 1) if Syria controls the Heights it has a strategic advantage looking down upon northern Israel either to initiate an offensive or to launch artillery barrages at northern Israeli towns and villages; on the other hand, when Israel controls the Golan Heights, it means its military is already sitting on the Golan plateau, only about 35 kilometers of flat, open territory away from Damascus; and 2) a major water resource, particularly important to Israel, runs through the Golan Heights as tributaries feeding into the Jordan River, the life-blood of Israel in terms of water capacity, itself running alongside the Golan Heights

The Syrian-Israeli Frontier

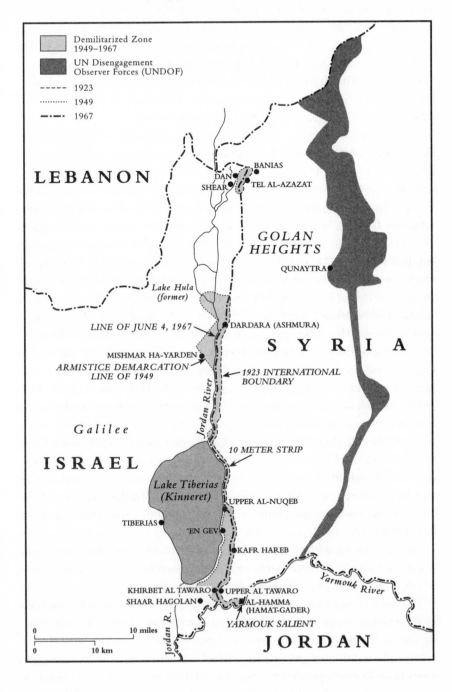

Demilitarized Zone
1949–1967

UN Disengagement
Observer Forces (UNDOF)

----- 1923

·········· 1949

—·—· 1967

LEBANON

BANIAS
DAN
SHEAR
TEL AL-AZAZAT

GOLAN
HEIGHTS

QUNAYTRA

Lake Hula
(former)

LINE OF JUNE 4, 1967

DARDARA (ASHMURA)

SYRIA

MISHMAR HA-YARDEN

ARMISTICE DEMARCATION
LINE OF 1949

1923 INTERNATIONAL
BOUNDARY

Jordan River

Galilee

ISRAEL

10 METER STRIP

Lake Tiberias
(Kinneret)

UPPER AL-NUQEB

TIBERIAS

'EN GEV

KAFR HAREB

Yarmouk River

KHIRBET AL TAWARO
SHAAR HAGOLAN

UPPER AL TAWARO
AL-HAMMA
(HAMAT-GADER)

YARMOUK SALIENT

Jordan R.

JORDAN

0   10 miles

0   10 km

and feeding into the Sea of Galilee (called Lake Tiberius in Syria, Lake Kinneret in Israel) on its northern shore and emerging again from its southern bank on down further into Israel, forming part of the border with the country of Jordan. The three main tributaries in the Golan Heights are the Dan, Hasbani, and Banyas rivers, all spring-fed by the western and southern slopes of the Mt. Hermon massif. Together the three tributaries contribute 500 million cubic meters of water per annum on average to the Jordan River, totaling some 30 percent of Israel's water requirements.

The 1974 disengagement agreement between Syria and Israel brokered by the United States following the October 1973 Arab-Israeli war established a demilitarized zone (DMZ) that runs continuously north–south along the eastern edge of the occupied Golan Heights on the existing Syrian border. United Nations Security Council Resolution 350 set up a UN Disengagement Observer Force (UNDOF) to patrol and monitor the ceasefire arrangement. The DMZ has been, relatively speaking, remarkably free of Israeli-Syrian confrontation since 1974, and the UN mission there is one of the great success stories in peacekeeping activities. Today there are about 1,050 UNDOF troops from six different countries stationed in and around the DMZ, along with scores of international and local civilian staff.[2] There are currently 33 Jewish settlements on the Golan Heights itself, numbering in total approximately 18,000 people. Qatzrin is the only town on the Heights, the other settlements largely being a mix of kibbutzim and moshavim. There are also about 17,000 Syrian Druze in four villages on the Golan Heights. They were "caught," so to speak, on the Golan during the Israeli capture of the territory, although most have become naturalized Israeli citizens since that time.[3]

The Golan Heights is at the center of the Syrian-Israeli dispute. Simply put, Syria wants it back, and Israel is hesitant and reluctant to return it either in part or in its entirety without certain guarantees for peaceful relations; indeed, Israelis and Syrians cannot even agree on the origins of the name "Golan" or "Jawlan." To the Jews, the name comes from the biblical reference to a city called Golan that was located in the region of Bashan, roughly the area of the Golan Heights today. To the Syrians, the name comes from the Arabic word *ajwal*, meaning "land filled with dust," a reference to the characteristic high winds in the Golan that frequently stir up dusty conditions.

The issue of the Golan Heights is a personal matter to the Asad family. Hafiz al-Asad was minister of defense at the time of the 1967 Arab-Israeli war; thus, he seemed to feel a level of personal responsibility for its loss as well as its return. The continuing struggle with Israel over the years as well as a healthy amount of domestic propaganda has made the return of the Golan Heights an obsession in Syria, something that almost every Syrian agrees upon no matter whether they support the regime in Damascus or not. As such, Bashar has become part and parcel of the consequences of a war that in many ways shaped the modern Middle East, one that occurred when he was not even two years old, yet that framed much of his world and may very well define his presidency.

Cataclysm

The 1967 Arab-Israeli war was one of those watershed events that forever changed the region and beyond. The war's dramatic brevity has been inversely matched by the long reach of its results. It was not one of those occurrences the important repercussions of which took years to become manifest. The actual and potential change wrought by the outcome of the war was almost immediately apparent to anyone who cared to take notice. It took six days of battle to produce the following: a) the creation of the occupied territories situation, with Israel acquiring the Sinai Peninsula and Gaza Strip from Egypt, the West Bank, including Arab East Jerusalem, from Jordan, and the Golan Heights from Syria—the Sinai Peninsula has since been returned to Egypt per the 1979 Egyptian-Israeli peace treaty, but the remaining territories are still occupied by Israel; b) the establishment of the principle of land for peace embodied in UN Security Council Resolution 242 passed in November 1967 and, therefore, the basis for a peace process that still remains the operative framework for peace today; c) the effective end of secular Arab nationalism with the convincing defeat of its standard-bearer, Egyptian President Gamal Abd al-Nasser—although, importantly, a strong sense of "Arabism," a less ideological construction of shared experience, heritage, and brotherhood, has remained very much a part of the Arab world's dynamic since then, fed in large measure by the Arab-Israeli dispute and the plight of the Palestinians; d) the resuscitation of Islamism, particularly its more virulently anti-Israeli and anti-West extremist variant, in the wake of the clear ineffectiveness of secular Arab ideologies in confronting Israel and the popular awareness of the secular Arab regimes' inability to manage their own economies and disperse power amid authoritarian and corrupt political structures—Syria became a classic model of this developing trend; e) the more intimate involvement of the two superpowers, the United States and the Soviet Union, in the Arab-Israeli conflict, a dangerous scenario that reached a climax in the near nuclear confrontation between the two during the latter stages of the 1973 Arab-Israeli war; and finally, f) the acceleration of political divisions within Israel revolving around the question of how much, if any, of the occupied territories should be returned to the Arabs in exchange for peace. In addition to all of this, the war affected Israel and the Arab states emotionally and culturally in a very deep and long-lasting fashion, embedded in the psyche of the populations of the Middle East through film, literature, art, and music. The environment in which Bashar was raised is one that sees Israel, the Palestinians, and, indeed, the entire Arab world through a prism shaped by the 1967 conflagration.

Interestingly, Syria almost escaped the war unscathed despite the fact that its actions prior to the war were probably the single most important factor in raising the level of Arab-Israeli tension to breaking point. An intra-Baath coup in February 1966 in Damascus brought a more radical wing of the party to power led by its strongman, Salah Jadid. It was an ideologically aggressive regime that welcomed the participation of the communist party in Syria in the government, a development the Soviets looked very kindly upon since communists in most of the other Arab states were persecuted in some form or fashion. The regime also adopted a more assertive position *vis-à-vis* Israel as part of its attempt to become the true vanguard of Arab nationalism to replace a hesitant Nasser in Egypt or compel him to implement more aggressive actions of his own that matched his rhetoric. As such, Syria intensified its support of Palestinian guerilla (*fedayeen*) raids on the border with Israel as well as through Jordan and Lebanon. It also directly confronted Israeli troops along the Syrian-Israeli DMZ set up under the armistice terms following the 1947–1949 war.

What elicited the DMZ tussles in an immediate sense was Israel's diversion of the headwaters of the Jordan River into Israel to increase its water resource capacity, especially to the south toward the Negev desert, a process that had begun in the late 1950s and reached near-completion by 1964. Nasser successfully conducted his own diversion in an Arab League summit meeting in Cairo in 1964 to discuss the Israeli actions. This was not, however, a water diversion; he wanted to divert momentum away from a war for which the Egyptian president was not ready, especially since he had some 80,000 Egyptian troops in Yemen trying to keep pro-Nasserist republican forces in power following a coup that overthrew the Yemeni monarchy in 1962. The creation of the Palestine Liberation Organization (PLO) following the summit meeting was one way to pass off the burden of directly confronting Israel, as was the sanctioning of Syrian attempts to divert the tributaries leading into the Jordan River, ergo providing less water for Israel before it even reached the Jewish state. The latter was a futile effort destined to fail, for Israeli forces easily prevented Syrian attempts to even begin any diversion. The PLO, however, did evolve into something more than just a showpiece of Arab confrontation; it morphed into an effective and popular guerilla organization over time, one that also became a diplomatic football between Cairo and Damascus and other Arab capitals over the next several decades in their respective attempts to gain more control over the Palestinian movement to serve their own propaganda and diplomatic purposes.

The raids and reprisal raids were growing more and more intense between Israel and Syria throughout 1966, a development that began to concern Moscow lest a regime it viewed favorably should become weakened to the point of being overthrown and replaced by a group less interested in cooperating with the Soviet Union. Toward this, Moscow helped engineer a defense agreement in November 1966 between the Arab cold-war rivals, Egypt and Syria, ostensibly to take the heat off Syria by threatening Israel with a multi-front war if it should take further military action against its northern neighbor. This placed Nasser in a difficult dilemma. He was the acknowledged leader of the Arab world, a position he, himself, orchestrated, so it was also to him that the Arab world looked in order to confront Israel. He had to do *something* in response to the deteriorating situation on the Syrian-Israeli front, and this was made all the more apparent when Israeli jets shot down some Syrian MIG jets and buzzed Damascus in April. In reaction to this and, according to most sources, Soviet disinformation that Israel was massing troops on the Syrian border in early May, Nasser engaged in a series of moves that put Egypt and much of the rest of the Arab world on a war footing, further escalating tensions with Israel throughout the remainder of the month, finally compelling Israel to launch its infamous pre-emptive strike first aimed at Egypt on June 5, 1967.[4]

Although the war lasted only six days, the outcome was actually determined within the first few hours. In this time, the Israeli air force dramatically crippled, if not destroyed, the Egyptian air force in a daring pre-emptive strike in Egypt. Without air support, Egyptian ground forces were no match for the Israelis. Such disruption did the initial Israeli air strike cause, that the other two primary Arab combatant states, Jordan and Syria, could be dealt with in succession by the Israel Defense Forces (IDF). By June 9, the Egyptians, after having lost the Gaza Strip and the Sinai Peninsula, and the Jordanians, after losing the West Bank, had agreed to UN-brokered ceasefires assiduously arranged by the United States and the Soviet Union. Syria still remained, and it was hoping for a ceasefire on its relatively quiescent front before it would lose any territory. But the Israeli high command was not about to let Syria get off scot-free; this was an opportunity to deal a crushing blow to Syria as well as get control of the strategic Golan Heights. As the United Nations dithered, in what many Arabs claim to be connivance between the United States and Israel to buy time for Tel Aviv to move against Syria, the Israelis in very difficult terrain involving hand-to-hand combat conquered the Golan Heights. A ceasefire on this front was finally reached on June 11.

The Arab world was as shocked as the Israelis were exuberant. Israel, it seemed, was invincible, and it finally confirmed its existence in the Middle East—Israel suddenly had the strategic depth it had been lacking since its creation in 1948, and it was clear it could not be pushed into the sea. The Arabs, on the other hand, were searching for answers and soul-searching. Nasser stepped down from office only to reinstate himself after the Egyptian people could not come up with an alternative, so dominant had he become in their consciousness.

Ironically, and against conventional wisdom, not long after the war Nasser began preparations for renewed conflict with Israel. He and the other Arab leaders believed they could not enter into any negotiations with Israel from such a position of weakness, a position confirmed at the August 1967 Khartoum Arab League summit meeting, at which the so-called three "no's" were adopted: no peace, no recognition, and no negotiations with Israel. Before they could attempt to regain the lost territories through either diplomacy or force, they had to improve their bargaining position. It was in this context that Nasser launched what came to be known as the War of Attrition, traditionally dated from March 1969 through August 1970. As the name suggests, it was a war designed to sap the strength of Israel in the type of incremental, drawn-out conflict that worked to the advantage of the Arabs, with their deeper pockets of overall resources when compared to Israel, which greatly preferred quick, mobile warfare that made use of its qualitative advantage in technology and tactics. By its conclusion, however, this "war" would have monumental repercussions in both Jordan and Syria.

Hafiz Becomes President

Syria was largely a bystander to the War of Attrition, but little did the Asad family know that it would trigger a series of events that would culminate in Hafiz al-Asad's assumption of power in November 1970. The war was characterized by a series of artillery exchanges across the Suez Canal (which was now the border between Egypt and Israel) and air combat that eventually resulted in losses on both sides, including Israeli bombing strikes in Cairo. Nasser was hoping to bloody Israel and maybe even establish a bridgehead of sorts on the east bank of the canal in the Sinai Peninsula, undermining Israel's already stretched-out defense of a territory that was five times larger than pre-1967 Israel itself; this would at the very least improve Egypt's bargaining position. As the war continued, drawing more and more attention from the superpowers anxious not to let it spiral out of control into a full-blown conflagration, both Egypt and Israel began to wear down to the point that by the summer of 1970 a ceasefire loomed as a mutually desirable outcome. Under the guise of what was called the Rogers Initiative (named after U.S. Secretary of State William Rogers), the United States brokered a limited ceasefire agreement between Israel and Egypt that brought the War of Attrition to a close in August.

But there were some in the Arab world who were mightily distressed by the ceasefire agreement, primarily factions within the PLO. Now headquartered in Jordan, the PLO essentially formed a state within a state, challenging King Hussein's power; indeed, Palestinians constituted a majority of the population in the Hashemite Kingdom after having absorbed the lion's share of Palestinian refugees from the 1947–1949 Arab-Israeli war. The main fear was the possibility that the Rogers Initiative could lay the foundation for an overall Arab-Israeli agreement that did not in the least take into account the PLO objective of regaining its homeland.[5] In no way, shape, or form did the PLO want a peace environment to emerge in the Arab-Israeli arena; it needed the Arab states at war with Israel because that was the only way it had any hope of defeating Israel. Any disruption to peace, engendered by the Rogers Initiative, would be welcome.

Two factions within the PLO, the Popular Front for the Liberation of Palestine (PFLP) led by George Habash, and the Popular Democratic Front for the Liberation of Palestine (PDFLP) led by Nayef Hawatmah, decided to disrupt things in a way that would not only serve the interests of the PLO in general, but also promote their own interests against those of Yasser Arafat's dominant Fatah faction within the Palestinian movement as well as the fortunes of the PFLP's and PDFLP's patron, Syria. When the Rogers Initiative was accepted by Israel and Egypt in August, Arafat was reluctant to act, while the PFLP and PDFLP called directly for Hussein's overthrow, not only because he was an easier target but also because he was viewed as complicit in helping to arrange the ceasefire. To make matters worse, the PFLP hijacked four European airlines and brought them to Amman, some twenty miles from Hussein's palace at an airfield. The passengers were released, but the planes were subsequently blown up live on television for the world to witness. Such an affront to Hussein's authority could not go unpunished, so he moved against the PLO in Jordan, launching on September 16 the Jordanian civil war or what the Palestinians have called Black September. With an appellation such as "Black September," one can certainly hazard a guess at who lost. By the end of the civil war on September 25, over 3,000 from both sides had been killed, including a number of civilians, especially in the Palestinian refugee camps. King Hussein successfully reasserted his authority, and by July 1971 all of the PLO organizations in Jordan had been effectively kicked out of the country, only to shortly thereafter establish a state within a state in Lebanon, where the al-Asad family over a decade later would become intimately engaged in another serious crisis involving the PLO.

The Jordanian civil war also involved Syria in a way that led directly, and quite unexpectedly, to Hafiz al-Asad's assumption of power. The radical Baathist regime of Salah Jadid, which led the way into the 1967 war, still held the reins of power in Damascus. It saw the crisis in Jordan as an opportunity to advance Syrian control of the PLO while also possibly undermining, if not getting rid of, King Hussein, considered to be a reactionary and hopeless lackey to the West. Damascus sent tanks into Jordan in support of Palestinian positions. Despite threats from the United States to withdraw from Jordan, Syria called the U.S.' bluff knowing full well it had the backing of its own superpower patron, the Soviet Union. The Israelis now were becoming concerned because although Jordan had been a reluctant combatant in the 1967 war, King Hussein was pro-West and he and his family had had secret discussions with Israeli officials over the years to establish at least a quasi-amiable relationship—Tel Aviv did not want to see him fall from power. As such, the Israelis, feeling less subject to Soviet deterrence, started to make threatening noises toward Damascus and promised Amman air support if requested. With this tacit backing, Hussein launched air strikes against PLO and Syrian positions. At this point, Jadid ordered Hafiz al-Asad, who was minister of defense and commander of the Syrian air force, to send air support into Jordan. Asad refused, fearful that the Israelis would at the very least destroy his air force and possibly even strike directly at Damascus—and he was probably correct. It is a caution that would come to characterize much of Asad's strategic diplomacy in coming years. In essence, this was the first shot fired at the regime of Salah Jadid, who was further discredited after the debacle in Jordan. By November 1970, Asad was able to remove Jadid and his closest supporters from the government and become the de facto leader in Syria, being formally elected as president of the Syrian Arab Republic in a referendum on March 12, 1971. In August he was elected as the secretary-general of the Baath party.

As one can see, the Jordanian civil war had repercussions far beyond its borders. It had a profound effect on U.S. foreign policy toward the Middle East, as the Nixon administration began to view Israel in a new light, i.e. as a strategic asset that could effectively thwart the expansion of Soviet influence in the region, as it had so clearly deterred Syria, a Soviet client-state. This is when the special relationship between the United States and Israel in terms of military and economic aid really took off, fitting very nicely into the Nixon Doctrine foreign policy paradigm of finding surrogates in the region that could represent U.S. interests in the cold war while it was bogged down in Vietnam—it is also when Iran under Shah Muhammad Reza Pahlavi assumed a similar role in the Persian Gulf. The crisis in Jordan also led directly to the death on September 28, 1970 of Gamal Abd al-Nasser, whose weakened body gave out under the stress and strain of desperately trying to negotiate an end to the civil war. It signaled the end of an era in the Arab world, only to have a new one begin in a few short years under his successor, Anwar al-Sadat. Nasser was a giant in his day, a hero to a generation of Arabs. Although he was too young to remember him, Bashar lists Nasser as one of his favorite leaders in recent history, even though he believes the Egyptian president was somewhat naïve by today's standards. Regardless, Bashar's life had forever changed—his father had just become the head of the country, and within a few years, reflecting this change, he would move uptown to a house in the more upscale Malki district in Damascus, where he remains today.

Contrary to popular belief, Asad's assumption of power signaled the departure of an ideologically based foreign policy to a much more pragmatic one prepared to resolve the Arab-Israeli conflict diplomatically but wholeheartedly committed to a full return of the Golan Heights. His primary intent in the area of foreign relations was to bring Syria back within accepted parameters inside the Arab fold, mainly by establishing a working relationship with Egypt and Saudi Arabia in order to coordinate policy toward Israel, a policy shift that would manifest itself in the 1973 Arab-Israeli war.

Domestically, Asad becoming president signaled a retreat from the radical economic policies of Salah Jadid's regime and the opening up of the economy to the private sector. Indeed, Asad's political program upon his ascension to power was called the Corrective Movement (*al-Harakat al-Tashishiyya*). This first opening, or *infitah*, paralleled a similar process in Egypt under President Anwar al-Sadat, one that especially gained steam after the October 1973 war, among the results of which was the near fourfold increase in the price per barrel of oil. While the profits largely accumulated in the pockets of the oil-exporting Persian Gulf states, the non-oil (or smaller oil-producing) states bordering Israel also benefited enormously from the new economic realities of the Middle East. The only way that countries such as Saudi Arabia and Kuwait could fight the Arab-Israeli conflict and still maintain their "Arab" credentials was to provide healthy amounts of financial aid and grants to the so-called "confrontation states." Countries such as Egypt and Syria also reaped the rewards of remittances from their citizens who were arriving by the tens of thousands in the sparsely populated Gulf countries as laborers.

The 1970s thus resulted in impressive growth in the Syrian economy. In fact, Asad's decision to open up the economy to allow more flexibility for the private sector was less a reaction to the inability of the public sector to accumulate capital (as would be the case in the 1980s), but more to find mechanisms to distribute the wealth that was suddenly pouring into the country. The growth was not structurally stimulated, but was due largely to Arab transfers. In addition, during the oil boom years of the 1970s, few states—and certainly Syria and Egypt were not among them—did anything to accumulate foreign exchange reserves or to direct remittances toward more productive activity. As such, changes in the regional and/or international economic environment could, and did, have deleterious repercussions for Syria, a country whose prosperity seemed to rely totally on the vagaries of the oil market and, as primarily an agrarian-based economy, seasonal rainfalls.[6]

For Syria the decade of the 1970s began with an impasse on the Arab-Israeli front, reached a level of near exuberance with its much-improved military showing in the 1973 war, and ended in dire straits on both the domestic and foreign policy fronts. The Nixon Doctrine's programmed role for Israel, i.e. staunch U.S. backing, only stiffened Israeli resolve to hold on to the occupied territories, or at least force the Arab states to come to the bargaining table on Israeli terms since it seemed obvious that the Arabs could not militarily defeat Israel or even through military pressure improve their strategic position. In addition, it was surmised, the Arab states would be forced to negotiate through the good auspices of the United States, a process that would exclude the Soviet Union. A stalemate on the Arab-Israeli front thus ensued by 1971/1972.

The Internationalization of Syria—The 1973 Arab-Israeli War

Relatively unknown at the time, Anwar al-Sadat knew that the legitimacy of his regime, following in Nasser's charismatic and dominant shoes, rested on his ability to return the Sinai Peninsula to Egyptian control, either through peace or through war. Not only was there the political and psychological necessity to reacquire the Sinai, but there were also a number of practical reasons. Three of the four pillars of the Egyptian economy at the time in terms of generating foreign exchange were directly or indirectly related to the level of tension in the Arab-Israeli arena. First, since most of the oil reserves in Egypt were located in or astride the Sinai Peninsula, this revenue-producer was obviously in abeyance while Israel held the territory. Second, Egypt relies heavily on Suez Canal tolls, but the canal had been blocked since 1967, and in any event, Israel held the east bank of the Suez Canal in the Sinai and could easily impede passing ships. Third, because of its unique pharaonic and Islamic history, Egypt counts a great deal on tourism; however, tourism declined sharply after the 1967 war and the War of Attrition, and it remained a depressed industry when Arab-Israeli tensions were high, which was certainly the case in the early 1970s. In addition, if a settlement with Israel could be reached, Egypt could redirect a significant portion of its defense expenditures toward more productive purposes—augmented by tremendous amounts of U.S. military and economic assistance; indeed, Egypt became the second largest recipient of U.S. foreign aid—second to Israel—following the 1979 Egyptian-Israeli peace treaty. For all of these reasons, Sadat was compelled to focus the entirety of his efforts on regaining the Sinai.

Sadat at first attempted to reactivate negotiations through diplomatic overtures, particularly the expulsion of some 15 to 20,000 Soviet advisors in July 1972. This actually had a salutary effect on Syria. Asad was in an enviable position *vis-à-vis* the Soviets because he knew they were desperate to recoup their loss in Egypt and shore up their position in the Arab world; therefore, he could and did extract a high price from Moscow. In fact, there were rumors of Egyptian pressure on Syria to also expel Soviet advisers in order to provide Sadat and Asad more leeway to choose to go to war without being obstructed by thousands of Soviet personnel.[7] Knowing Asad preferred to keep the Soviets at arm's length, the Kremlin was quick to shower the Syrian president with economic and military aid—for instance, a $700 million arms deal upon Asad's visit to Moscow in July 1972 following Sadat's move, whereupon the number of Soviet advisers in Syria rose from about 400 to 700 at the end of July 1972 to about 3,000 by the end of the summer.[8] The only problem for the Egyptian president was that Tel Aviv and Washington essentially ignored his gestures interpreting them as signs that the stiff negotiating posture was, indeed, working. The stalemate continued, and Sadat felt he had to do something to break it. If diplomacy could not be reactivated and the stalemate could not be broken by kicking out Russians, pursuing UN peace missions, or appealing to Washington, then maybe it could be accomplished through war. And this is exactly what Sadat did, initiating the next Arab-Israeli war on October 6, 1973, one that brought Syria once again to the front and center in war and peace in the Middle East.[9]

Sadat utilized the newly developed Cairo–Damascus–Riyadh axis to launch a simultaneous surprise invasion of Israel. Egypt attacked across the Suez Canal in the south and Syria moved through the Golan Heights in the north, all of which was backed up by Saudi influence in the Organization of Petroleum Exporting Countries (OPEC) to unleash, if necessary, the oil weapon: an oil embargo that would force the United States to intervene either to save the Arabs from total destruction if things turned for the worse or to enter the fray as an active mediator ready to pressure Israel to make the necessary concessions for peace—or both.[10] The Israelis were caught off guard by the attack primarily because they were convinced that the Arabs would not initiate an all-out war unless they knew they could win. However, Sadat did not launch the war to defeat Israel or even to regain all of the lost territories from the 1967 war; he did it to achieve the more limited objectives of reactivating diplomacy and improving, if possible, Egypt's bargaining position with Israel by at least establishing a bridgehead on the east bank of the Suez Canal. This the Egyptians accomplished in a remarkable military effort. As Nadav Safran wrote:

> The Yom Kippur War was an effort by an Arab coalition to defeat Israel by breaking through a gap in its security concept. It was an attempt by the vast standing armies of Egypt and Syria to overcome the inferior standing forces of Israel before its reserves could be brought into play, and thus gain a decisively favorable position from which to defeat those reserves as they came into play. The attempt depended critically on surprise so that Israel should be unable to mobilize and deploy its reserves before the Arab forces attacked.[11]

The only problem for Syrian President Hafiz al-Asad was that, according to him, Sadat never informed him that he entered the conflagration with only limited objectives in mind; Asad held no illusions about completely defeating Israel, but at the very least he wanted to gain the Golan Heights back in its entirety, a military objective he thought Sadat shared with regard to the Sinai. Syria and Egypt were thus fighting with two different strategic designs, which caught Asad by surprise and undermined his own efforts to engage in a successful offensive in the Golan. In other words, after Egypt was successful in establishing a bridgehead on the east bank of the Suez Canal, it essentially stopped and assumed a defensive posture, which was strategically sound in terms of not fighting the mobile type of war at which Israel excels, but it also enabled the IDF to concentrate more forces to the north to stall the more immediate Syrian threat. This infuriated Asad, and he would never forgive Sadat for it. Even the name Syria has given the war—the October War of Liberation (*Harb Tishreen al-Tahiriyya*)—suggests the clear objective of Asad to "liberate" the Golan Heights. The different war objectives precipitated a conflict of interests at various times during the war itself between Syria and Egypt and complicated Soviet efforts to arrange for a ceasefire agreeable to both.[12]

The initial Syrian offensive that pushed the Israelis back across parts of the Golan Heights stalled by October 8, brought to a halt by the full fury of the Israeli air force. By October 9 and 10 Israeli jets were bombing economic and military targets deep in Syria, and the IDF was able to push Syrian forces back to the so-called Purple Line that separated the Israeli-occupied Golan Heights from Syria proper. This prompted the Soviets to begin a massive airlift of arms and ammunition to Syria by October 9 or 10. Moscow was very fearful that the Israelis could focus their attention on Syria since Sadat had dug in along his bridgehead in the Sinai, and the Syrians had lost an enormous amount of material during the Israeli counteroffensive—as did the Israelis. The Soviets, however, always trying to balance need versus wherewithal, were careful to provide the Syrians only with that which was necessary to preserve their position and not try to initiate further hostilities against Israel that might bring the United States directly into the game. Despite this, the Israelis by the 13th had pushed on to create a salient toward Damascus beyond the Purple Line up to the village of Sasa on the road to the capital. By this time, Asad was fully aware of Sadat's more limited objectives, and he later even learned that Sadat had entered into diplomatic contact with U.S. Secretary of State Henry Kissinger from a very early stage of the conflict. To put it mildly, Asad was furious, and the tone of communication between Damascus and Cairo quickly deteriorated as he demanded Egypt do something to take the pressure off Syria.

The Soviet airlift soon elicited an American one to Israel by October 14, as Tel Aviv worried about losing by attrition at this point since its enemies were being resupplied. Thus the two superpowers became implicated despite pre-war pledges not to face-off against one another in Third World conflicts—neither Moscow nor Washington wanted another Cuban missile crisis and both wanted to preserve the détente policy that was a priority for each at the time; however, by doing so the United States and the Soviet Union, trying to preserve the gains of their client-states, came dangerously close to the face-off they adamantly wanted to avoid toward the end of the war. Only intense U.S. pressure on Israel to cease and desist in its efforts against Egypt after successfully turning the tables on Egyptian forces, as well as similar pressure by Moscow on Damascus not to re-engage in the conflict, finally brought the conflagration to an end by October 25 with the acceptance of the final version of UN Security Council Resolution 338. Interestingly, Asad was kept largely out of the negotiations surrounding the ceasefire, and Syria was virtually forced to accept it after Egypt did, not wanting to take on Israel by itself. The Soviets knew this, and they did not want Asad to be an impediment to ceasefire negotiations at a time when immediate implementation was necessary in order to save what was left of Egypt's position. Ironically, while Israel certainly considered itself to be in the catbird seat, Asad was reportedly eager to stage a counterattack at Israeli forces in the salient that in his estimation were becoming more and more exposed, especially as Syria had rearmed itself and continued to receive contingents of military support from other Arab countries, particularly Iraq. Despite the heavy losses in the war, however (6,000 men and hundreds of tanks, planes, and armored vehicles), Asad apparently was in good spirits, having fought Israel toe-to-toe early in the conflagration, bloodying the Jewish state, experiencing tangible battlefield success in the first stage of the conflict (even though the Israelis decisively turned the tide of battle and made their way halfway to Damascus by the end of the war), and showing Israel that Syria was a foe that had to be dealt with seriously.[13] These views tended to be replicated throughout the Arab world; indeed, in Damascus there is a grand modern museum dedicated to the feats and heroes of the October War of Liberation.

Bashar was still too young at only eight years old to fully understand what really was going on at the time. He remembers flashes from the period, but not much more than that, particularly as his family tried to shield the children as much as possible from the death and destruction; indeed, Asad's wife and children, as well as other family members, were evacuated to their Alawite home village of Qurdaha, east of Latakia in northwest Syria, out of harm's way during the conflagration. Typical of most children, Bashar recalled that the first thing he and his friends did was to celebrate that school was closed! But soon enough he started to comprehend a deeper meaning when he saw all the military equipment being hastily moved around and planes flying in the air before he left the city. He saw very little of his father during the conflict, but he remembered the concern in his face and the intensity of purpose in his eyes; obviously when your mother quickly rounds you up to escape a dangerous environment, it has an impact, and you begin to worry simply because you see everyone else worrying. When he returned to Damascus he encountered people who had lost fathers and sons in the war, and a mixture of grieving, exultation, and anger. This was not the world he left only a few weeks earlier. He started to ask himself and others about the meaning of war, about what it is, how it begins, and what results from it. These are questions a young boy normally should not encounter. They can lead to an introspective outlook on life, a more realistic version of childhood fantasy that yearns for explanation. It would be the first of many conscious encounters for Bashar with painful reality, family and national crisis, and violence—he could not escape it; after all, he was a son of the president.

Following the war Henry Kissinger set about his famous shuttle diplomacy in the Middle East to secure the tenuous ceasefires and guide the Arab-Israeli conflict toward a resolution according to his prescriptions: excluding the Soviet Union from the diplomatic paradigm as much as possible and giving priority to extracting Egypt completely from the Soviet camp and into step-by-step agreements with Israel. Asad met with Kissinger in many long meetings, something that would become one of the Syrian president's calling cards; indeed, Kissinger traveled to and from Damascus no less than 26 times and met with Asad for approximately 130 hours of face-to-face discussions.[14] Today we think of Hafiz al-Asad in terms of this wily, tenacious negotiator, but we must remember that he was still very green to this role in 1973 and 1974, and both Sadat and Kissinger regarded him as a junior partner in the talks. As such, while Asad saw the negotiations for a disengagement agreement as the first step toward regaining the entire Golan Heights, if not a comprehensive Arab-Israeli settlement, Kissinger viewed them within the construct of his primary regional objective of detaching Egypt from the Soviet Union—as did Israel, although in its case it was to detach Egypt from the rest of the Arab world. This had been a long-time policy priority for Tel Aviv, i.e. if a peace agreement could be consummated with Cairo, thus separating the most powerful and populous Arab country from the Arab fold, then it could virtually eliminate an Arab military option *vis-à-vis* Israel since no Arab coalition could even entertain the hope of defeating Israel militarily without the participation of Egypt.

Kissinger negotiated a disengagement agreement (Sinai I) between Egypt and Israel in January 1974, separating the forces in the Sinai with UN monitors interspersed between them. He also hoped the movement in negotiations would alleviate the Arab oil embargo put into effect during the war; this did, in fact, occur with the embargo's lifting in March 1974. All of this, however, made a Syrian-Israeli disengagement agreement less urgent, but Kissinger wanted to make sure Egypt was not portrayed in the Arab world as lurching out on its own and abandoning a coordinated Arab stance and the Palestinians. It was important at this stage to get another Arab state to sign along the dotted line in order to allow Egypt more flexibility to move forward even further. The Syrian-Israeli disengagement agreement was just such a vehicle for Kissinger, and an end to another means, while Asad considered it the first step. The Syrian president was wrong, and it was a lesson he learned early in his reign. He would be careful not to make this mistake again in the future—maybe Kissinger should share the blame for Asad's deliberate, suspicious, and incremental negotiating style that for better or worse would come to define his approach to diplomacy from here on out. The Israelis withdrew from their salient toward Damascus, and they even relinquished part of the Golan Heights captured in 1967 to allow the UNDOF to establish their positions. Ever since, the disengagement agreement has held up remarkably well. Sadat, for his part, signed another disengagement agreement brokered by Kissinger in September 1975 (Sinai II), moving Israeli forces back about halfway across the Sinai Peninsula, and the process seemed well on its way toward Sadat's destiny in 1979, confirming Asad's worst fears of virtually being alone to confront Israel.

Syria and Lebanon

It is in this context of increasing isolation that one can begin to understand Syria's obsession with its neighbor to the west, Lebanon. The civil war that began in Lebanon in 1975 and lasted effectively until 1991, including the seminal 1982 Israeli invasion that brought the IDF to Beirut, had a defining influence on Bashar al-Asad's life—as he told me, the series of crises in Lebanon "built my political consciousness. As children we read the press every day, and so we followed the Lebanese issue closely after 1975, which gave us a familiarity with Lebanon from a young age." It seems that ever since he became politically aware, Lebanon has been at the forefront of his country's and family's well-being, the two becoming dangerously intertwined in 1983 and 1984 when, amid the turmoil engulfing their neighbor, his father was debilitated by a serious illness, almost prompting a Syrian civil war as Bashar's uncle, Rifaat, attempted to snatch away his brother's throne. Bashar would become very familiar with Lebanon, and he was even given the important so-called "Lebanon file" by his father in the late 1990s to oversee the extensive Syrian economic, political, and strategic interests there. Lebanon has remained a high-priority issue in Bashar's presidency to date, more often in terms of generating potential trouble with Israel and the United States than in terms of providing tangible benefits for Syria. Washington, Tel Aviv, Paris, indeed the international community as a whole in addition to many in Lebanon itself, pressured Damascus to withdraw its troops from Lebanon, stop supporting the Islamist group Hizbollah (Party of God), and cease its interference in Lebanese domestic political affairs. This was easier said than done, however, as the motto popular in Syria regarding Lebanon, "One people, two countries," clearly indicates. There is, of course, the strategic factor, but Lebanon also provided Syria with an alternative labor market, generating approximately $2 billion a year in remittances and employing up to about 1,000,000 Syrians, relieving some pressure on Damascus to provide jobs. I asked President Bashar what benefits Syria brings to Lebanon, and with an immediate laugh he said:

I thought you might ask what benefits Syria could get from Lebanon! Actually, first of all it depends on what they want, of course mostly this deals with the security issue. We have provided security and stability since we intervened in 1976. This is most important. Second, I think we depend on each other economically. Thursday and Friday most of the Syrians living middle-class lives and above go to Lebanon to have fun, buy things, or go to the hotels. On Saturday and Sunday most of the Lebanese middle and lower classes come here to buy cheaper things, clothes, food, sometimes gasoline since it is much cheaper here. So we complement each other. We are becoming one market.[15]

Lebanon emerged, as did Syria, as an independent country following World War II after having been a French mandate territory since World War I. It had been effectively carved out of the Syrian hinterland by the French in order to protect the Francophile Lebanese Christian community and as part of Paris' divide-and-rule tactics of colonial rule. There have been some groups in Syria, such as the Syrian Social Nationalist Party (SSNP) in the 1950s, that have called for the reintegration of Lebanon as part of "Greater Syria." As Hafiz al-Asad stated in a speech upon the signing of the Treaty of Brotherhood, Cooperation, and Coordination between Syria and Lebanon on May 22, 1991:

We [the Syrians] did not create [that which binds] us to Lebanon—this is God's handiwork. We all share a common history, a common geography, and bloodties. Therefore, the ties we establish today between the two countries are a reflection of our common heritage. This heritage cannot be erased, nor will it disappear with the passage of time, for brothers are brothers, whether or not they live in the same house. We are one people, even if we live in two separate states. This is the truth, and no one can ignore it. Turning away from this truth does not serve the interests of either of the two independent states, or of the people who live in them.[16]

The French did implement a unified economic policy in the two mandates in terms of customs, currency, and taxation, and they maintained open borders for travelers and trade.[17] The National Pact of 1943 defined the political system under which Lebanon would operate. It would be a confessional democratic system of political apportionment based on a specious 1932 census possibly rigged by the French that counted the Maronite Christians as the largest religious sect in Lebanon, followed in order by the Sunnis, Shiites, and the Druze. As such, according to the pact, a Maronite Christian (the largest and most influential of the Christian sects in Lebanon) would be president, a

Sunni would be prime minister, and a Shiite representative would be speaker of parliament, and on down the line in the staffing of the government. The size of the political blocs in parliament would also be apportioned in a like manner.

The basic problem in Lebanon since independence has always been one of political representation. Since the 1932 census, the demographics have shifted considerably. Probably by the 1970s the Shiites (poorer and thus with higher birth rates) constituted the largest sect in the country (today approximately 32 percent) followed roughly equally by Sunnis and Maronites (approximately 20 percent each today)—altogether Muslims currently account for about 60 percent of the overall population of 3.7 million and Christians about 40 percent. There is also a significant Palestinian refugee population in Lebanon dating back to the 1947 to 1949 Arab-Israeli war. The Palestinians lived for the most part in UN-administered refugee camps and were not granted citizenship, similar to the plight of Palestinian refugees in Syria, Jordan, and Egypt. But the Maronites as well as other established interests, both Christian and Muslim, did not want to relinquish power, which would most certainly occur under a confessional system if they gave in to the calls to hold another census. The Maronites forcefully resisted.

As the demographic shifts became obvious, there would be political crises from time to time in Lebanon, such as that which occurred in 1958 that involved the landing of U.S. marines in Beirut to maintain stability. The confessional system of government tends to give the impression that the political disputes in Lebanon are based on religion, i.e. Christians versus Muslims. While this view is not entirely incorrect, the reality is, however, much more complicated than that, with Christian groups/individuals vying with other Christians, and Muslim groups vying with other Muslims or even allying with certain Christian groups with shared objectives. It has generally been a political labyrinth, and in acute situations it invites external dabbling in internal Lebanese affairs. Overall, however, the Lebanese experiment worked fairly well, as most parties in the equation were able to compromise or at least paper over the differences. As a result, Lebanon became the shining light of democracy and economic growth in the Arab world in the 1960s and early 1970s, with Beirut earning the sobriquet, "Paris of the Middle East."

Left on their own, the Lebanese may have been able to resolve these political problems eventually without resort to civil war. But being caught geographically between the vice of Syria and Israel, it was almost inevitable that Lebanon would become entangled in the Arab-Israeli conflict, especially when the destructive power of the 1973 Arab-Israeli war informed Syria and Israel that they might be better off fighting each other through proxies rather than head on.

Tensions started to rise domestically once again by the late 1960s as Muslim groups called for the "deconfessionalization" of Lebanon, but the situation started to spiral out of control upon the entrance of the PLO into the country by 1971 following its Black September expulsion from Jordan. The Palestinian population in Lebanon was already developing into a state within a state; now with the entrance of the PLO not only was the Palestinian position in the country reinforced, but Lebanon was automatically moved closer to the Arab-Israeli conflict, something it had been trying to avoid for years.

The situation finally burst out into open civil war in April 1975. Asad simply wanted stability in Lebanon so as not to create troubled waters in which the Israelis could fish at Syria's expense or generate sectarian strife that could spill over into his own country. Lebanon has also been a haven for a variety of Syrian opposition groups over the years, many of them funded by other Arab states and/or the great powers; therefore, extension of Syrian military-security influence, if not control, in Lebanon had been viewed as something of a strategic necessity. Israel, for instance, developed a relationship with the Maronites in Lebanon, seeing them as another non-Muslim minority in a Muslim-dominated region as well as conduits to advance Israeli interests *vis-à-vis* Syria. With Sadat heading out in his own direction, Asad saw the situation in Lebanon as an opportunity to gain more control over Lebanese politics as well as the PLO to utilize them as arrows in an increasingly bare quiver against Israel and in the inter-Arab arena. He also wanted to prevent these same elements from unwarrantedly precipitating an unwanted conflict with Israel.[18] With this in mind, Asad tentatively supported the so-called Rejection Front of Palestinian and Lebanese Muslim forces against the Maronites.

When the tide seemed to turn against the Maronites in early 1976, however, Asad abruptly switched sides against the Rejection Front, fearful as he was that the Israelis would intervene to save its allies in Lebanon—a stable balance of power largely under its control and keeping the Israelis out were the priorities for Syria. At the end of the day, the initial round in the sixteen-year civil war resulted in something of a modus vivendi between Syria and Israel. The latter maintained a presence in southern Lebanon through an allied Christian militia (the South Lebanon Forces of Saad Haddad) while the Syrians did not cross a "red line" in the south, commonly thought to have been the Litani River. Asad was successful in obtaining regional sanction for Syria's military presence in Lebanon at an Arab League summit meeting in Riyadh in October, establishing an all-Arab force, mostly composed of Syrians, stationed in the country ostensibly to maintain stability. It was something of a draw between

Syria and Israel; however, Lebanon was brought directly into the Arab-Israeli conflict, this episode being only the first manifestation of a string of disasters.

The Repercussions of Peace and Revolution in 1979

Things would not get better for Asad for the remainder of the decade. A former militant with the ultra-right-wing group called Irgun, Menachem Begin, became the first member of the right-wing Likud party in Israel to become prime minister in May 1977. A stalemate again ensued on the Egyptian-Israeli front as Begin accelerated the settlements process in the occupied territories, despite new U.S. President Jimmy Carter's foreign policy emphasis on finding a comprehensive solution to the Arab-Israeli conflict. Once again, Anwar al-Sadat, who had a flair for the dramatic, unexpectedly arrived in Israel in November 1977 to break the deadlock, the first official visit by an Arab leader to the Jewish state. Negotiations would tack back and forth between Israel and Egypt, surviving a major Israeli military incursion into south Lebanon to clear out PLO positions that were shelling northern Israeli settlements. Ultimately, Egypt and Israel needed the direct intervention of Carter in September 1978 to broker the Camp David Accords, which formed the basis of the Egyptian-Israeli peace treaty signed on the White House lawn on March 29, 1979. The Middle East was suddenly a dramatically different place and this altered Asad's conception of Syria's role in the region.

Faced with losing the leverage and threat of Egypt, Asad searched for allies to confront an empowered Israel that could now focus its attention to the north. The Steadfastness Front, including Libya, Algeria, and the People's Democratic Republic of Yemen, formed in large measure to counter what was feared to be an emerging Egyptian-led consensus of moderate Arab states, diplomatically fortified fellow member Syria to a certain degree, but these countries were largely on the fringes of the Arab-Israeli conflict. Asad even briefly flirted with an entente with his Baathist rival, Saddam Hussein of Iraq, in the aftermath of Camp David in order to shore up Syria's eastern front to contain Israel. It would be an association that inevitably floundered over continuing differences between the two countries, ranging from persistent Baathist elite and ideological quarrels and personal animus between Asad and Hussein to more practical matters such as water-sharing of the Euphrates River and the question of who should be the dominant partner in any planned union. The answer to this question would, in effect, determine who would fill the vacuum of power in the Arab world created by Egypt's departure from the Arab fold after it signed the peace treaty with Israel. Asad, always concerned with flanks and balances, was compelled to meet the strategic challenge.

Interestingly, although he was only in his fourteenth year at the time of the Egyptian-Israeli peace treaty, when I spoke with Bashar he struck a sympathetic tone toward Sadat, even though the Egyptian president was almost universally loathed throughout the Arab and Islamic world. He almost seems to admire the fact that Sadat had U.S. guarantees in place before signing along the dotted line and that there was a real peace process at work that produced the agreement as opposed to the current situation between Syria and Israel. Sadat did what he felt he had to do to get the Sinai Peninsula back, despite the vociferous critics in the Arab world who believed he had sold out the Palestinians and fatally weakened the Arab bargaining position *vis-à-vis* Israel. The Egyptian president believed his country had bled enough for the Arab cause, and he had seen how his predecessor became captive to Arab nationalism to his detriment in the end. Egypt had to consider its own interests and national objectives as paramount. His own country somewhat isolated and in severe economic straits, it is seductive to suggest that possibly Bashar might do the same under similar conditions.

The culmination of the Iranian revolution in February 1979 and subsequent Iraqi invasion of Iran in September 1980 obliterated whatever slim reed of hope existed for an Iraqi-Syrian rapprochement.[19] With the arrival of the Ayatollah Khomeini in Teheran along with his new Islamic republic as an avowed implacable foe of Israel and the United States, Asad saw a definite convergence of interests with Iran, taking steps even before the outbreak of the Iran–Iraq war to develop a relationship that still remains intact to this day; indeed, Iran is one of President Bashar's most important and influential allies. From Hafiz al-Asad's point of view, Iran provided some strategic depth now that the multi-front approach against Israel was defunct.

When Saddam Hussein invaded Iran, it made it that much easier for Damascus to openly side with Teheran. Asad believed that Hussein's follies were an untimely and misdirected application of vital Arab resources and assets away from the Arab-Israeli arena; but they also created an opportunity to weaken an inter-Arab rival, thus allowing Syria to play a leading role in the region and fill the shoes vacated by Egypt. This would not be the first time that Asad would adopt a pragmatic policy that on the surface was unexpected and against the grain—he would do so again ten years later during the 1990 to 1991 Gulf crisis and war. But because of its support of non-Arab Iran against Arab Iraq in the war, Syria became more isolated in the early 1980s in the Arab world. The Gulf Arab states, on whom Syria depended so much for financial and political support, were more concerned with matters of Gulf security and less with the Arab-Israeli arena. In addition, Syria had never quite repaired the damage done to its relationship with the PLO stemming from its switch over to the Maronite side during the 1975 to 1976 civil war in Lebanon. Despite Syria's frequent efforts to mend its relations with the PLO, especially after Sadat engaged in the peace process with Israel, the PLO never totally cut off its line to Cairo, much to the consternation of Asad. From PLO chairman Yasser Arafat's point of view, Syria was trying to turn the PLO into something of a protectorate in order to strengthen its own bargaining power and indispensability so as not to be left out in the cold again by another Arab participant in the Arab-Israeli equation.

Jordan also did not obediently follow Syria. Amman was typically caught between pressures from a variety of sources, including Syria, Iraq, Saudi Arabia, Egypt, and the United States, and of these, Jordan had the least to lose with Damascus. With this array of pressure, Jordan naturally gravitated toward the more moderate front within the Arab world, in the process of which it established closer ties with Iraq and mended its own fences with the PLO. Iraq, now ensconced in war with Iran, toned down its rhetoric and began cooperating with the moderate Arab states so as to buffer its ability to withstand an Iran that had weathered Iraq's initial attacks and by 1982 was clearly on the offensive. This emerging moderate bloc in the Arab world, due to a significant degree to the Iran–Iraq war, also allowed Egypt to rehabilitate itself and quietly reenter the Arab fold.

By the end of 1980, Syria seemed as isolated as it had ever been in the Middle East. Clearly, Hafiz al-Asad's diplomacy had failed. Egypt had signed a separate peace treaty with Israel and yet no serious coalition of Arab states would align their positions with Damascus. Worse still, the attention of most of the Arab states, indeed most of the world, was consumed with events in the Persian Gulf and South-Central Asia following the December 1979 Soviet invasion of Afghanistan, not with those in the Arab-Israeli arena.

Desperate Times: Isolation and Islamist Revolt

Syria had to make a tactical change if it was to contain what the Syrian regime perceived as Israeli pressure and carve out a role for itself in the Middle East. Israel's *de facto* annexation of the Golan Heights (in actuality extension of Israeli law) in 1981 reinforced Syria's assessment of its own weakened position in the region—it could not do anything about it. Something had to be done, and it seemed from Asad's perspective that Syria would essentially have to go it alone in the region for the time being. Asad began to put forward the possibility of attaining strategic parity with Israel, not so much to defeat the Jewish state but to act as an effective deterrent while at the same time strengthening Syria's bargaining leverage should a peace process develop. To do this,

Syria needed massive amounts of military aid from the outside—from the Soviet Union.

The Soviet Union and Syria began to build upon what had been a tenuous relationship, exemplified by the 1980 Treaty of Friendship and Cooperation signed between the two countries. Moscow also had its nose bloodied in the Middle East, with Egypt embracing the United States, and Iraq, against the wishes of the Kremlin, invading Iran and matriculating toward the moderate Arab camp to buffer its deteriorating position as the war progressed. In a sense, if not for the virtual disabling of Iraq and Egypt, the Soviets would not have been tempted to invest so much in Syria. For his part, Asad felt he had little choice but to draw closer to Moscow.

Syria's relative isolation in the Middle East was not its only problem in the early 1980s. Economically, the decade of the 1980s was as bad for Syria as the 1970s had been good. Not only were the structural defects and inefficiencies of Syria's state-dominated economy becoming obvious, but also the regional and international political and economic environments exacerbated already-existing problems. Most damaging was the precipitous decline in oil prices by the mid-1980s due to the world oil glut. This adversely affected Syria's own not-insignificant oil revenues, as well as reducing remittances from abroad and financial aid from the oil-rich Arab states in the Persian Gulf, who were already displeased with the decision by Damascus to support Iran against Iraq. Concurrent with this development was an unfortunate drought lasting half the decade, which devastated an agricultural sector that had already suffered under the regime's policy of import-substituting industrialization that favored manufacturing over agricultural enterprises. In addition, the general Third World debt of the early 1980s reduced capital inflow, and the recession in the industrialized countries had negative run-off effects on developing nations seeking foreign investment. Finally, the winding down and end of the superpower cold war by the close of the decade and subsequent retrenchment of the Soviet bloc deprived Syria of the military and economic aid it had been receiving in such large amounts earlier in the decade as well as reduced access for Syrian products in Soviet markets.

As a result, Syria developed in the 1980s a severe balance-of-payments and foreign-exchange crisis. It had become clear that the state could no longer be the engine of capital accumulation; therefore, the regime decided that the private sector had to be given more leeway to fill the capital void. The country as a whole had to create a more investor-friendly business environment to attract foreign investment. This second *infitah*, or economic "opening," was brought about by economic crisis and not economic largesse. With a series of decrees throughout the 1980s, Asad attempted to ameliorate the situation, launching

Syria on the road to what has been called selective liberalization—"selective" because if Asad liberalized the economy too much or too quickly he might undercut the public sector patronage system that helped maintain the regime in power. His subsequent zigzag approach to economic reform experienced some limited success, but on the whole, by the end of the decade, it produced disappointing results.[20]

Also confronting the Asad regime by the early 1980s was a very serious internal threat from the Muslim Brethren (MB or *Ikhwan al-Muslimun*), mirroring similar emerging Islamist movements in other Middle East states by the mid- to late 1970s. Causes for the rise of the Sunni MB in Syria as a serious threat were: 1) the avowedly secular nature of the Baathist regime, especially one led by a minority schismatic Shiite sect, the Alawites; 2) the economic difficulties and disparities that had become apparent by 1980 accompanied by rampant corruption; 3) the inspirational example of the Iranian revolution, which, although a Shiite one, still set the standard of an Islamist movement successfully overthrowing what it considered to be a tyrannical and non-Islamic regime; and 4) Asad's support for the Maronite Christians against the PLO within a year after the outbreak of the Lebanese civil war in 1975. No doubt the MB in Syria were also galvanized by the assassination of Anwar Sadat by Islamic Jihad elements in Cairo in October 1981, which, of course, only made Asad more wary of his own predicament and the severity of the threat. After enduring a number of attacks by Islamic militants against various representations of the regime, resulting in hundreds of deaths, Asad ordered a full-scale attack in February 1982 against the center of MB activity in the Syrian city of Hama. The result was the virtual destruction of a significant portion of the city of Hama, mainly the old part of town, with anywhere from 10,000 to 30,000 deaths, depending upon the source. There is no question that this was ruthless, but MB opposition essentially ceased to exist after this crushing blow; however, Syria's reputation suffered immeasurably, both regionally and internationally. This incident is employed by anti-Syrian (specifically anti-Asad) elements in the West as an example of the ruthless dictatorship built by Hafiz al-Asad, one that has been inherited—but not altered to any significant degree—by his son. It is certainly an obvious and convenient way to bludgeon the reputation of Bashar al-Asad and promote a more aggressive U.S. foreign policy to contain if not overthrow the regime.

One does not talk openly in public about this incident in Syria for fear of censure, imprisonment, or expulsion if you are a foreign visitor. This is part and parcel of the repressive nature of the regime, but it also reflects the fact that Hafiz al-Asad wanted to cultivate a different image for his country than that which was popularly held in the West. The incident served its purpose domestically in another sense as well, in that Hafiz restored what Syrian expert Joshua Landis terms as his "aura of invincibility," his *zaama* or leadership, after it had been so severely tested and to a degree usurped by the MB rebellion.[21] This is why the regime allowed foreign journalists to enter the destroyed parts of the city only days after the incident. Landis goes on to explain that "Zaama is crucial to leadership in Syria as it is in all patriarchal societies. But Syria is more patriarchal than most. Although tribalism in any kind of pristine form has disappeared from much of Syrian society, its forms and virtues remain very much alive."[22] Bashar, in a discussion revolving around what he felt was misguided U.S. policy *vis-à-vis* Islamic extremism (thus implying that Syria could teach the United States a thing or two in this regard), recounted to me the dire state of affairs in Syria at the time :

Syria has had a great deal of experience with the Muslim Brothers. We know how to deal with them. The first conflict with them was in 1964 in Hama, but the real conflict started in 1976, when they began to assassinate teachers in universities, doctors, and others. Between 1976 and 1977 we were not sure who was doing this because we thought it might be the Palestinians since we intervened in Lebanon on the side of the Christians in 1976. But we soon found out it was the Muslim Brothers, and my father negotiated with them to possibly become part of the government. They did not say no, but they said they wanted to discuss it. But they kept on killing while they were thinking about it. In the end they did not want to share power—they wanted to take power, and they wanted to transform Syria into an Islamic republic. It took us three years between 1976 and 1979 to understand their ideology—what do they want and how do they think. And there were many Syrians who were sympathetic to them because they were viewed as real Muslims. But they were not for Islam, and the people were naïve to think they were. So we began the conflict with them in 1979; if we started in 1976 we may not have been as successful. It was a difficult time, much worse than when Nasser was confronted by Muslim Brothers, because my father was not as strong as Nasser was at the time, and we were besieged and somewhat isolated in the region.

It was under these conditions that Syria encountered the next challenge to its position in the Middle East: the Israeli invasion of Lebanon in June 1982. As in most crises, there exists possible opportunity in the face of vulnerability, and Asad was determined to make the best out of a potentially catastrophic situation, but he would have to dig down deep into the resources available to him to weather another challenge to his position in the region. It was a game of survival that would be dramatically—and ruthlessly—played.

Syria and Lebanon, Part II

From the Syrian perspective, the Israeli invasion of Lebanon was the expected repercussion of the Egyptian-Israeli peace treaty. It was thought that Israel, freed up on its southern flank, could now concentrate on securing its position to the north. To Asad, the invasion was an attempt to outflank Syria, something Damascus had been wary of for years, a concern that, of course, precipitated its involvement in Lebanon in 1975 and 1976. Syria seemed to be vulnerable, with its regional isolation and domestic problems; for Asad, the timing of the invasion, coming just on the heels of the return of the final portion of the Sinai Peninsula to Egypt, was anything but a surprise. One could almost sense that this was something of a last stand for Syria, or at least for Asad's regime, and, as such, he would fight tooth and nail to prevent an Israeli victory in Lebanon, one that would complete Syria's isolation in the region.

As is well known, in response to PLO attacks into Israel from south Lebanon, what at first seemed to be a repetition of the 1978 Israeli sweep of Palestinian positions in the south escalated into a full-fledged invasion—or what has been described as Prime Minister Menachem Begin's and Defense Minister Ariel Sharon's hidden agenda, that is, the elimination of the PLO as a force in Lebanon, its removal as a viable negotiating partner regarding the disposition of the West Bank and Gaza Strip, and the placement in power in Beirut of a Maronite president, Bashir Gemayel (al-Jumayyil), who would then sign a peace treaty with Israel and remove Syrian troops from the country. Asad's troops were compelled to fight the Israelis alongside the PLO, and they suffered severe losses on the battlefield and in the air despite determined resistance. As the full scope of the Israeli plan unfolded and as casualties mounted inside and outside Beirut, the international community, led by the United States, attempted to bring the bloodletting to a close, just as the Israeli forces stopped on the outskirts of Beirut, hesitant to enter into a house-to-house struggle with PLO and Syrian forces. With the United Nations hamstrung by an expected Soviet veto, the United States, Britain, Italy, and France led a multinational force (MNF) into Beirut in August 1982 with the defined objective of escorting the PLO forces out of the city and guaranteeing the safety of Palestinian civilians left behind in the refugee camps. The former was accomplished in short order, followed by the departure of the MNF—the latter objective was not.

President-elect Bashir Gemayel was assassinated on September 14, less than a month after he was elected president. Most believe that Syria was responsible, in a last-ditch effort to prevent a Maronite-Israeli triumph in Lebanon. Shortly thereafter, in an act of revenge, Christian Phalangist militia units associated with Gemayel, apparently with a green light from Israeli forces, attacked two Palestinian camps in south Beirut, Sabra and Shatila, massacring hundreds, mostly old men, women, and children. The MNF, still anchored offshore, felt obliged to return to Beirut with the nebulous and ill-defined task of restoring order to the chaotic situation.

The longer the U.S.-led MNF stayed in Lebanon the more it began to be seen, certainly from Syria's perspective, as a pro-Maronite—and thus Israeli—prop. The attempt by the Reagan administration to broker an Israeli-Lebanese peace agreement negotiated in May 1983, without Syrian or Soviet participation, seemed to be a case of the United States trying to do diplomatically what the Israelis had tried to do militarily. This came on the heels of the Reagan peace plan put forward during the Israeli invasion in 1982. That plan attempted to take advantage of the PLO's and Syria's weakened position (thus excluding the Soviet Union), in what some have called an alternative version of Camp David, this time pushing for Palestinian-Jordanian cooperation for more Palestinian autonomy on the West Bank and Gaza Strip. Again, from the point of view of Damascus, this approach also seemed to be a flanking operation against Syria through diplomatic means, this time through Jordan. Wherever the direction of diplomacy brokered by Washington, Syria was left out, and if the supposed U.S.-Israeli plan were to succeed, Syria's isolation would be complete and its bargaining strength *vis-à-vis* a return of the Golan Heights would be virtually non-existent.

From this seemingly desperate position, Syria lashed out against the pincer movement any way it could. Fortunately for Damascus, the MNF presence and extended Israeli stay in Lebanon were vehemently opposed by a variety of Lebanese factions, such as the Druze, Shiite Amal, and the new Iranian-backed Shiite group, Hizbollah, thus producing a coincidence of interests that Syria could employ to its advantage. It is in this context that one should read the April 1983 bombing (over 90 killed) of the U.S. embassy and the October 1983 bombing of the U.S. marine barracks (241 military personnel killed) as well as French positions in Beirut—and countless other smaller attacks against what was perceived as a hostile and tendentious MNF. Under this continuous barrage, the MNF evacuated Lebanon by early 1984. The enhanced factionalization of Lebanon due to the breakdown of the state and the subsequent external interference by a multitude of powers made a chaotic situation worse. Opposition to the Israeli occupation increased, forcing Israel in early 1985 to withdraw further southward to the security zone it would maintain along the

Israeli-Lebanese border until its unilateral withdrawal from the country in May 2000.

Many have called this war Israel's "Vietnam"—for the first time in its brief history Israelis themselves perceived the invasion to be offensive in orientation, even imperialist, rather than defensive. Begin and Sharon tried to play kingmaker, and they got burned. In addition, maybe the single most important repercussion of the war was the alienation of South Lebanon's Shiite community, who generally welcomed the Israeli invasion initially because it liberated them from the clenches of and the dangerous environment created by the PLO. But the Israelis stayed on, and they were soon seen not as liberators but as occupiers, and they became a target. In the process, the radicalization of the Shiite community allowed for the entrance of the Shiite Islamic Republic of Iran into the fray, anxious to portray itself as a pan-Islamic force rather than just a Persian Gulf power. What was born was Hizbollah, a militant Shiite Islamist party that eventually forced Israel to leave Lebanon after a fifteen-year guerilla war, and having done so became a model to be emulated in the Middle East and a political force to be reckoned with in Lebanon. It also became another arrow in Asad's quiver in trying to find as much leverage as he could against Israel. The Syrian-Iranian alliance merged with Hizbollah's interests to make the latter that much more lethal and difficult to eradicate.

Asad had won. Through his strategic use of various Lebanese factions, rearming by the Soviet Union, and the commitment born by being pressed against the wall, Syria reemerged as the dominant power in Lebanon, its western flank secure. Syria's Arab credentials were somewhat restored for taking on Israel and the United States and not just surviving but emerging as the victor. Syria was the only player that could have provided some semblance of stability, and essentially the playing field was laid open for Damascus to try to do so. The October 22, 1989, Taif accord brokered by the Saudis was an important turning point in ending the civil war, as most of the Lebanese factions finally realized that the National Pact had to be amended, even though it still did not take into account the prevalence of Shiites in the country, by then making up over 30 percent of the populace. In theory the president, prime minister, and speaker of the house were placed on equal footing, with a rough parity in parliament between Christian and Muslim representatives. The Taif accord also called on Syria to withdraw its troops from Beirut to at least the Bekaa Valley within two years and for the disarming of the militias, presumably the security vacuum to be filled by the Lebanese Forces; in addition, in accordance with UN Security Council Resolution 425, passed in 1978, the agreement called on Israel to withdraw its troops from south Lebanon.

The 1991 Brotherhood treaty was, in essence, Syria's amendment to the Taif accord, putting its stamp on Lebanon following the Gulf war and the George H. W. Bush administration's de facto acquiescence to Syrian dominance in Lebanon. And Lebanon did, in fact, become much more stable under Syrian patronage. The economy improved with impressive growth rates for most of the 1990s while the inflation rate was lowered to less than 10 percent, and all the while foreign investment began to make its way into the country again and Beirut began to rebuild.[23] The irony of Syrian control in Lebanon is that neither Hafiz nor Bashar publicly expressed a desire to annex Lebanon—the touted goal had been to restore political and economic stability to the war-torn country by reestablishing a sound political and economic institutional foundation. The more stable the country, especially when that stability is at Syrian gunpoint, the more benefits accrue from Lebanon. This was achieved in large measure, but the very process of doing so created the framework within which many Lebanese felt they could do without the Syrian presence—they could go it alone, thank you very much; indeed, Hafiz's concentration on and success in Lebanon laid the very seeds of distress in Syria's neighbor that his son has dealt with over the past years.

Rifaat's Putsch

In the midst of the crisis in Lebanon in November 1983, Hafiz al-Asad became very ill, inaugurating a series of events that would soon pit the president against his brother, Rifaat, in a confrontation in Damascus that came perilously close to civil war. It was popularly thought that Asad suffered a heart attack since he was rumored to have heart problems. He did, indeed, suffer from diabetes and lived a very sedentary yet hard-working and stressful lifestyle. According to Patrick Seale, however, the Syrian president was simply exhausted from the stress surrounding the Lebanese situation—the fact that this crisis came on the heels of the MB uprising gave Asad literally no time to catch his breath.[24] Rifaat was one of the most powerful figures in Syria. He was charismatic, outgoing, almost the complete opposite in many ways from his brother. He had built up the formidable Defense Companies, something of a praetorian guard for the regime, and it was primarily he who protected the regime during the MB revolt, leading the onslaught on Hama itself in 1982. The Defense Companies were probably the best trained, paid, and equipped of any single unit in the Syrian military.[25] Because Asad's condition was unknown even to the higher echelons of leadership in Syria, many began to fear the worst. As such, a number of powerful figures in the country, particularly in the military, began to back Rifaat as the best alternative who would maintain the status quo in terms of political and economic privilege. But Asad recovered only to become furious that many of his orders had been ignored and superseded by Rifaat's.

The whole crisis came at a time of potential threat to Syria, especially as the United States rumbled away at Syrian positions with artillery and air force sorties in response to the marine barracks bombing in October. Although Asad was on the verge of victory in Lebanon, with the new Lebanese president, Amin Gemayel (the brother of Bashir), planning to pay homage to Damascus (something he would formally do in February 1984 with the abrogation of the May 1983 Israel-Lebanese agreement), there was still a very real possibility, in the view of the ever-suspicious Syrian president, that the United States could orchestrate his overthrow. As a result, Rifaat's actions, particularly as he was someone who was enamored with the United States and enjoyed close relations with U.S. allies in the region, seemed all too coincidental. Hafiz continued to recover in December, and he systematically tried to pull the noose around Rifaat's neck, hoping to contain and thwart any ambitions he might be seduced to entertain. Finally, military units supporting each brother went out into the streets of Damascus in late March 1984 and faced off against one another, with periodic and sporadic minor encounters for days. Ultimately, in quite dramatic fashion, Hafiz, in full military uniform, along with his eldest son, Basil, walked alone past Rifaat's lines of defense to his home in the Mezzeh district of Damascus. There, with their ailing mother as a witness, Hafiz basically demanded Rifaat stand down and heed his elder brother, which he did. The crisis had passed, and Rifaat would be systematically torn down to vestigial status by a combination of exiles and demotions, with his Defense Companies significantly reduced in size and strength.[26] But, as Seale astutely notes:

> Asad had triumphed, but in the crisis the institutions of his state had made a poor showing. At the moment of danger he had to go down into the street himself and clear the tanks away. Checks, balances, the People's Assembly, the Popular Organizations, indeed the party itself with it extensive structure in both the country and the army, were all of no avail when ambitious generals threatened to shoot it out. In the end it was his personal authority and that alone which held the country together. He was the only pole holding up the tent. It was not a good augury for the future.[27]

At the time, Bashar was in his second year of college at the University of Damascus. When the crisis erupted he remembers having two sets of feelings: one toward Hafiz al-Asad as his father, and one toward him as president. He wondered what would happen if he died. What would happen to the family? What would happen to the country? The students were all very concerned at the university; and even on campus, groups formed in support of Hafiz and others in support of Rifaat, reflecting similar divisions in the military that would soon be played out on the streets of Damascus. Bashar continued to go to class during the crisis and, according to his friends at the time, acted in an absolutely normal fashion, which amazed them because the tension in the city at the time was palpable. He had no extra protection and was typically calm even during the final showdown between his father and his uncle. Like most Syrians, he celebrated his father's recovery and the anti-climactic end to the crisis. But, it would be yet another lesson, another experience to be utilized and drawn upon in the future. Certainly if he became president he would not want the country to be teetering so delicately on the edge, to the point that an ill president could send Syria reeling into civil war. The state had to build up a firmer institutional foundation so that it could better withstand such internal and external disruptions—this was fantasy back then; now Bashar is slowly attempting to turn fantasy into reality. For Hafiz now, blood was not thicker than water, and he became ever more suspicious. He would further restrict the coteries of loyalists around him, become even more isolated than he had been in the past, and, importantly, he would turn more and more to Basil as his eventual successor—he could, after all, trust his eldest son.

By mid-1984, then, Hafiz al-Asad had passed two severe tests, one external and one internal. On the other hand, his attempt to take advantage of Arafat's weakened condition following the PLO's expulsion from Beirut paralleled a U.S.-Israeli push to do the same, albeit for different reasons. For Asad, the aim was to finally gain control of the PLO and eliminate his long-time nemesis, Arafat, as a viable force; for Washington and Tel Aviv, it was to exploit Arafat's desperate situation to compel him to adopt the path of least resistance, that is, the Jordanian option envisioned by the Reagan plan. While Asad won Lebanon, the United States and Israel, relatively speaking, would win the PLO.

Syria initiated in 1983 an uprising in Tripoli, Lebanon, against Arafat's Fatah faction, in the process of which it brought together traditional radical factions of the PLO (such as the PFLP and the DFLP) to establish the Damascus-controlled Palestine National Salvation Front. In the end, however, Arafat's popularity, or maybe it would be more appropriate to say his institutionalization, within the PLO as a whole prevented Asad's own outflanking attempt from succeeding. Syria's intervention against Arafat meant it lost many of the points in the Arab world that it had gained in Lebanon—the self-professed standard-bearer of the Arab cause does not foment intra-Palestinian discord that undermines the movement as a whole. Even though the

Jordanian option had fizzled out by 1986, by the end of the decade Arafat had clearly chosen a diplomatic resolution to the Palestinian problem and situated himself within the moderate Arab camp. The Palestinian intifada or uprising in the occupied territories begun in December 1987 further led to Arafat's revival as a negotiating partner, resulting in late 1988 in the PLO's recognition of Israel, acceptance of UN Security Council Resolutions 242 and 338, and the renunciation of terrorism. Much to Syria's consternation, the PLO had been added to the growing list of Arab entities that seemed to be striking out on their own toward potential peace agreements with Israel.

At the end of the decade Syria's position did not seem to be measurably better than at the beginning. Asad had prevented, for the time being, a Camp David consensus from emerging in the Arab world, yet because of the regional effects of the Iran–Iraq war and such episodes as the intifada, a moderate Arab consensus had developed, one that had rehabilitated Egypt, naturally resulting in the swinging of the power pendulum in the Arab interstate system toward Cairo and away from Damascus, bringing Jordan and the PLO along for the ride. Syria was successful in its attempts to avoid being outflanked either through Jordan or Lebanon, and it rose from the proverbial ashes in the latter to emerge as an indispensable powerbroker actively backed by the Soviet Union. Asad seemed to confirm Henry Kissinger's contention in the 1970s that in the Arab-Israeli arena there can be no war without Egypt, but there can also be no peace without Syria.

Cooperation with the United States: The 1991 Gulf War

In 1989, Syria's position seemed to take a turn for the worse. Iraq had emerged victorious in the Iran–Iraq war after Teheran reluctantly accepted a UN-brokered ceasefire in August 1988—and it was an Iraq that wanted to re-exert its influence in the Middle East. Saddam Hussein remembered Syrian support for his enemy and would make life as difficult as possible for Syria in Lebanon by supporting anti-Syrian groups such as the Christian militia led by Michel Aoun. He also would draw Jordan deeper and deeper into Baghdad's orbit through economic incentives. Furthermore, the pillar of Soviet support that had braced the Syrian regime for most of the decade virtually crumbled with the ascension to power of Mikhail Gorbachev in 1985 and the Red Army exit from Afghanistan by early 1989, both of which led to a dramatic reassessment of Soviet foreign policy that emphasized a drawing down of Soviet commitments abroad, more concentration on domestic restructuring, and improving ties with the United States. This did not bode well for Syria, as Moscow first urged and then backed the PLO's decision to pursue a negotiated solution, and the Kremlin also improved its relations with Israel. Gorbachev made it clear to Asad upon the Syrian president's visit to Moscow in April 1987 that Syria's "reliance on military force in settling the Arab-Israeli conflict has completely lost its credibility," and he went on to suggest that Damascus abandon its doctrine of strategic parity and seek to establish a "balance of interests" toward a political settlement in the Middle East.[28]

In addition to these problems in the foreign policy arena, Syria's economy continued to deteriorate, owing in large measure to the concentration of economic resources in the military in the attempt to achieve strategic parity with Israel. Compounding the continuing burden of an overly dominant public sector were a number of problems inhibiting economic growth, including the lack of a private banking system or stock market to organize capital; an inadequate regulatory regime and insufficient transparency; a private sector too fragmented to lead the way toward capital accumulation; rampant corruption creating proscribed entrances into the Syrian economy in connivance with government officials; falling oil prices, thus decreasing aid from oil-rich Arab states and remittances; and finally, perhaps the most damaging of all, a population-growth rate of about 3.6 percent per annum, placing more pressure on a dilapidated and corrupt system to create jobs and keep pace, the failure of which could lead to further socioeconomic dislocation and domestic political turmoil—this is a situation that, if anything, is worse today; this was Bashar's inheritance.

Because of his position at the end of the 1980s, Asad was again forced to change his policy in a dramatic fashion, much as he had done at the beginning of the decade—he took Gorbachev's advice. In December 1988, Asad "acknowledged the importance of Egypt in the Arab arena," the first time he had publicly praised Egypt since before the Egyptian-Israeli peace treaty. By the end of 1989 Damascus had reestablished full diplomatic relations with Cairo.[29] With an eye toward isolating Iraq as well as building bridges to the United States, Syria also began to improve its relationship with Saudi Arabia. While maintaining the link with Iran, partly to contain the Iraqi threat, partly to continue its relationship with Shiite groups in Lebanon, and partly to remain a credible military threat to Israel, Syria made a strategic choice to join the Arab-Israeli peace process, the ultimate objective of which was the return of the Golan Heights and a comprehensive peace.

To the rest of the world, the outward manifestation of this policy shift was Syria's participation in the U.S.-led UN coalition to expel Iraq from Kuwait in the 1990 to 1991 Gulf crisis and war. Not only was it participating in an alliance whose objective was to weaken, if not destroy, the war-making capacity of its arch-nemesis in the Arab arena, Syria was also clearly situating itself in the Arab world's moderate camp and opening up the economic doors of investment and aid from the West and grateful Arab Gulf states. To the United States, Syria's inclusion in the coalition, although mostly symbolic, was, in effect, the most important of all the Arab states. Since Syria had been at the vanguard of the "Steadfastness Front" of Arab states arrayed against Israel, its joining up made the coalition against Saddam Hussein seem as if it consisted of the entire Arab world rather than the usual pro-Western suspects, which, if the latter had been the case, Baghdad could have utilized to its own propaganda advantage.[30] It also broke a number of taboos since, although Israel was purposely excluded from the Gulf war coalition, Syria and the other Arab states were, in essence, aligned with U.S. and Israeli objectives *vis-à-vis* Iraq.

Syria's sponsorship of and participation in the Damascus Declaration security grouping shortly after the end of the Gulf war, consisting of the Gulf Cooperation Council (GCC)* states plus Syria and Egypt, demonstrated the regional thrust of its new policy. Ironically, just as Iraq's invasion of Iran compelled Syria to embark upon its own strategic path in the region, albeit with substantial Soviet assistance, so did Iraq's invasion of Kuwait accelerate Syria's backpedaling toward Egypt, Saudi Arabia, and the American-sponsored peace process, in a way rejoining the inter-Arab paradigmatic line-up of the early 1970s. For Asad, establishing a stronger link with Washington was very important, and to do this he had to go through Israel; indeed, some have accused Asad of engaging in the peace process not so much to redefine Syria's relationship with Israel as to improve Syria's ties with the United States and the West following the end of the superpower cold war. This would not only have economic benefits at a time when Syria desperately needed them, but Asad's engagement in a peace process brokered by the United States was his best defense against Israeli pressure, as Washington, it was thought, would act to curtail Israel in order to maintain Syria's involvement in the process, one that could lead to an entirely new American-dominated Middle East system. It also opened up possibilities of securing his position in Lebanon as a quid pro quo with the United States, as Washington cast a blind eye toward Syrian consolidation with the ousting of the Iraqi-supported Christian militia led by General Michel Aoun.

As such, Syria emerged as the key Arab player in the convening of the Madrid peace conference in October 1991, co-sponsored by the United States and the Soviet Union and including a Lebanese delegation (clearly acting under the direction of Damascus) and a Jordanian delegation that also con-

---

* A sub-regional organization formed in 1981 in reaction to the Iran–Iraq war, comprised of Bahrain, Kuwait, Oman, Qatar, Saudi Arabia, and the United Arab Emirates.

sisted of Palestinian representatives from the occupied territories, i.e. not the PLO. For the first time, Syrian officials publicly sat down with Israeli officials to discuss peace. The Bush administration was leveraging its newly found position in the region in the wake of the Gulf war and the end of the cold war to energize the peace process and move it to an entirely new level, as it had promised a number of participants in the Gulf war coalition it would do in the war's aftermath. As with the Gulf war coalition, Syria's participation was important because without it any conference held (which would have been unlikely in any event) would include only the pro-Western Arab states. That they got Asad to attend is a tribute to the diplomatic efforts of the United States as well as a number of Arab countries—and to the Syrian president himself, for he realized the shifting winds in the region. There existed now a window of opportunity to regain the Golan Heights and reposition Syria in the region both economically and politically. Even though the exchanges among the participants in Madrid were more acrimonious than cordial, a truly comprehensive peace process was under way. Arab parties would continue to meet separately with Israel in Washington, paralleled by multilateral talks at various locales focusing upon such issues as arms control, trade, and water-sharing.[31]

By 1992/1993, Israel's new prime minister, Yitzhak Rabin, and the new Clinton administration preferred to concentrate on the Israeli-Syrian track over the Israeli-Palestinian one, primarily because of the inherently less complex nature of the former in addition to the fact that Israeli leaders simply trusted Asad more than Arafat.[32] But progress with Syria was limited, and that track would soon be overshadowed by the September 1993 Israeli–PLO Declaration of Principles. The agreement was largely negotiated outside the Madrid process in what became known as the Oslo channel. Soon thereafter, as momentum built in the region, the Jordanian-Israeli peace treaty was signed in 1994. Asad was furious with both Arafat and King Hussein for, in his view, doing something very similar to what Sadat had done. It had been an axiom of Syrian foreign policy to maximize Arab bargaining leverage. In essence, the failure of Asad to corral Jordan and the PLO within Syria's orbit in the 1980s had now become manifest. On the other hand, now that the PLO and Jordan had signed accords with Israel, no longer would Damascus feel completely obligated to subscribe to the Palestinian or Arab nationalist line, for the PLO itself had compromised its position. Though bereft of some of its bargaining power, Syria now felt free to pursue its own interests to a greater extent than it had in the past, first and foremost, of course, the return of the Golan Heights.

Because Syria is a relatively weak country when compared to many of its neighbors, its foreign policies have tended to wax and wane based on perceived circumstances at any given time. Hafiz al-Asad pursued and implemented a very pragmatic foreign policy that went against the grain on several occasions, but he, his regime, and his country survived a multitude of internal and external threats. This compelled Syria to embrace partners, such as Iran and the Soviet Union, that produced immediate positive results but also complicated its regional and international standing. The Asad regime was more Bonapartist and less doctrinaire in both the domestic and foreign policy arenas. Hafiz al-Asad showed remarkable flexibility in some cases and utter ruthlessness in others in order to survive and advance Syria's interests. He had done an admirable job as far as dictators go. Despite siding with Iran, the Soviet Union, Hizbollah, and radical Palestinian groups, by the mid-1990s Syria was engaged in a peace process with Israel and developing a positive relationship with the United States.

It was amid this hopeful environment, possibly more propitious than at any other time since the creation of the state of Israel for finally putting to rest the Arab-Israeli conflict, that tragedy struck the Asad household with maybe the darkest day in Hafiz al-Asad's life—his eldest son was killed in a car accident. Bashar received the phone call in London.

Chapter 4

From Eye Doctor to Heir Apparent

Bashar cannot really say specifically why he chose the field of ophthalmology. It was just one of those things that appealed to him after he had tested the waters with a number of different subjects during his schooling. If it had been up to his father he probably would have become a cardiologist, but he liked the precision in ophthalmology, particularly in its surgical procedures. It is also fairly typical among the rich and powerful families in Syria (and elsewhere in the Arab world) for the second son to become a doctor while the eldest follows in his father's footsteps. But Bashar grew up in a Sunni environment in Damascus as the president's son as opposed to the minority Alawite environment in which his father was raised, so his opportunities were much more varied than his father's. As such, he chose to carve out a different type of career than his father or his older brother. Bashar very much enjoyed the healing side of ophthalmology in addition to its technical aspects. He liked the dramatic way in which patients heal, the way that a person who once could not see suddenly can. The results of his training and steady hands became manifest in a distinct and open fashion. If only the positive results of his presidency to date were as easily identifiable, so dramatic. This is probably one of the most frustrating aspects of his presidency: the absence of immediacy in terms of outcome and the inability to manipulate results directly with his own hands in a kind of societal surgery.

A Career in Medicine

In Syria, if a medical career beckons, you enter medical school directly from high school (secondary school in Syria). So Bashar was only seventeen when he entered the University of Damascus in September 1982. One specializes in medicine in the faculty of medicine at the university for six years rather than, as in the United States, undertaking four years of undergraduate school and then attending medical school. As such, Bashar received his degree in ophthalmology in 1988—he was a licensed ophthalmologist. Following this, the now Dr. Bashar al-Asad had a four-year internship at Tishreen (Liberation) Military Hospital in Damascus—he was an army doctor. At Tishreen, he engaged in major surgeries, including cataracts and glaucoma, and he assisted in retina and cornea transplants. He even did some plastic surgery.

For the most part Bashar enjoyed his time at the university, although, as mentioned in the previous chapter, he had to deal with problems associated with being the president's son that went far beyond the usual challenges of a college student. Certainly the Israeli invasion of Lebanon only a few months before he began college as well as the crisis between his father and uncle in his second year made life on campus a kind of escape from the politics and tensions that permeated even Hafiz's valiant attempts to shield his family from the repercussions, positive and negative, of his job. Bashar kept a small circle of friends at the university among a diverse and larger group of friends with whom he "hung out" on campus. Most of his college friends continued on in their chosen medical professions, some practicing in Syria, others having moved to Europe or the United States to pursue their medical careers.

Bashar was popular among his college friends, and they often went out on the town to restaurants and cafes in the evenings. As with his elementary-school classmates, his university friends saw him as a very loyal friend who did not in any way lord it over them; indeed, it was usually quite the opposite— some of his friends at times wished he would take on some of the trappings that one would expect a child of a powerful Syrian family to have. Bashar used to drive a four- to five-year-old Peugeot to campus, as he lived only about ten to fifteen minutes away. The other sons of the rich and powerful in Syria would have a Mercedes or BMW, or were even chauffeured to campus. The type of car one has is very important in terms of status in the Arab world among the elite classes; indeed, it is a very hierarchical society, where the lines between classes are distinct with regard to style and behavior. The Asad family's approach was the complete opposite of this, almost a reverse snobbery. During Bashar's first year of college, even though the incident at Hama had occurred earlier in 1982, there still remained security concerns. As a result, students could not park their cars in many of the parking lots they had normally used on campus. A number of children of the Syrian elite were allowed to park in special areas on campus for security reasons, and certainly Bashar could have used his father's pass. He refused to do this, parking outside along with his friends and walking to campus. He wanted to fit in, he wanted to be thought of as normal, and he was almost neurotic about it. This would remain a signature characteristic even during his presidency.

Bashar apparently liked ophthalmology. Many of his classmates at medical school, a good portion of whom presumably were compelled by their parents to enter medicine more for status than interest, openly disdained their studies and their anticipated occupation. But Bashar was never like this, according to his friends—he was satisfied with his chosen profession. Moreover, he was good at it. He was popular with patients, displaying a caring, jovial bedside manner that contrasted with that of other physicians who viewed the day's rounds as nothing but toil and drudgery. Bashar was also quite successful with his surgeries, and it is this aspect of the field that truly interested him; indeed, today he says this is what he misses most about his former career—the surgery, the new techniques and innovative equipment, and procedures such as laser surgery. He tries to keep up with the new medical procedures by reading professional journals, but he has scant time to do so as president.

It was after his four-year stint honing his specialty at Tishreen Hospital that Bashar decided to go to the next level of ophthalmology. There were several countries he could travel to in order to learn new procedures and essentially become the equivalent of board certified. He even considered the United States, which so soon after the Gulf war did not seem to be as outlandish an option as it would have been a decade earlier (or later). But he decided to go to England, where the exams, according to some of his medical colleagues, are much tougher to pass than in the United States or some other countries in Europe. Only about one-quarter of the doctors pass the first time they take the exam compared to about 70 to 80 percent in the United States; indeed, Bashar failed the first time he took the exam. Also, his second language, after Arabic, is French, and he only had at best a halting command of English when he embarked upon his new adventure in London. This was definitely not the easy choice, but Bashar seemed to be up to the challenge, and he relished the opportunity to prove his worth under such potentially difficult circumstances. There was never any doubt, however, that—in contrast to some of his college mates—he would return to Syria to practice ophthalmology, if anything as a civic contribution to society. The Syrian education system is sorely lacking in training in all fields when compared to that of more developed countries. For many it is necessary to go abroad to learn the latest techniques and ideas and then bring them back to the home country. Unfortunately for Syria, most Syrians, indeed most Arabs, who study abroad, tend to stay abroad following the completion of their programs. Throughout the Arab world, particularly in Syria, bringing back expatriates has become a major policy objective, not only to bring their money back for local investment but also, more importantly, to bring back their skills and knowledge. Bashar was always coming home.[1]

Bashar in London

Bashar entered into what was, in effect, a residency at the Western Eye Hospital in London. The hospital is part of the St. Mary's National Health Service (NHS) Trust, located in the Paddington district in northwest London, and the Western Eye Hospital itself is situated in the central London area of Marylebone, a few blocks east of St. Mary's Hospital. Although the area is relatively upscale, the hospital itself is a rather modest, old five-story building. Originally known as the Western Ophthalmic Hospital, it began its medical life in 1856, the current structure having been built in 1936. The hospital is a mix of old and new in the inside—actually mostly old, and it is a little beaten up in places—though it has been strategically modernized. The Trust advertises itself as providing "a wide range of general and specialist hospital services from the world famous St. Mary's Hospital and the Western Eye Hospital." It is a large complex, employing over 3,500 staff and physicians. The system has a long history and is home to two Nobel Prize winners, including Sir Alexander Fleming, who discovered penicillin in 1928. So this was not some pseudo-school of medicine in a glamorous location; it was a well-known medical facility—a serious place for serious doctors. The Western Eye Hospital conducts approximately 3,500 major operations per year, but it is slated to close within about five to seven years because it is so old; a new facility, also to be called the Western Eye Hospital, is being built as part of the St. Mary's Hospital complex.

Bashar moved to London in the fall of 1992, spending less than two years there. He lived by himself in a flat located in Lennox Gardens near Sloane Street, just south of Hyde Park in the upscale Royal Borough of Kensington and Chelsea area of central London. The flat was on one floor of a nice four-and-a-half-story red-brick town house that was part of a row of town houses circling Lennox Gardens. He appeared to fit seamlessly into one of the bastions of the Western world. Interested in computers, he found the freedom of Internet access in London positively enlightening, especially since the Internet would not enter Syria for several more years to come; indeed, every morning the first thing he did was surf the Internet, especially the Top 40 Billboard chart to see which songs were popular. He enjoyed very little social life in London, primarily because he was either working or studying for exams, and he did not really mingle with the large Arab community in the city for the same reason. It was an eye-opening experience for Bashar. He learned a great deal about the level of technological modernization necessary in an increasingly globalized world, something he would assiduously work to duplicate in a small way in his homeland.

At the Hammersmith Hospital, another teaching hospital in London, a Syrian friend of Bashar's approached one of the ophthalmology surgeons, Mr. Ed Schulenberg, a South African who had been in Britain for twenty years, and asked him if he would take on someone as a trainee.[2] He arranged for Bashar to meet Schulenberg in a Middle Eastern restaurant in London in early 1992. Bashar made a very good impression, and Schulenberg agreed to take him on, awarding the future Syrian president with an unpaid, self-funded fellowship. It was a propitious time for such an endeavor; Mr. Schulenberg informed me that today it would have been very difficult to accept Bashar in such an informal manner—it is now much more competitive, limited, and regimented. Bashar was officially accepted as a trainee in the eye department at St. Mary's Hospital, training to become an eye surgeon in what in the United States would be the equivalent of a residency. The ultimate goal of Bashar's stay was to receive Fellowship of the Royal College of Ophthalmology, or the FRC. One undergoes clinical and academic training in order to pass the written and practical examinations. Bashar ended up spending less than two years in the program, but if he had continued his studies, he probably would have remained in London for another three years (five in total) before receiving the FRC.

While at the Western Eye Hospital, Bashar did surgery twice a week in one of the four theaters (operating rooms) in the facility, beginning with minor cases but then assisting a doctor in major eye surgery toward the end of his stay. There were then three days of outpatient treatment in the clinic and one day of inpatient follow-up—and studying for exams whenever he could find the time. Bashar would attend teaching programs, classes, guest lectures, or clinical presentations in the morning, and in the afternoon he would work in the A & E department ("accident and emergency," the equivalent of an emergency room), where he would encounter all sorts of situations. He was kept very busy; in fact, a few months before he returned to Syria he approached Mr. Schulenberg, his immediate supervisor, and told him that he could not expect to pass the exam and continue his work schedule—he needed more time to study. He was granted his request and given time away from the hospital to concentrate on his studies—he would then return to surgery following the exam, or at least that was the plan. He had just returned from Syria after the New Year's holiday as a student cramming for the first of two sets of exams (three sets today) in the FRC process when the news arrived that forever changed his life.

It was during the process of studying for a second crack at this exam, one that Schulenberg believes he would have easily passed, that Bashar received the news of Basil's death and returned home—and he suspected that it would be for good this time. His career as an ophthalmologist was over almost before it had begun.

Mr. Schulenberg remembers Bashar as a gentle, sympathetic doctor with a wonderful bedside manner that distinguished him from most of the other doctors. He was a very good time-keeper, always punctual (he continues to be this way today). He was apparently very popular with the staff at the hospital, as he was known as an honest and compassionate individual, a "real nice chap" as one former staff member fondly recalls. He was just "one of the guys" at the hospital, and he never had any bodyguards at the facility. Schulenberg opines that Bashar would have been "a very good doctor. He had an amazing amount of respect for everyone around him." When Bashar met the Queen of England and Prime Minister Tony Blair in London in 2003, he made a special point of visiting the hospital again to see all of those with whom he had worked. Schulenberg, of course, saw Bashar upon that visit and remembers that he had not changed at all since his days in London. Bashar clearly enjoyed his time at the hospital.

Groomed to be President?

It is at this point that there exists a clear divergence in Bashar's trajectory toward the presidency as depicted in the West—actually, almost anywhere outside Syria—and as portrayed in Syria itself among the president's closest associates, friends, and family. The commonly accepted picture is that Bashar was summoned back to Syria by his father following Basil's death. Almost immediately Bashar was systematically integrated into the military, taking a crash course in military training and courses for command and staff as well as tank battalion command. He advanced quickly through the ranks by the end of the decade through the Syrian officer corps, much as Basil had been elevated in the late 1980s and early 1990s. Upon Bashar's return from London he was at the equivalent level of a captain (*naqib*), yet by mid-1997 he had been promoted to lieutenant-colonel (*muqaddam*) followed by a promotion to full colonel (*aqid*) in early 1999.[3] He had also assumed Basil's role as brigade commander in the elite Republican Guard.

According to this line, Bashar was given other increasingly important posts in the government and a higher profile in society at large as the decade wore on; he went from being chairman of the Syrian Computer Society in 1994 to being handed the very important Lebanese "file" by 1998 (overseeing Syria's vital relationship with Lebanon) and heading an anti-corruption campaign to weed out those elements that may be opposed to his succession. His father orchestrated this march into politics by pushing aside older officers in the military and promoting a tranche of younger officers about the same age as Bashar who would presumably be more loyal and remain subordinate to him. Hafiz remembered that even during the height of his power, when he fell ill in 1983, a number of his most senior and loyal generals and government officials briefly backed Rifaat until it was clear the president had recovered—he knew that they were most interested in retaining their political and economic power positions, i.e. the *status quo ante*. Mandatory retirements were therefore suddenly enforced and long-fallow anti-corruption laws were selectively applied to clear a more secure path for Bashar.

It almost seemed to be a race against time: that is, did Hafiz have enough time to prepare the ground for a smooth succession for his young and inexperienced son before his health finally gave way? In essence, Hafiz had barely secured enough support and had gotten rid of just enough opposition for Bashar to take over in June 2000. However, there had not been enough change to allow the new president to implement the type of reform measures necessary to put Syria on the road toward more rapid economic and political development. There were still too many of the *status quo ante* "old guard" and not enough of the "new guard." As one foreign-embassy official exclaimed to me in Damascus, "For God's sake, he [Bashar] had an office right next to his father's in the [Rowda] palace downtown; so much went through him—he *had* to expect it." Bashar was clearly being groomed for the presidency since his return from London—he knew it, and he embraced the anticipated role.

But there is quite a different picture painted in Syria itself, especially among those who were associated with Hafiz and, of course, among those who are now associated with President Bashar himself. It is that Bashar in no way, shape, or form was being prepared to succeed his father—he neither expected it nor did he actively seek it; indeed, it really was not until his father died and the people clamored for him—and elements in the government and military-security apparatus gave the green light and paved the road—that Bashar realized once and for all that he was going to become the next president of Syria. Furthermore, many of these same people strongly suggest that this also held true for Basil, that he, too, was not being specifically groomed for the presidency, a notion that almost everyone outside Syria finds totally unbelievable.

On this subject Bashar says:

I never expected to be president. It was mentioned in the press and magazines everywhere but I never thought about it. He never mentioned it or tried to push me to be president. I wanted to work in the public domain and I was a member of the [Baath] party, but I did not expect to lead the party. He did not plan for me to lead the party; if so, he could have arranged that much earlier. There was a party conference already scheduled to be held the next week [the first such regional party congress meeting in fifteen years], and they wanted to cancel it, but I said no, and at the conference I was elected as head of the party. He [Hafiz al-Asad] never tried to get me to do anything presidential. It was my ambition to work in the public domain. But he never prepared me to be president.

I asked the president about his entrance back into the military after returning from London, to which he replied:

I went back in because I was a military doctor. My father told me, "are you going back to London?" and I said "no." Then he asked me what I was now going to do. I told him that I am military now, and in the military you have the right to change specialties, such as toward engineering or officer school. For weeks he said that I can go back to London or stay in Syria as a doctor, but I said I wanted to go into the military, and eventually he was convinced of this and he said OK. I did not think of politics [meaning government since there really is no politics in a traditional sense in Syria]. For years I only wanted to work in the public domain. In 1998 I started to become involved in politics for several reasons. One reason was that people would always come up to me wherever I was to ask for help and tell [me] about their problems. I would tell them that I am not an official and could not help, but because of my family position I thought that if I could help I should. I have always believed that I should not use my position to help myself but to help others. This is how I started thinking about politics. This is when I started to involve myself more and more with the people, attend their lectures, learn what they want, and what they are thinking. This is the most important thing, so I began to get involved in all the details and get involved in different sectors of society. I was only involved in politics by being asked by the people and by being asked by [foreign minister] Farouk al-Sharaa to visit France in 1999 to meet with President Jacques Chirac. I was also invited to Lebanon and made a trip to Saudi Arabia, during the course of which I made the hajj [pilgrimage to Mecca]. It is not that I did not have any desire [to get involved in politics]. I just never really thought about it. Sometimes you don't like to think about it. Am I qualified? How can you know if you are qualified unless you try? And you won't have the answer until you are fifty or sixty years old. Studying medicine in the last year of medical school you cannot think that you will be in a position in the following year to fix somebody's eye, to take that responsibility, but you do it. I never expected myself to cut into an eye, but you do it. You don't know if you have the potential unless you try. I had some confidence—you like your country, you understand what the people want, but it is only in theory. It doesn't mean that you are confident that you can do it or that you have the tools to do it. It is very complicated, but I said I would do it.

I told him that in the West the presumption was that he was, indeed, being groomed after he returned from London in 1994, especially when he was given the Lebanon file and headed an anti-corruption campaign ostensibly, it was thought, to help clear the way for him to become president by using it as a device to remove potential obstacles to his succession. In response he said:

How do you fight corruption if you are not part of the government or the judicial system? Fighting corruption means everything, bringing corrupt people to justice and having a new administrative system. It was known about me that I am against corruption. I have close relations with people who are against corruption, particularly writers, and I was encouraging them to write about it in newspapers. Concerning Lebanon, I already had relations with the Lebanese. I have always been interested in Syrian-Lebanese affairs. I was invited to visit Lebanon [in 1999]—I was not sent by my father. Actually, my father thought that my visit could be misperceived, and I told him that maybe he was right, but that I had already accepted the invitation. I cannot say no to my father, but I was invited [by the Lebanese government]. It was really just public relations.

Maybe his father did some things to prepare the way for him without his knowledge, I suggested. Bashar said: "Definitely, every father would like his son to be successful, but he was never emotional, he was never affected by emotion. He was an emotional person but he never let this emotion show, so if I wanted to be a doctor, that would be fine—the most important thing is to be successful."

Still, Bashar's claim continues to strain credulity in the eyes of many, so I asked him again about his decision in 1994 to go in a completely different direction from ophthalmology, to which he responded:

We live in a political family. This is our normal environment in which we live. Second, I am a person who has a vision for his country, as a son of the president, you always have a vision. It's the family code that you are not allowed to have a private job or business or private clinic—you must never use your position for your own interests, you must use it for the government or for the public, and you were brought up with this idea—always be for the public and always feel for the people. So that makes you exposed to large sections of Syrian society, thus giving me a larger vision. This became part of my nature, and Basil was the same way, but he was already in the public domain so there was no need for the president to bring him in. But when he died I thought it was my duty to get involved. And there was a strong desire on my part that now that I have authority I can apply my vision—before I did not have any authority. Basil was young when he died, and since my father was not ill at the time, we did not talk about who would be the next president. [Basil] was into sports, equestrian, the Syrian Computer Society, which I headed later. He was not that involved in politics at the time of his death, similar to my situation before I became president. Basil was a very ambitious person, but in our house we never talked about this. I could not even talk about it because it would look like I am seeking this position. We *never* talked about it in our house—it was not a good idea.

I asked Bashar if he thought his father would be pleased that he became president, and he responded, "I never talked to him about that, and in any case he was not the type of person who ever said 'bravo' or good job—he rather told you about the things you should not do, the negative." Bashar's very active and cosmopolitan wife, Asma, is also adamant that he was not being groomed at the time, nor was there even a discussion concerning succeeding his father. He went to the university to go to school and he went into the military to become an officer, not to be groomed to take over. Bashar was never brought up as the president's son and he was never brought up to be a president, something that she hopes to replicate with their own three-year-old son, Hafiz; indeed, she is absolutely insistent that her children should be kept out of the limelight, that they will not be brought up or prepared in any role that they do not want to take or do not choose themselves.

Farouk al-Sharaa, Syria's long-time foreign minister (since 1984), who has reached iconic status in the region for his tough, steadfast negotiating style, has an interesting take on Bashar:

I think Bashar was not at all thinking about this [succeeding his father], although Basil definitely expected it. I have this analogy between him [Bashar] and Rajiv Gandhi [prime minister of India from 1984 to 1989]. Rajiv also had no idea he would become the prime minister of India. But because his elder brother died in an airplane accident, he had to take the job. He was not prepared for this, yet he became a brilliant prime minister, a really brilliant leader. From the time I really got to know Bashar [which he says was in the two years preceding the death of Hafiz al-Asad] I saw that he is an able man, a clever, smart person, having charisma, a sense of responsibility, a sense of leadership. He wants to know, he is open, transparent, and he would like to understand the people's experiences and other countries' experiences, so I drew this analogy between him and Rajiv.[4]

Regarding whether or not Bashar was specifically being groomed, he stated:

I don't think so because I still remember that even after the death of Basil he [Bashar] did not even visit any countries informally—he was not in a position to do that. He [Hafiz] did not encourage that, he did not like that. So I do not think he was very enthusiastic to see his son replacing him, simply because perhaps he never thought he was going to die. I am telling the truth, it is not because he did not like his son; quite to the contrary I have been to see him many times when he was in the residence, and Bashar would suddenly come rushing out and he closed the door and always talked to him, so he loves him, but he did not want to rush him.

Dr. Bouthaina Shaaban has been a long-time, close confidante of the Asad family. She is close to Bushra, and she was the translator (and sometime adviser) for Hafiz in the 1990s. As such, she became a close adviser to and translator for Bashar, until she took up the position as minister of expatriates in September 2003. I asked her if she had any idea that Bashar would become the next president, and she replied:

No, no. I am close to the family, and I know they are a very close family, a great deal of love for each other. So when he came back after he lost his brother, it was not surprising that he did not return to London—Bushra told me he was not returning. President Bashar felt he had to stay with his parents after the tragedy and comfort them. He said he is not going back— he is going to stay with his parents.

After Basil's death in 1994, there were pictures all over the country of Hafiz, Basil, and Bashar together, with the inscription, "the Leader, the Example, and the Hope," respectively. Even today in the country you still see these signs, although not nearly as prominently displayed as they had been before Bashar took power and consciously tried to prevent any personality cult from developing around him as it did his father—which embarrassed Bashar while growing up. The Syrian demi-god was simply his dad. But the posters, billboards, and pictures of the three certainly implanted the idea that Bashar was next in line, that he was being purposely elevated in the regime propaganda to embellish and heighten his status. Most Syrians I spoke to at the time certainly expected Bashar to succeed his father. Bashar and his father were aware of such speculation, but there was not much dissuasion of this notion from any government quarters. Some pictures had Bashar look much more muscular than his current trim physique; some had him look older, and thus wiser, than his youth indicated. Shaaban has an explanation for all this, one that is similar to that given by other Syrian officials who have commented on it:

> I think it was something that people just did because they love Hafiz al-Asad so much that when he lost Basil they felt so sorry for the family and wanted to make him feel that he had another son that we would love to get into government because Basil was really more engaged in the country and with the people. Bashar was always studying although socially he was active, he had his own IT [information technology, presumably a reference to his role in the Syrian Computer Society], and his own activities, but I think it was a natural response of people to support the president and his wife, that Bashar is the hope.

Dr. Imad Moustapha is the Syrian ambassador to the United States. He was appointed to this position personally by Bashar al-Asad in early 2003. He has a long academic background, is an accomplished scholar and a former dean at the University of Damascus. He came to Bashar's attention when he gave a public lecture in April 1997 at the National Library on how Syria should change its attitudes toward the Internet, advocating much wider access to it beyond the restricted fortunate few who were then allowed into it. This obviously caught Bashar's eye as the chairman of the Syrian Computer Society and long an advocate of just such change in Syria. A short time after he became president, Bashar established the Faculty of Information Technology at the University of Damascus by presidential decree, and Dr. Imad was chosen as the dean. Dr. Imad is certainly not a career diplomat nor a member of the Baath party; indeed, he was known as a serious proponent of reform, but he began to become increasingly involved in Syrian-American dialogue at various conferences over the next couple of years until he was assigned to the Syrian embassy in Washington as chargé d'affaires, from which he rose to ambassador. President Bashar meets with the ambassador often when the latter is in Syria, and he certainly values his advice on the important and troublesome American-Syrian relationship. Even though Dr. Imad was not in the government in the 1990s, nor when Bashar became president, I believe he has a great deal of objective insight into Bashar al-Asad. When I asked him whether he thought Bashar was being groomed for the presidency he said:

> This is a very difficult question. I will never be able to tell you exactly, so I will tell you only what I think. Syria has a highly centralized presidential system. Mere access to the president means that person has tremendous influence. What I would tell you is the following: yes, the perception in Syria is that the son would be one of Hafiz's closest advisers and he would have a great deal of influence. And Bashar at that time probably thought he had an important role to play in the system, but not as a successor—and he did play an important role. Lots of people thought of him as a breath of fresh air in politics and thought maybe he can deliver things that for one reason or another the regime could not do because Hafiz was very ill. He seemed at that time as a forthcoming, honest person with high moral integrity, with modesty and determination to help modernize Syria, so lots of people supported him. So on the one hand you have this person who belongs to the family of the president, the president was not in the best of health, so by default he would have lots of influence in Syria because of the political system whether you like it or not. On the other hand, you had lots of people in Syria, especially the intellectuals, the intelligentsia, people who were usually outside of the political system gathering around him and get-ting as close as possible to him and placing responsibility on him that he should deliver things—so he knew he was in a position where he could play an important role. My personal guess would be that there was no explicit grand plan for him to become the successor, but that it was the nature of the events that occurred, especially the sudden death of Hafiz al-Asad. We all knew that he was not in the best of health, but it was still a shock when he died. Suddenly the system that Hafiz had built [was in danger of crum-bling and some people feared this] and the majority of the people wanted to see that open-minded, earnest young man become leader of Syria. Both desires came very close to each other, and I think Bashar becoming president was the natural result of this.

One of the mantras of the new regime has been "change within continuity," which reflects the dialectic at work in a country such as Syria. There is a recog-nition that change must occur but also a reluctance to bring about that change in a dramatic fashion for fear of undermining the very bases of power too quickly and/or causing too much societal disruption. There is almost too much societal inertia economically, culturally, and politically to bring about change in anything but an incremental fashion. In this way, it seems, many

Syrians, conditioned to the static, were almost relieved that Bashar, another Asad, had come to power. On this point, Dr. Imad adds:

Here in the Middle East sometimes people are dismayed or shocked when a leader dies and there is fear that there will be an absolute change in policy, like what Sadat did after Nasser. Even those who did not like Hafiz al-Asad respected him because he did not cave in and play the Middle East game. He was steadfast throughout and did not go for an easy peace with Israel by forgetting our claims on the Golan or the Palestinians. So at least there was this consensus that whether you liked or disliked the regime of Hafiz al-Asad, on this one particular issue they felt comfortable with Hafiz, so when Bashar came to power there was this sense that he would not betray his father's heritage on national and pan-Arab issues, so at least they thought there would not be another Sadat. Now when I meet with him he has more and more grown into it, and he is becoming a professional and experienced politician.

A couple of Bashar's friends from his college and elementary-school days say that he did, indeed, take on extra responsibilities during the period between 1994 and 2000—no one disputes this. He was doing many of the same things that Basil did—chairman of the Syrian Computer Society, rising military officer, etc.—so the assumption was natural that Bashar would be in a position, like Basil, to extend a great deal of influence in Syria even if he was not the de facto anointed successor. Hafiz was burned by Rifaat in 1983–1984, so this is why he wanted everything to go through Basil. Basil was in front and Bashar, as the second eldest son, was in the back, although he was involved in various aspects of society and gained some political experience even at college and at medical school, contrary to the idea that he was totally untested. Bashar's friends comment that when Basil died, Bashar simply moved to the front, and as such he was more exposed. One friend remembers that in the 1995–1996 period he met Bashar in a restaurant in Damascus after which they went to a house to attend a party. At the party Bashar sat in a seat and heard the complaints of many people who were there, almost as if he was playing the traditional role ascribed to a tribal *shaykh*. Already he was starting to play a role that was quite different from the more "out-of-the-spotlight" one he had not only been used to but also relished in the past.

One of Bashar's close friends, someone who was also very close to Basil, responding to the popular perception that Bashar's rise to power was carefully orchestrated, commented that:

I can understand how in the West they thought this. But that is not what happened. The late president worked eighteen hours a day, yet he never took politics inside his home, and Bashar is from that same background. The father did not talk about Bashar becoming president, but maybe as a son of a president you naturally think of politics at some level. Why don't people get upset about the Gandhi family in India or the Bush family in the United States when they essentially succeed each other? Bashar and his brothers and his sister are very proud to be the children of Hafiz al-Asad, and it is natural that they would want to carry on his tradition and legacy, although perhaps in a different way.

In this sense, it almost seems as if Bashar's assumption of the presidency was a kind of psychological pacifier for a country so accustomed to someone who had ruled for thirty years. The propaganda surrounding Hafiz, the conscious and unconscious personality cult, and the mystical nature of his rule driven by his own reclusiveness and paranoia created a routinization if not a kind of dependency that found solace in the fact that another Asad was coming to power. Bashar's last name did provide him with a certain amount of legitimacy dividend, at least for a time. After Syria's turbulent post-World-War-II internal domestic history, marked by a succession of coups, had for the most part come to an end with Hafiz al-Asad's rise to power in 1970, continuity may have been the most important element in the drama that arose with Hafiz's illness and eventual death. As Bouthaina Shaaban comments:

> It was very difficult for us to know that someone who was with us so long is now gone. It was a shock—really, you don't want anything to change. It was frozen, and you just want the country to remain frozen without anything changing. So this is probably what everyone wanted, and Bashar was the obvious choice who could make us feel that Hafiz al-Asad didn't die— there is continuity, we are fine, and the country is going to be OK.

Continuity for the public—and continuity for those in power who had benefited from Hafiz's regime.

So which version is correct? Even with this information from the horse's mouth, so to speak, most would still scoff at the notion that Bashar was not being readied to become president. If, in fact, there was some coordinated, concerted effort by regime officials and friends to put forth the alternative view of Bashar's succession, then the question is why? Maybe it was done to reinforce the notion that Syria is not a monarchy; it is, indeed, a republic.

Bashar the crown prince was not being prepared for the throne by his father the king—it was sudden and dictated by the circumstances, and, after all was said and done, he was elected by the people in a referendum and by the Baath party. Then it could be said that the institutions of the state apparatus played their role and Bashar became president as the result of a process and not lineage. Such a charade could also be intended to help buy some time for Bashar, i.e. since he was not being prepared, since he did not expect to become president, maybe the people would be more forgiving if any expected salutary effects of the transition were delayed—after all, since it was so sudden and unexpected, one must give him some time to learn on the job. In addition, the dramatic reversal in his career could be brought more into focus if he were simply upholding Arab family tradition as the next eldest son; it would certainly generate more sympathy and popularity for Bashar if he were thought to have sacrificed his career as an ophthalmologist for the good of the country.

Or perhaps Bashar and the others are simply telling the truth—or at least not a blatant falsehood. I do not in any way want to discount this. As we know by now, the West can misunderstand or misread Arab dynamics because their assumptions are grounded in Western paradigms. However implausible it may sound, it is possible that Hafiz never *literally* talked about succession to either of his two eldest sons. As one Syrian pointed out, Basil was only thirty-one when he died, yet the Syrian constitution, although it could be easily amended as in Bashar's case in 2000, stipulated that the president must be at least forty years old. As such, maybe Basil and later Bashar were indeed being groomed, but not for the presidency in specific terms, just for positions of influence and power on which an increasingly paranoid Hafiz al-Asad, rattled by Rifaat's attempted coup, could readily depend. Those in the West have a difficult time understanding the role of family in the Arab world, how strong the bonds and obligations are. It is not implausible that Bashar could have returned on his own from London out of a sense of duty to his dead brother and his grieving father, much less the country as a whole. Those that support this version ask why many doubt this so much? Do they doubt it because it more conveniently fits stereotypical impressions of an Arab leader, an Arab ruling family, or the Asads in particular? Why do they attribute to the Asads less than altruistic motives? Enough people believed President George W. Bush's avowed sense of duty, patriotism, and belief to make him president—why does Bashar deserve less consideration for espousing similar motives? Is it an attempt to cast him as illegitimate? Maybe he is when weighed against political culture in the United States, but in Syria, what exactly is illegitimate? Has any ruler in post-World-War-II Syria built enough of a political and societal institutional foundation even to suggest a legitimacy that could then be used as a barometer to measure illegitimacy? This may be the failing of successive Syrian regimes, it may be the weak legacy of his father, but it is certainly not Bashar's fault. Within the Syrian experience, whatever one might think of it, Bashar's coming to power was accepted by the vast majority of Syrians; however, this does not mean that Bashar has a free ride in perpetuity—at some point even an Asad has to deliver the goods, a subject to be taken up later in this book.

Climbing the Ladder

Bashar did return home and took on more and more responsibility in the country. As mentioned, he quickly succeeded Basil as chairman of the Syrian Computer Society (SCS), a non-profit organization based in Damascus with branch offices in all of the major cities in Syria. The primary objective of the SCS is to effectively promote and contribute to the diffusion of information technology in Syria. Better and wider access to computers and to the Internet in Syria have been two of Bashar's closely held goals, even if they do run against the stream of control of information that existed under his father; ultimately, he believes that the overall economic and cultural benefits will outweigh any societal restlessness fueled by knowledge of what is going on elsewhere in the world. Access is still relatively limited, but mostly by economics rather than by state interference, i.e. most people still simply cannot afford a computer much less an Internet service provider. But Internet cafes have sprouted up in the major cities in Syria and there are dozens of ISPs listed in the Damascus phonebook (although still controlled by the government), whereas five years ago one could not find any. The universities now have much greater access to the outside world, made possible by, in some cases, a 1,000 percent increase in the number of computers provided since Bashar came to power. Bashar is well aware of the general ineptitude of the Syrian system, its relatively archaic techniques and mechanisms, and the danger of the country falling behind even further in the globalization process. He sees the expansion of computer equipment, knowledge, and technology as an important remedy to the country's systemic ills. Commenting on the importance of the SCS, Bashar said:

I have always seen the problems caused by chaos and corruption, and these problems can be fought with the computer. And if you use a computer, you must be organized—you cannot be chaotic and be good with a computer, so it has two effects. The technology was created to make things easier and faster, and we need to make things easier and faster in this country. Every domain in the world now depends on the computer—publishing, communication, education, administration . . . everything

depends on the computer. Knowing how to read and write is not enough—
you must know how to use the computer, to be computer literate. That's
why I became a part of the Syrian Computer Society.[5]

Bashar brought a number of people from the Syrian Computer Society into
the government—they can be found in almost all of the government and
Baath party organs. They were usually Ph.D.'s with an academic background
who, for the most part, were forward thinking and vociferously supported
Bashar's vision of a modernized Syria and the power of the computer bringing the country right into the twenty-first century. One such person is the
minister of tourism, Dr. Saadallah Agha al-Kalaa, who is a vast improvement
over prior ministers of tourism, who barely had a clue as to how to begin to
mine the huge wealth of Syria's historic tourist sites for the benefit of the
country. Dr. Saadallah is one of the founders of the SCS, and, of course, he got
to know Bashar through his involvement there. He recalls how seriously
Bashar took his new position as chairman of the organization—this wasn't
some fat-cat son of the president who received a sexy title yet never showed
up for meetings or provided input into the program. Immediately Bashar
arranged for the SCS to have a real headquarters and a place to conduct their
weekly meetings, which up until then had been in a room in the Al-Asad
National Library in Damascus. The minister added that:

> During his [Bashar's] tenure at SCS he used to have regular meetings on
> the status of technology from 9:00 a.m. to 1:00 p.m., then have a short
> break, and then we would continue until 5:00 p.m. He always came exactly
> on time, when the meetings were supposed to start. And, of course, now
> everyone had to show up on time whereas before many would come late.
> He was very serious about his job. I remember going out to Deraa for a pro-
> gram on IT, and all of us had to be there ahead of time, at a quarter till eight
> in the morning. At the meetings he tried to emphasize the positive ele-
> ments, and he was always listening and asking poignant questions, the type
> of questions that showed that he was listening. Building a dialogue to dis-
> cuss common elements is very important to him. Since he is an ophthal-
> mologist, a physician, he must first diagnose the problem and then make a
> decision. And dealing with the eye, which is so fragile, he has become good
> at analyzing fragile situations.

In the period 1994–2000, Bashar also worked his way up the military ladder, something he was committed to doing—and, of course, had to do if he
were ever to become president. Most believe his quick rise through the ranks

was all part of the plan. As stated earlier, when Bashar returned from London he held the equivalent rank of captain (*naqib*); in July 1997 he was promoted to the rank of lieutenant-colonel (*muqaddam*), and in January 1999 he became a full colonel (*aqid*). Finally, on June 11, 2000, one day after the death of his father, Bashar was promoted to lieutenant-general and Supreme Commander of the Armed Forces. As a result of this, Bashar would develop a bastion of loyalty within the military, especially among officers of his own generation.

In addition, there were forced retirements and removals of various officers—in large measure as a result of an anti-corruption campaign—that from the outside seemed to further pave the way for Bashar's ascension in the military, facilitate the rise of younger middle-level officers loyal to the president's son, and remove potential "old guard" obstacles who could prevent Bashar's succession and/or shift the presidency as well as important military-security apparatus posts away from the near monopoly the Alawites had in these areas. The climax to this process appears to have been the pensioning off in July 1998 of General Hikmat al-Shihabi, the Sunni Arab long-serving chief of staff of the Syrian military, someone many considered to be the country's number-two man and a legitimate candidate to succeed Hafiz al-Asad. An Alawite, Ali Arslan, the long-time deputy chief of staff and member of the Kalbiyya tribe to which the Asads belong, was chosen as Shihabi's successor. What is interesting about this episode is that Shihabi was retired by selectively employing a provision in the Military Service Law that stated that a general (*imad*) is required to retire at the age of sixty-seven, which was the age of Shihabi at the time, whereas Arslan, who was sixty-six at the time, enjoyed a subsequent amendment to the law that raised the mandatory age of retirement to seventy.[6] It is also interesting that at about this time Hafiz al-Asad was quoted in an interview with French television, in response to the question of whether Bashar was being groomed, as saying:

> I am not preparing my son to take my place, nor have I ever heard him speak of this matter. It seems to me that the fact that such a possibility is mentioned derives from his activity, which earns him the esteem and love of his colleagues, as well as respect among the residents of the country. As for the issue of succession, there is no clause whatsoever in our constitution that gives the right of succession to family members.[7]

Vice President Abd al-Halim Khaddam, another Sunni Arab who had long served Hafiz al-Asad, also seems to have been somewhat marginalized in the Syrian hierarchy, although he retained his position for the time being. It was he who "gave up" the Lebanon file to Bashar in 1998, and there were investigations into some possible wrongdoing—they did not result in any charges but very well could have been a "shot across the bows" to let the vice president know the precariousness of his position. Some suggest that, had Hafiz al-Asad not died when he did, Khaddam might have fallen prey to the anti-corruption campaign in due course.[8] Even though he was officially the "acting president" in accordance with the constitution, Khaddam was practically invisible at Hafiz al-Asad's funeral; indeed, the foreign dignitaries attending the funeral all met with Bashar.[9]

General Intelligence Chief General Muhammad Bashir al-Najjar was removed from his position at about the same time and sentenced to a twelve-year stint in prison on charges of corruption. In addition, Rifaat al-Asad was formally stripped of the title of vice president in February 1998, soon thereafter going into exile in Europe. And there was the dismissal of the cabinet and formation of a new one in March 2000, during which Prime Minister Mahmud Zubi was accused of corruption along with several other cabinet ministers—Zubi was dismissed from the Regional Command of the Baath party shortly thereafter and was sent home, where, according to Syrian authorities, he committed suicide. It certainly seems as if a path was being cleared, but maybe the path had less to do with Bashar and more to do with the maintenance of Alawite control in the military-security apparatus and, therefore, retaining their hold on power.

The Alawites, as discussed in chapter two, were a persecuted minority—destitute and powerless. Although Hafiz had constructed an alliance of sorts between Alawites and the Sunni business class that some have called the "military–merchant complex," the Alawites were not about to relinquish their near-monopolizing hold on power and all of the political, social, and economic benefits that accrued from this; in fact, it can be surmised that they were not even prepared to accept a dilution of that power that the succession of a Sunni president might portend. As Christopher Hemmer notes, "Although the Asad regime is broader than an Alawi dictatorship, there is no doubt that as one moves through these organizations, from the formal government, to the party, and to the military and intelligence agencies, and as one moves up each organization, the Alawi presence becomes more and more predominant."[10] Possibly, Bashar rode into power less on the name of Asad than on the aspirations of the Alawite sect. Since most of the Alawites remained behind the scenes in important posts in the military and in the *mukhabarat* (intelligence/security directorates), Bashar, as the president's eldest son and with his increasingly open role in Syria, was the public face of the Alawites—there was really no other choice. Whether Bashar, or even his ailing father, was completely and explicitly aware of this is the question—it certainly seems as though he should have been, but he may not have completely understood that this Alawite ground preparation would lead directly to his becoming the Syrian president so rapidly and with such apparent ease after his father died.

The Death of Hafiz al-Asad

There exist a number of different stories recounting the day of Hafiz al-Asad's death and the machinations of various regime insiders to arrange for Bashar to come to power. We may never know the full truth because even President Bashar may not have been fully aware of the maneuvering and decision-making in the military-security apparatus nor among the stalwarts of his father's regime. From the outside, Bashar's succession went very smoothly, almost without a hitch, to the point where it has become something of a model for some of the former Trans-Caucasus and central Asian republics of the Soviet Union that are now independent and facing similar potential succession crises.[11] Bashar himself says he never saw or sensed any succession struggle; he only read of such things in foreign newspapers. He believes that there were many who wanted to be a part of the decision-making process, and there may have been some who harbored some ambitions until they saw the parliament, party, and people clearly articulate who they wanted as president in the immediate aftermath of his father's death. To Bashar, it was very important that the people spoke up and let it be known who they wanted as president—it was important for him to have that imprimatur. Also, evidence of at least the outlines of some institutional process was important—the Baath party, the parliament, a referendum, no matter how arranged this might have seemed from the outside. According to the constitution, Vice President Abd al-Halim Khaddam should have at least been the interim president during the interregnum, but this was barely perceptible—which may have been a reflection of his lessened standing vis-à-vis Bashar and the fact that he was Sunni. That Khaddam continued to hold the position of vice president seems to have been the quid pro quo for giving up his claim and that of his supporters for the presidency.

According to Bashar, during the day in the hours after his father died, several high-level members of the Baath party came to speak with him about becoming the next president. He was not thinking about this particularly, but more about what his future was going to be, what his role would be. He knew he wanted to play an important role—he had already acquired a good amount of influence, and he believed this would continue if not be enhanced. He really did not have any time to be emotional. From all accounts he was very much in control of himself, very calm and focused on what had to be done next. The same could not be said about the country at large. People were in shock, mesmerized by the sudden dramatic events taking place since they had been unaware of Hafiz's condition. A number of Syrians commented on how they felt lost at the time, even some among those who were less enamored of his regime. But he had been in power for thirty years. The surrounding cult of personality and dominant control he had exhibited had, in a way, conditioned the population to believe he would live forever. All one has to do is visit the government-sponsored website *www.assad.org* to gaze at the very strong lingering effects of this man and the tall shadow he has cast over the country, much like the statue along the main road between Damascus and Homs. On the website Hafiz is called the "Saladin of our Modern Time," named after Salah al-Din al-Ayyubi (anglicized as "Saladin"), the twelfth-century figure who led Islamic armies to defeat the Crusader forces at the Battle of Hattin in 1188 and subsequently liberate Jerusalem from the Crusaders. Born in Tikrit in modern-day Iraq and of Kurdish stock, Saladin is entombed adjacent to the grand Umayyad mosque in the old city of Damascus.[12] On the home page of the website, the following passage is prominently displayed: "The day of his departure is a day of sadness and sorrow in every home, school, university, farm, factory, and quarry. The legacy of President Assad's accomplishments and ideas is a star that will shine not just on this generation but also on coming generations." Despite all this, in Damascus everyday life did not come to a screeching halt. There were the requisite black banners and bunting, the Quranic verses played over and over again on television, more police and security on the streets than usual, but overall things proceeded in an orderly fashion. In Damascus at the time of Hafiz' death, Michael Hudson, a Middle East specialist at Georgetown University, noted: "The mood in general was somber and respectful rather than deeply emotional. One did not sense the grief or hysteria that we observed . . . in the funerals of King Hussein of Jordan or King Hassan of Morocco."[13] It seems as though the controlled environment in Syria that Hafiz established in life also followed him in death.

Reflecting a more emotional reaction, one Christian Arab Syrian mentioned to me that Hafiz was bigger than life, a kind of Santa Claus figure who watched over the nation and kept it stable and independent. One almost senses a psychological dependency to some degree, and no doubt much of the crying and the distraught configurations in the crowds following the announcement of his death was genuine and spontaneous. There was a great deal of uncertainty, concern, and fear about the future—what would happen to the country? While some of it could have been arranged easily, there was some kind of natural emotional wave that compelled many Syrians to demand publicly that Bashar become president; they surrounded the national assembly and held vigils calling for the son to succeed the father. The fact that he did, and that it appeared to go smoothly without any overt signs of a succession struggle, was very comforting to a grieving and shocked nation. Perhaps Bashar was the only figure who could have engendered calm while also providing some confidence to those who saw in him a potential new direction for the country. He was viewed as a young, educated, compassionate, man of the people in a way his father never had been—he represented the next generation, yet he was still an Asad. It was an effective combination that no one else possessed in the country. The fact that the succession occurred so smoothly probably has less to do with any institutions that facilitated the transition—in fact, there really was no institutional foundation in Syria for what had just happened—and more to do with the personage of Bashar himself; indeed, he was the "hope."

A number of former Western diplomats in Damascus at the time comment that long-serving Defense Minister Mustafa Tlas and Vice President Abd al-Halim Khaddam played key roles in the transition process. They reportedly called the generals and key figures in the *mukhabarat* to make sure everything was secure before announcing Bashar's "candidacy." These two stalwarts of the regime had been very loyal to Hafiz al-Asad, and as such have also been loyal to his son, which is why the two remained in their posts when Bashar came to power, Mustafa Tlas only retiring from his position in early 2004. The sons of Tlas and Khaddam are also said to be close to Bashar, and they, too, play an important role in the current regime, leading some critics to suggest that in Damascus there is only a new-generation oligarchic elite rather than a new generation of change.

A number of possible obstacles had been removed from the intelligence directorates in the couple of years preceding Hafiz al-Asad's passing, replaced by personages who were close to Bashar, such as Dr. Bajhat Sulayman, Asef Shawkat (who is married to Bashar's sister, Bushra), Ghazi al-Kanaan, and Major-General Hassan Khalil (who replaced the powerful head of one of the main intelligence directorates, Ali Duba, in February 2000). In the fall of 1999, approximately 1,000 of Rifaat al-Asad's supporters were rounded up across Syria and later suppressed by force; Rifaat still entertained hopes of returning triumphantly to Syria, and some believed that the uncle felt his nephew did not have what it takes to keep him away—he was wrong.[14] As one Syrian analyst mentioned at the time, "He [Bashar] sent in the tanks, and the message was: if you want to play hard, I will play hard. It was important, and it showed Bashar's strength."[15] Or as one senior Arab official stated, "[Hafiz al-] Asad took power thirty years ago by putting his rivals in jail and getting the party to back him as leader. Bashar used modern concepts of democracy and anti-corruption to reach the same goal."[16] Many were wondering whether it was politics as usual in Syria, but just operating underneath a different, albeit a more modern and possibly less overtly abrasive, veneer. This was certainly not democracy at work.

It seems clear that Bashar, with or without his knowledge, was being systematically prepared for succession in the several years preceding Hafiz' death; however, we cannot casually dismiss the possibility that Bashar is telling the truth regarding his version of whether he was or was not being groomed. He was definitely aware that it was being talked about in the press both in and outside Syria, although in the country the state-controlled media was never specific about it. Bashar is quick to emphasize that Syria must have functional institutions that go beyond familial, religious, or tribal affiliations. This is the sine qua non of a society that actually works. But there was only a façade of institutionalism present at the time of Hafiz al-Asad's death, and the constant reference to how the institutional apparatus brought Bashar to power is disingenuous, and, at best, wishful thinking. Syria is far from establishing such an institutional foundation; indeed, had such a foundation been actually in existence in 2000, the succession probably would have been a much more ugly affair. One could say that the seamless succession was due more to the system of dictatorship Bashar's father established rather than any functioning institutional basis. As former American ambassador to Syria Theodore Kattouf told me, "Hafiz al-Asad made the regime, but the regime made Bashar." What can at least be said is that the transition to the post-Hafiz order was anticipated by powerful figures in the Syrian hierarchy for a variety of reasons—loyalty to Hafiz, maintenance of Alawite control, prevention of dramatic change to the status quo ante, ensuring national stability, hope for a new generation of leadership, etc.—with or without Bashar al-Asad. Obviously a critical mass within the regime concluded that all of these things could best be achieved with Bashar in power. They did their job exceedingly well. Hudson observed that, "Whatever doubts that Syrians in the ruling circles or the general public might have about this relatively untested young man, there seemed to be a general tacit agreement that this was not the time to air them."[17]

Chapter 5

Seasons in Damascus

On June 11, 2000, Bashar was unanimously nominated by the Baath party for president. There were no other nominees. The national assembly quickly amended article 83 of the Syrian constitution that stated that the president of the republic must be forty years old—it was changed to thirty-four years old, the exact age of Bashar. On June 24 he was elected as secretary-general of the Baath, in effect the head of the party, at the 9th Regional Congress meeting, the first such gathering of the Baath party to be held in fifteen years. It was already scheduled before Hafiz al-Asad's death, but Bashar agreed to still hold the meeting; in a way, it was fortuitous because it allowed for the further public "deputization" of Bashar amid the lingering emotion of recent events. Three days later the Syrian parliament voted "yes" to the nomination, and in a nationwide referendum, Bashar received 97.29 percent of the total vote (99.7 percent of valid ballots cast), which was slightly less than the 99 percent his father had regularly received. According to the Syrian minister of the interior, of the 8.69 million votes cast, only 22,439 said "no" to Bashar in the "yes" or "no" referendum.[1] His seven-year term began, at the end of which he has said he would like to hold a presidential election rather than just a referendum—time will tell.[2]

Inauguration and Hope

President Bashar al-Asad officially took the constitutional oath of office and delivered his inaugural speech on July 17, 2000, in Damascus. By Syrian standards, it was a remarkably enlightened speech that deigned even to criticize certain policies of the past. It served to confirm the suspicions among many in and outside Syria, especially the pro-reform and pro-democracy elements, that indeed Bashar was a breath of fresh air who would lead the country in a new direction. In his speech he made economic reform a clear priority; indeed, the frankness of his criticism of the prior system was unprecedented.

The new president declared that the state bureaucracy had become a "major obstacle" to development, and he admitted that economic progress had been uneven, due in large measure to the state-dominated economy: "Don't depend on the state. There is no magic wand. The process of change requires elements that are not the preserve of one person. . . . Authority without responsibility is the cause of chaos." He went on to say, "We must rid ourselves of those old ideas that have become obstacles. In order to succeed we need modern thinking . . . some people may believe that creative minds are linked to age and that they can frequently be found with the old, but this is not quite accurate. Some young people have strong minds that are still lively and creative." And in a very gentle fashion, he seemed to set the foundation for embarking on a different path from his father by exclaiming that "the approach of the great leader, Hafiz al-Asad, was a very special and unique approach and therefore it is not easy to emulate, especially as we remember that we are required not just to maintain it but to develop it as well." Although his speech in many ways charted a new course for Syria, particularly in the economic and technological spheres, he did say that it would be impossible for Syria to become a Western-style democracy, calling instead for "democracy specific to Syria that takes its roots from its history and respects its society." On the subject of democracy, he added the following:

> We cannot apply democracy of others onto ourselves. Western democracy, for example, is the outcome of a long history that resulted in customs and traditions that distinguish the current culture of Western societies. In order to apply what they have, we have to live their history with all of its social significance. As this is obviously impossible, we have to have our democratic experience that is special to us and that is a response to the needs of our society and the requirements of our reality.

Regardless of whether one thinks that Bashar's views on democracy provide him with an "out," so to speak, to delay political reform in lieu of more immediately needed economic reform measures, he is really only reflecting modernization theories that are generally acknowledged in social-science circles in the West as they developed in the post-World-War-II era: progress and modernization are not unilinear, as was once thought—it is a multilinear process where in each case the pace and type of modernization reflects the history, culture, and experience of that particular country. Bashar's ideas regarding democracy are not fully developed, which one might expect given that he grew up in an authoritarian environment. They are certainly secondary to his thoughts on the need for modernization and economic improvement, both of which he sees as more immediate needs. Indeed, for obvious reasons, there has been very little discourse or debate regarding the implementation and growth of democracy in Syria. This has, in fact, been one of the demands of pro-democracy elements in and outside the country: a discussion on political pluralism and democracy, so long repressed, needs to begin.

But there was a genuine air of exuberance among many who had longed for change in Syria. Bashar had also nurtured a collaborative relationship with elements in the intelligentsia upon returning from London in 1994, especially in his capacity as chairman of the Syrian Computer Society. A number of these were brought into the government by him, people who could legitimately be called reformists. This added to the anticipatory environment, although the new reformists in the government were more along the lines of technocrats than pro-democracy elements. They were tasked with the job of modernizing Syria, implementing administrative reform in the various ministries to which they were assigned, and examining the economic weaknesses of the system and devising ways to correct it; they were not there to enact political reform.

Nonetheless, there was noticeably more political openness in the months after Bashar took office, during what many have called the "Damascus spring." This is akin to the "Prague spring" in Czechoslovakia that lasted from January to August 1968 during a period of political liberalization under the leadership of Alexander Dubcek before it was crushed by 200,000 Warsaw Pact troops and 5,000 tanks under the application of the so-called Brezhnev Doctrine.[3] During the seven to eight months of the Damascus spring the political opening was marked by general amnesties to political prisoners of all persuasions, the licensing of private newspapers, a shake-up of the state-controlled media apparatus, the provision of political forums and salons in which open criticism and dissent was tolerated, and a discarding of the personality cult that surrounded the previous regime.

Spring in Damascus

Reports by Amnesty International (AI) and Human Rights Watch (Middle East Watch) have generally been harsh on Syria over the years. In 1991, for instance, Middle East Watch reported that the "Asad regime has been a gross violator of human rights and its practices remain repugnant. . . . Having killed at least ten thousand of its citizens in the past twenty years, the Asad regime continues to kill through summary executions and violent treatment in prison. It routinely tortures prisoners and arrests and holds thousands without charge or trial."[4] According to most reports, Syria's record improved along these lines during the remainder of the 1990s as the threats from the perspective of Damascus receded in the wake of the 1991 Gulf war and Syria's involvement in the Madrid peace process with Israel. In addition, one of Hafiz al-Asad's goals ever since coming to office had been to improve Syria's international image, not only for economic and business reasons but also for the sake of prestige and international acceptance. He generally did a poor job of balancing this desire with what he viewed as the situation on the ground in terms of perceived threats. However, the end of the cold war, combined with Syria's participation in war and peace on the side of the West, meant that Syria's judicial and human rights records needed to be cleaned up in order to attract the type of foreign investment and international goodwill that Hafiz was seeking.

Despite these improvements, however, in its annual 2001 report to Congress on human rights practices, the State Department concluded that the human rights situation in Syria remained poor, and the government continued to restrict or deny fundamental rights, although it noted a few improvements in certain areas. It further stated that Syrian citizens do not have the right to change their government and that there is no organized political opposition, the rubber stamp, Baath-dominated Progressive National Front notwithstanding. According to this report, serious abuses include the widespread use of torture in detention; poor prison conditions; arbitrary arrest and detention; prolonged detention without trial; fundamentally unfair trials in security courts (Supreme State Security Courts or SSSC), especially the continuance of martial law; an inefficient judiciary that suffers from corruption and political influence; infringement on citizens' private rights; denial of freedom of speech and of the press, despite a loosening (at the time) of censorship restrictions; denial of freedom of assembly and association; some limits on freedom of religion; and limits on freedom of movement.[5]

The report delineated the pattern of prisoner releases, which picked up after Bashar became president. One of the hallmarks of the Damascus spring was the release in November 2000 of some 600 political prisoners, an act the State Department believes was the first time the Syrian government acknowledged holding prisoners for political reasons. This became something of a pattern for the regime, i.e. general amnesties were granted to prisoners on the November 16 anniversary marking the ascension to power of Hafiz al-Asad as well as on July 17, the anniversary of Bashar's assumption of the presidency.[6] According to Amnesty International, most of those released were Muslim Brethren (MB) in addition to various members of two communist parties. The report also noted the release of forty-six Lebanese political prisoners.[7] AI estimated that the number of political detainees amounted to approximately

1,500, bringing the total number down to about 900 after the November 2000 releases, with another 140 political prisoners released in late 2001. AI also commented in its 2001 report on Syria that there were fewer instances of torture in the year 2000, although "the system allowing for its application remained intact and there were apparently no investigations into previous allegations of torture and ill-treatment."[8] There were more releases (approximately 250) announced by the regime in July 2004. It is estimated that since November 2000, the regime has released over 800 political prisoners.[9] When compared to other Middle East states, including some that have close relations with the United States, Syria fares quite well in absolute numbers as well as per capita totals of political prisoners; indeed, Syria today probably has considerably less than 1,000 political prisoners, putting it on a par with Tunisia and well below the 18,000 of Egypt, the 4,000 to 7,000 of Algeria, and the 10,000 to 20,000 thousand in Turkey as reported by Amnesty International.[10]

The State Department report also offered the following:

> Syria supports freedom of religion and women's rights to a greater degree than do many Middle East governments. Aside from Lebanon, Syria is the only Arab-speaking country whose constitution does not establish Islam as the state religion, although it does require that the President be a Muslim. In accordance with the largely secular philosophy of the ruling Baath party, the country's Christian community and tiny Jewish minority have been free to practice their religion without interference; some Christians have held high-level positions in the government and armed forces. Syrian law specifies equal rights for women; government policies stipulate equal pay for similar work; the government discourages conservative religiously-based restrictions on women; women serve in governmental and diplomatic posts (twenty-six women won seats in the most recent parliamentary elections).[11]

The change in atmosphere in the months after Bashar came to power was most overtly on display with the proliferation of political forums and salons, in effect the resuscitation of the civil society movement. Indeed, even before the death of Hafiz al-Asad, almost in anticipation of what possibly lay ahead, a segment of the intelligentsia—writers, professors, artists, and media and film personages—many of whom had agitated previously for more civil society freedoms and were jailed because of it in the early 1980s, set against the MB uprising, and formed in May 2000 the Committees for the Revival of Civil Society in Syria.[12] The anticipation was high among the long-dormant groups of civil society activists. They believed in Bashar's sympathetic predilections, which were confirmed by his inaugural speech. Riyad Seif, a well-known civil society activist and parliamentarian, formed in August a political forum called the Friends of Civil Society in Syria. The mission statement of the organization, as outlined in Alan George's book *Syria: Neither Bread Nor Freedom*, called on the necessity "to revive the institutions of civil society and achieve a balance between their role and that of the state in the context of a real partnership between them in the higher national interest." The statement emphasized the "importance of freedom of opinion and expression, respect for opposing views, active and positive individual participation in public life and the adoption of dialogue, positive criticism and peaceful development to resolve differences, as being among the most important foundations of civil society." Finally, it pointed out that "the rule of law, the independence of the judiciary and the abolition of special courts, martial law and emergency legislation also constitute a solid basis for civil society."[13] The "martial law" refers to Decree no. 51 as amended and implemented on March 9, 1963, one day after the Baath came to power. It declared a "state of emergency" that was ostensibly designed to thwart the military threat from Israel, but, of course, it has been used to stifle and arbitrarily eliminate internal challenges to the regime. It is still in place, its removal being one of the primary objectives of the civil society groups.

The formation of the Friends of Civil Society and its mission statement are interesting in a number of respects. The goals and objectives outlined in the manifesto became pretty much the mantra of the various organizations that formed as part of the civil society movement, some more vociferously expressed than others. But it is clear from the relatively mild and accommodating tone of the statement that the civil society activists were at the same time wary of a regime that could still pounce on them in a heartbeat if necessary and aware that they did not want to provoke Bashar al-Asad too much— they were calling for "positive criticism" and "peaceful development." Knowing that stability was the sine qua non of any modern Syrian regime, they did not want the new president and leading officials to feel as if the civil society activists were fomenting a revolution. With Bashar at the helm, progress in the development of civil society freedoms could proceed within current societal parameters.

In fact, as Alan George points out, since Decree no. 39 of 1958, Syria's Law of Association requires every civil organization to register and obtain a license from the Ministry of Social Affairs. Riyad Seif actually directly approached Vice President Abd al-Halim Khaddam seeking permission for his association as well as showing him the mission statement. According to Seif, Khaddam reacted in a "very, very negative" way, saying, "it's a coup. You want to destroy the system and take over." Seif apparently also approached a leading general in the *mukhabarat*, who George believes was Bajhat Sulayman, the Alawi head of the General Intelligence Directorate and a close ally of Bashar, and he received a similarly negative response.[14] The Lebanese newspaper *Al-Hayat* reported that Khaddam and Sulayman, despite their misgivings, informed Seif of two "red lines" that his organization would be forbidden to cross: no relations with Westerners, and no secrets from the government.[15]

While this clearly shows that some powerful forces in the regime were uncomfortable with the formation of these civil society organizations, it is also clear that the immediate political atmosphere had changed, i.e. at least Khaddam and Sulayman, if in fact these contacts took place, were listening and not definitively saying "no" at first; again, compare this with the environment that existed in Iraq under Saddam or that still exists in countries such as North Korea, Burma, or Uzbekistan—or Syria in the early 1980s. Despite the clear reluctance on the part of the regime as a whole, as well as the retrenchment that would soon follow, in some very important ways the Rubicon had been crossed—that is, unless this was just an attempt to expose the identity of the pro-democracy elements, which is unlikely, but possible; however, within the first six months of Bashar's tenure, hundreds of these civil society and pro-democracy forums were established, many operating out of people's homes. Importantly, to the consternation of the regime, the Qatar-based satellite news agency al-Jazeera covered the phenomenon and interviewed many leading civil society activists, much of which was beamed back into the satellite-dished homes of Syrians, having a multiplying effect.[16]

Encouraged by these developments, civil society elements drafted in September 2000 what became known as the "Statement (or Manifesto) of 99," a statement signed by 99 Syrian civil society activists reiterating many of the goals of the nascent movement outlined above. Again, it was carefully worded. As George notes: "There was no demand for the wholesale democratization of Syrian institutions; no ideological flavor; no attack on the manner in which Bashar al-Asad had come to power. None of the signatories had significant histories of anti-regime activism and the authorities were thereby denied the chance to condemn them as 'well-known enemies of the state' or 'agents of Israel.'"[17] More bold was the so-called Manifesto of the 1,000, also known as the Basic Document by its supporters, that was leaked to a Lebanese newspaper in January 2001. While reinforcing many of the earlier civil society and pro-democracy objectives, it went even further by explicitly attacking the foundation of Baathist rule and advocating, indeed demanding, a multi-party political system, countering the regime's China-model mantra of economic reform before political reform by stating that the former would fail unless "preceded and accompanied by a comprehensive package of political and con-stitutional reform."[18] Along with some other internal and external events the regime encountered during this time frame, the Manifesto of 1,000 seems to have been something of a turning point for those elements in the regime who were hesitant about the political openings to begin with. By, in essence, call-ing for the installation of a different system altogether, however much it was sugar-coated to placate the regime, the civil society activists had gone too far.

There are a number of non-governmental organizations (NGOs) in Syria, which leads many in the government to scoff at the notion that their country does not have a vibrant civil society. Ironically, considering she is the presi-dent's wife, one of the leading voices for these NGOs is Asma al-Asad. Among many other things in which she is involved, Mrs. al-Asad was the organizing force behind the creation of FIRDOS (Fund for the Integrated Rural Development of Syria, or "paradise" in Arabic), an impressive organization that facilitates rural development in Syria through educational programs, micro-finance, and guidance to empower people in villages and towns to take the initiative to improve their own infrastructure and services available in their communities. One of its prime objectives is to reverse the dominant trend in recent decades of migration toward the cities by investing more in the rural areas of the country.

All NGOs, however, must register with the government. Critics of the regime point out that having NGOs, clubs, and charitable organizations does not equate to a vibrant and free civil society, the basics of which require civil liberties, freedom of expression, and some semblance of a democratic process as well. Most Arab countries have numerous such organizations, but they are closely tied to and/or monitored by the government—take for example FIRDOS. This is why in a number of these and other Islamic countries Islamist organizations have proved to be quite popular, filling the void left by the inadequate service provided by the government and existing civil society. The Syrian regime has recognized the important role NGOs can play; perhaps it is trying to walk that fine line between effectiveness and control—however, the two should often be mutually exclusive if NGOs are to truly fill the void created by government inefficiency before other more threatening and oppositional forces do.

There were a number of other manifestations of the Damascus spring that confirmed that the moniker was aptly deserved. Two human rights organiza-tions opened up in Syria: the Syrian Human Rights Association and the Defense of Democratic Freedoms and Human Rights. There were also some important press freedom gains characterized by the emergence of private and party-run newspapers as well as a more rambunctious state-run press after some shake-ups in the state-controlled media apparatus and Ministry of Information. The highlight of this process was the January 2001 licensing for the publication of *Al-Dumari* (The Lamplighter), the satirical weekly owned by renowned political cartoonist Ali Farzat, which was the first privately owned newspaper to be published in almost four decades. The 75,000 copies of the first edition were quickly bought by a populace starved of unrestricted news and politics. The progress and fate of this newspaper would be a long and winding one over the next couple of years, reflecting the push and pull between the government and the civil society movement. In addition, a loyal opposition communist party in the National Progressive Front was permitted to publish its own newspaper, allowing criticism of Syrian policies, especially in the economic sphere. And, of course, one of the hallmarks of the Damascus spring, as mentioned previously, was the release of political prisoners. Symbolic of this new mood, the infamous Mezzeh prison in Damascus, built by the French in the 1920s and often the jail for political prisoners since the regime of former Syrian President Husni al-Zaim came to power in 1949, was closed down four days after the November 2000 prisoner release.

Bashar acknowledges that one of the primary demands of the civil society activists has been to put an end to the state of emergency in place since 1963— as well as the subsequent establishment of the extra-legal Supreme State Security Courts. He admits that the law has been abused by the government on a number of occasions as a form of repression against political dissent. But he doesn't back down from the necessity of having the emergency law, basically stating that while in such a dangerous neighborhood Syria has needed it: with the Muslim Brethren, Israel, and the ongoing situation in Lebanon, the country has constantly been in a precarious situation. Now, of course, the instability engendered by the situation in Iraq has reaffirmed to many the correctness of keeping the law on the boards, but, "we cannot use it as an excuse for something depending on our mood. It cannot be employed in the wrong way." He also pointed to a parallel in the United States after 9/11 with the Patriot Act being passed, legislation that also deals with internal security: "People in the United States now understand the need to have this law, whereas before they would not have accepted it." In essence, as long as there is no peace with Israel, the situation in Iraq remains unstable, and the United States continues to adopt a threatening posture the emergency law will remain in effect. Bashar has stated that, "the emergency law is not used to suppress freedoms but to suppress terrorism, and there is a huge difference. Frequently in the past this law was used in the wrong way."[19] He points to the "terrorist" act that shockingly occurred in Damascus in March 2004, when four men encountered police near an empty United Nations office building in an upscale area of Damascus that houses a number of embassies and swank restaurants. There was an exchange of fire, with rocket-propelled grenades destroying the façade of the building and two people killed in the process. Bashar called it the "first terrorist experience in nineteen years" in Damascus, and he claimed that it was a result of the heightened instability due to the repercussions of the war in neighboring Iraq.[20]

I believe Bashar recognizes that he may have gone a bit too far in his inaugural speech, especially considering the self-image that he and others promoted of a modernizing agent of change before and after he became president. He told me:

Using the reference to Prague spring is incorrect for two reasons: 1) the Prague spring was in large measure imported from the outside—we did not have that here; and 2) the Prague spring was a political movement against the government, while in Syria I *started* it as president. I did not give a speech regarding political openness to get elected—I gave it after I was elected. Stability is important. We have our goals, and we go in one direction to try to achieve them, and if there are difficulties or problems with this path, then we go back and try a different way. We are very cautious—I am very cautious, and when you talk about achieving stability, you do it in steps, not very big steps. We take small steps, and if we do it wrong, we take another step. So in some things we go back—we did not take the right way. But I do not use the word "spring."

But I think it is also clear that many civil society activists assumed too much in the beginning, even though they tempered their earlier statements and even contacted regime figures. After all, they did not rebel outright against the regime. This, however, captures the dilemma of the reformers: how much can they agitate and bring about real reform instead of bringing about regime repression—and the reformers were divided on the issue. As Alan George comments: "Some felt that the best strategy was a tacit alliance with the reformers within the regime, and that to demand too much too quickly would alienate those, including Bashar, upon whom ultimate success would depend. Others were uncompromising and insisted that the system was incapable of reforming itself and that the movement should therefore press on regardless of the regime's attitude."[21] Bouthaina Shaaban, commenting on the assumptions and misassumptions of Bashar's speech, said:

I think in certain ways some people probably understood it to mean do whatever you like, anyway you like, anytime you like, and I don't think that is what it was meant to be. So at the beginning they opened salons, which is not new. In 1920 the first women's salon was opened, and there have been many literary and intellectual salons—these are not new to our culture. But the new ones were political—that's the difference. I read the statements by some of these societies and I felt that all they wanted was a coup d'état to get into power—there was no agenda, no constructive criticism, so perhaps it was a combination of a misunderstanding and wanting to do things too fast along with not knowing where we are heading and what we are planning to do. Now having said this, I think in certain areas there is room to do things more quickly; personally, I believe this because every political party in the world gets old and needs to refresh itself and needs to be reformed. And the Baath party has gotten old and the people are stuck. It will be good for the country to do this, and it will be good for the president as well.[22]

But the reformers may have assumed that all of the talk regarding modernizing Syria, economic reform, and technological progress would be matched with political reform. The latter may come as a result of the former regardless of what the regime does over time, but it will be less of a conscious policy decision than evolutionary structural change. After all, unlike in the Soviet Union where the reverse occurred, the China model of perestroika without glasnost, i.e. reform or restructuring without political opening, that has been touted so much by Bashar and the regime did indeed produce economic dividends, but it also led to incremental political change, some of it intended, some of it unintended. However, many developing countries admire China and want to replicate the China model not so much because of the economic reforms—what needs to be done economically is known widely—but because of how China implemented them. This is what separates China from other states—successful implementation. The lesson drawn is that in order to implement, if not impose, these reforms a strong central government is necessary.

The pro-democracy and civil society activists do not feel that one can adequately separate economic progress from political progress, understanding that such basic things as foreign investment require the transparency, regulatory regime, and independent judiciary that Syria currently does not have. But what they haven't digested is that the regime believes it can make maximum progress economically while making only minimum progress politically—and in areas that facilitate economic progress rather than free and fair elections, true political parties, or a free press. When all is said and done, after a peace agreement with Israel, if Syria, however unlikely, can stake out a comparative advantage in some industry area that feeds into the wealth of the industrialized world, as China and India have done in different ways, then the lack of certain democratic practices will be forgiven or at least overlooked in the West.[23]

Snowfall

A number of former diplomats who were in Syria at the time believe that the regime was caught off guard by the growth of the civil society organizations combined with the prisoner releases and other measures implemented by Bashar. They believe that some of the stalwart elements in the regime—who many have termed the "old guard," those who had reached positions of power under and been loyal to Hafiz al-Asad—basically approached Bashar and warned him of the deleterious effects of the evolving situation in Syria. As one former U.S. official who has spent a great deal of time in Syria told me: "Some of the tough guys in the regime came to Bashar and essentially said: 'Hey kid, this is not how we do things here.'" Now it is obvious that even the toughest guys in the regime would not be so brusque with the president, but they were certainly detecting clear trends that could soon be harmful to their positions and the regime in general. Serious political reform could jeopardize the predominant position of a number of status quo elements who had established sinecures in the system that had brought them economic, social, and political benefits for years. They had seen the violent end that had befallen many of the "old guard" in some of the former socialist regimes in Eastern Europe following the conclusion of the superpower cold war. They had witnessed the instability that can occur when a country's center rapidly erodes, as in Yugoslavia, the Sudan, Somalia, and now even in Iraq. And stability has been—and obviously continues to be—a priority for the regime and for most Syrians.

Many point to an interview that Bashar gave to *Al-Sharq al-Awsat* (The Middle East) out of London on February 8, 2001, as a turning point, when the Damascus spring began to turn into what the activists saw as a "Damascus winter." Bashar stated that the "intellectuals" were a "small elite" that were not representative of the Syrian people at large. Then Bashar stated what became an oft-repeated rationale for cracking down on the civil society elements:

> When the consequences of an action affect the stability of the homeland, there are two possibilities . . . either the perpetrator is a foreign agent acting on behalf of an outside power, or else he is a simple person acting unintentionally. But in both cases a service is being done to the country's enemies and consequently both are dealt with in a similar fashion, irrespective of their intentions or motives."[24]

Khaddam as well as members of the Baath party 21-member Regional Command then toured the country, holding meetings in cities and at universities condemning the civil society movement and reiterating the notion that to continue along the same path would be to court disaster, to tear apart the fabric of the country. This could be taken advantage of by those perceived to be a threat to Damascus, such as Israel and the United States.

These iterations made by Bashar and his regime representatives reflect a paranoia both genuine and artificial that is found all too often in the Arab world, a paranoia that emerges from a paradigm of secrecy and control that characterizes the authoritarian regimes in the region. It is not totally made up—many people really do believe in these paranoia-fed conspiracy theories that see Israel and the United States as responsible for everything that goes wrong, and not just the uneducated commoner, but also many of those who are cosmopolitan and educated in the West. There has been just enough external manipulation, mostly from the experience with European imperialism and cold war machinations, to lend a hint of credence to such claims. Certainly all one has to do is read about the "struggle" for Syria in the 1950s or revisit the Lebanese imbroglio next door to Syria in the 1970s and 1980s to understand how multi-ethnic and multi-religious societies in an immature polity can be exploited by a plethora of external powers trying to advance different agendas, all the while just enhancing and widening the internal fissures in the countries in which they are trying to extend their influence.[25]

One must also remember the timing of the onset of the Damascus winter. The Palestinian intifada (uprising) of September 2000 began largely as a result of the polarization in both Israeli and Palestinian societies toward a more hardline position following the failed Camp David summit meeting between President Bill Clinton, Palestinian Authority President Yasser Arafat, and Israeli Prime Minister Ehud Barak the previous July. By the end of the year observers were describing the level of violence between Israelis and Palestinians in terms of a civil war. It had become apparent to most that, despite continued serious discussions between Palestinian and Israeli negotiators in January 2001, the Oslo process was dead; indeed, the Madrid process as a whole, with the intifada following so soon upon the failed Geneva summit meeting between Clinton and Hafiz al-Asad in April 2000, seemed to unravel before our eyes, even with the new president in Damascus. The hardening of the Israeli mindset toward a negotiated solution with the Palestinians led to the landslide election victory of Likud leader Ariel Sharon as the new Israeli prime minister in February 2001. This came less than a month after George W. Bush came to power in the United States, with Damascus warily observing a number of elements who had long advocated a tougher policy *vis-à-vis* Syria being brought into the administration, a subject that will be examined more closely in the next chapter. As such, a regime that had traditionally been very cautious in reaction to international events began to act as if it really were the continuation of the legacy of Hafiz al-Asad and not the advent of a new age in Syria that some had hoped for. In such perceived threatening circumstances, Damascus tends to wait and see where the winds will blow—not necessarily an imprudent move. From the viewpoint of the regime, it may not have been a time to be experimenting with nascent democracy.

Soon after Bashar's interview and the anti-civil society tour of various government and party figures, the Ministry of Social Affairs announced that forums could only meet by first receiving permission from the ministry itself (as opposed to receiving a license to organize meetings), the granting of which would only come after the provision of specific information as to the location of the meeting and who was to attend. Another key moment was the passage of Decree no. 50/2001 on September 22, 2001. The decree enables privately owned newspapers, magazines, and other periodicals to seek licenses to publish but essentially only at the discretion of the government, as the prime minister can deny licenses for reasons "related to the public interest." In addition, among other things, the decree prohibits articles and reports about "national security, national unity, and details of secret trials." It also establishes harsh criminal penalties for publishing "falsehoods and fabricated reports."[26] As a result of the increasing pressure, *Al-Dumari* ceased publication in April 2003 after almost two years of a tug-of-war with the government; again, however, the fact that it lasted this long, with some issues extremely critical of the regime, may say more about cracks appearing in the armor of those who want to maintain the level of political repression of past years than about the current regime being atavistic. The government also authorized in 2002 the licensing of the first private radio (FM) stations in Syria. Although they are barred from airing news or political programming, these are the types of baby steps Bashar has been advocating. No matter how controlled, once allowed it is that much more difficult to go back to the status quo ante.

A number of leading political activists, many of whom had been in and out of prison over the preceding twenty years, were again arrested, including parliamentarians Riyad Seif and Mamun al-Humsi. The trials of several of them in the Supreme State Security Courts were open to certain journalists and representatives of foreign embassies. Most of these activists were imprisoned again, although under less harsh terms and in less harsh conditions than their previous stays. As Riyad al-Turk, a leading opponent of the regime who was imprisoned by Hafiz al-Asad in solitary confinement for seventeen years, stated, "I would like to describe the prison as a five-star jail compared to prisons during his father's time."[27] Also, the world is watching more closely than ever before. In one notable case, Haythem Maaleh, the director of the Syrian Human Rights Association, was released after the Supreme State Security Courts dismissed the case against him and four others of distributing unauthorized copies of a human rights magazine.[28]

The civil society, pro-democracy, reform activists, whatever one might call them, have not backed down completely. They are certainly more circumspect, but they have also continued to maintain the pressure on the regime. The fear factor that existed under Hafiz al-Asad seems to have dissipated somewhat—and this is not necessarily a bad thing. This has proved worrisome to a number of regime stalwarts. As Najib Ghadbian states: "What Bashar and his supporters, the old guard and reform-minded alike, may realize is that once the phantasm of fear is shaken off by the people, it can't be reconstituted. One incidence of public dissent tends to encourage others and dissent becomes a less terrifying prospect each time."[29]

On the other hand, there has generally been a more politically relaxed—as opposed to more open—atmosphere in Syria, especially when there is not an acute crisis, in comparison to that which existed under Bashar's father. As Ali Farzat, who was editor of the satirical daily newspaper *Al-Dumari*, said in 2003, "There are some limits known to everyone, such as talking about military secrets or defaming people or making groundless accusations, but now we clearly can criticize things such as official institutions and ministries."[30] In other words, do not compare what has transpired—the Damascus winter—over the last few years with the Damascus spring. Under this juxtaposition the former obviously does not compare favorably with the latter. But when you position it with the more overtly repressive political and social environment in the 1980s and even in the 1990s, it is clear that Syria is moving slowly in the direction of a more free and transparent civil society. This may be a case of seeing the glass as half-full rather than half-empty (and leaking), but there are a number of silver linings in the clouds. Even some activists have realized that although he is not implementing reform as quickly as they would like, Bashar represents their only hope. In a Reuters report in August 2004, Aktham Naise, head of the Committees for the Defense of Democratic Freedoms and Human Rights in Syria, and someone who has been in and out of jail over the past few years, stated that, "there is a reform current within the regime that is working, albeit slowly, and we must encourage it. I now see that only the regime has the ability to implement this reform and we have to bet on this."[31] I asked Syrian ambassador to the United States Dr. Imad Moustapha, an academic by training who has long been considered a reformist, a question on whether or not the pro-democracy intellectuals still support Bashar:

> In one way or another, yes, I believe they still do. They believe that Bashar is capable of moving Syria into a new age. So, no, Bashar has not lost them yet. But you must remember that these liberals or pro-democracy elements are a minority. The overwhelming majority of Syrians are traditional or religious, who care more about the national struggle against Israel rather than about liberal or democratic values, which, by the way, is not good— but what they really care about is the issue of Israel and the rights of the Palestinians. And they are living in terrible conditions so they care more about administrative and economic reform. I think the crushing majority of Syrians would like to see a government that is not as heavy-handed as it used to be so that they can have more freedom, not so much in terms of rights but more freedom. They care more about improving their livelihood and their welfare, and they have staunch opinions on the Palestinian problem and the return of the Golan. So when they see Bashar appointing technocrats to top positions, who are highly educated, competent, non-Baathist, and have a high degree of integrity, then the people are very pleased with this. They believe these guys will reform the corrupt system and deliver on the economic front. It's really not necessary for them to have Western-style elections—this is not their top priority. Getting rid of corruption, improving the economy, and preserving Syria's nationalistic policies are the top priorities.[32]

Bashar inherited an exceedingly ossified system, and he has been in power for only about five years. They have been years marked by incredibly profound regional and international events—the intifada, 9/11, the subsequent war in Afghanistan, and, finally, the war in Iraq in 2003 and resulting instability next door amid a deteriorating relationship with both Israel and the United States. He has yet to establish the legitimacy that his father painstakingly built up over the years, although having the last name of "Asad" has given Bashar something of a legitimacy dividend. He does not have his father's power base nor has he really organized a base of support around him to implement the reforms as quickly and in as dramatic a fashion as he would have liked. His father ruled in many ways by consensus among the elite, but he was able to shape and manipulate that consensus when necessary; Bashar does not have this type of credibility yet. We tend to measure progress in four-year increments in the United States based on the four-year presidential election cycle. This cannot be applied to Bashar's first four years in office, primarily because of the dilapidated condition of the polity and economy he inherited as well as the legacy and personnel he inherited from his father. Many believe that Bashar does not have the time to reform Syria in an incremental manner—the system may come crashing down before enough is done to turn it around in a positive direction rather than just maintain it and muddle through; however, for now, as Aktham Naise has recognized, the latter may be the best the Syrians can hope for. The clear implication is: give Bashar some more time.

Suggesting that democracy is a process best accomplished as an incremental, home-grown evolution and not imposed from the outside, Bashar noted in his interview with the *New York Times* on November 30, 2003:

> I hope we can make better steps toward democracy in our country, but that takes time. But no one in Syria, or maybe in the region if I want to exaggerate a little bit, asks for help from any country to have his own democracy. I think before the war on Iraq some thought about this, but after the war they changed their minds. Only a small percentage of people used to think before the war that the war on Iraq would help democracy in the region. Most of them now think this is a bad example of bringing democracy.[33]

Chapter 6

The "Rogue State" and the United States

During the last decade scores of congresspersons, think tank and NGO representatives, and Middle East experts who have testified and commented before congressional committees assessing the regimes of Hafiz al-Asad and his son Bashar have, for the most part, concluded that Syria is, indeed, a so-called "rogue state." It is argued that from the viewpoint of Washington, Syria supports terrorism, possesses weapons of mass destruction (WMDs), and generally deviates from the accepted norms of the international community. In the 1980s and 1990s terminology such as "rogue states," "backlash states," or "states of concern" became fashionable in U.S. foreign policy discourse to describe countries that went beyond internationally sanctioned behavioral patterns. In the post-9/11 environment, with the United States taking upon itself the task of evaluating countries as being for or against terrorists, the term "rogue state" has again found a receptive audience. The appellation "repressive states" was employed by George W. Bush in his State of the Union speech in February 2005, in which he specifically mentioned Syria as a country that "still allows its territory, and parts of Lebanon, to be used by terrorists," and he called on Syria to "end all support for terror and open the door to freedom." Ever since the beginning of such foreign policy categorizations deemed inimical to U.S. interests, Syria has been at the forefront, as well as on the outside looking in.

Pressure from Congress

In 1996, at what turns out to have been the midpoint of the Oslo and Madrid peace processes, commenting on whether Syria was a "peace partner or rogue regime" on the House Committee on International Relations, Representative Dan Burton (R-IN) stated,

I do not think many mafia characters or Al Capone ever shot anybody directly. I think usually they hired somebody to do it, and they insulated themselves. To say that Syria is not actively involved or directly involved in terrorism is splitting hairs, as far as I am concerned. . . . We keep licking Assad's [then Syrian President Hafiz al-Asad] boots and urging him to end his terrorist activities and begging him to get into the peace process.

At the same committee hearing, investigative journalist and terrorism expert Steven Emerson commented, "Were Syria to abandon terrorism, the regime of Hafiz al-Assad would collapse. Mr. Assad's only hope of surviving both internally and externally is through a systemic policy of instilling terror in his own population, as well as spreading it in the population of neighbor states." He went on to say, "As is the inherent nature of other states who sponsor terrorism, Syria also manifests similar characteristics: It is a repressive dictatorship bent on squandering its precious few resources on acquiring the poor man's atomic bomb—chemical and biological weapons. The regime is prone to routinely torturing or killing political prisoners, even liquidating without any hesitancy thousands of civilians on a whim."[1]

In testimony before the same House committee in September 2002 on whether or not to pass the Syrian Accountability Act (House Resolution 4483), Rep. Dick Armey (R-TX) proclaimed, "Our inaction on holding Syria accountable for its dangerous activities could seriously diminish our efforts on the war on terrorism and brokering a viable peace in the Middle East . . . Syria should be held accountable for its record of harboring and supporting terrorist groups; stockpiling illegal weapons in an effort to develop weapons of mass destruction; and transferring weapons and oil back and forth through Iraq." In support of H.R. 4483, co-sponsor Rep. Eliot Engel (D-NY) asserted, "We will not tolerate Syrian support for terrorism. We will not tolerate Syrian occupation of Lebanon. We will not tolerate Syria making weapons of mass destruction; and we will not tolerate Syria's lack of compliance with the oil embargo against Iraq." Attempting to link Syria with the specter of 9/11, Engel quoted a line from President George W. Bush's speech before the UN General Assembly that same month: "If an emboldened regime were to supply weapons of mass destruction to terrorist allies, then the attacks of September 11th would be a prelude to far greater horrors." Engel then stated, "That's our President, and I agree with him. . . . I do not want to witness horrors worse than 9–11. I urge the Administration to get tough on Syria." At the same hearing, Rep. Gary Ackerman (D-NY) said, "This is not too big a nut to crack. Syria is a small, decrepit, little terror state that has been yanking our diplomatic chain for years." Rep. Robert Wexler (D-FL), specifically commenting on Bashar al-Asad, said that "he, individually, presents what may be . . . the most dangerous obstacle in the Middle East; both with respect to Iraq, both with respect to Hizbollah and his absolute condemnation, by action, of any kind of peace process whatsoever." Alluding to President Bashar's background in ophthalmology, Rep. Shelly Berkley (D-NV) stated,

> I don't care if he's a doctor, a lawyer, a plumber, a carpenter—this is not a kinder and gentler leader. This is a kinder and gentler terrorist, and we don't need another one of those. He is no different from his father; perhaps, even worse because he should know better. This is a disgrace that this country isn't standing up to this terrorist and making sure that this type of behavior is not only condemned, but eliminated.

Matthew Levitt, a senior fellow at the Washington Institute for Near East Policy, said before the committee:

> Syrian support for terrorism under Bashar al Assad has become far more brazen and direct than it was under the rule of his father. . . . Failure to hold Syria accountable for its support of international terrorism after repeatedly articulating this message will further dilute America's already diminished credibility in the eyes of men like Bashar al Assad, Yasir Arafat, and Saddam Hussein. Bashar is waiting to see if the United States will actually act on all its talk, or if in fact it's all just *kalam fadi*, empty words.[2]

In testimony a year later, the chair of the subcommittee on the Middle East and Central Asia, Congresswoman Ileana Ros-Lehtinen (R-FL), opened up the hearing by detailing that "the Subcommittee held an oversight hearing to assess the impact of foreign investment that Iran's energy infrastructure has had on the Iranian regime's ability to finance its nuclear program, its development of long-range ballistic missiles, and its continued sponsoring of terrorist organizations. Unfortunately, we see a similar pattern emerging with respect to Syria." She went on to state,

> Just as ties between Iran and Syria appeared to be strengthening, governments focused on appeasing these two terrorist regimes are also expanding their ties with Iran and Syria. . . . It appears to me that over the 2 decades, and particularly since the September 11th attacks, Syria's overall actions have not been those of a state that shares our commitment to nonproliferation and combating terrorism. It should be the end of the line for the Syrian regime.

Finally, Eliot Engel chimed in with, "I have often said, and I say it again, that Syria's record on terrorism, in my estimation, is even worse than Iraq's."[3]

Terrorist activity has long been associated with Syria, less because of direct involvement in terrorist actions than because of its support for what Washington terms as terrorist organizations, such as Hizbollah, Hamas, Palestinan Islamic Jihad, and some Kurdish groups over the years, such as the Kurdish Workers' Party (PKK), which has targeted U.S. friend and NATO ally Turkey. Many believe that Syria was behind the 1983 bombings in Beirut: that of the U.S. embassy in April, killing over ninety people, and that of U.S. marine barracks in October, which took 241 American lives. In terms of direct involvement in terrorist activity, the last reported incident concerning Syria was an abortive attempt to place a bomb on an El Al airliner in London in 1986 (the so-called Hindawi affair), after which the United States withdrew its ambassador to Syria for a year. As such, there are those who believe that Syria has been wrongfully kept on the state-sponsored terrorism list, and that it is being used by Washington as a bargaining chip *vis-à-vis* concessions on the Arab-Israeli front. Others, however, do not see a distinction between direct and indirect action, i.e. support for terrorist groups such as Hamas and Hizbollah is reason enough to keep Syria on the terrorism list and, indeed, take more concerted action against the regime. By late 1998, Syria agreed to expel PKK members (most especially PKK leader Abdullah Ocalan) under Turkish political and military pressure—the so-called Adana Accord—and the State Department believes that Syria has "generally upheld its agreement with Ankara not to support the Kurdish PKK."[4] Some in the United States have held out Turkey's military pressure against Damascus as a model for the Bush administration to follow—military pressure begets results; however, others believe this to be a misplaced assumption, for as Hemmer states,

> Any hope of using the Turkish model to get Syria to cut its ties to Lebanese and Palestinian terrorism is likely to be as misguided as any hopes that Hizballah's success in chasing the Israelis out of southern Lebanon can serve as an effective guide for driving the Israelis from the Golan Heights or the West Bank. Just as the Golan and the West Bank mean far more to Israel than southern Lebanon, Syria gains far more from Hizballah and Hamas than they did from the PKK.[5]

Following the 9/11 attack, President Bashar sent a cable to President Bush offering his condolences in which he "condemned the terrorist attacks that targeted innocent civilians and vital centers in the United States." In a radio broadcast he also called for "international cooperation to eradicate all forms of terrorism and guarantee the protection of basic human rights, notably the right of humans to live in security and peace wherever they are." It is at this time that Syrian propaganda began to compare the U.S. war on Islamic extremism with its own struggles against the Muslim Brethren in the 1980s. According to many reports, Syria cooperated with the United States in investigating al-Qaida and persons associated with it. Reports in June 2002 outlined Syrian assistance to the United States in providing information gained from an interrogation of a key figure in the 9/11 plot, Muhammad Hayder Zammar, who was extradited from Morocco to Syria. Bashar told reporters that Syria had provided information to the United States on a planned al-Qaida operation targeting U.S. personnel.[6] On June 18, U.S. Assistant Secretary of State William Burns informed a congressional panel that "the cooperation the Syrians have provided in their own self-interest on al-Qaida has saved American lives."[7]

Syria does not deny claims of support for Hizbollah, Hamas, and Islamic Jihad, viewing that such operations constitute legitimate resistance and not terrorism; indeed, Damascus often views Israeli activities *vis-à-vis* the Palestinians and its actions in Lebanon as terrorism. At the Arab League summit meeting in Beirut in 2002, Bashar explained that "there is a difference between terrorism and resistance . . . the difference between one who has a right and the other who usurps this right."[8] President Bush said in a speech on April 4, 2002, that "Syria has spoken out against al-Qaida. We expect it to act against Hamas and Hizbollah as well," and on June 24, Bush added, "Syria must choose the right side in the war on terror by closing terrorist camps and expelling terrorist organizations." These statements have been used by supporters in Congress of the Syrian Accountability Act to persuade the Bush administration to sign the legislation, which it finally did in December 2003.[9] While not disputing the accusations leveled at Damascus, the Bush administration, particularly State Department officials, testified against passage of the act. They believed that at such a critical phase in the Middle East it would reduce the administration's flexibility to pursue various policy options in Iraq as well as on the Arab-Israeli front.

As one can see, U.S. relations with Syria are complex and oscillating, primarily between those groups who believe the U.S. should remained engaged with Damascus and those who feel that Washington should place more pressure on Syria, containing it if not generating regime change. On the one hand, Henry Kissinger famously stated in the 1970s that there could be no war in the Middle East without Egypt but there could also not be any peace without Syria, therefore affirming the centrality of Damascus in any sort of comprehensive settlement in the Arab-Israeli arena. On the other hand, there have been a number of powerful voices, much more prevalent in the last few years, that have written off the Asads, condemned Syria as a rogue state, attempted to marginalize and isolate it, and advocated a more aggressive policy of confrontation with Damascus. These voices officially want a change of behavior on the part of the Syrians, not necessarily a change of regime. However, U.S. rhetoric and actions of late point to a clear desire to destabilize the regime in what some U.S. policymakers have oxymoronically termed, "constructive instability." It is, therefore, little wonder that Damascus, more often than not, prefers to err on the side of caution and circle the wagons against anticipated and potential adversaries.

Syria in the Crosshairs

It has been common practice with regard to the designation of rogue regimes to focus on individual leaders, in many cases with good reason since most are, in fact, ruthless, bonapartist dictators whose prime objective is the maintenance of power. We have spoken as much, if not more, of dictatorial and totalitarian regimes and leaders as we have of states and peoples—it is the regime of Saddam Hussein, the war against Saddam, or the Iraqi regime; the Iranian regime or the regime of the ayatollahs; or Kim Jong-Il's tyranny, the North Korean regime, and so on. This focuses attention on specific threats in order to drum up domestic support for a stout foreign policy while making any action more palatable with international conventions and regional allies. It also fits in with the strategic desire to win over the people in a targeted state (as happened in Afghanistan and in Iraq) so as to deplete the resources upon which a rogue regime can draw support and/or to create internal coalitions that will assist in weakening and/or overthrowing said regime. As Michael Klare comments regarding America's civilian and military leadership at the end of the cold war between the United States and the Soviet Union:

> At the same time, they began to ascribe to the leaders of these states [WMD-equipped Third World powers] violent and immoral intentions of a sort long identified with Soviet leaders. The officials hoped in this fashion to define a strategic environment that would compel legislators to relinquish dreams of a substantial peace dividend in return for enhanced national security.[10]

So it has generally been the case with Hafiz al-Asad—and now his son, Bashar.

It is imperative to understand Syrian history under Hafiz al-Asad because this same history has been constantly referenced by powerful forces in Washington since the mid-1990s who have advocated containment of Syria, if

not outright regime change. Therefore, it is necessary and beneficial to provide some historical context to these references and, more importantly, to
acquire some perspective on how Damascus viewed the world during the
same time frame, whether one thinks its positions on this or that issue were
legitimate or not.

Syria is a charter member of the original State Department list of states that
sponsor terrorism, as articulated in the 1979 Export Administration Act
passed by Congress.[11] But as opposed to the other six members of what
became the officially sanctioned and oft-mentioned State Department list of
state-sponsors of terrorism (North Korea, Iraq, Iran, Cuba, Libya, and Sudan),
Syria was generally spared official opprobrium from successive U.S. administrations throughout the 1980s, 1990s, and into the first years of the presidency
of George W. Bush, and it was (and continues to be) the only country on the
list that has diplomatic representation in Washington at the ambassadorial
level. In 1985 President Ronald Reagan delivered a speech in which he named
Iran, Libya, Cuba, North Korea, and Nicaragua as "outlaw states" that were
subverting U.S. interests.[12] The Clinton administration assiduously avoided
grouping Syria publicly with the usual suspects of state-sponsors of terrorism;
indeed, Anthony Lake, Clinton's national security adviser, wrote a seminal
essay in *Foreign Affairs* in 1994 outlining the threat to global security from
what he termed the "backlash states." Syria was nowhere to be found in the
article; only North Korea, Libya, Iran, and Iraq were named.[13] Syria was also
subject to less stringent terms and application of antiterrorism legislation
throughout the 1990s in comparison to other members on the State
Department list.[14]

Syria narrowly avoided inclusion in the Iran–Libya Sanctions Act in 1996
that extended more restrictions on U.S. interaction with both of these countries. U.S. sanctions against Syria were applied nonetheless, pursuant to the
Anti-Terrorism and Arms Export Act of 1989, with bans on economic aid
(including U.S. support in international forums for multilateral economic
assistance) and military sales, and limits on the sale of dual-use items. But
these allowed at least a modicum of private economic and cultural interaction
as well as leaving the door open to diplomacy. The sanctions studiously did
not cut U.S.-Syrian ties anywhere near as deeply as these acts and their sup-
plements did in the cases of Libya, Iran, Iraq (before the 2003 war), and North
Korea. At times the doors of diplomacy between Washington and Damascus
were wide open, as evidenced by over twenty trips to Syria made by U.S.
Secretary of State Warren Christopher during the height of the peace process
in the first four years of the Clinton administration. In fact, Clinton was the
first sitting president since Nixon in 1974 to visit Syria, arriving in Damascus

in October 1994 to energize the peace process. He definitely believed that Syria was the key to a comprehensive Arab-Israeli peace. Echoing the view of many in the Clinton administration, Anthony Lake wrote in May 1994:

> A decisive Syrian-Israeli agreement would allow Jordan and Lebanon to resolve their differences with Israel in short order. An Israeli-Syrian peace would thus shore up the agreement between Israel and the PLO and greatly advance U.S. efforts to widen the circle of peacemakers, bolster the network of Middle East moderation, and construct a bastion against backlash states.[15]

The prevailing decision by the Clinton team regarding Syria was to engage Damascus rather than actively contain it through economic sanctions and/or military pressure. This made a great deal of sense considering the fact that, as mentioned previously, Syria joined the U.S.-led UN coalition to liberate Kuwait in the 1991 Gulf war and played a key role in convening the Madrid peace process later in the year.

Hafiz al-Asad seemed to be serious about peace—the regional and international winds drawn by the Gulf war as well as the end of the superpower cold war gave Damascus little choice but to enter into the peace process and improve its relationship with Washington. In addition, both Clinton and newly elected Israeli Prime Minister Yitzhak Rabin, who along with his Labor party was favorably disposed to the land-for-peace framework outlined in the 1967 UN Security Council Resolution 242, initially preferred the Syrian track rather than the Palestinian track since the former was, at least on the surface, more direct and less complicated. After the PLO signed the Declaration of Principles with Israel in 1993 and Jordan signed a peace treaty with Israel in 1994, Asad was furious that both went ahead of him rather than in tandem, thus, in his view, diluting the leverage on the Arab side of the negotiating equation. On the other hand, he also felt free to carve out his own deal since Syria was now less wedded to the Palestinian and pan-Arab cause. While there were certainly doubts as to the sincerity of the Syrian regime in entering the Madrid process, some seeing it as more of a diplomatic maneuver to get closer to Washington, improve relations with the Gulf Arab states—who, grateful for Syria's participation, would now (and did) invest in the faltering Syrian economy—and/or buy time to strengthen the regime in terms of acquisition of weapons of mass destruction, the Clinton administration chose to give Damascus the benefit of the doubt. In any event, it probably does not make any substantive difference what brought Syria to the peace table, or any country for that matter; just as long as it was serious about it once it was engaged—

and from everything we know today, Damascus was very serious. Every country enters into a peace process to gain something—no one does it just for the sake of peace in and of itself; Syria is no different. As President Clinton stated on Hafiz al-Asad's death in 2000: "While we had our disagreements . . . I always respected him . . . because I felt he meant it when he said he had made a strategic choice for peace."[16]

But there was an influential chorus that began to make its voice heard in the mid-1990s categorically denouncing Syria as a partner in peace. Essentially, the belief was that Syria's involvement in the process was fraudulent and that the U.S. policy of engaging Damascus was misguided, if not dangerous to both U.S. and Israeli interests. This chorus rang out from within a strain of the Republican Party. The turning point was the 1994 midterm congressional elections that brought the Republicans a majority in both the House and the Senate. Most remember this Republican "revolution" led by, among others, Newt Gingrich, for its domestic policy repercussions, especially over welfare reform and the budget, including the shutting down of the government in late 1995. However, it also established the foundation for important shifts in foreign policy if and when there arose a sympathetic administration in the White House and/or a more propitious environment, both of which occurred with George W. Bush coming to power in 2001 followed swiftly by the repercussions of 9/11. As James Zogby, president of the Arab-American Institute, wrote in 1997, "This new Republican leadership is not from the traditional pro-business moderate wing of the Party once represented by Texans like George Bush [George H. W. Bush, the forty-first president of the United States and the current president's father], James Baker, and John Connaly. The new Republican leadership in Congress is an alliance between ideological neo-conservatives and the Christian fundamentalist movement."[17]

A seminal representation of this emerging viewpoint was a six-page report prepared by the Jerusalem-based Institute for Advanced Strategic and Political Studies in 1996, entitled "A Clean Break: A New Strategy for Securing the Realm."[18] As the report states, it was compiled from discussions among the "Study Group on a New Israeli Strategy Toward 2000," consisting of, among others, Richard Perle, Douglas Feith, David Wurmser, and Meyrav Wurmser (David Wurmser's Israeli-born wife). All of these people have or had important positions either in the Bush administration itself or in entities that are closely aligned to various elements in the administration. Richard Perle has been called a godfather of the neo-conservative movement as it has been applied in the Bush White House—he is an adviser to the Department of Defense who sat on the Defense Policy Board. Feith is undersecretary of defense for policy and was one of the main proponents of the war in Iraq.

David Wurmser, a neo-conservative scholar with close ties to the Israeli right, was appointed in September 2003 to join the national security team of Vice President Dick Cheney, led by his national security adviser, Lewis "Scooter" Libby. And Meyrav Wurmser heads the Middle East studies section at the Hudson Institute, a conservative think tank in Washington, DC, and, along with the American Enterprise Institute, one of the bastions of neo-conservative thought in recent years. The report was constructed for Likud party leader Benjamin Netanyahu in the immediate aftermath of his election victory as Israeli prime minister in 1996 offering recommendations regarding Middle East policy; indeed, the report even has passages in bold print marked "TEXT" to highlight what are suggestions for a "possible speech" by the new Israeli premier. In many ways, this report has become a blueprint for the Bush administration's foreign policy toward the Middle East. Along with Iraq, a—if not the—primary target in the estimation of the authors is Syria, or more to the point, the Asad regime, and the implementation of Bush's Middle East policy appears to have followed many of the recommendations made in this report.

The report contends that "efforts to salvage Israel's socialist institutions—which include pursuing supranational over national sovereignty and pursuing a peace process that embraces the slogan, 'New Middle East'—undermine the legitimacy of the nation and lead Israel into strategic paralysis and the previous government's [that of Yitzhak Rabin and Shimon Peres] 'peace process.'" In order to "secure the nation's streets and borders in the immediate future," the authors of the report suggest Israel do the following:

1) Work closely with Turkey and Jordan to contain, destabilize, and roll-back some of its most dangerous threats. This implies a clean break from the slogan "comprehensive peace" to a traditional concept of strategy based on balance of power.
2) Change the nature of its relations with the Palestinians, including upholding the right of hot pursuit for self-defense into all Palestinian areas and nurturing alternatives to Arafat's exclusive grip on Palestinian society.
3) Forge a new basis for relations with the United States—stressing self-reliance, maturity, strategic cooperation on areas of mutual concern, and furthering values inherent to the West. This can only be done if Israel takes serious steps to terminate aid, which prevents economic reform.

The report states that Syria "challenges Israel on Lebanese soil," and calls on Israel to seize the strategic initiative by engaging Hizbollah, Syria, and Iran as "the principal agents of aggression in Lebanon" in the following manner: 1) strike Syria's drug-money and counterfeiting infrastructure in Lebanon;

2) establish the precedent that Syrian territory "is not immune from attacks emanating from Lebanon by Israeli proxy forces"; and 3) strike Syrian military targets in Lebanon, "and should that prove insufficient, striking at select targets in Syria proper." Describing the Syrian regime, the report goes on to say:

> Israel also can take this opportunity to remind the world of the nature of the Syrian regime. Syria repeatedly breaks its word. It violated numerous agreements with the Turks, and has betrayed the United States by continuing to occupy Lebanon in violation of the Taif agreement in 1989. Instead, Syria staged a sham election, installed a quisling regime, and forced Lebanon to sign a "Brotherhood Agreement" in 1991 that terminated Lebanese sovereignty. And Syria has begun colonizing Lebanon with hundreds of thousands of Syrians, while killing tens of thousands of its own citizens at a time, as it did in only three days in 1983 in Hama [actually 1982, only one of the many factual errors in the report]. . . . Indeed, the Syrian-controlled Bekaa Valley in Lebanon has become for terror what the Silicon Valley has become for computers. . . . Given the nature of the regime in Damascus, it is both natural and moral that Israel abandon the slogan "comprehensive peace" and move to contain Syria, drawing attention to its weapons of mass destruction program, and rejecting "land for peace" deals on the Golan Heights.

The report proffers that

> Israel can shape its strategic environment, in cooperation with Turkey and Jordan, by weakening, containing, and even rolling back Syria. This effort can focus on removing Saddam Hussein from power in Iraq—an important Israeli strategic objective in its own right—as a means of foiling Syria's regional ambitions. . . . Most important, it is understandable that Israel has an interest supporting diplomatically, militarily and operationally Turkey's and Jordan's actions against Syria, such as securing tribal alliances with Arab tribes that cross into Syrian territory and are hostile to the Syrian ruling elite.

Other than the report's recommendations regarding Israel's economy and weaning away from U.S. aid, its contents are highly questionable. It could be dismissed if it were in fact not so serious in that a number of the recommendations have come to pass with, in my opinion, disastrous short-term and long-term results for the United States, Israel, much of the rest of the Middle East, and the global war on terror. The report closes with the following ominous bold print "text" suggestion: "Israel will not only contain its foes; it will transcend them." Interestingly, Netanyahu visited Washington in 1996 advocating a policy of what was called "triple containment," i.e. the containment of Iraq, Iran, and Syria. This was very much in line with "A Clean Break," and in a way has appeared again in current U.S. policy toward the region.

In May 2000 a pro-Israeli (specifically pro-Likud) research group called the Middle East Forum (MEF) along with the United States Committee for a Free Lebanon (USCFL) released a study entitled "Ending Syria's Occupation of Lebanon: The U.S. Role?" The report was officially the work of the "Lebanon Study Group," which was co-chaired by Professor Daniel Pipes, the president of the MEF, and Ziad Abdelnour, an expatriate investment banker from Lebanon who established the USCFL in 1997.[19] The USCFL describes itself as a "non-profit, non-sectarian think tank" that wants to get rid of "dictatorships, radical ideologies, existential conflicts, border disagreements, political violence, and weapons of mass destruction" from the Middle East. These are all laudable goals. Largely reflecting the program of Lebanese Christian groups, the USCFL has been a leading advocate of removing Syrian troops and deleterious influence from Lebanon, and it has been a remorseless critic of both Hafiz al-Asad and his son Bashar.[20] The report explicitly calls for the use of military force to eliminate weapons of mass destruction from Syria and end its "occupation" of Lebanon. It also asserts that "Lebanon occupies a strategically vital corner of the world," and states that "preserving Lebanon's Christian communities ... becomes the cornerstone for safeguarding the country's special freedoms that uplift all its communities."

The study sanctions a more aggressive U.S. policy in Lebanon:

> the Vietnam legacy and the sour memories of the dead American marines in Beirut notwithstanding, the U.S. has entered a new era of undisputed military supremacy, coupled with an appreciable drop in human losses on the battlefield. But this opportunity will not wait, for as WMD capabilities spread, the risks of such action will rapidly grow. If there is to be decisive action, it will have to be sooner rather than later.

Among the signatories of the document were: Richard Perle; David Wurmser; Douglas Feith; Michael Ledeen from the American Enterprise Institute, who has been a leading voice of neo-conservative foreign policy toward the Middle East; Elliot Abrams, who is in charge of Middle East policy on the U.S. National Security Council; Frank Gaffney, a former aid to Perle in the Reagan administration who now heads the Center for Security Policy; former UN ambassador Jeanne Kirkpatrick; and David Steinmann, chairman of the Jewish Institute for National Security Affairs (JINSA). All except Kirkpatrick have played key roles in and outside the Bush administration in the development of its Middle East policy, including, of course, during the 2003 war in Iraq. While most agree that it was time for Syria to get out of Lebanon, its presence there became something of a lightening rod for those who advocate a more aggressive policy against Damascus. It represents a merger of interests between Lebanese Christian émigré groups and pro-Israeli groups. As the Turks and others have learned, one of the optimum ways in which a group and/or country can advance its objectives in Washington is to attach itself to the pro-Israeli lobby on issues of mutual concern, in this case, the weakening or replacement of the regime in Syria.[21] In this way, the powerful pro-Israeli lobby, in return, will support Turkish, or Greek, or Indian, or indeed almost any policy on issues that are important to these countries and that do not conflict with Israeli interests.

These anti-Syrian and, indeed, anti-Asad reports and claims are more often than not analysis by assertion. They fail to fully consider the strategic position from the viewpoint of Damascus at a particular time and tend to lay everything that's wrong at the feet of Hafiz and Bashar al-Asad. One glaring example is the focus on the bombing of the marine barracks in Beirut in October 1983. This incident comes up repeatedly in reports and congressional testimony by anti-Syrian organizations, scholars, and pundits as a prime example of how Syria is not a friend of the United States; quite to the contrary, it is responsible for the deaths of many Americans—something that they feel needs to be drummed into the public's psyche to counter the State Department mantra that Syria has actually helped save American lives with the sharing of intelligence on al-Qaida following 9/11. It is astonishing to me that when speaking of the marine barracks attack carried out by groups aligned with Syria, they almost always fail to mention that it was the Israeli invasion of Lebanon in June 1982 in the first place that precipitated the chaos that soon enveloped the country, creating the conditions in which such tragic events could occur. As detailed in chapter three, the invasion became an albatross for Israel. It was Israel's disastrous decision to stay on in southern Lebanon that radicalized the Lebanese Shiite community and created fertile ground for the rise of Hizbollah—all of this after the Shiites initially welcomed the Israeli invasion to expel the despised PLO military units. Although well-intentioned at first, the U.S.-led MNF combined with exclusionary cold war American diplomacy—that relied too much on Amin Gemayel—exacerbated a deteriorating situation.

To say that Syria was responsible for the outright mess that became Lebanon in ensuing years is to confuse current myopic policy intent with real-

ity, playing upon most people's ignorance of history and the current prejudi-
cial climate to anachronistically advance an agenda. Quite to the contrary, the
first Bush administration, as an unofficial quid pro quo for Syria's participation in the Gulf war coalition, is widely believed to have given Damascus the
green light to consolidate its position in Lebanon in 1990 and 1991, leaving
the al-Taif agreement to be interpreted and implemented by Syria, thus leading to the 1991 Brotherhood treaty. Did Syria stay on in Lebanon for too long?
Yes. Has it taken political and economic advantage of its position there?
Absolutely. One critical, but fairly accurate, assessment of the Syrian role in
Lebanon characterized the situation thus:

> [It is a] creeping Anschluss to absorb a country no pan-Syrian or pan-Arab
> nationalist has ever really accepted as a stand-alone entity. Another, equally
> important, reason [for Syria's continued presence in Lebanon] is the craven
> corruption of much of the Lebanese political class, who interlock as clients
> with the Syrian nomenklatura in their shared pillage of what should be a
> much more vibrant economy. Far from withdrawing, Damascus reconse-
> crated the pre-war sectarian system in a way designed to highlight its own
> role as indispensable arbiter and bulwark against a relapse into conflict.
> It cultivated political clients, including warlords and rival forces within
> each community, using lucrative patronage and divide-and-rule tactics to
> prevent the emergence of a cross-confessional national force.[22]

But there is need of an accurate reading of history in order to understand
how Syria arrived in Lebanon, what its role has been, and why it was reluctant
to leave. From the time when Syria first sent troops into Lebanon as an Arab
League-mandated action at the beginning of the Lebanese civil war in
1975/1976, it has probably played more of a stabilizing role there than the
obverse, particularly during the late 1980s and early 1990s when Lebanon had
literally come apart at the seams. Syrian influence, when weighed against the
alternative, was an ameliorating one.

Syria, at least publicly, did not express interest in annexing Lebanon,
although former Lebanese president Amin Gemayel disagreed: "Syria considers its presence here not as something temporary, not as a foreign occupation, but as something natural. They think that Lebanon is a part of Syria."[23]
Or as one Lebanese journalist said: "They gave us security, but what a price
we've paid for this security. They took our money, they took our democracy."[24] Despite popular perception, however, Syria's stabilizing role in the
aftermath of the destructive civil war actually better enabled the Lebanese to
increase their independence from Damascus. Bashar al-Asad understood

this, and realized over the years that Syria would not remain in Lebanon in perpetuity. In fact, in a "background note" on Syria from the State Department in August 2004, commenting on the 1991 "treaty of brotherhood, cooperation, and coordination" between Syria and Lebanon, it was stated that "The treaty provides the most explicit recognition to date by the Syrian Government of Lebanon's independence and sovereignty"—this is quite a different view from the supporters of the Syrian Accountability Act and the like who saw the treaty as further proof of Lebanon falling further into the bosom of Syria.[25] Set against what was publicized most of the time, there were those in and outside Lebanon who were not as anxious to see the Syrians leave or support the 2003 Syrian Accountability Act. As former CIA Middle East analyst Martha Kessler noted, "Lebanon has really never healed since its civil war. It still has a huge Palestinian community that is deeply disenchanted and disenfranchised. The stability of Lebanon is a big unknown should Syria withdraw."[26] Even so, Syria can still wield preponderant influence in Lebanon without the troops and security agents it had stationed in the country.

In addition, both Syria's participation in the 1991 Gulf war coalition and its direct involvement in the Madrid peace process tends to be glossed over and/or trivialized by anti-Syrian organizations, when in fact they were vitally important to U.S. interests and helped reshape the regional balance of power that for about a decade came very close to establishing the paradigm for a comprehensive Arab-Israeli peace. The fact that both the Madrid and Oslo processes failed to achieve their ultimate objectives does not diminish and certainly does not negate the Syrian contribution and role. Hafiz al-Asad was indeed serious about peace with Israel, and by most accounts the two sides traversed about 80 percent of the distance toward peace as a result of intense negotiations in 1995–1996 and in late 1999 and early 2000. Concrete issues were discussed regarding timing for withdrawals, security arrangements, and normalizing relations. Negotiations were complicated by the issue of whether or not Israel would withdraw from the Golan Heights to the line drawn on June 4, 1967 but some say that the late Yitzhak Rabin indicated that he was prepared to withdraw to the June 4 line. And regarding the 1999/2000 discussions, one only has to read Clinton's autobiography as well as U.S. lead negotiator Dennis Ross' account as outlined in his book *The Missing Peace* to learn that it was not only the Syrians who were to blame for the breakdown, but also the Israelis. The fact that Lt. General Moshe Yaalon, the Israeli army chief of staff, commented in August 2004 that Israel would be prepared to give up the Golan Heights in return for peace with Syria suggests that Syria is not the dire threat to Israel and the region as a whole that it has been portrayed as of late. Yaalon gave an interview to the Hebrew-language daily *Yedioth Ahronoth*, also in August, in which he indicated that if a peace agreement with Syria is reached in which the Golan is given up, the IDF would be able to defend Israel without it.[27]

Perceptions

With Hafiz al-Asad it was always the strategic situation internally and externally at a particular time that dictated his foreign policy direction rather than a tightly articulated ideology. To him, groups such as Hizbollah, Hamas, and Palestinian Islamic Jihad were always the opposite side of the coin to the peace process, to be delicately utilized as leverage against Israel in order to exact the necessary concessions. They were also functional elements of his asymmetrical military posture *vis-à-vis* Israel—after several wars, he knew he could not fight Israel directly, a situation made even more disparate with the end of the cold war, the termination of Soviet largesse, and the further deterioration of Syria's economy and armed forces. These strategic alignments and realignments, a strategic chess game if you will, were very much part and parcel of who Hafiz al-Asad was, and he tended to be quite good at it given Syria's relative weakness. Bashar is also trying to deal with no less a strategic threat from the perspective of Damascus, although whether or not he will be as adept as his father in playing this game remains to be seen.

This aspect of the equation is almost totally lost or ignored when discussing or analyzing Syria from the U.S. perspective, i.e. the view from the other side. In the post-World War II era, Syria has seen itself as threatened from a variety of directions. It touts itself as a crossroads of history, and indeed it is. While this is good for tourism, it is bad for the national psyche because it means Syria has been invaded and conquered on numerous occasions throughout the millennia; it provides grist for the mill when painted against more modern manifestations of perceived threats. Whether legitimately or not, Syrians honestly believe Israel is an aggressive, threatening state—and it is perception rather than reality that counts. The 1982 Israeli invasion of Lebanon was perceived in Damascus as a flanking operation intended to isolate Syria. And just as there have been enough Syrians touting the Greater Syria plan over the decades to make Israelis (as well as Lebanese and Jordanians) worry, so have there been just enough Israelis countenancing expansionist visions to make Syrians worry. To say that the Asad regime over the years has utilized the idea of the Israeli threat—and the role of the victim—for propaganda purposes and domestic political advantage would be accurate; to say that it was a totally fabricated illusion would be inaccurate.

So when many of the people who have been writing anti-Syrian tracts and countenancing military action to pressure, if not remove, the regime in Damascus are in high places in the Bush administration, and when many of these very same people successfully marshaled forces in and outside Congress to pass the Syrian Accountability Act in December 2003, Syrians have had to wonder seriously over the last few years if they have been targeted. Syria *has* been targeted. Many administration hawks were hoping that the war in Iraq might provoke turmoil in Syria that would overthrow the regime, something they were also hoping for in Iran. The administration was also concerned that the U.S. debacle in Lebanon not be repeated, i.e. Syria would not be allowed to play a destabilizing role in Iraq. This heightened belligerency toward Syria became especially noticeable as the United States shifted its strategic modus operandi in the post-9/11 era to that of preventive war as articulated in the Bush doctrine (National Security Strategy of September 2002) and as applied in Iraq in 2003. Indeed, it is a strategy that advocates when necessary a preventive war though pre-emption. The use by al-Qaida of the failed-state environment of Afghanistan to build up its terrorist network convinced policymakers that the United States could no longer wait for a threat to become manifest. It was now compelled to deal with countries that from the viewpoint of Washington facilitated terrorist activities before the actual threat emerged. Syria has been identified as either one of or close to being one of these types of states.

The war on terror engulfed Syria. Entities Damascus considered to be resistance groups fighting against Israeli occupation eventually became grouped with terrorists of all shapes and colors, including al-Qaida. Ross Leonard Fisher wrote:

Whilst September 11 created new reasons for the US to engage Syria [by sharing intelligence on al-Qaida], it also heightened Damascus' increasing exposure in US foreign policy calculations. For one, the heightened US intolerance for terrorism after September 11 produced a more hostile operating environment for Syria to continue supporting terrorist groups. From the outset, Syria apparently became targeted in neoconservative proposals to extend the US war on terror beyond al-Qaeda to states sponsoring terrorism.[28]

Indeed, the Bush administration's focus more on Iraq than on Arab-Israeli peace upon coming to office tended to diminish Syria's utility in the eyes of many in the administration who were already suspicious of Syrian motives in the 1990s. But it was also important to keep a line open to Syria because it could still play an important role in the containment of Iraq, especially after it gained a seat on the UN Security Council. In addition, it might help keep a lid on Hizbollah. Doing so could limit Iranian influence in the region through the Syrian connection. As such, one could still hear positive comments on Syria emanating from administration figures, usually in the State Department. For instance, in responding to an inquiry on why he included a visit to Syria in his tour of the Middle East in February 2001, Secretary of State Colin Powell stated, "Syria is an important nation in the region . . . and so I thought it was very, very appropriate for me as part of this quick trip through the Middle East . . . to stop in Syria for a few hours."[29] I believe Syria's growing opposition to U.S. military preparations against Iraq in late 2002 and early 2003, despite their voting for UN Security Council Resolution 1441 in November 2002, provided grist for the mill for those who had already adopted an anti-Syrian posture, the crowning blow coming with the accusations of Syrian support for elements fighting against U.S. forces in Iraq in April and May 2003. The transition was complete, and the Kissinger admonition regarding Syria no longer applied in foreign-policymaking circles in Washington. This became readily apparent when then White House spokesman Ari Fleischer on April 14, 2003, bluntly stated that "Syria is indeed a rogue nation."[30]

Fundamentally speaking, the United States believed it could more assertively "go after" what it considered to be rogue regimes from the end of the cold war because the possibility of eliciting a Soviet response, which often acted as a deterrent to American military calculations, had been eliminated— the 1991 Gulf war was the first manifestation of this post-cold war military flexibility. The Gulf war also reflected a level of cooperation with Moscow that had been apparent since the last days of the Iran–Iraq war. Certainly during the heady days of military success during and immediately after the war in Iraq, that is, until the situation in postwar Iraq evolved into the quagmire that it is as of this writing, elements in the administration and in the punditocracy were essentially labeling Syria (as well as Iran) as next on the hit list. Pentagon officials were dropping hints to Syrian officials that the United States could very well move on from Iraq toward other venues close by since the troops and tanks were already in the area—that the main cost of war is not the fighting itself but getting all of the men and materiel to the theater of combat.

Syrian ambassador to the United States Dr. Imad Moustapha assessed the Bush administration and its policies in the following manner:

This administration has played a very negative role in the region— wherever you look. I mean, look at the situation in the Middle East they have created, in Iraq, in their refusal to help Syria resume peace negotiations with Israel. Let me tell you this, and I am not a conspiracy theorist, but ten years ago people who now belong to the neo-cons published articles and books lambasting the United States for supporting the peace process between Israel and the Arabs, saying the United States should never pressure Israel to give back its territories to any other state. Now these people today are a part of this administration—they are key officials in this administration. So they are not a special interest group lobbying the administration, they are *in* the administration. As I said, I am not a conspiracy theorist, but what can I say when these people are running the show. Senator Rockefeller asked David Satterfield [deputy assistant secretary of state for Near Eastern affairs] a public question at a congressional committee meeting about how the United States could play an objective role in the region when the chief political officer for [Vice President Dick] Cheney is well known for advocating that Israel should never give back any of its territories. This was a public question, so the Arabs are not delusional when they say these things.[31]

While trying not to incur the wrath of the United States, which was basking in the fruits of victory next door, the Syrians would do what they could in terms of supporting low-level resistance in Iraq to contribute to the failure of the Bush doctrine—to them it was a matter of survival in the face of a clear and present danger. It is, therefore, not a surprise that Syria was more cooperative by spring–summer 2004 regarding the new interim government in Iraq—to the point of welcoming Interim Prime Minister Iyad Allawi to Damascus and pledging a cooperative relationship—only when it became clear that the United States was ensconced in Iraq, that domestic support had decreased for Bush's policies *vis-à-vis* Iraq, and that the Bush doctrine seemed to be consigned to a one-time application for the time being. This is not an excuse for political repression. But supporting groups labeled as terrorist and/or engaging in activities intended to thwart U.S. success in Iraq need to be placed within the context of being threatened.[32] Maybe, then, a distinction needs to be made between rogue-state type activities in a threatening environment and those in a non-threatening environment measured against the asymmetry of forces between those who believe they are genuinely threatened (Syria) and those perceived to be threatening (the United States and/or Israel). Libya under Muammar al-Qadhdhafi is certainly considered to have been a rogue state. Yet it is far removed from the Arab-Israeli conflict, or any consistent threat for that matter. Its behavior in terms of support for terrorist groups and acquisition of WMD is more difficult to justify. Syria, on the other hand, is in a much more threatening environment, at least from the perspective of

Damascus. Given its relative weakness and the fact that it has been virtually surrounded by antagonistic states for most of the past several decades, Syria's foreign policy choices are easier to understand regardless of whether or not the foundation on which these choices are based is faulty.

I asked President Bashar about Syria being labeled a rogue state. He said,

> Some see me as bad, some see me as good—we don't actually care what terms they use. It is not right to apply this term to Syria—I mean, look at the relationship that Syria has with the rest of the world; if you have good relations with the rest of the world you are not a rogue state just because the United States says you are.

When I asked the same question to Ambassador Imad Moustapha, he responded by saying:

> I do not immediately get offended because I understand how misinformed Americans are about the issue. I will tell you this: we are not in breech of any UN resolutions, whereas Israel is in breech of something like 72 UN resolutions. We do not occupy parts of Israel, Israel is occupying part of Syria. We have a small country, Israel is very powerful [rather than referring literally to size, since Syria is some ten times larger than Israel, the ambassador apparently uses the word "small" to indicate Syria's relative military weakness]. Rather than deny the negative, I stress the positive; this so-called rogue state [Syria] has been calling for the resumption of negotiations—we have declared many times that we want a peaceful resolution of the Middle East conflict. It was us who went to the Security Council last year and submitted a draft resolution asking to declare the whole Middle East free from weapons of mass destruction and to allow the Security Council to impose modalities and mechanisms that will ensure that this will be. It was the United States that blocked this resolution, it was not Syria. So at least understand these realities, and if Americans insist on calling us a rogue state, then so be it.[33]

Long-time Syrian foreign minister Farouk al-Sharaa had a more biting response to the same question:

> You happened to have different teachers in school. One you respect and one you do not respect just because the style or conduct of that person is not attractive to you. But the one that you respect, if he just winks at you angrily you spend the whole day upset because you respect him; but if you

do not respect him, even if he says "go to hell," you do not accept it. You say to a friend that this man I do not respect, so whatever he says to me I am not going to respect. It would have been very harsh if it [calling Syria a rogue state] was directed at us by a respectable nation. How dare they put us in accountability, especially now with what is going on in Iraq.[34]

It is difficult to say whether Syria has been a rogue state over the last fifteen years. The actions of Hafiz al-Asad's regime in the 1970s and 1980s, especially as it was on the opposite side of the cold war as well as at the forefront of anti-Israeli hostility, established a paradigm for assessing Syria from the vantage point of Washington within the rogue-state pattern as determined, delineated, and defined by the United States. Because of the asymmetry of power between Syria and Israel (and certainly between Syria and the United States), Damascus felt compelled to adopt asymmetric means in order to, from its perspective, survive. Thus it was easier, so to speak, to label Syria a rogue state because asymmetric warfare by its very nature falls within the definition of a rogue state, i.e. a state that is involved in terrorism and has (or is seeking to obtain and/or proliferate) weapons of mass destruction.

Syria joined the U.S.-led UN coalition that evicted Iraq from Kuwait in 1991—although most Syrians will say they joined the coalition to stand by the Kuwaitis, not the Americans. Syria was a key to the convening of the Madrid peace conference in October 1991, and it negotiated *seriously* with Israel throughout much of the decade, although Damascus did not engage in the multilateral talks held in tandem with the Madrid process in which a number of countries in and outside the region, including Israel, discussed a host of issues such as water-sharing, arms control, and economic cooperation. On October 8, 2001, the United Nations General Assembly elected Syria to a non-permanent seat on the UN Security Council. In this capacity, and despite severe reservations, Syria voted for UN Security Council Resolution 1441 on November 8, 2002, which cited Iraq as remaining in "material breach" of its obligations and authorized the return of UN inspections to Iraq—the Security Council vote was unanimous.

Although not terribly enthusiastic about it, at an Arab League summit meeting in March 2002 Syria joined other Arab states in endorsing a peace initiative by Saudi Arabia's Crown Prince Abdullah calling for full Israeli withdrawal from Arab territories occupied in the 1967 war in return for normal relations in the context of a comprehensive peace. During Bashar's presidency, Syria consistently scaled down its forces in the Lebanon by over 50 percent until all were withdrawn in April 2005. Syria has also cooperated with the United States regarding intelligence on al-Qaida, including, according to a number of reports, receiving terrorist suspects for more vigorous interrogation through third-party nations in what have been termed "extraordinary renditions."[35] Bashar al-Asad frequently calls and visits President Husni Mubarak of Egypt, Crown Prince Abdullah of Saudi Arabia, and King Abdullah of Jordan to consult and coordinate policy on a variety of Middle East issues—all three of these countries and their leaders are close allies of the United States.

Pope John Paul II visited Damascus in May 2001, and President Bashar returned the visit to the Vatican in February 2002, atttending, as well, the Pope's funeral in April 2005. British Prime Minister Tony Blair met with Bashar in Damascus in 2002, and, again, Bashar made a return visit to Britain to meet with Blair, as well as Queen Elizabeth II.[36] In May 2004 the so-called Middle East "quartet" (United States, Russia, European Union, and the United Nations) entrusted with the implementation of the "road map" to peace held a meeting in Dublin, Ireland, to discuss the modalities of an Israeli withdrawal from the Gaza Strip—various proposals were discussed during a two-day meeting of EU foreign ministers and their counterparts from Algeria, Egypt, Israel, Jordan, Lebanon, Morocco, the Palestinian Authority, Turkey, Tunisia, and *Syria*.[37] Iyad Allawi, Iraq's interim prime minister, visited Damascus and Beirut on July 26, 2004, to improve relations with Iraq and garner more widespread support within the Arab community for the interim government—while in Damascus, Allawi stated "it is clear that our visit here is the beginning of a bright chapter in relations between our two brotherly peoples. We are opening a new page with Syria." A number of economic accords were signed between the two countries on the visit as well as pledges to cooperate regarding the infiltration of anti-coalition militants into Iraq.[38]

Where Syria Stands

We can go on with various examples of Syria's cooperation with and integration into other manifestations of the international community—it is not a pariah state by any means, and it is certainly not Iraq, despite attempts by anti-Syrian interests to link Syria with Iraq and to group Bashar al-Asad with the likes of Saddam Hussein or Yasser Arafat. This is an illusion, and is total fabrication for the purposes of promoting a misguided foreign policy agenda. The vast majority of countries, including some of America's closest allies, engage Syria at a number of different levels and hold fast to the opinion that Syria is not a rogue state. Are they all wrong? Maybe they are, and the United States will be proven correct in the long term—but I think not. Syria has WMD—most likely chemical and biological weapons.[39] It supports groups that are deemed terrorist by the United States. Syria did, indeed, outstay its welcome in Lebanon and manipulated the political process there, particularly with its clumsy intervention in August 2004 in extending pro-Syrian Lebanese President Emile Lahoud's term in office by three years.[40] Syria is not a free, open, and pluralistic society. And there still exist political repression and human rights violations in the country. But Syria is in a dangerous neighborhood virtually surrounded by what it perceives to be, and largely are, real threats. The domestic political and economic environment is improving, even if it is at a slower pace than many had expected. These were very unrealistic expectations to begin with given the corrupt, inefficient, broken-down system Bashar inherited. Even the pro-democracy opposition elements to the regime have, for the most part, recognized that the best hope for reform in Syria lies with Bashar al-Asad for the time being, even if it be at a decelerated rate.

The United Nations in 2004 ranked Syria as the third safest country in the world in terms of the incidence of crime (after Singapore and Malaysia). The Syrian government and the people have made a Faustian bargain of sorts between freedom and security/stability, and only if you spend a good deal of time in Syria do you realize that most Syrians willingly accept this arrangement, although the margins for freedom are much wider than popularly perceived. In essence, the United States has its own Faustian bargain in the opposite direction, but many of the less desirable repercussions of America's unbridled freedom and capitalism are unacceptable to a number of other cultures and societies.[41] There is an abstract question to address regarding whether or not the United States should be the determining element in defining who is and who is not a rogue state, much less what a rogue state is. Today a great many people outside the United States, if asked which country in the world exhibits more rogue-like behavior than any other, would likely answer America. If the definition of a rogue state revolves around possessing WMD, supporting what Washington has officially labeled as terrorist groups, being politically repressive to at least some degree, then, yes, Syria is a rogue state.

I believe the term "rogue state" requires a more nuanced definition that is not generated through the prism of Washington. There are a number of close allies of the United States who currently meet some or all of the criteria for rogue states and/or repressive regimes, such as Egypt and Pakistan (and many Arabs would include Israel as well), but they are not classified as "rogue" because they are currently aligned with U.S. interests. One of the objectives of the "rogue state" label is to batter a country into submission through sanctions or the threat of sanctions (or even military action) to compel a change of behavior toward that which is much more in line with U.S. interests. On

Bashar's position *vis-à-vis* the United States in recent years, Ambassador Imad Moustapha has said the following:

First, he [Bashar] understands the nature of the circumstances. Second, he knows that what happened between Syria and the United States was in a way inevitable. We told them [U.S. officials] everything regarding WMD in Iraq, the supposed tie—or lack thereof—with al-Qaida, etc., and our analysis was offered at every meeting, and it is in the minutes of every meeting. Their analysis is far from reality and [we told them] that if they invade Iraq they will end up in a messy situation—they will inflame Iraq and the region. And you see this today. At the time they were so scornful of our analysis—they felt we were just bullshitting. Every single thing we told them before they invaded has become a reality, and look at the situation today. President Bashar said this to me a month ago about how all the things we thought would happen in fact did happen. We were astonished at how accurate our analysis of the situation was. We told them, "don't believe those who are misleading you," but they did not heed our advice; on the contrary, they accused us of misleading them. And this, of course, culminated with the Syrian Accountability Act. But what can you do? What can you actually do? Everything they are discussing with us today has nothing to do with bilateral U.S.-Syrian relations. This is my mantra—that this has nothing to do with bilateral relations. You are the world's only superpower, and you have allowed your policies to be hijacked by a certain country [presumably Israel]. Do we wait for another administration—I don't know, but what we are doing is to keep talking to this administration. The only way out of this situation is a comprehensive Middle East peace, and we have been saying this for a long time. And we will keep on saying this to them. At least we can tell them, "Look, there will always be a political disagreement between Syria and the United States, and you will always be staunch supporters of Israel. We are not saying do not support Israel. We are saying help Israel find the right way. But we maintain a constructive dialogue with this administration.[42]

Foreign Minister Farouk al-Sharaa, again, has a more pessimistic view of the relationship. When I asked him if he initially had high hopes when the Bush administration came to power, he said:

I was fairly optimistic at first because I thought perhaps he would follow in the footsteps of his father [President George H. W. Bush]. We were somehow friendly with his father, and we had a good understanding. In fact, of course, we worked together against the Iraqi occupation of Kuwait, and we sent troops there to help liberate Kuwait. But I am very suspicious of American policy, to tell you the truth, which has nothing to do with specific people. I mean, [President Bill] Clinton was very nice. I met with him perhaps ten times with many meetings lasting several hours. But I am talking about the general feeling—the general assessment of American administrations. They do not keep their word very much. Deep inside they do not respect others. They prefer to use others rather than build bridges, find common ground, or exchange views. This sense of arrogance is there. They can even say to that that this is a new administration; the only country in the world that says the current administration has nothing to do with the previous is the United States, because even in the Third World, where regimes change often by force, the first thing the new regime must say is that they respect all the signed agreements of the previous regime—it is the first announcement, the first public statement. While with the United States—and it happened to me just a few weeks ago—they say this is a new administration; Clinton is finished. I think if the United States wants to maintain an international leadership position, it cannot do so. This is regardless of blunders and mistakes—this goes to the essence of credibility. They lack credibility—they kill it. In Iraq they did kill it.[43]

President Bashar believes that Syria and the United States share some important common interests regarding Iraq, global terrorism, and Middle East peace and stability that should constitute a foundation for a reasonably good relationship. He also mentioned that, even though Syria is a small country, a trade relationship could develop, which would obviously have a much greater positive impact on Syria than the United States. He stated, "We do not seek confrontation because we do not compete with the United States in any field. If you have common interests, you do not end up in conflict over those interests." He described the U.S.-Syrian relationship over the years as "fluctuating" from administration to administration, reminiscing fondly about the Nixon administration, when the United States first established an embassy in Damascus as a result of the 1974 disengagement negotiations between Syria and Israel; the first Bush administration, due to its cooperation in Lebanon and, of course, the U.S.-led UN coalition to evict Iraq from Kuwait in 1990/1991; and the Clinton administration, because of the close high-level peace negotiations throughout most of the 1990s. Indeed, he has very high praise for President George H. W. Bush (1989–1993) as well as the people in his administration; but while he highly praised Bill Clinton, he was less enamored with his team of negotiators. He obviously does not hold a very favorable view of the George W. Bush administration, but he recognizes how the United States changed after 9/11:

> It [9/11] was a very important lesson. The position of the United States in the world is a leading one, but you cannot live without the world. You cannot lead in peace if the world doesn't believe in you. The oceans do not protect countries anymore unless you want to live apart from the rest of the world, but you cannot, and I will tell you that Syria was one of the first to deal with this type of thing with the Muslim Brethren in 1982. 9/11 placed security at the top of the policy agenda, so the United States sees everything through security—that's normal, but it is not correct. It was a reaction, but you cannot live for years in a reaction to September 11th—you have been in a state of reaction for over two and a half years now. They should analyze it, learn from it, and don't keep it as the basis of conflict. Security is very important, very important, but you should not see everything through security. And don't see all the world through bin Laden and what happened in New York and Washington.[44]

History has shown that Syria's internal policies often are elastic with external and internal threats to the regime and societal stability—it is not a surprise that Decree 50/2001 was promulgated only eleven days after 9/11 and in the same year hardline right-wing elements came to power in both Israel and the United States. When the pressure is perceived to be less, as it was during most of the 1990s and during Bashar's first year in power, the regime is more inclined to undertake political and economic reform. As Andrew Tabler of the Beirut *Daily Star* wrote,

> The primary casualty in this contest of wills could very well be the Syrian people. Their widely expressed hopes for greater consensus building and economic reform could easily fall victim to an American failing to deal effectively and realistically with the symptoms or origins of terrorism in the region, a Syrian state that is unlikely to reform under the barrel of a gun, and opponents of the Syrian regime to whom spleen venting takes priority over constructive criticism.[45]

Members of Congress even tried to mount more pressure on the Syrian regime. In April 2004 two leading supporters of the Syrian Accountability Act, Representatives Eliot Engel (D-NY) and Ileana Ros-Lehtinen (R-FL), announced that they were drafting legislation, the "Syria and Lebanon Liberation Act" (or SALLA), calling for a "transition to free, democratic rule in Syria" and establishing "a program of assistance to independent human rights and pro-democracy forces in Syria and Lebanon," including funding for independent media broadcasts. This is very similar to the Clinton administration's adoption of legislation in 1998 calling for the overthrow of the regime of Saddam Hussein, i.e. the Iraq Liberation Act. For this reason alone, because of the controversy surrounding the Iraqi exiles, such as the Iraqi National Congress, who pushed for the legislation and were supported by two U.S. administrations, this proposed legislation is unlikely to be approved by the Bush White House unless U.S.-Syrian relations deteriorate and Washington is looking for another screw to tighten the noose around Damascus. One of the disturbing aspects from the perspective of Damascus regarding such things as SALSA and SALLA is the broad bipartisan support in Congress for ratcheting up the pressure on Syria. Certain Republicans in the administration and in Congress have been the most vociferous antagonists, and their control of congressional committees has given them opportunities to set agendas, push through legislation, and focus attention on the subject. Having said this, some high-level Syrian officials have told me that in their private discussions with a number of legislators, the latter have said that they really did not support the SALSA, but they could not be seen to vote against it in the post-9/11 political environment in Washington and be perceived as being "soft" on terrorism. As such, there continues to be a duality in U.S. policy toward Syria; however, the clear emphasis now is to maintain the pressure while leaving only the slightest bit of daylight for improving relations. The fact that President Bush, as one of the two sanctions he chose in implementing the SALSA, picked the ban on overflights of U.S. territory by Syrian airlines, something that never occurred in any case, suggests the White House was leaving some room for maneuver with Damascus.

On Hafiz al-Asad, terrorism expert Steven Emerson stated that "Mr. Assad's only hope of surviving both internally and externally is through a systemic policy of instilling terror in his own population, as well as spreading it in the population of neighbor states."[46] While exaggerated to make a point to some extent, this line of thought does not apply to Bashar—this will not work, and he knows it. But he also needs some time before we can definitely declare whether he is a true reformer or a Bonapartist interested only in regime maintenance. In international standing, Syria is on an entirely different level when compared to countries such as North Korea or Libya—it displays nowhere near the abhorrent behavior of these and other countries, or Iraq prior to the war. Treating Syria as a rogue state is counterproductive, and I strongly recommend a policy of measured engagement rather than containment or regime change toward Syria. The fact that Condoleeza Rice surprisingly omitted Syria from a list of six "outposts of tyranny" during her January 18, 2005, Senate confirmation hearings on her nomination as the new secretary of state was a positive sign for Damascus. This was done almost simultaneously with reports emanating from Washington that administration hardliners were considering launching military strikes against selected targets in Syria due to the latter still being accused of not doing enough to halt support for insurgents in Iraq (and also possibly being disruptive on the Palestinian front following the election of Mahmoud Abbas as the new Palestinian Authority president on January 9, 2005). The harder line was reflected in various sympathetic media outlets such as the *Washington Times,* the *Weekly Standard,* and the *Wall Street Journal.* The neo-conservative editor of the *Weekly Standard,* William Kristol, wrote that, "we could bomb Syrian military facilities . . . we could go across the border in force to stop infiltration; we could occupy the town of Abu Kamal in eastern Syria, a few miles from the border, which seems to be the planning and organizing center for Syria activities; we could covertly help or overtly support the Syrian opposition."[47] And, as mentioned earlier in the chapter, President Bush specifically singled out Syria in his State of the Union speech in February. Rice later did include Syria in discussions during her European tour in early February. In Rome she stated, "It is time for Syria to demonstrate that it does not want to be isolated, that it does not want to have bad relations with the United States. Syria has been unhelpful in a number of ways."[48] All of this reflected the continued ambiguity in U.S. policy toward Damascus at the time as well as administration attempts to construct an overall policy direction in the Middle East itself. The countries included on Rice's list on January 18, 2005 (Cuba, Burma, North Korea, Iran, Belarus, and Zimbabwe), may represent a shift in administration foreign policy that President Bush repeated in his inaugural speech later that month: that the United States would "stand with oppressed people on every continent," calling on the spread of freedom and liberty to undermine tyranny and repression, which in themselves create a facilitating environment for terrorism.[49] It seems that both sides are still trying carefully to calibrate pressure and opportunity with each other, trying not to step over imagined lines of behavior. All the while, however, the level of tension is ratcheted upward, as the foreign policy success or failure of the second-term Bush administration will be measured in the Middle East; in these circumstances, Bashar needs to be very, very careful. One misstep could give administration hawks the ammunition they need to push forward a more aggressive policy *vis-à-vis* Syria. The United States, on the other hand, needs to give President Bashar a chance—he is probably the only person in Syria who has the necessary legitimacy (for the time being) to implement reform and pursue peace with Israel. As opposed to with a real rogue state such as Libya, a country that habitually acted outside the norms of commonly acceptable international behavior, a more positive relationship with Syria would be tremendously advantageous to the United States with regard to its position in the Middle East and the global war against terrorism.

The Assassination of Rafiq Hariri

On February 14, 2005, Rafiq Hariri, a former Lebanese prime minister and architect of Lebanon's reconstruction following the end to its civil war, was assassinated in a massive car bomb explosion in downtown Beirut.[50] A billionaire Sunni Arab businessman, Hariri took several turns as prime minister.[51] For the most part, he maintained a relatively cordial relationship with Syria over the years, and he made frequent visits (as have all Lebanese prime ministers since 1989) to Damascus for consultations. Although certainly having his enemies in and outside Lebanon, and despite his Keynesian economic policies that produced a massive public debt and budget deficits, he was a popular figure in the country for having been the prime mover in the rebuilding of Beirut after its desolation in the civil war and for attracting much-needed foreign (especially Saudi) investment.

Immediately cries rang out in Lebanon and throughout most of the international community holding Syria responsible, either directly or indirectly. Vociferous demonstrations spontaneously erupted in Beirut and other Lebanese cities directly accusing Damascus and its pro-Syrian allies in Lebanon. It was unprecedented open criticism accompanied by calls for Syrian troops and intelligence agents to leave the country. What had been a growing opposition to Syria's presence and influence in Lebanon before the assassination became that much more galvanized afterward, emboldened by what it felt was blatant interference in Lebanese affairs beyond the norm. No one in Lebanon or in the international community seemed to believe claims by the Lebanese government that the attack was carried out by al-Qaida-like Islamic militants who claimed responsibility for the assassination, saying it was due to Hariri's close ties to the Saudi royal family.[52] Most believed this was a smokescreen planted by Syrian and Lebanese intelligence to divert responsibility for the murder in another direction. An estimated 200,000 people gathered in Beirut for Hariri's funeral procession two days after his death. It was a wildly anti-Syrian crowd, chanting and carrying signs that said such things as "Syria Out!" "No to the hegemony of the Syrian regime and its agents," "It's obvious, no?" and "Bashar, Lahoud, we have prepared coffins for you." Walid Jumblatt, the long-time Druze leader in Lebanon, was careful not to specifically blame Bashar personally or the regime in Damascus directly. He laid blame at the feet of the Syrian-Lebanese military-security apparatus running the country by saying, "I charge the Lebanese-Syrian police regime with responsibility for Hariri's death. This is a regime of terrorists and terrorism."[53]

The Bush administration was also careful not to accuse Damascus directly for the incident, preferring to pass judgment until an internationally sanctioned investigation into the killing ran its course. However, administration officials did publicly hold Syria responsible in a general sense since it was the primary powerbroker in Lebanon, ostensibly there to provide stability and security. It also became immediately clear that the assassination and ensuing pall it cast on Syria's position in Lebanon gave added ammunition to those who had been calling for the evacuation of Syria. The U.S. representative at Hariri's funeral, Assistant Secretary of State William Burns, stated that, "Mr. Hariri's death should give—in fact it must give—renewed impetus to achieving a free, independent and sovereign Lebanon. And what that means is the complete and immediate withdrawal by Syria of all of its forces in Lebanon."[54] As a clear sign of Washington's linking of the assassination with increasing pressure on Syria, the Bush administration recalled its ambassador in Damascus the day after the killing. However, again being careful not to accuse the regime of Bashar al-Asad directly, Secretary of State Rice noted that the assassination was the "proximate cause" of the ambassador's recall, while also saying that the administration was reviewing whether further sanctions against Damascus should be enacted.[55] Both Washington and Paris strongly renewed their calls to implement UN Security Council Resolution 1559, co-sponsored by the two countries and passed in 2004, calling for the withdrawal of all foreign forces from Lebanon (see Appendix for text of resolution). It passed the Security Council with no negative votes and six abstentions, including Russia. All of this was also intended to show immediate support for Lebanese opposition groups to maintain the pressure on Syria from within. Emboldened by this, anti-Syrian demonstrations in Lebanon continued throughout February and into March.

The regime in Damascus immediately stated that it was in no way responsible for the assassination and roundly condemned the killing. In what is very unusual for Damascus in such cases, Syrian officials appeared on a variety of news programs to counter the accusations. On CNN Imad Moustapha claimed that anti-Syrian groups were using the incident to "score some points against Syria." He went on to state, "It should be very clear to everyone that if anybody is insinuating about a Syrian role in the criminal atrocity that happened in Beirut, I think they are lacking in logic. Syria has nothing to benefit from what has happened."[56] The Lebanese information minister, Elie Ferzli, rejected claims that Syria or the pro-Syrian government in Lebanon could have been responsible: "We consider that the assassination of Hariri is against stability. And we consider that stability is our concern. So, this action is against us."[57] Those willing to absolve Damascus of blame point out that Syria was in no position to "rock the boat" like this, knowing that it would be held responsible for the killing even if it were not behind it. They point to Israel, however unlikely, or anti-Syrian (particularly right-wing Christian Phalangist) groups in Lebanon as benefiting the most from the assassination, so it follows from there that the trail of responsibility should lead away from Damascus and its allies in Lebanon. In a February 27 interview with Italy's *La Repubblica*, Bashar al-Asad stated that Syrian involvement in the killing "would be like political suicide."[58] But Washington was skeptical to say the least. An unnamed State Department official told the *New York Times* after the assassination, "We're going to turn up the heat on Syria, that's for sure. It's been a pretty steady progression of pressure up to now, but I think it's going to spike in the wake of this event. Even though there's no evidence to link it to Syria, Syria has, by negligence or design, allowed Lebanon to become destabilized."[59]

The turning point for Hariri as well as Syria's almost thirty-year presence in Lebanon seems to have been the extra-constitutional extension of Emile Lahoud's term in office in September 2004. Two wrongs do not make a right, but it is ironic that the United States attempted something quite similar in 1958 to extend the term of pro-American Lebanese President Camille Chamoun, precipitating a constitutional and sectarian crisis that required the presence of U.S. marines to stabilize the situation.[60] The Lahoud extension was widely condemned by the international community, leading to the passage of UN Security Council Resolution 1559, which succeeded in bringing the United States and France together on a Middle East issue, something rare of late to say the least.

According to Bashar, he started to hear rumors of the possibility of something like resolution 1559 back in May 2004, and that the French were behind it. Bashar said the Syrians heard these ruminations from their European friends who had had discussions with French President Jacques Chirac. Chirac, with whom Hariri was quite close, apparently had grown weary of Syria's opposition to many of Hariri's policies when he was Lebanese prime minister, and, according to Bashar, he did not like Lahoud at all. Bashar believes that the French were using the situation in Lebanon to repair relations with the United States. Faced with what he figured was inevitable clash over Syria's position in Lebanon, Bashar said that he made the decision to extend Lahoud's tenure in order to make sure he had a strong ally in Beirut to confront what was to come. As Bashar told me, "We didn't have any other choice but to support Lahoud. He has always supported Syria—he never changed. He is a strong person, and I know him well as a person. If we did not have him there, we thought we would have a lot of problems. The UN resolution really had nothing to do with the extension of Lahoud. It was coming anyway."[61] This mistake by Syria internationalized the issue, gave ammunition to anti-Syrian hawks in the Bush administration, galvanized the Lebanese opposition, alienated a traditional friend in Europe (France), and, maybe most importantly in retrospect, it alienated Rafiq Hariri. Up until this point, Hariri had had a working, if not always a smooth, relationship with Damascus. According to a number of reports, Hariri was summoned to Damascus and told in no uncertain terms to support the extension of Lahoud's term in office. Hariri complied, but then he resigned from his position as prime minister in protest.[62] Subsequently, he reportedly encouraged the United States and France to push through the resolution in the United Nations, and he began to cooperate more with opposition leaders in Lebanon, such as Walid Jumblatt.

Hariri's opposition to Syria increasingly placed him in a dangerous position. This was driven home even further by an assassination attempt in October 2004 on Marwan Hamadi, an opposition politician who had voted against Lahoud's extension. Hamadi survived the attempt but was severely wounded. In addition, with parliamentary elections in Lebanon due to take place in May 2005, Hariri was preparing the ground for an electoral challenge that might return him to office. Many believe that whoever killed Hariri was sending a strong message, as Abdelwahab Badrakhan wrote in the Lebanese daily al-Hayat: "What happened . . . was a clear and strong warning to the opposition. Hariri was the strongest opposition leader and the most internationally protected. His killing sends the message that no one is protected."[63]

It also may have been a message sent to someone else: Bashar al-Asad. I do not believe Bashar personally ordered the assassination; indeed, he probably did not know anything about it. While not eliminating the groups that could have carried out the assassination, I suspect that elements within the Syrian and Lebanese military-security apparatus independently ordered and arranged it. They had seen the pressure on their lucrative positions in Lebanon increase following the bungled Lahoud affair. They overstepped their bounds by convincing a young president to follow their lead. After having realized how much it backfired, Bashar attempted to wean himself away from the foreign policy way of the past—and the elements in the regime associated with it. Throughout the fall of 2004 and into early 2005, Bashar became more cooperative with the United States, clearly signaled his readiness to reenter peace negotiations with Israel, and stepped up efforts to prevent insurgents from entering Iraq. A turning point in this regard may have been the handing of the important Lebanon file to Syrian Deputy Foreign Minister Walid

Mouallim in January 2005. Mouallim visited Beirut on February 1 in what many Lebanese politicians, pro-Syrian and opposition alike, heralded as indicating a possible shift in Syrian policy in Lebanon in terms of meeting international demands to remove Syrian troops from the country. Mouallim is known for being a moderate in terms of his views of the West and Israel. As Syrian ambassador to the United States at the time, he was a key figure in the Israeli-Syrian negotiations in the mid-1990s as part of the Madrid peace process.

There are as many theories on who was behind the assassination of Hariri as people to express them. It could be that the assassination had multiple objectives: to get rid of a powerful Lebanese opposition voice, to intimidate remaining opposition elements in Lebanon, and may be to send a shot across the bows of Bashar al-Asad not to go any further with possible existing plans to vacate Lebanon and/or appease the United States. Hariri was, after all, one of the richest and best protected of any leading Middle Eastern figure: if the assassins could get to him, they could get to anyone. As many diplomats and Syrian experts concur, it would be a mistake to regard Syrian policy as a unified structure emanating from the president's office. Bashar has yet to "keep a leash" on Syria's many intelligence agencies and elements in the military, particularly those involved in Lebanon, which, in their view, practically became an independent fiefdom. For many powerful Syrians, Lebanon has been as important as or even more important than the Palestinians, the Golan Heights, and Iraq. As well-respected Lebanon expert Augustus Richard Norton comments, "Uncomfortable though it may be for Syria in international opinion, in certain quarters of Syria the stakes in Lebanon are existential, and existential challenges may be deemed to justify existential solutions."[64] The Hariri incident is very similar to the 1982 assassination of Lebanese President Bashir Gemayel, probably by Syrian and/or pro-Syrian Lebanese elements. There is one difference, however: with Hariri, the hand of the Syrian president was most likely not there. As the status quo beneficiaries in the Syrian regime did when Bashar went a bit too far during the Damascus spring, many of the same people in a more indirect fashion could have been sending a signal that he had better change direction regarding Lebanon, and if not, the direction would be changed for him.

Other theories include the following: that it was an indirect attack against the Saudi regime, with which Hariri had forged close ties. If this is the case, then al-Qaida becomes a prime suspect since the Saudi monarchy has been one of its primary targets. In addition, in this scenario, most would naturally point fingers at Syria, thus weakening a secular regime that has been at odds with al-Qaida and Islamist groups in general. There is still no definitive evidence signaling whether the bomb was set off below or above ground, although initial investigations indicated that it was above. If below, then this would be a more sophisticated operation that would seem to suggest the support of a state apparatus, thus pointing more toward Syria. However, if it was set off above the ground, then it was most likely a suicide bomber, a less sophisticated operation that opens to door to a myriad of potential perpetrators (as Bashar told me, "There are, unfortunately, lots of suicide bombers in the Middle East"[65]). Another theory suggests that the Syrian regime—and possibly even Bashar himself—was directly responsible, the rationale for carrying out the assassination being an attempt to weaken the Sunni element in Lebanon and by extension in Syria itself; after all, the most prominent Sunni official in Damascus, Vice President Abdul Halim Khaddam, was close to Hariri. Indeed, Khaddam was the only high-level Syrian official to attend Hariri's funeral, and he has been someone within Syria who has been rumored to be at odds with Bashar. After all, the sine qua non for Bashar's presidency is to maintain the predominant Alawite position in Syria, even preventing a reverse Sunni "crescent" from emerging in Lebanon and Syria linked to Jordan and Saudi Arabia. According to this theory, the writing was on the wall for a Syrian withdrawal from Lebanon if Hariri continued to add his weight to the opposition.

The Syrian regime, thus, had little to lose by eliminating him and possibly a great deal to gain if not for the international and domestic Lebanese outcry, both of which Damascus underestimated. Another less plausible theory, but one nonetheless that was making the rounds in some circles in Damascus, was that Rafiq Hariri was killed by his son, Saad Hariri; the fact that Saad has taken up the mantle of his father's political ambitions in the aftermath of the assassination has lent some ex post facto (and too convenient) credence to this assertion. The specifics may never be uncovered. A UN fact-finding mission was authorized and sent to Beirut following the assassination to "report urgently on the circumstances, causes, and consequences" of the incident. The team was headed by Patrick Fitzgerald, a deputy police commissioner from Ireland. The "Fitzgerald report" was issued on March 24, and while it stated that, "it is clear that the assassination took place in a political and security context marked by an acute polarization around the Syrian influence in Lebanon and a failure of the Lebanese state to provide adequate protection for its citizens" and that Syria "bears primary responsibility for the political tension that preceded the assassination," it could not assign direct blame for the killing. The report noted that the local investigation was deeply flawed and inept, and it accused the Lebanese security services of "serious and systematic negligence" to the point of deliberate obstruction. The report called for a full-fledged independent commission to uncover the truth. Only reluctantly did the Lebanese government give its assent for an international investigation.[66]

It has been interesting to witness Bashar's reaction to all of this. If the assassination was carried out by Syrian and pro-Syria Lebanese elements without his knowledge, which direction would Bashar take? Will he heed the warning and retrench as he did with the Damascus winter, or will he exploit the international outcry and threatening U.S. posture to strengthen his own position in Syria by using it to continue to weed out elements that have consistently retarded his efforts on a variety of fronts? Either way, it is a critical moment for Bashar.

What emerged from Damascus in the aftermath of the Hariri assassination was a mishmash of policy directives indicating a great deal of confusion, if not division, within the regime over how to react to the enhanced level of pressure. On the one hand, Bashar clearly made some moves to placate the Americans, wisely recognizing that the Bush administration gave him a little bit of rope by not accusing the regime of being directly responsible for the bombing in Beirut. According to a number of reports, at the end of February, Syria captured and handed over to Iraqi authorities Saddam Hussein's half-brother, Sabawi Ibrahim al-Hassan al-Tikriti, as well as twenty-nine fugitive members of Saddam's regime. Sabawi reportedly was one of the leading organizers and financiers in Syria of the insurgency in Iraq, and he was number thirty-six on the list of the fifty-five most-wanted Iraqis compiled by U.S. authorities. In interviews with the Italian newspaper *La Repubblica* and with *Time* magazine Bashar stated that Syria was prepared to withdraw troops from Lebanon. To the Italian newspaper he stated that the withdrawal could occur by the end of 2005, and he attached it implicitly to a peace agreement with Israel, which Damascus has always seen as the quid pro quo: "From a technical viewpoint, the repatriation [of Syrian forces] could happen by the end of the year. But from a strategic viewpoint, it will only happen if we get serious guarantees. In a word, peace."[67] Under even more pressure from the United States and others who demanded a more immediate timetable, he amended his earlier remarks in his interview released the next day with *Time*, reducing the period for a possible withdrawal to a few months:

It [withdrawal] should be very soon and maybe in the next few months. Not after that. I can't give you a technical answer. The point is the next few months. I could not say we could do it in two months because I have not had the meeting with the army people. You need to prepare when you bring your army back to your country. There are two factors: The first is security in Lebanon . . . and the second thing, which is related to Syria, is that after withdrawing we have to protect our border.[68]

Soon after Sabawi's handing-over to Iraqi authorities, some Syrian officials began to deny that they had anything to do with it, fearing that such an admission would prove that Syria was harboring Iraqi insurgents and could at the blink of an eye round them up if it decided it really wanted to.[69] Then there were a multitude of regime voices, including that of Bashar, who were making different and often conflicting comments and clarifications regarding whether and when Syria would withdraw from Lebanon. Prime Minister Naji al-Otri, visiting Teheran at the time of the Hariri assassination, stated that Syria and Iran must form a "common front" against their mutual threats, i.e. the United States. When told of this in his CNN interview on February 15, the day after the assassination, Imad Moustapha said he had heard nothing of this and could not comment on it. Otri's comments were later amended to indicate simply that Iran and Syria face similar pressures. Unfortunately, the lack of discipline in the regime and the different sinecures of power came into full view in this crisis situation.

Bashar appeared to take some steps to make clear to the international community that he was dealing with some of those regime elements who "allowed" the assassination to occur. While distancing himself personally from the act, this also gave him an opportunity to push aside some questionable personages within the regime and surround himself with more true loyalists as he tightened up his inner circle and consolidated his position *vis-à-vis* the security services in the face of potential threats from without and within. To others, it was a de facto admission of ultimate Syrian responsibility, especially since neither Damascus nor Beirut was repeating anything regarding the possible al-Qaida connection behind the killing. On February 18, Bashar replaced the chief of military intelligence, General Hassan Khalil, whose retirement had been postponed more than once, with Brigadier General Asef Shawkat, the Syrian president's brother-in-law and close adviser. There were also reports in early March that Bashar planned to fire Rustum Ghazal, the head of Syrian intelligence in Lebanon and a focal point of Lebanese anger over the assassination.

Ghazal was not relieved of his duties, but he departed Lebanon with the remaining Syria troops on April 26. As important to the Lebanese opposition were demands that the Lebanese government replace security officials that had been tainted by their cooperation with Syria over the years. In late April, Major General Jamil Sayyed, director-general of the Ministry of Interior's General Security Directorate and someone considered to be Lebanon's powerful security chief, handed in his resignation. Another security official, Major General Raymond Azar, the director of Lebanese military intelligence, announced he was taking a one-month administrative leave in late March, and he subsequently left the country along with family.[70] In retrospect, the Hariri assassination precipitated an intra-regime battle for the soul of Syria. Only Bashar and his inner circle know the precariousness of their situation internally, but perhaps this is the jolt he needed, on top of the Emile Lahoud fiasco, to finally cleanse the regime. On the other hand, as an Israeli newspaper noted, "The next question will be whether the Syrian establishment will seek to punish the young president for losing Lebanon."[71]

The maelstrom in which Damascus found itself continued. A suicide bombing in Tel Aviv on February 26 killed four and wounded scores of Israelis. The attack, claimed by Palestinian Islamic Jihad, threatened to unfurl the February 8 cease-fire agreed to by Israeli Prime Minister Ariel Sharon and newly elected Palestinian Authority President Mahmoud Abbas upon their joint summit meeting in Sharm al-Shaykh, Egypt, alongside Egyptian President Husni Mubarak and Jordan's King Abdullah. Israeli Defense Minister Shaul Mofaz blamed Syria for the suicide bombing, stating that he "sees Syria and the Islamic Jihad movement [which has offices in Damascus] as those standing behind the murderous attack in Tel Aviv."[72] The Israeli deputy defense minister, Zeev Boim, said, "There is no doubt that Syria is a center of terrorist activity, this time against Israel, but also regionally. Operations by us against Syria are certainly possible. We have done it in the past [a reference to Israel's strike against a purported Islamic Jihad camp outside Damascus in October 2003]. If Asad needs another message from us, then he will certainly get it."[73] The Bush administration chimed in by stating through the White House press secretary, "We do have firm evidence that the bombing in Tel Aviv was not only authorized by Palestinian Islamic Jihad leaders in Damascus, but that Islamic Jihad leaders in Damascus participated in the planning."

Maintaining the pressure on Syria, Condoleeza Rice, in a joint news conference with French Foreign Minister Michel Barnier, stated that France and the United States were speaking with one voice on Lebanon and that the two countries would support the sending of observers and monitors for the May elections as well as consider international peacekeepers to oversee Syria's troop withdrawal. She stated that "The Syrians are out of step with where the region is going and out of step with the aspirations of the people of the Middle East."[74] President Bush, referring to Rice and Barnier, reiterated these sentiments by saying in a news conference that "Both of them stood up and said loud and clear to Syria, 'You get your troops and your secret services out of Lebanon so that good democracy has a chance to flourish.'"[75] Another blow to Syria's position in Lebanon occurred on February 28, when the government led by pro-Syrian Prime Minister Omar Karami, who had taken over for Hariri when the latter resigned the previous fall, submitted its resignation, bowing to the demands of thousands of demonstrators who continued to openly and defiantly agitate against Syrian influence and its Lebanese "lackeys." Jubilation swept through much of Lebanon as people heard the news. A caretaker government was appointed by President Lahoud until the elections in May and June. Amid some confusion, Karami returned to his post for about six weeks, but he was unable to form a cabinet and was compelled to give way once again to popular demand, with Najib Mikati assuming the post of prime minister in April. Mikati was a compromise figure acceptable to pro-Syrian and opposition elements in Lebanon, and he formed a cabinet composed of individuals drawn from both groups. Analysts as well as prominent Lebanese admitted that while the assassination was the straw that broke the camel's back for many in Lebanon, the so-called "orange" revolution in Ukraine in the fall of 2004 and the much better than expected election process and results in Iraq and within the Palestinian Authority in January 2005 emboldened the opposition to press forward with their demands, especially as the international limelight, including the crucial support of the Bush administration, was shining upon them for the moment.

In the face of all of this, Bashar seemed to run toward any Arab cover he could find. This was difficult, however, since some of his traditional friends, such as Egypt, Jordan, and Saudi Arabia, all strongly encouraged him to remove Syrian troops from Lebanon and set a timetable for doing so. Even before the Hariri assassination, Bashar had tried to improve his relationship with Jordan and Egypt in an attempt to persuade them to advance Syria's cause *vis-à-vis* any emerging peace process that might develop in the wake of the Sharm al-Shaykh summit meeting (to which Asad was not invited). The proceedings at the summit meeting seemed to have been the quid pro quo for Syrian assistance in persuading the Palestinian militant factions over which Damascus has influence to tacitly accept the February 8 Israeli-Palestinian cease-fire. According to Egyptian sources, Syria was very helpful in this regard.[76] At the summit meeting itself, both Mahmoud Abbas and Husni Mubarak mentioned that Israeli-Palestinian progress must lead to the implementation of the Middle East "road map" and a comprehensive peace by reactivating the Syrian-Lebanese track. Mubarak even employed Hafiz al-Asad's own words by saying that the Arabs had made "a strategic choice for peace."[77]

The February 26 Palestinian Islamic Jihad bombing in Tel Aviv coming so soon on top of the Hariri assassination obviously disturbed Bashar's attempts to form a common front with Egypt and Jordan. Having said this, however, Egyptian and Saudi officials stepped in to, as one Arab diplomat in Cairo put it, "save Syria from a serious conflict that will pitch it against the whole world."[78] In order to help Syria, they wanted to regionalize the situation in Lebanon rather than have it remain at the international level—an open conflict between Syria and the United States, Europe, and the United Nations does nothing but harm the position of other Arab states trying to come to grips with and stabilize the Israeli-Palestinian and Iraqi situations. Syrian Foreign Minister Farouk al-Sharaa met with his Egyptian and Saudi counterparts following the Tel Aviv bombing in an attempt to coordinate action regarding Lebanon. Syria reportedly returned some disputed territory to Jordanian jurisdiction on February 28, most likely to enlist Jordanian assistance.[79] However, the reaction that Syria received from Saudi Arabia was very cool. Bashar visited Riyadh on March 3 in an attempt to strengthen his hand vis-à-vis the international community. According to most reports, he was singularly rebuffed. The Saudi leader, Crown Prince Abdullah, was reportedly furious over the assassination of Hariri, someone who was close to the Saudi royal family. Apparently, he informed Bashar in no uncertain terms that Syria should withdraw its troops from Lebanon and present a timetable for doing so—either that or "face strains in its relations with the kingdom."[80] Syria seemed resigned to the fact that it must remove its troops from Lebanon, but it wished to do so in a phased manner and under the guise of the 1989 Taif Accord that originally called for their removal rather than solely under UN Security Council Resolution 1559. If this were arranged with the help of some Arab states, then at least on the surface it would seem as though Damascus had not bowed to international, particularly American and French, pressure. It would be withdrawing in accordance with an existing Syrian-Lebanese agreement. This is, however, pure fiction and window-dressing, especially as Syria became more and more isolated in the inter-Arab arena.

Bowing to the unrelenting pressure, Bashar gave a speech to the Syrian National Assembly on March 5.[81] The speech began by pointing out Israeli intransigence regarding the peace process and the recklessness of American policy in the Middle East. The second half dealt with Lebanon, and throughout there was barely a mention of any domestic reforms—it was clearly a speech dedicated to foreign policy. In the speech he stated that Syrian troops would withdraw from Lebanon, first to the Bekaa Valley and then to the border. Bashar declared, "In so doing, we will have implemented both the Taif accord and UN Security Council resolution 1559. We started the withdrawal in 2000, and pulled back almost sixty percent of our troops. The number was 40,000 and at present there are only 14,000." While saying that the "pressure and targeting" of Syria would continue, he admitted, "we made some mistakes in Lebanon."[82] He added that it must be "a coordinated withdrawal" and said, "if you, as the UN, think we should immediately withdraw, not withstanding any negative impact on Lebanon, you tell us, you decide."[83] Bashar also noted that, "we would not stay one day if there was a Lebanese consensus on the departure of Syria . . . our way is a gradual and organized withdrawal."[84] In a not-so-veiled threat to the United States and Israel, Bashar declared, "I'll tell them [Lebanese 'brethren'] another 17th of May is looming on the horizon. I want you to be prepared to bring it down as you did before." This is a reference to the Israeli-Lebanese May 17, 1983, agreement brokered by the United States (and pointedly excluding Syria) that was scuttled primarily by Syrian efforts in Lebanon, including the October 1983 bombing of the U.S. marine barracks in Beirut. Many saw this as an implicit call on pro-Syrian forces in Lebanon, especially Hizbollah, to again rise up against foreign interference if Damascus is forced out. It was also a reminder and warning to Washington that Syria cannot be easily dismissed.

Most Lebanese opposition parties as well as the international community were not particularly pleased with the ambiguities in Bashar's speech. But perhaps this is as far as Bashar felt he could go without incurring too much opposition within Syria itself. Again, it seems as though Damascus was carefully trying to calibrate the minimum it could do to assuage the United States and France. If pressure continued to build, it would give in some more, little by little. Russian Foreign Minister Sergei Lavrov was quoted as saying that "Syria should withdraw from Lebanon, but we all have to make sure that this withdrawal does not violate the very fragile balance which we still have in Lebanon."[85] The key phrase is "violate the very fragile balance," something about which the Syrian regime has been warning in its exhortations about the difficulties and dangers of withdrawing too precipitously. Damascus seemed to have been latching on to this as a way to slow down the process so that down the road it may not have to fully withdraw from the country. It is clear Bashar was trying to buy some time and deflect some of the mounting pressure on his government.

Anticipating this, however, the Bush administration, expressing its disappointment in Bashar's speech, rejected the phased approach and again reiterated that Syria must withdraw its troops and intelligence services from Lebanon as soon as possible and certainly no later than the May elections. A State Department spokesman followed this by saying, "It's clear to us, not just the United States, but the international community, that his [Bashar's] words are insufficient. We have not heard the words: immediate and full withdrawal."[86] Washington was drawing a line in the sand. It may have given some leeway to Bashar, but it did not give any to the Syrian position in Lebanon—there did not seem to be any middle ground. As Joshua Landis reported from Damascus:

> The president [Bashar] gave no time table for withdrawal. He accepted none of the blame for Syria's isolation and explained the sudden consolidation of the Lebanese opposition only in terms of foreign influence and manipulation. He continued to describe the world from a Baathist perspective, as a battle between the forces of good and evil, pitting himself and Syria against George Bush and his nefarious plans for the region. Rather than laying out a vision for Syria's future by announcing an agenda for reforms, he dwelt on old battles and history. He is carving an ever clearer image of himself as the anti-Bush."[87]

This "us against the world" approach is anachronistic and ultimately unhelpful to Syria's position. While it might rally some domestic support, it further places Bashar in the cross hairs of those in Washington and elsewhere who want to weaken if not topple the regime in Damascus as part and parcel of the winds of change sweeping across the Middle East. Ultimately, of course, Bashar succumbed to the pressure and made the correct decision to withdraw from Lebanon. For the most part, the Syrian public has not blamed the regime for the loss, preferring to blame external forces for the departure, primarily the United Nations and the United States. There has also been something of a nationalistic response against the Lebanese after witnessing on television the throngs in Beirut demonstrating against Syria. As such, despite the economic and socio-cultural integration, there will probably be a temporary lull in day-to-day Lebanese-Syrian cordiality.

Bashar as well as his father had long hoped to utilize Lebanon as a bargaining chip in negotiations with Israel over the Golan Heights. Their bargaining position had now been clearly weakened, but it has not totally dissipated. Hizbollah is still a powerful force in Lebanon with an estimated 20,000 troop militia, and it will probably remain so for the foreseeable future as it has successfully transformed itself from a pure guerilla resistance organization into a political movement. As a clear sign of this, Hizbollah organized large pro-Syrian rallies in Lebanon on March 8, 2005, to counter the anti-Syrian demonstrations. According to most estimates, there were approximately 500,000 pro-Syrian demonstrators in Beirut (Syrian sources reported 1.6 million). Even if a substantial portion of the throng were paid or forced to attend by pro-Syrian Lebanese groups, it clearly reinforced Bashar's implicit warning embedded in his May 17 comment in his speech. Certainly the Shiites in Lebanon, constituting the largest sect in the country, about 30 to 35 percent of the 3.7 million population, tend to see the Alawite regime in Damascus as more co-religionist and as a protector of their hard-won concessions over the years. In addition, because of the overall socio-economic integration between Syria and Lebanon, Damascus can still wield a tremendous amount of influence over its Arab neighbor to the west regardless of whether or not its troops are stationed there. This is something of which the Bush administration has to be wary. Its policies in Lebanon could backfire if it is seen to be trying to use the Hariri assassination to disarm and disband Hizbollah, a difficult task at best at the current time. In early March, Washington seemed to appreciate this. The *New York Times* reported that a diplomat "close" to U.S.-French consultations on the situation stated that "the main players [U.S. and France] are making Hezbollah a lower priority. There is a realization by France and the United States that if you tackle Hezbollah now, you array the Shiites against you. With elections coming in Lebanon [in May], you don't want the entire Shiite community against you."[88]

The Bush administration seems to have accepted the view of France and others in Europe (who have not designated Hizbollah a terrorist organization as Washington has) that in such a fractured society it would be dangerous to antagonize Hizbollah too much. Similar to efforts regarding Hamas in the Palestinian territories, the United States and Europe appear to be encouraging Hizbollah to shed its militancy altogether and integrate itself totally in the political process. The U.S. experience in Iraq may also be informing Bush administration policy. In Iraq, the United States tacitly cooperated with the majority Shiite population in carrying out the election process that culminated in the Shiites gaining the most seats in the new Iraqi constituent assembly in the January 30, 2005, election. The Shiites generally did not oppose the U.S. presence in Iraq since they knew they were poised to gain power in Iraq via the ballot box. It will be interesting to see if Lebanon develops along these lines as well, all of which would represent a major shift in the Middle East policy of the Bush White House, more sympathetic toward Shiite or Islamist groups in general in the region, a point of concern to Sunni regimes in the area, such as Jordan and Saudi Arabia.

There is the possibility that Syria will surreptitiously destabilize Lebanon in the aftermath of the withdrawal simply to prove what it has been saying all along: that the Syrian presence was necessary in order to stabilize Lebanon's fissiparous tendencies. The fact that several bombs ripped through the predominantly Christian areas of Beirut in late March, combined with the assassinations of two leading anti-Syrian figures in June, only reinforced the notion that this was an attempt by Syria and its loyalists to sow fear of sectarian strife as well as intimidate the opposition. There is also concern among the Lebanese opposition that Damascus will try to "remote control" its interference in the country's politics through pro-Syrian parties. Lebanon could realistically—and dangerously—become a fractured polity once again. The fact that Lebanon's leading anti-Syrian Christian figure, General Michel Aoun, returned to Beirut in early May 2005 after fourteen years in exile only confirmed this possibility. Amid a raucous and roaring welcome in Beirut by throngs of his supporters, Aoun began to minimize the contributions of Walid Jumblatt and the repercussions of the Hariri assassination to the Syrian withdrawal, instead trumpeting his own efforts in helping Chirac construct resolution 1559, which, according to Aoun—and to the severe distaste of Hariri's and Jumblatt's constituencies—was the real driving factor in Syria's evacuation. The parliamentary elections in May and June produced a victory for the anti-Syrian coalition, composed of an amalgam of Christian and Sunni parties as well as Walid Jumblatt's Druze led by Saad Hariri, the son of the slain politician. However, although winning a majority of seats (72) in the 128-member parliament, it was still not the two-thirds needed to remove Emile Lahoud from the presidency. In addition, Shiite parties, particularly Hizbollah and Amal in the south, continued to win a substantial bloc of seats (35), and Nabih Berri, the long-serving speaker of parliament and leader of the pro-Syrian Amal, was again appointed to the position for his fourth four-year term. And in an ironic twist, Michel Aoun actually allied with pro-Syrian elements in the elections, garnering 21 seats in assembly. Even though Syria's influence in Lebanon has clearly been reduced and codified with the victory of the anti-Syrian coalition, with Lahoud still in power, the Shiite parties are still a force to be reckoned with, and with opportunistic politicians such as Aoun always available, Damascus still has viable conduits through which it can continue to promote its interests.

The so-called "old guard" elements that may have been behind the assassination of Hariri are as clumsy as they are ignorant of the changing regional and international environment. Then again, maybe after decades of honing their repressive craft under Bashar's father they know no other way. They always count on some other regional or international event allowing Syria to fade into the back pages of the newspapers unnoticed or regain some value in the West as it did during the Gulf war and Madrid process—then they can dabble in Lebanon again. Ultimately, this will not benefit Damascus, as the world will be watching carefully. If the U.S. position in the Middle East falters, especially from the perspective of the Arab street, Damascus could also try to delegitimize the Lebanese opposition by depicting it as an American lackey.

The leader of Hizbollah, Shaykh Hassan Nasrallah, already started playing this card in the March 8 demonstrations, saying that a Syrian pullout would be doing the bidding of Israel and the United States.[89] Both the Lebanese opposition and the Bush administration must be careful in this regard.

But Syria's ability to "dabble" in Lebanon is much more circumscribed than it was in the past. With the French on board, the Europeans might be inclined to pass their own version of the Syrian Accountability Act, with far more effectiveness than U.S. sanctions since the preponderance of Syria's trade is with the EU countries. UN envoy Terje Roed-Larsen met with Bashar on March 12, 2005, and reportedly informed him that "if he doesn't deliver [on withdrawal], there will be a total political and economic isolation of his country. There is a steel-hard consensus in the international community."[90] A UN official commented that there was "remarkable" support for a showdown with Syria over Lebanon, including that of Arab states such as Egypt, Jordan, and Saudi Arabia.[91] Beyond this, military strikes against a weak and isolated Damascus are always an option, as Syria has been labeled in Western circles as "low hanging fruit": a country that can more easily be pressured via economic sanctions and/or military action than a country such as Iran, which poses more difficulties. Syria is an easy target, and it has become a somewhat fashionable one in certain circles in Washington as a cause of much of what ails the Middle East.

It is hoped that the withdrawal does not become a whirlpool of violent sectarian contestations by various groups attempting to fill the vacuum of power created by the Syrian departure. The Bush administration has to be careful and not fall prey to any eagerness by neo-conservative elements to press the issue against Syria too vigorously. As one European diplomat commented:

> The US should not overestimate the extent of its influence in a situation that has its own dynamics. . . . the killing of Hariri . . . provoked an unprecedented and unexpected wave of outrage that shattered people's fears of Syria and united many Christians and Muslims in the country. The active role of Jacques Chirac . . . in the mounting pressure on Syria has given the international policy more credibility. Washington's departure from the international consensus would harm the improvement . . . in Lebanon."[92]

Syria is almost as sectarian as Lebanon, and if the center should precipitously fall with Bashar's overthrow or political incapacitation, the country could devolve into violent sectarian strife. What would emerge after the dust settles down could very well be a polity that is Islamic extremist, one on the border with Israel and one that could make common cause with like-minded elements in Iraq and Lebanon. This is certainly not in anyone's interest. In fact, there is something of a debate regarding the prospects of who or what would come to power in Syria should the regime of Bashar al-Asad fall. Many in Syria, including Bashar, see the regime, more specifically the Baath party, as the last bastion of secularity against a seething, rising tide of radical Islam in Syria. Critics of Bashar in Washington claim this is self-serving and only being iterated by Damascus as a way to soften America's current hardline approach for fear of giving an unintended rise to an Islamist polity in Syria. The fact of the matter is we do not really know what would happen should there be regime change. The more radical salafists in Syria are certainly a force to be reckoned with, more so than the Muslim Brotherhood, toward which Bashar has taken a fairly moderate position, releasing most imprisoned MB members since coming to office. The salafists are also Sunni and have given vocal and probably real support to the insurgency in Iraq. This is why the regime has had to tread carefully in cracking down on Syrian support for insurgents, i.e. doing enough to meet American demands but not enough to stir up the boiling pot of radical Islam in the country. Most who have visited Syria and know the country would agree that a radical Islamist trend is real and influential in Syria, whether or not it might fill the void caused by regime change.[93] As such, as Egypt and Saudi Arabia seem intent on doing, the United States and its European friends could maintain some pressure on Syria while making sure it does not reach a level that might foment an internal coup against Bashar. The continued pressure could be mixed with the carrots of economic aid, the lifting of sanctions, and engagement in the peace process. Syria is in a tight fix economically and is more vulnerable than ever to international pressure and sanctions—and it appears there will not be any cheap Iranian oil as during the Iran–Iraq war, or the Gulf Arab largesse that followed Syria's participation in the 1991 Gulf war to move the limping Syrian economy along. But Bashar is waiting for some sort of quid pro quo from Washington. He is very frustrated by the fact that Syria received very little, if any, credit for the assistance it has provided Washington on the terrorist front, its withdrawal from Lebanon, or its willingness to engage with the United States on a host of issues, from the Iraqi border situation to peace talks with Israel. CIA officials visiting Damascus have been very appreciative, but they have pointed out to Bashar that they are not involved in politics. The last time I visited with Bashar, in May 2005, there was, unfortunately, an air of resignation that seems to have come over him regarding the United States, i.e. that no matter what he does it will not be enough. As such, earlier in the year he discontinued Syrian cooperation with the CIA regarding global terrorist organizations, most particularly, of course, al-Qaida. This was certainly a blow to U.S. intelligence efforts in this regard, but ultimately it could also hurt Damascus, for the intelligence community in the United States was one of the few entities that tended to support a policy of engagement with Syria as well as provide something of a brake on those elements in the Bush administration that wanted to embellish—or even manufacture—intelligence about Syrian activities, especially in the area of WMD. It is a shame to lose this conduit, but Bashar felt he was getting nothing in return, absolutely no delineation from the Bush administration of what he could get in return; indeed, from his vantage point, what he got was quite the opposite. If Bashar can survive internal dissension over the loss of Lebanon, this could be the turning point for his presidency and for achieving his stated objectives. As such, many people in and outside of Syria in the spring of 2005 pointed with a great deal of anticipation and hope to the Baath party congress in June as the vehicle for dramatic change in Syria. The loss of Lebanon could also be the beginning of the end. One thing is for sure: in this whole process we will see what type of leader he is, where he really wants to go, and how much authority he really has.

Chapter 7

A "Strategic Choice" for Peace

Syria has been at the forefront of the Arab-Israeli conflict for over half a century. It has been at war with Israel ever since it hesitantly and quite incompetently entered the first Arab-Israeli conflagration that formally began upon Israel's declaration of independence on May 15, 1948.[1] Armistice lines and demilitarized zones were agreed to by the combatants in the war at negotiations in 1949 on the island of Rhodes and brokered by UN representative Ralph Bunche, an American who received the Nobel Peace Prize for his efforts. The agreements, however, were not peace treaties nor did they consist of Arab recognition of Israel. Thus, the period between 1949 and 1967 on the Syrian-Israeli front was characterized by sporadic raids and reprisals between the two adversaries, with the utilization by Damascus sometimes of Palestinian refugees and at other times of regular forces. While still formally at war with Israel, Hafiz al-Asad made what he called a "strategic choice for peace" in the early 1990s, reflecting the changed domestic, regional, and international circumstances in which Syria found itself following the end of the superpower cold war and in the wake of the 1991 Gulf war. The "choice" was to pursue a peace agreement with Israel, one centered, from the Syrian perspective of course, on a return of the Golan Heights. This remains Syria's official position.

Hafiz al-Asad's rise to power marked a shift in Syria's approach toward Israel. The 1967 Arab-Israeli war convinced most Arab leaders that the Jewish state could not be defeated militarily and that diplomacy from a position of strength was the optimum way to recover the occupied territories. UN Security Council Resolution 242 has crystallized this approach, otherwise known as the land-for-peace framework. Most of the Arab combatants accepted Resolution 242 in one way or another over the next decade, Syria doing so implicitly by accepting UN Security Council Resolution 338 at the close of the 1973 Arab-Israeli war. Resolution 338, in addition to outlining a cease-fire, called for a resumption of negotiations over the occupied territories explicitly based on Resolution 242. The basic problem for the Arab states was how to get to a position from which they could negotiate with at least some strength; of course, this was the whole idea behind Nasser's War of Attrition (1969 to 1970) and Sadat and Asad's "War of Liberation" (October 1973). In this they were fairly successful, especially as the United States finally realized the explosive potential of all-out conflict in the Middle East that could escalate into a superpower confrontation.

Recognizing the shifting winds following the 1973 war that built upon his own more pragmatic foreign policy, Asad agreed to the May 1974 disengagement agreement with Israel, brokered by Henry Kissinger's shuttle diplomacy. The agreement on the Golan Heights involving UN observer forces has been assiduously adhered to by both sides. With the destructive potential revealed by the 1973 war so recently in their memories, neither Israel nor Syria wanted to confront the other directly. Even though Israel had (and continues to have) clear military superiority, Syria had (and presumably still has) the ability to cause just enough unacceptable damage to Israel to force the latter also to seek alternative ways to achieve foreign policy objectives *vis-à-vis* the other. Unfortunately for Syria and Israel's mutual neighbor, this alternate path as the 1970s progressed more often than not went through Lebanon, the culmination of which was the 1982 Israeli invasion that brought the IDF all the way to Beirut. Lebanon became the proxy battleground caught inextricably between the two, a fate, as pointed out previously, made all the more inevitable when the PLO relocated there from Jordan by 1971.

The end of the superpower cold war by 1989, the Iraqi invasion of Kuwait in August 1990, and the subsequent liberation of Kuwait in the Gulf war in 1991 compelled Hafiz al-Asad by circumstance and opportunity to engage in what became known as the Madrid peace process, launched by a plenary session of the participant countries and sponsors in the Spanish capital in October 1991. Asad and other Arab leaders in the Gulf war coalition had stressed to the Bush administration that the United States must address the Arab-Israeli situation after evicting Saddam Hussein from Kuwait. It was an unspoken quid pro quo on which the Bush team made good with the Madrid process. As American negotiator Dennis Ross noted, "Asad's choice put him in the center of post-Gulf War diplomacy," while Yasser Arafat's tacit support of Iraq sidelined the PLO leader.[2]

Asad had indeed made, as he stated, a "strategic choice" for peace with Israel—he really had no other alternative. Gorbachev had informed him several years earlier, even before the Soviet Union was on its last breath, that this was the way to go, thus changing the cold war dynamic that had for over three decades allowed Syria, in its advantageous regional position, to siphon political, military, and economic aid from its superpower patron. The economy was in tatters and desperately needed an influx of aid and investment, and for political and economic reasons Syria needed to continue to build upon the bridge it had already constructed with Washington as a result of its participation in the U.S.-led UN coalition that evicted Iraq from Kuwait—the roads to the Golan, to economic recovery, and to protection from an Israel that was getting stronger as Syria grew weaker all went through Washington. Paradoxically, the road to Washington went through Tel Aviv. Ultimately, this is why Syria made some important concessions to launch the Madrid process.

As has been the case with most Arab states, Syria strongly prefers negotiations to be held in a multilateral, international setting, with the direct involvement of the superpowers and the United Nations. The more countries involved, as the thinking goes, the more leverage and pressure can be brought to bear on Israel to make concessions. To obviate this possibility, Israel over the years has wanted the exact opposite, i.e. direct, bilateral negotiations with an Arab state, so that Israel's leverage is at its most advantageous and it is relatively free from international pressure. While the opening meeting in Madrid was, indeed, an international gathering, the subsequent negotiations broke off into bilateral meetings between Israel and the respective Arab parties, with one track, the Israeli-Palestinian one, abandoning the Madrid framework altogether to produce the Oslo process and accords leading to the Israeli–PLO Declaration of Principles signed on the White House lawn in September 1993.[3]

Syria and the Madrid Peace Process

The Syrian-Israeli track of the Madrid peace process proceeded in fits and spurts, the pace being affected by progress (or lack thereof) on the other Arab-Israeli tracks, especially the Israeli-Palestinian one, elections in Israel and in the United States, wild cards thrown in to the mix such as the 1993 Oslo accords and the 1995 assassination of Israeli Prime Minister Yitzhak Rabin, and, finally, the psychological and political parameters (or even constraints) within which the Syrian and Israeli leadership believed they could operate. The Syrian track for Rabin and President Bill Clinton was preferable to the Palestinian track because it was a much more direct set of circumstances revolving around a land-for-peace exchange—it was, in a word, easier. To the Israelis, Syria was a more dangerous threat than the Palestinians, the latter being seen more as a nuisance than something that could inflict severe damage upon the country. In addition, gaining ground in Washington was the idea that Syria was the key to an overall Middle East peace. If Syria would sign

1 Bashar at three.

2 The Asad family meeting with President and Mrs. Nixon upon the Nixons' visit to
Damascus in 1974. Front row *(left to right)*: Bashar, Maher, Majd, Basil; back row
(left to right): Anisa al-Asad, Pat Nixon, Bushra, Richard Nixon, Hafiz al-Asad.

3 Bashar (aged 10) and Basil, with their parents.

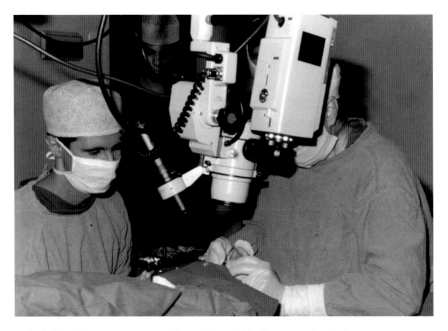

4 Assisting with eye surgery at Tishreen Hospital in Damascus in 1992.

5 Surrounded by a crowd in Homs when following up on the progress on a construction site in June 2003.

6 With his wife, Asma, and children, Hafiz and Zein, returning from a visit to Turkey in January 2004.

7 With the family, relaxing in summer 2003 at a resort outside of Damascus.

8 The most popular portrait of Bashar, seen throughout Syria and Syrian publications.

9 With the former Spanish prime minister, José Maria Aznar, in Spain in 2001.

10 President Bashar with US secretary of state, Colin Powell, in May 2003.

11 Pope John Paul II visiting Damascus in May 2001. A meeting in the ornate People's Palace reception room.

12 With the British prime minister, Tony Blair, upon Bashar's visit to London in 2002.

13 President Bashar with Saudi King Abdullah in Saudi Arabia in 2005.

14 President Bashar with Egyptian president, Husni Mubarak in Sharm al-Shaykh, in 2005.

15 With Libyan leader, Muammar al-Qadhdhafi, at the Arab League summit meeting in Algiers in March 2005.

16 With the Lebanese president, Emile Lahhoud.

17 With the Russian president, Vladimir Putin, in 2005.

18 The author with President Bashar in the Rowda presidential building in June 2004.

19 Photographs such as this are usually taken on national occasions every year, particularly military ones.

along the dotted line, so would Lebanon and Jordan in an immediate sense. All of this would open the door for Saudi Arabia and the rest of the Arab Gulf states to enter into peace agreements with Israel—and at the same time, Saddam Hussein's Iraq would be isolated and the PLO, with little Arab leverage behind it, would be compelled to seek a more rapid and conciliatory peace with Israel.

This is not to say that a Syrian-Israeli peace agreement would be easy to consummate, but there were—and still are—some important differences with the situation in the West Bank. There are considerably fewer Israeli settlements and people in the Golan Heights when compared to the West Bank. There is little geographic intermingling between the Israeli settlements and Arab villages in the Golan Heights, while it is quite the opposite in the West Bank. There is less religious significance attached by Israelis to the Golan Heights than to the West Bank (or Judea and Samaria as the more nationalistic Israeli Jews are apt to call it). In addition, an agreement on the Golan Heights rests primarily on issues concerning border demarcation, security arrangements, and the pace and nature of normalizing relations, i.e. all things that can be negotiated in a tractable fashion. In the West Bank, on the other hand, there are the much more intractable issues of what to do with the numerous Israeli settlements, the status of Jerusalem, and the question over the return of Palestinian refugees within pre-1967 Israeli borders. It is little wonder, then, that American and Israeli leaders consistently sought to explore the prospects of a Syrian-Israeli peace before a Palestinian-Israeli one.

Labor party leader Yitzhak Rabin, who became Israeli prime minister in 1992, was prepared to focus on the Syrian track for all the reasons just mentioned in addition to the fact that he was skeptical that Yasser Arafat could "deliver in the end through the Oslo channel."[4] As opposed to his hardline predecessor, Yitzhak Shamir, Rabin agreed that UN Security Council Resolution 242 applied to the Golan Heights. But as with most Israeli leaders, Rabin felt the Israeli public could absorb only so much at one time, i.e. a peace agreement on one track, but not on the other until sufficient time had passed—it would be diplomatic overload to try to consummate both at the same time. Rabin's initial explorations regarding peace negotiations with Syria through American intermediaries, however, did not proceed fast enough.

Hafiz al-Asad was renowned for his methodical and incremental negotiations, born as much by suspicion as by style or strategy. Some progress was made by both sides in terms of signaling willingness to enter into peace negotiations, and, especially, there was an Israeli willingness to withdraw from the Golan Heights, which is what really caught Asad's eye. But things bogged down over the definition of "full withdrawal" from the Golan Heights and the extent of "normalization" of relations between the two states. Hafiz al-Asad insisted that full Israeli withdrawal meant to the border as it existed on June 4, 1967, i.e. the day before the so-called Six Day War began. Israel prefers a return to the 1923 international border demarcation between mandatory British Palestine and mandatory French Syria. The June 4 line would, at least in theory, provide Syria with direct access to the Sea of Galilee, whereas the 1923 line is, at its closest point, about ten meters off the shore of the Sea of Galilee. The June 4 line represents Syrian advances during the Arab-Israeli war of 1947 to 1949 and Syria's border thereafter, prior to 1967. It is popularly suspected that one of the reasons for Asad's insistence on the June 4 line is so that Syria would appear to have more territory returned than that which Sadat received in the 1979 Egyptian-Israeli peace treaty, which itself was based on a 1923 demarcation by European powers. Since Asad held out so much longer than Sadat, so a certain line of thought expounds, he should expect a little bit more for his steadfastness. Additionally, the 1923 border, from the Syrian perspective, was the colonial border drawn arbitrarily by the European mandate powers; therefore, it was really not legitimate to begin with in the eyes of most Syrians. All of these issues, however, would be negotiable, as time would tell, but for the moment Rabin was disappointed in Asad's hesitancy and gave the green light to proceed with the Oslo channel with the Palestinians, all of which placed the Syrian-Israeli track on the back burner for the time being.

Syrian-Israeli prospects would again brighten by 1994, as the Israeli-Palestinian track, even in the aftermath of the Oslo accords, tended to periodically run smack into a number of obstacles on the road—to the point where both Syrian and Palestinian negotiators accused the Israelis of purposely playing one track against the other in order to extract more concessions on each. In the period 1994 to 1996 the basic parameters for a Syrian-Israeli peace were laid, and serious progress was made on a host of important issues; indeed, if a Syrian-Israeli peace should materialize in the foreseeable future, it will no doubt be based largely on the progress made at a series of discussions between the two sides brokered by the United States during this period. There were a number of important issues discussed. The timing and extent of a withdrawal of Syrian and Israeli forces after a return of the Golan Heights was a crucial obstacle to be overcome. Since Israel is much smaller than Syria, the former wanted an asymmetrical withdrawal—Syria keeping forces and certain types of armaments further away from the new negotiated border than Israel—in a longer, more phased approach, and Syria, while eventually agreeing to asymmetrical demilitarization, wanted a more rapid, total withdrawal. Security measures in the form of early-warning stations were negotiated—where they would be located and who would man them. Also discussed was the exact nature of the peace, in that Israel wanted full normalization with an exchange of embassies as well as trade and cultural interaction as part of the process of withdrawal (as it had done with Egypt) in order to build up a level of trust with Damascus and in order to measure the extent to which Syria really wanted peace. Syria, on the other hand, at least at first, spoke of "normal" relations, something falling short of an integrative relationship, saying that full normalization could occur over time, after an agreement was reached. In this regard, critics would accuse Asad of simply trying to create what was essentially a non-belligerency pact. There were the matters concerning adequate water-sharing, water protection procedures, and mechanisms for the tributaries traversing the Golan Heights, an issue that was central to Israeli concerns. Finally, of course, there was the question of where exactly the new Syrian-Israeli border would be located. While Asad stuck to his June 4, 1967, line, the Israelis sought to amend the border somewhat to keep Syria from the shores of the Sea of Galilee, possibly in exchange for some other territory adjacent to the Golan Heights (such as the al-Hamma area that juts out like a finger from the Golan toward Jordan).[5] According to lead U.S. negotiator Dennis Ross, however, there does not exist a map delineating the actual disposition of forces on the day of June 4, 1967.[6] In addition, the Israelis under Rabin made a commitment through the Americans (so that it could be plausibly denied if negotiations broke down), that was passed on to the Syrians, that they would be willing to implement a full withdrawal from the Golan Heights.

In the 1993 through 1996 period, the momentum toward an overall Arab-Israeli peace was being put together piece by piece. First there was the Declaration of Principles, then direct Syrian-Israeli negotiations at the military chief of staff level, and then the Jordanian-Israeli peace treaty signed in October 1994. Together with all of this there was also a great deal of progress made in terms of integrating Israel economically in the Middle East, marked by groundbreaking economic summit meetings in Casablanca and in Amman that involved Arabs, Israelis, and the international community attempting to create what the former Israeli prime minister and foreign minister, Shimon Peres, called a Middle East common market; indeed, a number of Arab countries dropped the secondary and tertiary economic boycotts toward Israel, and some even the primary boycott, dealing directly with Tel Aviv in a number of industry areas. Even with the PLO and the Jordanians breaking away from the Arab bloc and making deals with the Israelis on their own, something that had been anathema to Asad for years, Syria was not about to be left behind, so it continued negotiating. Ross puts it more harshly: "Asad justified making his own deal with the Israelis on grounds that the Palestinians had left him. But, in fact, he was ready to make his own deal from the beginning. He was willing to leave the Palestinians out in the cold, but not the Lebanese."[7]

The tragic assassination of Rabin in November 1995 did not block the Israeli-Syrian track; indeed, if anything, it accelerated it because his successor, Shimon Peres, was someone who was known to be more prepared to exchange land for peace with the Arabs and quicken the pace of negotiations. He certainly felt he could utilize the post-assassination atmosphere to push forward with the Syrians and finish what Rabin had begun. The momentum was broken, however, by two Hamas suicide bombings in Israel in February and March 1996. Since Hamas locates its political offices in Damascus, Tel Aviv expected Hafiz al-Asad to publicly condemn the attacks, which he chose not to do; indeed, Syrian exhortations over the radio tacitly supported the bombings. This was a major diplomatic faux pas. The meetings between Syrian and Israeli negotiators at the Wye Plantation in Maryland were subsequently called off. This episode certainly paints in stark relief the totally different wavelengths of Syria and Israel with regard to public diplomacy. Asad always wanted to play his cards close to his vest, never giving up any cards until he absolutely had to. The pace of Peres' march toward a Syrian-Israeli agreement was already uncomfortably fast for the methodical Syrian president. The Israelis, who had in mind the overtly dramatic public gestures of Anwar al-Sadat that jump-started the Egyptian-Israeli peace process, notably his visit to Jerusalem and speech in front of the Knesset in November 1977, expected Asad also to do something in the public arena that might reassure the Israelis about his sincere desire for peaceful relations.

Asad was a notoriously private man. He was consciously devoid of the dramatic flare of Sadat, who he felt relinquished his most expensive bargaining chips by de facto recognizing the Jewish state *before* an agreement. The Israelis may have expected too much from Asad in this regard and never really appreciated the fact that even though he was at the apex of an authoritarian state, he also had a constituency to play to among the Syrian elite, the Syrian population, and in the wider Arab world. Beyond that, various elements in the Syrian leadership were not shy about firing some warning shots across the bows through state-controlled media outlets to send subtle and not-so-subtle signals to Asad that he needed to rein in his march toward peace with Israel to a certain degree. He could not go too far out in front of them just as Rabin, Peres, and later Ehud Barak could not be seen to be too far out in front of their own respective domestic constituencies. But Asad's hesitancy, including Syria's failure to participate in the multilateral talks, fed into the claims of those Israelis who from the beginning doubted the sincerity of Syria's interest in peace. This is where Syria's traditional role at the vanguard of Arab nationalism and its oft-stated commitment to the Palestinian cause possibly hampered its ability to break out from this self-professed paradigm and embrace the ameliorating opportunities such as that which existed following the suicide attacks.

With Syrian-Israeli relations deteriorating, Hizbollah began to launch Katyusha rocket attacks against towns and villages in northern Israel, coupled with intensified operations against Israeli forces in the Lebanese security zone. Although Hizbollah acts with more independence from Syria than most perceive, it is still utilized as necessary leverage by Damascus in an indirect fashion against Israel. Asad considers Hizbollah to be the other side of the peace-negotiation coin, to be cashed when necessary to pressure Israel in the only way possible. This shows Tel Aviv that there is something to be gained—i.e. the quelling of the Hizbollah threat—by returning the Golan Heights and something to be lost by not doing so. Hizbollah as well as its other state sponsor, Iran, provide Damascus with some strategic depth in case of war with Israel, a military consideration that was a central feature of Hafiz al-Asad's overall strategic conception vis-à-vis Tel Aviv.[8] Israel, however, tends to see Syrian influence over Hizbollah as a threat that must be met with force in order to convince Damascus to de-link itself from the Shiite Islamist group or compel it to stand down. Since Shimon Peres had perhaps ill-advisedly called for new elections in May of 1996, he could not sit back and do nothing in response to the Hizbollah attacks in the midst of what was in effect an election campaign against Likud party leader Benjamin Netanyahu.

Peres' response was to launch Operation Grapes of Wrath in April in Lebanon as punishment for the rocket attacks. It was directed not only against Hizbollah positions but also against various manifestations of the Lebanese government, such as power grids, to convince Beirut that it would suffer too by not attempting to control southern Lebanon—the hope being that the general Lebanese population would then turn against Hizbollah even more for bringing the wrath of Israel down upon them. It turned out to be a public relations disaster, as it led to the displacement of over 400,000 civilians and the deaths of over 100 non-combatant Lebanese due to an Israeli artillery barrage that hit a refugee camp in the village of Qana on April 19—of course, all of this destruction was instantly shown to the world through the global media. This weakened Peres' position and fed into a more propitious domestic political environment for the election of Netanyahu—much as the Palestinian intifada in 2000 undermined Barak's position, leading to the landslide victory of the more security-minded Likud leader at that time, Ariel Sharon. Significantly, Israeli actions angered a great many Israeli Arabs, who make up almost one fifth of the population of Israel and 12 percent of the electorate.

Many of them had relatives in Lebanon. They certainly did not vote for Netanyahu, but they stayed at home in droves, depriving Peres of much-needed votes. Following his election, Netanyahu, who came into office with the mantra of "peace with security" replacing that of "land for peace," showed little overt interest in continuing the Syrian-Israeli track, or even the Palestinian-Israeli track for that matter. The Syrian-Israeli peace process was moribund.

The Netanyahu years (1996 to 1999) did, indeed, dampen the prospects for a comprehensive peace, and the Israeli prime minister often clashed with the Clinton administration on issues related to the negotiations (or lack thereof). It is not a surprise that Clinton's lead Middle East envoy, Dennis Ross, made not a single visit to Damascus during Netanyahu's tenure. It is, however, very interesting to note that behind the scenes Netanyahu sanctioned the efforts of Ronald Lauder, an American businessman, to secretly explore the modalities of a peace agreement with Syria on several visits to Damascus to meet with Hafiz al-Asad and other Syrian officials. Although in the end nothing concrete came of his efforts, primarily because Netanyahu's vision of an agreement with Syria was substantially less from the perspective of Damascus than the Rabin and Peres model, they did betray the continued preference of both Likud and Labor regimes in Israel for peace with Syria over a final peace accord with the Palestinians. For reasons that will be discussed later, this no longer seems to be the case today; indeed, Syria is desperately trying to re-enter the peace process framework from which it has largely been shut out in recent years.

A New Opportunity for Peace

New Israeli Labor party leader Ehud Barak won the election as prime minister in May 1999. He was a protégé of Yitzhak Rabin and cut out of the same mold. He, too, had been chief of staff of the IDF, and along with Netanyahu reflected the rise to power of a new generation of Israeli leaders. As was the case with Rabin (and as opposed to Peres), with his military background Barak was someone in the Labor party who most Israelis could trust not to give up land for peace without adequate security measures. Although misrepresented considering his role at the epicenter of the creation of the Israeli defense establishment as well as its nuclear capability, Peres was cast as a hopeless peacenik who was too eager to consummate accords with the Arabs. Barak also had some Anwar al-Sadat in him, prone to the dramatic, bold move to secure a peace agreement—and his place in history. But this was also the antithesis of Hafiz al-Asad's negotiating style, to which a succession of U.S.

Middle East envoys, secretaries of state, and negotiators can attest. Ross notes that "Asad did not like to rush under any circumstances; it was not his style. He was never in a hurry lest it appear that he needed an agreement more than the other side. And that, of course, was the very message Barak would be sending—he was anxious, and if so, why would Asad concede anything?"[9] The differences in negotiating style would prove to be fatal under the bright lights of international attention and expectations by early 2000.

Barak was especially keen to engineer an Israeli withdrawal from Lebanon. Long ago it had become a quagmire from which the majority of Israelis wanted their country extricated, especially as the deaths of Israeli soldiers accumulated over the months and years due to Hizbollah's effective guerilla campaign. But the new Israeli prime minister wanted the withdrawal to be part of an overall settlement with Syria. In this way Israel would not be seen as cutting and running and Hizbollah would not be perceived as winning. In addition, Syria could be brought on board as a guarantor of security along the Israeli-Lebanese border. If there was an Israeli-Syrian peace agreement, what need then would Damascus have of Hizbollah *vis-à-vis* Israel? In addition, Barak seemed to prefer dealing with Asad rather than Arafat, whom no Israeli leader ever really trusted. Asad was, from the Israeli perspective, difficult to deal with as well. The Syrian president once commented that "Our stance in the battle for peace will not be less courageous than our stances on the battle-field."[10] And Shimon Peres observed that Asad was "conducting the peace process just as one conducts a military campaign—slowly, patiently, directed by strategic and tactical considerations."[11] Given this, however, Asad could be trusted to comply with any agreement reached, and he was more straight-forward with regard to the issues that needed to be discussed. As Ross states, Barak "knew that what mattered to the Syrians was the land, and that what most mattered to Israelis was security and water."[12] In addition, Bashar had praised Barak following the election, and many Israelis believed this to be a signal from his father, thus encouraging even more attention to this track.

The Syrian-Israeli track, therefore, began to heat up again with behind-the-scenes contacts during the summer–fall of 1999, especially as the second-term Clinton administration was eager to broker a comprehensive Arab-Israeli peace before it left office in January 2001. This would be the capstone of Clinton's presidency, creating a legacy apart from the scandals and impeach-ment that rocked his administration in its second term. In addition, Hafiz al-Asad may have wanted to make a deal with a willing Israeli prime minister while he could, so that his son Bashar could inherit a more congenial regional environment when the time came. Hafiz' deteriorating health, which outside observers had been commenting on for years, appeared also to become an issue of increasing concern. But he was so reclusive by this point that even high-level Syrian officials were kept in the dark as to the status of his health. Bashar, however, knew that his father's condition was worsening, and a reshuffling of the cabinet in the spring of 2000 as well as an intensified anti-corruption campaign in Syria presented some possible hints that change was in the offing. Moreover, American negotiators could see for themselves that Asad was getting more gaunt and frail in late 1999 and into 2000. They had also heard reports from other Arab state officials that his ability to engage in everyday affairs was limited and that even his lucidity was called into question at times. One sensed that the momentum building toward direct Syrian-Israeli negotiations in late 1999 would be a last-ditch attempt to orchestrate an agreement before being overtaken by events, particularly the death of Hafiz al-Asad.

The climax came in January 2000, when Barak and his support staff met with Syrian Foreign Minister Farouk al-Sharaa and his staff at a retreat in Shepherdstown, West Virginia, about an hour and fifteen minutes from Washington by car. Camp David was specifically not chosen because the Syrians in no way, shape, or form wanted to be associated with Sadat and the Egyptians at Camp David in 1978, and the Wye Plantation was no longer a viable option since it had been used by Arafat to produce the Wye accords in October 1998. Yet Shepherdstown was still close enough to Washington, DC, for Clinton to fly back and forth via helicopter to mediate the talks when necessary. A good deal of progress was made on the preceding set of 1994 to 1996 negotiations, and, according to Dennis Ross, with an impressive display of flexibility on the part of the Syrians that showed the seriousness with which they were pursuing a peace agreement; indeed, while acknowledging that there was enough blame to go around for the failure of a definitive agreement produced at Sheperdstown, Ross explicitly states that "Barak was more at fault than the Syrians."[13] It seemed as if a peace agreement was definitely within earshot, or, as Bashar believes, they were at least 80 percent of the way there, especially with a U.S. president who was willing to take some risks in the pursuit of an agreement.[14]

An ill-timed leak of a draft agreement between Syria and Israel crafted by the Americans at Shepherdstown soon after the parties adjourned from West Virginia inestimably complicated the progress that had taken place. It is highly likely that the draft was intentionally leaked by someone in the Barak government as a trial balloon, for Barak was very concerned about public support for his position. It could also have been designed to drum up domestic support for Barak in the negotiations as well as in an Israeli public referendum. The leak, which confirmed some significant concessions by Damascus, embarrassed, if not infuriated, Asad, who would receive indirect criticism in Syria for having gone too far without enough guaranteed returns. It compelled him to lurch backward away from the negotiating table.

This episode again placed in stark relief the incongruity of the perception that both sides had of each other in terms of understanding what is necessary for each to do in order to garner domestic support. Despite this, contacts continued at the insistence of the United States, and President Clinton threw the full weight of his office behind it all by meeting personally with Hafiz in Geneva, Switzerland, in March 2000 in what appeared to be a last-gasp attempt to salvage an accord. Stories differ on all sides on what happened at Geneva that resulted in a failed summit. The Syrians believe they were promised an agreement that confirmed Israel's withdrawal from the Golan to the June 4 line, and when something less than this was offered by Clinton, they backed away.[15] Others believe that Asad, his health having deteriorated even more, was not really interested at all in peace negotiations at that moment because he was concentrating more specifically on preparing the way for Bashar to come to office with cabinet and military personnel reshuffling. Domestic politics was the immediate priority, and he could not be locked into another protracted round of negotiations with the Israelis. He attended the summit meeting with Clinton, according to this view, as a show of strength to those who had been criticizing him at home, that is, as Ross states, he would "stand up to the President of the United States and not compromise vital Syrian interests," shoring up the support of powerful elements within Syria that would help ensure Bashar's succession.[16] After the disastrous summit, and without any prospects for a deal with Syria in the near future, Barak decided to unilaterally withdraw Israeli forces from Lebanon in May. Hafiz al-Asad died in June.

Bashar and Israel

In his inaugural address, Bashar spent the majority of his speech focusing on internal affairs in Syria, especially the need for economic reform and accountability. It is only toward the end of his speech that he addressed relations with Israel, introduced through nationalistic statements regarding Lebanon, revealing the Lebanese link in the Syrian-Israeli dynamic. In retrospect, this clearly shows that the young president was first and foremost interested in dealing with domestic problems in Syria, economically and politically, and in shoring up his power base before even thinking about embarking upon another set of negotiations with Israel. He was hesitant to do so in any case after witnessing what had happened in the previous six months, after which, in many ways, the Syrian side felt betrayed by Barak. When he did arrive at the subject of Israel, he said the following:

Ending the civil war in Lebanon, establishing national reconciliation in addition to defeating the Israelis in the 1980s and 1990s, and finally, their worst defeat last May [with the withdrawal from Lebanon] are clear evidence of the importance of [Syrian-Lebanese] solidarity. All of these achievements were based on the solidarity and unity of the Lebanese people and state. . . . We in Syria shall always stand by Lebanon and support it in all its national causes, especially concerning the return of its full territory [a reference to the Shebaa Farms[17]] and the return of its prisoners locked in Israeli jails and in its brave stand in the face of repeated Israeli threats. . . . Such threats to do not serve the cause of peace in the region; rather they keep the tensions hot . . . as well as placing obstacles and impediments in the way of achieving a just and comprehensive peace in the region. In this regard, Israel still occupies our Golan. . . . The liberation of our territory is at the top of our national priorities and is as important to us as the achievement of a just and comprehensive peace that we have adopted as our strategic choice, but not at the expense of our territory nor at the expense of our sovereignty. Our territory and our sovereignty are a matter of national dignity and no one at all is allowed to compromise any of them. We were very clear in dealing with peace issues, firm in our stand since the beginning of the peace process in Madrid in 1991—unlike Israeli policy that fluctuated sometimes and erected obstacles at other times . . . they have not given us any proof that invites confidence that they have a true and genuine desire for peace. Rather they have been suggesting different versions in order to hide what they truly want to do, so they ask us to be flexible in order to press the borders, making ours smaller in a way that meets their objectives, or they send us envoys who ask us to agree to a modified June 4th line and ask us to call this modified line the June 4th one, as if the difference is about naming the line. Or they suggest giving us 95% of our land, and when we ask about the remaining 5%, they say it is only a problem of a few meters and that this should not be an obstacle in the way of peace. If those few meters are not a problem and should not be an obstacle to peace, then why don't they return to the June 4th line and give us the 5% of territory? . . . We call upon the United States to play its complete role as an honest broker and a co-sponsor of the peace process. Pressure has to be exerted in order to implement the resolutions of international legitimacy with all the legitimate rights for the Lebanese, Syrian, and Palestinian peoples. We would like to stress here that we have the desire to reach a state of peace, but we are not ready to give up an inch of our territory nor do we accept our sovereignty being impinged upon. We would like to achieve peace because it is our strategic choice and because the Syrian people have always been, throughout history, a peace-loving people.[18]

His language regarding Israel in the speech did, indeed, consist of fairly harsh rhetoric, although he did reaffirm on two occasions Syria's "strategic choice" for peace. It was probably to be expected that a young, relatively untested leader such as Bashar would stake out a tough line vis-à-vis Israel, if anything to show that he was in control, that Tel Aviv should not expect that he was going to be soft in any negotiations that may resume, and to reassure those powerful elements within his regime that had so recently fired some warning shots across his father's bows that he was not going to willy-nilly make concessions nor repeat the mistakes made at Shepherdstown. Unlike his father at Geneva, Bashar did not see a peace agreement with Israel as a way to consolidate his power in Damascus; quite to the contrary, it seemed that he would first have to consolidate his rule in Syria before embarking upon another round of talks with the Israelis. In this vein, many in the West, with their expectations that the ophthalmologist president would immediately engage in the peace process because he was a young, Western-educated modernizer who liked Phil Collins' music, failed to appreciate the inner dynamics of Syrian politics.[19] Even someone as much in control as Bashar's father had to tread delicately on the issue of Israel, much less an inexperienced leader with a very small power base that he could call his own. They also failed to realize that the so-called Western-educated ophthalmologist had only spent a grand total of less than two years of his entire lifetime of education in the West, and although he loved London, his brief stay there does not necessarily translate into instant "conversion." He is Syrian. He has spent most of his life in Syria. He has spent most of his life being directly affected by the Arab-Israeli conflict, viewing Israel as an antagonist and with suspicion, and championing the return of the Golan Heights and the rights of the Palestinians. To expect anything different from Bashar is wishful thinking.

This antagonistic attitude toward Israel would only heighten following the outbreak of the so-called al-Aqsa intifada in September 2000, when Ariel Sharon provocatively visited the Haram al-Sharif (Temple Mount), on which sit the al-Aqsa mosque and the Dome of the Rock, thus making Jerusalem, for most Muslims, the third holiest site in Islam after Mecca and Medina. The Palestinian uprising ignited by the visit as well as the Israeli response devolved into a virtual civil war as the year came to a close. In many ways the violence reflected the frustration of both the Palestinian and Israeli populations following the failed Camp David summit meeting between Arafat, Barak, and Clinton in July 2000. This meeting was an assertive, all-encompassing attempt by the Clinton administration to once and for all bring about an Israeli-Palestinian agreement that would settle the final status issues (the question of Jerusalem, the exact borders of a Palestinian state, what to do with the Israeli settlements in the West Bank and Gaza Strip, and the fate of Palestinian refugees who wanted to return to pre-1967 Israeli proper). The public failure of the summit emboldened the more hardline elements on each side of the equation who either were against the peace process or had been suspicious of it; at the same time, it severely weakened the peace camps on each side. It became clear to many that the Oslo process was dead, if not a futile effort to begin with, and that the only thing that would resolve the situation would be military pressure and violence. The stage was set for the devastating defeat of Barak in February 2001 and the rise of the more security-minded former military hero and godfather of the settler movement, Ariel Sharon, as Israeli prime minister. The Arab world was inflamed by the course of events, as the Palestinian cause still resonated on the Arab street if not with all of the Arab governments, the former compelling the latter to at least pay lip service to the plight of Palestinian suffering. Leading the way was the young president of Syria, a country that had traditionally considered itself at the forefront of the Arab and Palestinian cause.

Actually, Syria is one of the few countries in the Arab world that can play— or at least try to play—both sides of the fence. Its Arab nationalist credentials are intact since it has not yet signed a peace treaty with Israel. It still confronts Israel, even if indirectly through Hizbollah and its support of Palestinian groups such as Hamas and Islamic Jihad. It has, therefore, historically been at the vanguard of the "steadfastness" front in the Arab world arrayed against Israel. So it can legitimately adopt, at least rhetorically, a rather radical position *vis-à-vis* Israel when it is politically correct in the Arab world to do so without being seen as hypocritical, as opposed to countries such as Egypt and Jordan, who have both signed peace treaties with the Jewish state and have close relations with the United States. On the other hand, because of its track record of serious involvement in the Madrid peace process and its participation in the Gulf war coalition in 1991, Syria can also hop over to the other side of the fence when necessary and re-enter peace negotiations with Israel and/or adopt a more cooperative stance with the United States when and if the regional environment dictates it. Because Syria has been seen in Washington as an important conduit to those Arab countries who have yet to sign a peace agreement with Israel, many of whose leaders have publicly stated that they will only do so after Syria signs along the dotted line, the United States has traditionally tended to cast a blind eye toward the "radical" side of the fence while trying to nurture Damascus toward the more cooperative side.

As such, at an emergency Arab League summit meeting in October 2000 to discuss the intifada, Bashar al-Asad became a leading voice in the castigation of Israel and a strong advocate of concrete steps being taken to support the Palestinian cause. Stating that the Israelis were taking aggressive action against the "Arab nation," he specifically exclaimed that Israel threatened "the very existence of the Palestinians." Bashar reiterated that the Arabs continued to search for peace, but the Israelis wanted war, and that while Syria had chosen peace as a strategic option, Israel approached it as a "tactical option."[20] He urged the Arabs to "take pride" in the "heroic Lebanese experience" of resisting occupation and called on the Arab states to "halt all forms of cooperation with Israel and reactivate the Arab boycott."[21] In November, at the Organization of the Islamic Conference summit in Doha, Qatar, Bashar equated the Israeli action against the Palestinians as racism, stating,

al-Aqsa with its Islamic dimension and al-Quds [Jerusalem] with its Arab dimension, both Islamic and Christian, have become a danger to historical Zionist expansionism; therefore, they are perpetually endeavoring to obliterate those dimensions. Israeli arrogance and practices, which have no connection whatever with the ethics and teachings of any heavenly religion could not have happened without encouragement and support from other states [a reference to the United States]. They curse the old Nazis, yet they exercise the practices of a new Nazism about which is never read in the history books.[22]

Continuing the vitriolic rhetoric, at a speech in Amman, Jordan, in March 2001, Bashar stated that "Israel is a racial society and is a more racist one than Nazism," adding that "the Israelis have no desire for genuine peace." He confirmed Syria's commitment to a "just and comprehensive peace based on the Madrid terms of reference," meaning that negotiations would begin at the point they left off during the Madrid process, including the concessions Damascus believes Israel made, primarily the withdrawal from the Golan Heights to the June 4 lines. This has been a consistent position adopted by Damascus, reiterated by Bashar in his speech to the Syrian National Assembly in March 2005. When I asked President Bashar about his references to the Israelis as Nazis, particularly on the occasion of the Pope's visit to Damascus in 2002, he said the following:

How do you define the Nazis in the world? As killers, killers. If you kill them by gas chamber or if you kill them by bullet or if you kill them by bombs, it does not matter—they still lose their lives, but it is a systematic way of killing. And the way they act toward the Palestinians has been systematic following the intifada. I was asked in Spain . . . about this statement, and I told the journalist that one Israeli minister said the Arabs are snakes and should be killed—this is racism, and the Nazis were racists. What I said in front of the Pope, I was talking about Sharon. I said he was a Nazi, and I said as long as Israelis elect someone like Sharon with 70 percent of the vote, someone who is a criminal, they need to take the responsibility of electing someone like him. That is what I meant. What I said in front of the Pope [regarding the Jews being responsible for the death of Christ] was not to attack the Jews. One of the first things I did upon becoming president was to receive a delegation of Jews in Syria. You cannot be a Muslim and be against Judaism or Christianity because they are all part of each other, and as I told you about the movie *The Passion of the Christ* [which he saw at a public theater in Damascus], what happened two thousand years ago is not relevant today in terms of the Jews and the Romans, who were actually responsible for the death of Christ. I was talking with the Pope about the peace process and I told him that what has happened to the peace process is that it has been betrayed, like the betrayal of Christ and the betrayal of the Prophet Muhammad at one point, and I explained this to the Jewish senators from the United States who came to Syria . . . yet in your media it was portrayed as me attacking the Jews.[23]

Unfortunately, this type of verbiage has become commonplace in Arab discourse when criticizing Israel. It is obviously meant to touch a sensitive nerve in the Jewish state because of the experience of the Holocaust at the hands of the Nazis. In my personal view, it is totally irresponsible to equate what happened in World War II, the systematic genocide of six million Jews, with the Arab-Israeli conflict and the tactics of the Israeli occupation, no matter how tragic and/or wrong the latter may be. This type of rhetoric wins points only among those Arabs who have accepted such a characterization as a result of extreme frustration, educational brainwashing, and/or repetitive usage. In the West and in Israel, this does nothing but reinforce negative stereotypes of Arabs and Muslims and creates the image of Israel as a victim of wild propaganda rather than an aggressor.

Because of the asymmetry of power arraigned against them, the only weapon that many Arab leaders have at their disposal to confront Israel are angry words. The fact that Bashar made these comments in Madrid on May 3 and in front of the Pope on May 6, 2001, only a few weeks after Israel, in response to a Hizbollah attack on April 14, bombed a Syrian radar station in Lebanon on April 16 killing three Syrian soldiers is not a coincidence—what else could he do? But the Arab world can vehemently criticize Israel legitimately on a host of issues without resort to venal comparisons with Nazism. Bashar al-Asad, a man known for his humility and compassion, needs to exercise more leadership and not fall prey to the mob. However, he saw that Israel was changing the rules of the game *vis-à-vis* Syria, Hizbollah, and Palestinian groups, and perhaps he felt he had to lash out in as dramatic a way as possible in order for Syria not to look as impotent as it actually was. As Yotam Feldner observes,

> According to these rules, Israel retaliated in the past only against Lebanese targets (particularly Hizbollah targets in South Lebanon). A few times, when the casualties were high, Israel retaliated by destroying the Lebanese infrastructure. Since the withdrawal from South Lebanon, and despite threats, Israel refrained from escalating its retaliation, fearing, apparently, the fate of the Israeli hostages held by Hizbollah, and trying to avoid the creation of a new front. According to the Syrians, the attack on the Syrian radar was a turning point and an Israeli signal that Jerusalem wants to cancel these old rules of the game and to create a new equation in which the Israeli response to all Hizbollah attacks will be retaliation against Syrian targets in Lebanon.[24]

After the tragic event of September 11, 2001, there seemed to be a brief opportunity for a dramatic reversal in the Arab-Israeli arena. The Bush administration understood that it needed as many allies as possible, especially in the Muslim world, to go after the Taliban and al-Qaida in Afghanistan and fight the now enhanced threat of global transnational terrorism. It appeared to distance itself from Israel at first and draw closer to the Arab states, including Syria. Washington received condolences, letters of sympathy, and promises to help in the fight against global terrorism from leaders the world over, including Bashar al-Asad; indeed, it is at this point that Syrian officials expressed their sympathy for the United States by describing how their country had already experienced Islamic extremism in the late 1970s and early 1980s—and, of course, dealt with it swiftly and effectively.[25]

Since Syria is a secular, Baathist regime and the ruling hierarchy is largely made up of and controlled by a minority Muslim Shiite schismatic sect (Alawites), Damascus has been no friend of the ardently Sunni al-Qaida organization and its supporters throughout the region. It was in Syria's interests to assist U.S. intelligence in finding out more about al-Qaida operatives, and, indeed, Damascus provided some very helpful, if not crucial, information to U.S. officials regarding al-Qaida members and groups in order to thwart possible further attacks against American interests in the Middle East.[26] There was a great deal of official concern in Israel at the time that George W. Bush would emulate his father, George H. W. Bush, in trying to placate the Arab states in order to enlist them in the fight against terror and the war in Afghanistan (that began in October 2001). The Gulf war of 1991 excluded the Israelis and led to the Madrid and Oslo peace processes. The Israelis had for a number of years been concerned that the United States would lessen its commitment to the Jewish state, particularly by reducing military and economic aid (Israel is the largest recipient of U.S. foreign aid). It was quite possible that at the end of the superpower cold war Israel would no longer be seen as a valuable strategic asset in the region to contain Soviet expansionism. Both Labor and Likud officials in Israel attempted to depict Israel as the front line against the new global threat of Islamic terrorism, and as such, it could serve as useful a role for the United States as it had played during the cold war.

Fortunately for Ariel Sharon and his supporters, there were powerful elements in the Bush administration that began to view threats to Israel and America as one and the same. The events of 9/11 married the neo-conservative philosophy of power as a strategic asset with the promotion of democratic change in the Middle East to drain the swamp of Islamic extremism. In this vein, a strong Israel was seen as strategic necessity. After the flush of quick military victory in Afghanistan that resulted in the expulsion of the Taliban in fall 2001, a rumble could be heard in Washington regarding regime change in Iraq as the next objective. Soon enough Israeli and American officials were beginning to equate Yasser Arafat with Osama bin Laden, and the PLO with the Taliban. Despite Syria's intelligence cooperation, voices began to be heard regarding Syrian support for terrorism, and in their view there was no difference between groups such as Hizbollah and Hamas and the transnational al-Qaida terrorist network. Movement toward the Syrian Accountability Act began in earnest. All of this would hit a crescendo with the war in Iraq in March/April 2003.

Even by the end of 2001 and into early 2002 Syria felt itself placed more and more on the defensive. There were still mixed signals emanating from the United States. Congress was well on its way toward constructing the Syrian Accountability Act, elements in the Pentagon were becoming more vociferous in their complaints about Syria, and pressure groups, including Christian Lebanese, Syrian exiles, Christian evangelicals, and right-wing neo-conservative think tanks in Washington, heightened their anti-Syrian rhetoric while trying to convince the administration that Syria belonged with Iran, Iraq, and North Korea in the axis of evil that was announced in President Bush's State of the Union address in January 2002. However, the State Department, the CIA, and the Bush administration itself still believed that engagement with Syria was important, not so much for Syrian participation in a moribund peace process but for Damascus' assistance in destroying al-Qaida, especially as Lebanon was seen as a possible locale where al-Qaida might attempt to regroup, and in drumming up support in the Arab world for a possible war in Iraq.[27] As such, the Syrian regime probably believed that U.S.-Syrian relations would remain status quo and that the policy of engaging Syria would stay in place.

It was argued that Damascus may have grown a bit too complacent, secure in the knowledge that the State Department mantra—Syria had saved American lives—would insulate the country from the post-9/11 merger of assertive nationalists and democratic imperialists in the Bush administration.[28] Essentially, Bashar al-Asad and his foreign policy advisers did not adequately adjust to the important underlying changes in American foreign policy as a result of 9/11. Damascus thought the old rules of the game were still in place, and State Department and other administration officials led them to believe that such was the case, but at the same time the new rules of the game were being written in Washington in the corridors of Congress, the Pentagon, and in influential conservative think tanks by those who saw Bashar and his regime as part of the problem rather than the solution. The focus of power in the Bush administration in foreign policy matters had shifted to the Pentagon because the United States was at war in Afghanistan, then in Iraq, and globally against terrorist organizations. This naturally led to a more bellicose posture toward Syria (and Iran). State Department officials, including Secretary of State Colin Powell, would make comments from time to time that probably led Damascus to think the old rules still applied, but these statements by a weakened government department would carry little weight in the U.S. foreign-policymaking apparatus. Because of this, Bashar's continued verbal assaults on Israel well into 2003 played right into the hands of the ascending group of American foreign policy ideologues, whose positions seemed to mirror the security concerns and methodology of Ariel Sharon. Little did Bashar know that with each and every passing day he and his regime were becoming more of a target.

Even though Bashar expressed lukewarm support for Saudi Crown Prince Abdullah's comprehensive Arab-Israeli peace plan that was officially unveiled at the Arab League summit meeting held in Beirut in March 2002, Syria still tried to maintain its distance from any new peace process with Israel that might emerge.[29] Syrian officials successfully watered down some aspects of the Saudi plan, particularly by replacing the term "normalization" in the phrase "normalization of relations", part of what Israel would receive in return for the occupied land per UN Security Council Resolution 242, with the word "normal," which entails something less than full integrative relations with the Jewish state, essentially just a state of non-belligerency. Bashar's father believed that one should begin with "normal relations" (*alaqat tabiyya*), the bare minimum of diplomatic interaction, and build up over time toward "normalization." The Israelis, on the other hand, want normalization of relations, with economic and cultural exchanges occurring concurrently with the exchange of land and implementation of security arrangements, as was the case with the Egyptian-Israeli peace treaty.[30] This is important to the Israelis as a sign that an Arab state truly wants peace along with the fact that an integrative, interdependent relationship would be an additional guard against a resumption of hostilities; to many Syrians it is simply distasteful to engage in friendly relations after so many years of war and recrimination—this would be something that would take getting used to.

Progress, however, had been made on this issue during the negotiations in the 1990s, so Bashar's efforts at the Beirut summit seemed to indicate a measure of backtracking by the Syrians. To his critics, it seemed to confirm the contention that his and his father's regime do not necessarily want peace, i.e. a virtual state of war with Israel justifies Syria's authoritarian structure, heavily reliant as it is on the bloated military-security apparatus, as well as the perceived necessity of remaining in Lebanon. This assertion should not be discounted entirely. Given the heightened regional tensions by March 2002 as well as the unsettled internal environment in Syria, which was still dealing with the change of "seasons" from the Damascus "spring" to the Damascus "winter," Bashar most likely believed that he had very little room to maneuver *vis-à-vis* Israel and more to gain regionally and domestically by adopting a more hardline position—he was still playing both sides of the fence, although to Israelis and Americans he seemed to be planting himself squarely on one side of it.

At the 2002 summit meeting, in which Bashar was the de facto host, he termed the intifada a "movement for independence," and again called on Arab nations to sever relations with Israel until the realization of a just and comprehensive peace." He pointed out that "the Palestinian intifada was legitimate resistance against occupation," and closed by saying that, "for us, terrorism comes from Israel."[31] In television coverage of his opening speech Bashar seemed to speak extemporaneously and from the heart, not from prepared notes—unlike most of the other Arab representatives. In an interview with Reuters in October 2002, President Bashar, in response to a question regarding the revival of peace negotiations with Israel, stated, "I haven't met anybody who mentioned the possibility of making peace with Sharon. What we see of him is only killing." On the state of Syrian-U.S. relations, he commented that "we have no problem with the United States, we are neither for nor against the United States."[32] The problem for Bashar was that more and more American officials were hypothetically saying the following: "We have a very serious problem with the Syrians, we are no longer for them—we are against them."

Syrian Isolation from the Peace Process

The war in Iraq in March/April 2003 severely strained U.S.-Syrian relations. As such, the regime of Bashar al-Asad became increasingly marginalized in the eyes of the Bush administration as not-so-subtle threats were being hurled at Syria by top U.S. officials during and after the war for its alleged support of elements in Saddam Hussein's Iraqi regime and of the subsequent Iraqi insurgency. Syria was now being accused of *costing* and not saving American lives. The increasing antagonism provided momentum for the Syrian Accountability Act and grease for the gears for those elements in Washington who were advocating regime change in Syria. No longer was it the case, as had long been the argument of the State Department and others who favored the engagement approach, that the differences separating the United States and Syria (such as Syrian support for what Washington termed as ter-rorist groups, its troop presence in Lebanon, and its development of weapons of mass destruction) could be resolved *after* an Israeli-Syrian peace treaty. As a result of the clear and more open shift in the U.S. official attitude toward Syria as a result of the Iraqi conflagration, Syria now had to meet all of these U.S. concerns *before* negotiations could even begin with Israel. Syria consid-ered that the price for acquiescence on all of these issues was a peace treaty with Israel that addressed its primary concerns, mainly withdrawal to the June 4 line; now, Washington and Tel Aviv were setting the price for just such a peace treaty—and the price had to be paid beforehand and not afterward. This was a fundamental shift in U.S. policy toward Syria with regard to the Arab-Israeli arena, one that seemed to catch Damascus off guard.

Confirmation of this marginalization came in the form of the "road map" to peace announced in June 2003, sponsored and crafted by the so-called "quartet," the United States, Russia, the European Union, and the United Nations. The "road map" was meant to resuscitate the peace process in the Middle East in the wake of the failed Madrid and Oslo peace processes. Elevated by the apparent military victory in Iraq, the Bush administration sought to utilize what it thought to be its new-found leverage to advance the cause of peace in the Middle East: it would show that it was not just in Iraq for its oil and strategic position, much as Bush's father had done in establishing the Madrid peace process following the 1991 Gulf war. The Europeans were also pressing the United States to show its commitment toward and make forward progress in the Arab-Israeli arena to parallel the evolving situation in the Gulf. The Arab-Israeli arena could not be separated from the Persian Gulf arena, a generally accepted line of thought that goes all the way back to the Arab oil embargo during the 1973 Arab-Israeli war.

In order to ameliorate if not quell what would most certainly be seen in the Arab street as American usurpation and occupation of Iraq the longer the troops stayed, progress on the Palestinian issue had to proceed. The road map called for reciprocal steps leading to the creation of a Palestinian state by 2005. The only problem from the point of view of Damascus is that the road map did not say a word about Syria. The Syrian track seemed no longer to exist in the eyes of Washington despite the attempts by the EU to call for another road map to be drawn up for Israel and its neighbors, presumably Syria.[33] Bashar criticized the United States for not inviting Syria to the talks held at the Egyptian resort of Sharm al-Shaykh to discuss the road map. At the summit meeting, President Bush met with Arab leaders from Egypt, Jordan, Saudi Arabia, and Bahrain, and representatives from the EU and the United Nations. Trying to rationalize the situation, Bashar stated in an interview on the Dubai-based Arabic television channel al-Arabiyya that, "the summit was concerned with the Palestinian track and the road map. I think the Syrian track for them [the United States] now has been delayed. We don't know why, but for now it's not on the table."[34] It almost seemed as though Bashar was being relegated to pariah status and isolated, à la Yasser Arafat in his Ramallah compound in the West Bank. It was a considerably lonely and disturbing period for Bashar, now excluded from the Middle East peace process and over a hundred thousand American troops next door in Iraq. And things would get worse.

On October 5, 2003, Israel launched an air strike against what it claimed was a Palestinian terrorist training camp at Ain Saheb just northwest of Damascus. It was the first Israeli strike in Syria itself in almost thirty years. The camp was apparently abandoned, although some sources claim it was being renovated for future use by the Popular Front for the Liberation of Palestine General Command, one of the Palestinian groups said to be supported by Syria. The attack was in retaliation for a Palestinian suicide bombing that killed twenty people in Haifa, Israel, the previous day carried out by Palestinian Islamic Jihad, another Palestinian group, along with Hamas, supported by Damascus. Dore Gold, one of Ariel Sharon's foreign-policy advisers, pronounced after the attack that "no one can strike Israel with impunity."[35] Syrian officials claimed the camp had been long abandoned and was, in any case, a civilian facility.

While dramatically venturing inside Syria, the Israelis knew the camp would be empty and apparently meant the attack to be mostly a symbolic albeit a strong and direct message to Asad to desist Syrian support for Palestinian groups carrying out suicide bombings against Israelis. Not only did it deliver a message to Damascus, but it also conveyed to a jittery Israeli public a strong response by an Israeli government that was having a difficult time stopping the Palestinian attacks. The Bush administration was conspicuously mute in its response, only saying that Israel "must not feel constrained" in defending itself; indeed, the general anti-Syrian tone adopted by a Congress on the precipice of convincingly passing the Syrian Accountability Act as well as an administration that had been consistently warning Syria in nebulous terms regarding its behavior no doubt emboldened the Israelis to believe that they could get away with the raid without American censure or opprobrium. Syria also could not muster up the necessary support in the United Nations for a resolution condemning Israel. The "old rules" of the game were definitely out the window.[36]

It is under these circumstances that Bashar tacked in the direction of openly advocating a resumption of peace negotiations with the Israelis—the regime finally completely understood that rather than the United States protecting Syria from Israel, it was now at least casting a blind eye toward, if not sanctioning, a more assertive Israeli policy. In any event, Syria was now basically surrounded by U.S. allies and friends: Iraq, Turkey (with whom Damascus had markedly improved its relationship by then), Israel, and Jordan. But would anyone be listening?

Bashar's first overt indication along these lines was an interview he gave to the *New York Times* on November 30, 2003. On the subject of negotiations with Israel and the Golan Heights, he said the following:

Some people say there are Syrian conditions, and my answer is no; we don't have Syrian conditions. What Syria says is this: negotiations should be resumed from the point at which they had stopped simply because we have achieved a great deal in these negotiations. If we don't say this, it means we want to go back to point zero in the peace process. This would also mean wasting a lot more time, and every day we waste more people are being killed and more violence erupts in the region.[37]

Recognizing that Syria's relations with the United States had been in a state of flux, he pointed to the coincidence of interests that both countries had in the region: "If you take the Israeli element out of the picture, I cannot see the difference between Syria and the U.S.; there are no differences between Syria and the United States about what we want to achieve in the region."[38] Bashar's response from the United States came in the form of the Bush administration's signing of the Syrian Accountability Act into law in December, although it would not be activated until May 2004. Israeli officials also responded coolly to Syria's peace overtures. Israeli officials were reportedly somewhat divided over how to respond to Bashar's olive branch, only agreeing that it was prompted by U.S. pressure on Damascus as well as the fall of the fellow Baathist regime of Saddam Hussein.[39] Ariel Sharon was certainly on the more cautious side, while some other Israeli ministers and military officials, including Finance Minister Benjamin Netanyahu and Foreign Minister Silvan Shalom, believed that it might be a mistake to rebuff Bashar at a time when Syria was in a relatively weak position, allowing Israel to strike a deal to its own advantage.[40] Sharon reportedly told a U.S. senator on his way from Israel to Damascus to inform Bashar that Israel was not interested in being the Syrian president's "springboard to the White House."[41] In other words, was Bashar serious about peace or was he just trying to relieve Syria of U.S. pressure. In addition, while the Sharon government was dealing with its announced intention to unilaterally withdraw from the Gaza Strip, it would, again, be overloading the Israeli public by simultaneously engaging in both tracks. There are those in Israel who just want to hang on to the Golan Heights for strategic reasons as long as possible, if not in perpetuity; indeed, Ariel Sharon, a military commander known for his commitment to holding the high ground strategically, would be hard-pressed by this fact alone to give up the Golan.

Maybe the Golan Heights would become a new Alexandretta for Syria, i.e. the sliver of territory along the northwest coast of Syria above Latakia that Turkey (which calls the area Hatay) received from France in 1939 as payment for remaining neutral in World War II. The longer it becomes part of the status quo the more the Syrians will reconcile themselves to the fact that they will never get the land back; considering the vehemence with which Syrians view the Golan issue, if, indeed, this time should ever come, it will be far into the future. Besides, many Israelis felt that they should just stay put and ride the new American posture *vis-à-vis* Syria to pressure Damascus to abandon its policies that are inimical to Israeli interests—why short-circuit U.S. pressure before it had run its course? The voices against reacting positively to the overture in Israel, however, outmatched those who wanted to explore it. Even so, reflecting divisions within the Israeli government over how to respond, Israeli President Moshe Katsav publicly offered to meet with Bashar personally in a place of Bashar's choosing in order to assess the prospects for peace.[42] Bashar was not about to accept the invitation given the fact that Anwar al-Sadat was so roundly criticized for his dramatic visit to Israel in 1977 without getting any guarantee of a return, i.e. he relinquished his most expensive bargaining chip—recognition—before the actual negotiations began. Regarding the invitation, Bashar said:

> It was like a maneuver because when I told the *New York Times* about peace, it created some discussion and controversy in Israel, and it was embarrassing to them. They said you should respond to President Asad. So Katsav said he would invite me, and if Asad says no, then it is just a line—he really does not want peace. But why go? Just to shake hands, have dinner? If you want peace, we have criteria, and you start by saying the Golan should be returned to Syria and you start negotiating.[43]

Bashar would continue to indicate publicly that he was ready to renew peace talks with Israel throughout the summer of 2004. In July he was quoted as telling UN Middle East envoy Terje Roed-Larsen that "we must find a mechanism to re-launch talks. Syria has not requested that any party be included in the roadmap because the Syrian track is based on [UN] Security Council resolutions and on the principle of land-for-peace."[44] Both Israeli and Syrian officials visited Ankara, Turkey, at the same time in July, fueling speculation that at least some third-party contact (through the Turks) might be possible.[45] The Israeli army chief of staff Lt. General Moshe Yaalon commented in August that Israel would be prepared to give up the Golan Heights in return for peace with Syria and that the IDF could defend Israel without the Golan. Israeli writers were warning that the current situation with Syria reminded them of that which existed prior to the 1973 Arab-Israeli war. Before then Sadat had been making peace overtures that had been ignored. Ultimately, even though he knew he could not win militarily, he chose to go to war with Israel to reactivate diplomacy at the very least—some believe that history, however unlikely, could be repeating itself with Bashar al-Asad if the Syrian president were to continue to be rebuffed, although Syria's military capability now is significantly less than what Egypt's was in 1973.[46]

After meeting with President Bashar in October 2004, former U.S. assistant secretary of state and ambassador to Israel Martin Indyk indicated that the Syrian president was offering to make peace with Israel and was ready to cooperate with the United States in stabilizing Iraq: "Something is going on in Syria and it is time for us to pay attention." He observed a "clear change" in

Syria's position, saying that Bashar had offered to hold talks with Israel without preconditions, whereas previously he had always insisted that the talks should begin where they left off during the Clinton administration. Indyk also stated that Bashar had dropped the demand that Israel reach an agreement with the Palestinians before resuming negotiations with Syria.[47] Former Democratic presidential nominee Senator John Kerry met with Bashar in Damascus for two hours in January 2005. After discussing a host of issues, Kerry remarked, "I leave here with a sense that we can improve our relationship. There are significant possibilities, particularly with the elections in Iraq and . . . in the West Bank. This is the moment of opportunity for the Middle East, for the U.S. and for the world. I hope that we would seize that opportunity." In response, the Syrian official news agency reported that Bashar stressed "the importance of dialogue between the two sides."[48]

In October 2004, Israeli Foreign Minister Silvan Shalom stated, "I think that peace with Syria is a strategic goal for the State of Israel . . . it would mean that all the countries we share a border with would be at peace with us and of course that would also make future negotiations with the Palestinians easier."[49] Shalom did add, however, that Syria must first stop aiding Palestinian militants and end its logistical assistance to Hizbollah, saying that "President Asad can't hold the stick from both sides . . . the seriousness of intentions will be proven if he acts on these issues."[50] There was some discussion in Israel regarding the idea of sanctioning a "regional agreement" that would negate altogether the idea of a Palestinian state, "which means abandoning the failed attempt to share the land with Arafat and his cohorts and a return to the solution of the 1948 truce agreements. Egypt will take the Gaza Strip, Jordan the West Bank and Syria the Golan Heights, and Israel will obtain stable agreements with the countries responsible in exchange for conceding territories."[51] There was even some speculation that secret negotiations had already begun between Israelis and Syrians. As Gabriel Ben-Dor, director of the University of Haifa's National Security Studies Center, stated:

> There have been persistent rumors that negotiations are going to be renewed, that the groundwork is being prepared very meticulously, or that talks might already have started surreptitiously . . . although this is unlikely to happen until after the U.S. [presidential] election. If the administration of President Bush survives, it is conceivable there might be a turn to the Syrian track because the situation with the Palestinians is a mess and the Americans, to counter criticism over Iraq, would probably like to demonstrate they have not given up on trying to bring peace and stability to the Middle East.[52]

While the Bush administration after its second-term election victory has gone in the other direction, i.e. tightening the screws even more on Syria, the fact that the Palestinian situation became infinitely more murky after the death of Yasser Arafat in November 2004 could have also led to a resuscitation of the Syrian track. As Yezid Sayigh writes:

> Yassir Arafat's personality and intentions will long be debated, but his death may not offer the widely trumpeted opportunity to reform Palestinian national politics and, crucially, relaunch the peace process. This is partly because his domestic legacy of patronage-based politics and bloated bureaucracy had time to solidify during his decade as president of the Palestinian Authority (PA) and will not be transcended easily. It is also because resumption of a credible peace process depends just as heavily on Israeli and US policy, neither of which gives cause for optimism.[53]

Overall, the Americans will assess whether or not the death of Arafat has actually created an opportunity for peace by removing one of the main obstacles to restarting negotiations from the policy perspectives of Bush and Sharon, or whether it will lead to a prolonged period of uncertainty, if not chaos, in the Palestinian movement that will only complicate the prospects for a resumption of talks in the foreseeable future. Sharon made several conciliatory moves to facilitate the Palestinian election that took place on January 9, 2005, including a stated willingness to begin negotiations with the new Palestinian leadership even if it has not terminated Palestinian terrorist attacks; therefore, this may indicate that Sharon might be willing to do the same with Syria with regard to Hizbollah and its alleged support of Palestinian groups—at the very least not adopting this same attitude toward Syria would appear to be inconsistent.[54] In addition, as Robert O. Freedman points out, from the perspective of Tel Aviv, being engaged with Syria in a peace process may alleviate fears of retribution against Israel through Hizbollah if Israeli leaders feel compelled to strike militarily at Iran's nuclear installations, as it is conjectured that Teheran is attempting to develop a nuclear capability. As such, Syria would have more to lose by unleashing Hizbollah to retaliate for Israeli actions in Iran than by restraining any retributive bent by the Lebanese Islamist group and remaining in ongoing peace negotiations.[55] As of this writing, however, the successful election of Mahmoud Abbas and his concerted action to rein in Palestinian attacks has combined with reciprocal responses from the Sharon government that have placed the Israeli-Palestinian track front and center again—and with the support and interest of the Bush administration. Reflecting a more pessimistic tone regarding a resumption of negotiations with Israel, Bashar told me in May 2005 that, "We do not have any peace negotiations. There is nothing, really, and I don't see any negotiations or peace in the near future because the Bush administration is not interested in it."[56]

Despite some of the positive signs during the summer of 2004, including better Syrian-U.S. cooperation regarding Iraq and reports that Syria was moving to expel Palestinian militants from the country, Israel maintained the pressure on Damascus.[57] After two Hamas suicide bombings in Beersheba that killed sixteen people on August 31, 2004, Israel publicly held Syria responsible. Raanan Gissin, a senior aide to Sharon, stated that "the fact that Hamas is operating from Syria will not grant it immunity."[58] In a possible retaliatory move, a Hamas mid-level official, Izz al-Din al-Shaykh Khalil, was assassinated in Damascus on September 26 in an explosion set off in or near his car. Israeli army chief of staff Moshe Yaalon had gone on record as saying that "anyone who is responsible for terrorism against us should not sleep quietly."[59] Although Israel did not explicitly claim responsibility for the assassination, it did nothing to deny it or dampen rumors that it carried out the attack. Apparently, this was the first time since Israel set up a spy ring in Egypt in the 1950s that such an operation had been successfully executed in an Arab country with which Israel was still embroiled in conflict.[60] Israel was obviously sending another message to Syria saying that it no longer enjoys immunity and that it must expel Palestinian militant groups—the new rules of the game were continuing to evolve. Syria responded by calling the assassination a "terrorist act that constitutes a dangerous development for which Israel bears responsibility."[61] An adviser to Syria's information minister, Ahmad Haj Ali, stated that "this is not the first warning Israel has tried to convey to Syria. What happened indicates that Israel's aggression has no limits."[62] Some in Syria believe that Israel carried out the attack in order to undermine budding improvement in U.S.-Syrian relations that emerged out of the Emile Lahoud fiasco in Lebanon and the need in Washington to secure the Syrian-Iraqi border from infiltration by insurgents.[63] Again, however, there was little Bashar could do in concrete terms—he could only utter angry and exasperated words. The fact that he was already under severe pressure from the United States as well as Europe for manipulating the extension of pro-Syrian Lebanese President Emile Lahoud's term in office by three years made it that much more difficult for the regime to react in an assertive fashion. It had to tread carefully. It appears as if the nature of Syria's involvement in any peace process would be determined as the outcome of factional in-fighting among competing foreign policy groups in Washington and in Israel.

Does Bashar Want Peace with Israel?

When talking extensively to Bashar on the subject, I come away with a clear sense that he does want peace, although he is certainly not yet ready to give up anything beyond what his father was prepared to give. The line that Bashar repeats over and over is that Syria will return to the negotiating table with Israel without conditions. This is always paired with comments about beginning any talks under the Madrid terms of reference, which strikes some as placing conditions on the negotiations. Damascus, however, does not want to start at square one again, a position he accuses the Israelis of adopting; in other words, the two sides should build upon the progress made in the 1990s and not start from scratch. Bashar said as much in his speech to the Syrian National Assembly on March 5, 2005.

Bashar's domestic political environment as well as the tense regional atmosphere, almost from the day he came to office, limited his flexibility in pursuing any peace initiatives *vis-à-vis* Israel, especially as the United States became more bellicose toward Damascus. If one of the reasons for pursuing peace with Israel was to get closer to Washington for economic and strategic concerns, then it did not make much sense to be forthcoming if the United States was adopting a more anti-Syrian posture regardless of what Bashar did or did not do. The pressure from the United States—and, importantly, even France in the Lahoud affair—may have convinced many in the regime that tacking toward a more cooperative stance was advisable. Amid reports in January 2005 regarding possible U.S. military strikes against Syrian targets, Foreign Minister Farouk al-Sharaa on January 24 invited Israel to renew contacts with Damascus, promising complete calm on the part of Syria in exchange for an Israeli withdrawal from the Golan Heights.[64] He also congratulated Mahmoud Abbas for his election victory on January 9 as the new Palestinian Authority president, adding that Syria would like to see progress in "other channels" as well, a reference to the fact that Damascus is leery of the Syrian-Israeli track being ignored or left behind while the Israeli-Palestinian track progresses. The offering of "calm" also suggests that Damascus is portraying itself as having influence over Palestinian militancy as well as, of course, Hizbollah, either or both of which could be utilized to disrupt any emerging Palestinian-Israeli rapprochement that has become an important foreign-policy objective of the Bush administration—again, these types of bargaining chips are as important to Bashar as they were to his father, and astutely utilized they could indeed prevent the diplomatic isolation of Syria on the Arab-Israeli front; however, indelicately employed they could just as easily lead to the further diplomatic isolation of Syria. In an attempt to break out of this isolation and acquire some international leverage, Bashar held a summit meeting with Russian President Vladimir Putin in late January 2005, the first state visit to Moscow by a Syrian head of state since 1999. One scholar mentioned to me that Bashar's trip reminded him of Gamal Abd al-Nasser's visit to Moscow in 1970 seeking protection from Israeli air strikes during the War of Attrition—in the former case, however, there are only threats circulating against Syria rather than actual military action. In addition, Russia seems to have placed renewed importance on its relationship with Damascus, as Putin himself stated, Russia plans to "use the Syrian route" to enhance its influence in the Middle East peace process.[65] Emblematic of this new stance, reports indicated that the Kremlin was prepared to do something it has been reluctant to do for over a decade despite persistent Syrian entreaties, i.e. write off most of the $12–13 billion cold war debt Damascus owes Moscow (while Russia would maintain its naval port—its only foreign naval outpost in the world—at Latakia). The *Kommersant* business daily in Moscow commented that "Russian diplomats hope that the young Syrian leader will help Moscow assume a respectable place in the Middle East and this way gain back its status as a world super-power."[66] With relations with the United States strained over Chechnya and the contested election in the Ukraine in late 2004, as well as a cooling of Moscow's ties with Israel over Russian support for the building of a nuclear reactor in Iran, the Kremlin's opposition to Israel's construction of a security fence/wall to separate itself and some settlements in the West Bank from Palestinian territory, and its efforts to reinvigorate the role of the so-called "quartet" in Middle East peacemaking, Putin has, in an almost cold war-like fashion, attempted to align his position closer to that of the European Union as well as former Soviet allies, first and foremost among them Syria.[67] Responding to U.S. and Israeli criticism over its planned sale of anti-aircraft missiles to Damascus, Russian Foreign Minister Sergei Ivanov stated that, "It is the United States that lists Syria as a sponsor of terrorism. Russia does not."[68] This has allowed Bashar to position himself closer to the center of international diplomacy and at times cultivate his more conciliatory position *vis-à-vis* Israel.

This new cooperative tone among some of the regime stalwarts seems to have temporarily brought them in line with Bashar's thinking on the Israeli front; in addition, it must be said that the international outcry as well as some negative feedback even from the Syrian public regarding the regime's actions in extending Lahoud's term may have convinced Bashar that he needed to listen to a new set of foreign policy advisers, new voices in the regime that are not entirely ensconced in the old paradigms that define the Arab-Israeli conflict. The Hariri assassination could accelerate this trend or reverse it.

Whatever the case, Syria's foreign policy in the coming years will be watched with great interest, especially as the country either is pitted against or develops a cooperative relationship with the Bush administration. Will only sticks be used against Syria or will there also be some carrots? Damascus believes it has really extended itself *vis-à-vis* American concerns, yet it has received very little, if anything, in return. This cannot go on indefinitely. Bashar needs to have something to show for the more moderate position he has adopted of late; if not, his position domestically will be that much more weakened, compelling him to tack in the direction of confrontation in order to shore up the base of his regime. In a way, it may be fortuitous for Bashar that a peace agreement with Israel was not consummated in the last days and months of his father's life; in this sense, he bought some more time against implementing dramatic change internally because of the continued regional tensions; most importantly, he may need the added legitimacy and credibility gained from a peace agreement that he himself has negotiated (as long as he is seen as not giving up too much), which he can then use as leverage for the economic and political reform he advocated in his inaugural speech. The dilemma for Bashar may be that Israel may only accept the type of peace that Sadat gave, including the type of public diplomacy at which neither he nor (especially) his father have been particularly adept. It seems, however, that Bashar is not being given any choice at all regarding what it will take to resume peace negotiations with Israel. U.S. and Israeli attentions are elsewhere, and that which has been given to Syria has not been particularly conducive to developing a conciliatory posture.

Chapter 8

Syria is Not Iraq

Syria and Iraq have had considerably less than amicable relations for most of the period since World War II. Both countries are products of the European mandate system, both play central roles in the development of Arab nationalism, and both claim a leadership position in the inter-Arab arena. It is little wonder, then, that the two developed more as rivals than as neighborly countries sharing a 400-mile (600-kilometer) border. Despite the centripetal forces of shared enmity against Israel, opposition to Western imperialism, the commonality of secular Baathist Arabism, and regional familiarity, the centrifugal forces of border and water-sharing disputes, Baathist ideological rivalry, and struggles for centrality in the Arab world more often than not separate rather than congeal the interests and objectives of the two countries.

The U.S.-led invasion of Iraq in 2003 that removed from power the Baathist regime of Saddam Hussein has placed Syria in an awkward and dangerous position *vis-à-vis* the United States. Bashar has had to balance competing interests in the face of the maelstrom of criticism and pressure from the Bush administration regarding Syria's purported role in aiding the insurgency fighting U.S. and coalition troops in Iraq. This situation has produced one of the most trying points to date in Bashar's presidency, primarily because it has brought Syria square into the cross hairs of elements in Washington who wish to effect regime change in Damascus. Bashar could very well emerge from this having learned valuable lessons about regional and international politics as well as gained much-needed diplomatic experience. But this is not school. This is the real thing. He could utilize the situation to improve his position domestically and even construct a new relationship with the United States. It could also easily lead to his removal from power.

Inter-Arab Politics

For most of the 1950s Iraq and Syria were constantly at odds with one another, with the former involved in a succession of schemes in the latter to help engineer the rise of like-minded regimes that would enhance Baghdad's overall position in the region. Before its 1958 revolution, Iraq was, at least officially, situated with the West in the emerging cold war in the Middle East. The regime in power in Baghdad was the pro-Western monarchy that had been placed there by the British after World War I. The pro-West Iraqi strongman at the time, Nuri al-Said, who resumed his position as premier in 1954, envisioned Iraq as the link between the Arab states, the non-Arab northern-tier countries bordering the Soviet Union, and the West, thus enhancing his country's status in all these spheres and making it indispensable as a military bulwark against the USSR and Israel. If successful, Iraq would have automatically reduced Egypt's (and Nasser's) status to that of a junior partner in the contest for Arab leadership. This is why Syria became the key to Iraq's success: if Egypt was able to wean Syria into its own camp, Iraq would be isolated in the Arab world. On the other hand, if Iraq was able to win over Syria (through an alliance or even possible union), Jordan and Lebanon would most likely follow, resulting in Egypt's isolation. The culmination of this effort resulted in the pro-West defense alliance called the Baghdad Pact (formally known as the Central Treaty Organization or CENTO), formed in 1955. This was a struggle Nasser would win—by leveraging the immense popularity in the Arab world that he acquired by surviving the tripartite invasion of Israel, France, and Great Britain in the 1956 Suez war, snatching political victory from the jaws of military defeat. He then set the tone of Arab nationalism (or more simply, "Nasserism"). By doing so he isolated Iraq, as no other Arab state deigned to join the Baghdad Pact. Nasser's sangfroid in the American-Syrian crisis of 1957 secured his assets in Syria, leading to the formal merger of Syria and Egypt in February 1958 into the United Arab Republic (UAR)—Iraq had lost this particular Arab cold war.[1]

The violent coup that overthrew the monarchy in Iraq in July 1958 seemed to portend a major turning point for Arab nationalism, coming so soon on the heels of the formation of the UAR. The new Iraqi leader, however, Abd al-Karim Qassim, emerged as more of an Iraqi nationalist than an Arab nationalist, and he soon displayed an independent bent that was considerably different from Nasser's. The vehemence of the rhetoric going back and forth between Cairo and Baghdad, when the two regimes on the surface appeared to be alike, exceeded that which had existed prior to the Iraqi revolution, when the two regimes appeared to be polar opposites. Syria itself, particularly the Baath party, was caught in the middle of this struggle, which Malcolm Kerr termed the "Arab cold war."[2] Syrians expected Iraq to join the UAR, but it chose not to do so. Qassim, with his Iraqi nationalist bent, and others in Iraq did not want to sacrifice their independence nor subordinate themselves to Nasser. The Baathists in Syria, then, had to wonder what they had given up their independence for, and in the case of the Baath, what had they given up their very existence for in the face of Nasser's domineering ways and reluctance to allow any other foci of power in the UAR. If the culmination of Arab nationalism meant only the union of two countries, then perhaps they needed to reconsider the situation. That they did, and the merger of Egypt and Syria proved to be anything but a good fit at a number of different levels. Syria seceded in September 1961.

The Baathist coups in Iraq and Syria in 1963 again seemed to augur a period of cooperation between Damascus and Baghdad; indeed, flush with excitement, the new Baathist Arab nationalist leaders spoke of integral union between the two countries, and they almost immediately flew off to Cairo to convince Nasser that now was the time to consummate the tripartite merger that would envelope the entire Arab world. Nasser, however, having learned his lesson with the UAR, played it very coyly, erecting such difficult conditions for an actual union that Syria and Iraq begged off the proposed venture and headed home amid mutual recriminations.

At an ideological level it seemed almost inevitable that two countries right next door to each other and with a history of competition in the inter-Arab arena would also struggle over which Baathist regime was more pure, steadfast, and uncompromising than the other. The Iraqi and Syrian regional branches of the Baath National Command morphed into vicious rivals, although, if truth be told, both Baathist leaderships evolved into entities that were far removed from the original ideological thrust of Baathism that espoused socialism, freedom from imperialism, and Arab unity. Baathism became chastened by the development of authoritarian single-party regimes—in 1968 in Iraq, with Hasan al-Bakr and Saddam Hussein coming to power, and in 1970 in Syria, with Hafiz al-Asad—as well as foreign policies that were dictated more by circumstance and pragmatism than by ideological purity. Iraq would send significant military contingents to help Syria in both the 1967 and 1973 Arab-Israeli wars, but this would not overcome the differences between Baghdad and Damascus that reared their heads whenever Arab-Israeli issues were not paramount. Bashar believes the primary difference between the two Baathist regimes is that Syria has institutions, while "in Iraq after Saddam came to power there was no Baath party, there were just people who were called Baathists—he killed the real Baathists and destroyed the party; no Baath party, just Saddam."[3]

Most point to the decision by Hafiz al-Asad to side with non-Arab Iran against Iraq in the 1980–1988 Iran–Iraq war as the outward manifestation of the differences between Baghdad and Damascus. However, there were clear signals of antagonism prior to this. On the surface, Syria and Iraq seemed to cooperate as they formed a combined front in the face of Egypt's negotiations with Israel at Camp David in September 1978. The two Arab League summit meetings convened to discuss Egypt's portending departure from the Arab fold—one after Camp David, the other in March 1979 amid the signing of the Egyptian-Israeli peace treaty—were held in Baghdad, clearly signaling Saddam Hussein's intent to fill the vacuum of power in the Arab world created by Egypt's peace treaty with Israel. Below the surface, this made Hafiz al-Asad increasingly wary.[4] But never are differences revealed more than when two parties are closest together, and the brief entente between Syria and Iraq was but a distant memory by the summer of 1979. It was then, when Saddam Hussein formally became president of Iraq in July, that the animus came out into the open. Saddam immediately convened a Baath party regional congress meeting, at which scores of high-level Iraqis were openly accused of plotting against the regime. They were removed from the conference meeting, and many of them were summarily executed. The Iraqis quietly accused Syria of backing the plotters, although a majority of the condemned were Shiite Muslims, long suspected by the Sunni Arab ruling clique in Iraq as something of a fifth column in the country even though they make up about 55 to 60 percent of Iraq's population. The incident contributed to the souring of Iraqi-Syrian relations, thus making any real possibility of an alliance or union even more remote than it already was.

As surveyed in chapter three, Hafiz al-Asad took the rather unusual step of siding with non-Arab Iran against its Arab brethren and fellow-Baathist neighbor in the eight-year-long Iran–Iraq war; and again, for primarily pragmatic strategic reasons and economic necessity, the Syrian president swam against the tide by joining the U.S.-led UN coalition in 1990/1991 that evicted Iraq from Kuwait in the Gulf war. By default a weakened—and less dangerous—Iraq improved Syria's strategic position in the region. Ever a believer in a strong eastern front to contain Israel, Hafiz continued to develop Syria's relationship with Iran. Although this tacit alliance with Teheran associated Damascus with a country considered to be a pariah or rogue state in the eyes of Washington and many European capitals, Hafiz was able to utilize the relationship to enhance his strategic position in Lebanon via Hizbollah, contain a resurgent Iraq if necessary, broaden his strategic depth *vis-à-vis* Israel, acquire some leverage as a conduit to Teheran, especially from the point of view of the Arab states in the Persian Gulf, and obtain cheap oil (and boatloads of tourists) from Iran. Bashar describes Syria's relationship with Iraq before the fall of Saddam as

> full of conflict, many conflicts. We had a honeymoon period around 1978 before he [Saddam] came to power, and we improved our relations for a time. But he first got rid of Hasan al-Bakr and then he accused Syria of conspiring with many of his officials, and he got rid of them. So we then began a period of very bad relations, and he was responsible. All of Syria, not only myself, believe he was a very bad leader.[5]

Syrian-Iraqi Rapprochement

There was no love lost between Iraq and Syria, or, for that matter, between Saddam Hussein and Hafiz al-Asad, but perceived necessity can eliminate hesitation and reluctance. With the UN sanctions in place against Iraq following the Gulf war, Iraq's military decimated, and two-thirds of the country overflown by American, British, and French aircraft, by the late 1990s Iraq ceased to be a serious strategic threat to Syria. The economic opening in Syria and its attempts to attract foreign investment in the 1990s had not panned out as well as it was hoped, all of this amid record-low oil prices for a country that was producing about 600,000 barrels per day. If it were not for the grants and investment by grateful Arab countries in the Persian Gulf for its participation in the Gulf war, Syria would have been in even more dire economic straits beyond the stagnant growth it was already experiencing. Under these conditions, Asad began to see Iraq as a potential economic palliative, especially an Iraq that was desperately seeking ways to raise hard currency apart from the blanket of the UN sanctions regime. By 1997, Asad was exploring avenues of economic cooperation with Baghdad. He did this at first through fairly low-level official contacts, especially as Damascus wanted to keep such interaction as low-key as possible since it did not want to run afoul of the United States while the prospects of regaining the Golan Heights was still a possibility; however, with the hardline Netanyahu government in power in Israel, Asad probably believed he was not risking too much anyway by that point. These contacts would continue, and eventually they would be raised to much higher levels as the Syrian-Israeli track unraveled by early 2000.

In the first year of Bashar's tenure in office, Syria and Iraq reopened their borders, eliminated visa requirements, signed various agreements on transport and communications, and increased bilateral trade. This, of course, benefited the Syrian economy in a direct and immediate fashion, and Damascus also began to carve out a stake in the Iraqi economy before the UN sanctions regime arrayed against Baghdad came to a close, which at the time seemed to be a very real possibility, as countries such as France and Russia were pushing for the lifting of the sanctions regime in order to take advantage of their own economic investment in Iraq. In this sense, Syria would not be left out in the cold regarding the potential regional economic bonanza that a rebuilding of Iraq could provide. Since the United Nations did not have monitors in Syria at the time, Iraq viewed the enhanced trade and cooperation with Damascus as a way to undermine and circumvent the sanctions while acquiring much-needed hard currency, products, and equipment.[6]

Iraqi Vice President Taha Yasin Ramadan and Syrian Prime Minister Muhammad Mustafa Miro signed a tariff reduction accord on January 31, 2001, to reduce and gradually eliminate a number of trade restrictions between the two countries. The Syrian Arab News Agency called the accord "a starting point towards turning over a new leaf in Syrian-Iraqi cooperation."[7] Each of the two countries also agreed to de-escalate the usual level of vitriolic rhetoric aimed at the other as well as crack down on dissident groups that had until then been tolerated and supported by the respective governments in attempts to undermine the other. There were also some reports of military cooperation, or at least plans to improve strategic cooperation and even some military equipment sales. For Syria, with the situation continuing to deteriorate with Israel, acquiring more strategic depth became an additional reason to explore better relations with Baghdad.

The most controversial decision made by Bashar al-Asad regarding Iraq has been to reopen in late 2000 a 500-mile oil pipeline that runs from the oil fields in Kirkuk in northern Iraq to the Syrian port of Baniyas, transporting approximately 150,000 to 200,000 barrels of oil per day in apparent contravention of the UN sanctions against Iraq. Syria purchased the Iraqi oil at a discount price of about $10–$15 per barrel for domestic consumption and then exported its own oil at (higher) market prices, thus pocketing the difference. Partly as a result of this, Syria's GDP rose precipitously by 5.9 percent in 2001.[8] The United States, desperately trying to keep the sanctions regime in place in the face of pressure from other countries in the United Nations, began to take serious notice of the opening of the pipeline, to the point where Secretary of State Colin Powell visited Damascus in early 2001 to inquire as to the nature of the pipeline and reportedly won Bashar's agreement to allow UN monitors to keep tabs on it. Most consider Syria's explanation for all of this disingenuous. The regime contends that it was testing an old pipeline from Iraq and for this purpose simply bought the oil that was already in the pipeline. Regarding Powell's visit and U.S. accusations against Syria that it was violating international sanctions, President Bashar said the following:

About the oil, we talked about this with Mr. Powell, and we told the Iraqi government that we are going to use it [the pipeline] because it is a very old facility and it needs maintenance, so we used it and tested it, but what are we going to do with the oil [that was presumably already in the pipeline]? Well, we are not going to send it back! Maybe from the Iraqi point of view they see it as bribing the Syrians—that's OK, we will take the oil [laughter]. But we are going to build another pipeline [from Iraq], but if you want us to put it under UN resolutions we want preferential treatment, like Turkey has. If it is like Turkey, then we will do it. Powell asked me three times this question, and he didn't do anything, so we kept using that pipeline, which actually wasn't a very good one. The quantity was limited and we had lots of problems with it. We are negotiating with the French and the Russians to build a new one.[9]

One report somewhat supports Bashar's explanation. Relying on Lebanese journalist Ibrahim Hamidi's piece in *Al-Hayat*, this report states that Hamidi "explained that there was a misunderstanding between Washington and Damascus, because Secretary of State Powell mistakenly understood from President Assad that Syria intends to include the existing oil pipeline in the framework of the UN resolutions, while the Syrian president referred to the new pipeline it plans to lay down."[10] The Bush administration, however, never really bought the explanation that the Syrians were simply "testing" the old pipeline; it believed that Damascus was playing a kind of shell game, thinking the United States might continue to look the other way because of Syria's assistance *vis-à-vis* al-Qaida. Perhaps from Bashar's perspective, the ability to close down the pipeline, if in fact it was being utilized in the way Washington believed, could be used as a bargaining chip to be cashed in at some future date on some other issue, maybe continued tolerance of Syria's position in Lebanon—all the while, Syria would gain economic benefit from the oil while also skimming off some goodwill domestically and in the Arab world for "helping" the trampled Iraqi people suffering under punitive UN sanctions. For Bashar, the benefits economically and politically of deepening Syria's relationship with Iraq outweighed the potential costs—especially as it seemed from Damascus as if there would be very little, if any, cost. In any event, oil from Iraq was being shipped illegally—usually overland via trucks—through Turkey and Jordan, two U.S. allies, yet Washington had been looking the other way on those two fronts. From the viewpoint of Damascus, Syria was not doing anything beyond what other countries on the border of Iraq were doing, except that Syria was not a U.S. ally.

On the other hand Syria, despite severe reservations, did vote for UN Security Council Resolution 1441, passed on November 8, 2002, which cited

Iraq as remaining in "material breach" of its obligations and authorized the return there of UN inspectors.[11] Bashar said that Syria voted for the resolution because he thought it would delay the war by giving the inspectors a chance. He was fairly certain that there were no WMD in Iraq, if only the inspectors had the time to complete their investigations. The Syrians, because of their commercial relations with Iraqi entities, the close ties they have with common tribal elements in Iraq, and the numerous exiled Iraqi Baathists in Syria, as well as from their own intelligence, were apparently convinced the Iraqis had gotten rid of their WMD. Bashar agrees with those who contend that if the United States had allowed the inspectors more time, the pretext for war would have dissipated if not disappeared altogether, since no WMD would have been discovered. This back and forth relationship with Iraq and its effects on Syria's relationship with the United States reflected the ambiguity in Washington regarding Syria. There were still the fluctuating arguments championing engagement or confrontation *vis-à-vis* Syria. That is, until the United States invaded Iraq in April 2003.

The War in Iraq—Confrontation with the United States

The Syrians were shocked at how easily the regime of Saddam Hussein fell. It appears as though they expected the Iraqis to put up a stiffer fight that would make the United States think twice about extending the Bush doctrine elsewhere in the region. As it was, American forces steamrolled to Baghdad. The sleek make-up and rapid methodology of U.S. forces in doing so, however, contributed to the difficulties the United States experienced in the post-war environment in terms of stabilizing Iraq and dealing with a lethal insurgency. The Syrian leadership also may have expected the Baath leadership in Iraq to remain intact in some form or fashion even if Saddam Hussein was removed from power. The relative early decision by the U.S. occupation authorities for the "de-Baathification" of Iraq was not a welcome sight in Damascus—the Syrian regime did not want to be the last Baathist outpost on the planet, especially when the term "Baath" itself had become associated with such negative connotations in U.S. policymaking circles. The bottom line is that Syria did not want to see U.S. forces in Iraq for any substantial length of time. Moreover, it was imperative in Damascus that the application of the Bush doctrine in Iraq fail, or at least run into such problems as to make its application elsewhere—such as in Syria—questionable logic at best in Washington, even among the neo-conservatives pushing for the extension of American power toward Iran and Syria amid the immediate afterglow of military victory.

The threats aimed at Syria from Washington, and even London, started to mount during and immediately after the conflict.[12] British Foreign Secretary Jack Straw stated on April 14, 2003, that "now the new reality in the Middle East is that Saddam has gone . . . but that carries with it its own imperatives, and it is crucial that no country in the region harbors fugitives of Saddam's entourage, nor allows itself to be a sponsor of terrorism."[13] This was a clear warning to Damascus. Syria was being accused on an almost daily basis of allowing armed groups and individuals to cross the border into Iraq during and after the war to fight coalition forces; there were also unsubstantiated reports that Syria was harboring members of Saddam's ruling clique as well as stashing weapons of mass destruction that coalition forces had been unable to find in Iraq. Although offering no evidence, on April 13 President Bush explicitly stated that he believed Iraqi officials had been offered safe haven in Syria and that the United States "believes there are chemical weapons in Syria."[14] Syria has consistently denied the allegations, saying that the accusations were misinformation intended to divert attention away from the growing postwar problems of coalition forces in Iraq; Damascus also challenged the United States, demanding proof of such activities rather than just rumor and hyperbole. As it turns out, Charles Duelfer, the head of the former Iraq Survey Group (ISG) and the Bush administration's senior weapons inspector, stated in a report released on April 25, 2005, that "it was unlikely that an official transfer of WMD material from Iraq to Syria took place. However, ISG was unable to rule out unofficial movement of limited WMD-related materials."[15] Despite the vitriol of Straw's initial statement, he stated in the April 14, 2003 news conference that "as far as Syria being next on the list [for application of the Bush doctrine], we made it clear that it is not."[16] British Prime Minister Tony Blair spoke directly with Bashar at about the same time and Straw met with Syrian Foreign Minister Farouk al-Sharaa on April 11. Despite strong British support for the war in Iraq, London maintained its links with Damascus and urged the engagement rather than confrontation approach, as had most of Europe. The European Union foreign policy chief Javier Solana urged Washington to tone down its harsh statements regarding Syria: "The region is going though a very difficult process and I think it would be better to make constructive statements to see if we can cool down the situation in the region."[17]

These more reassuring words from European capitals may have assuaged some of Syria's fears, but the regime may not have adequately understood how little influence the Europeans, even the British, had over the direction of U.S. foreign policy, especially an ideologically driven administration, many elements of which were clearly emboldened at that moment by their apparent success in Iraq. Administration officials were appearing on a host of television talk shows maintaining the pressure on Syria. U.S. Secretary of Defense Donald Rumsfeld stated in a television interview that Syria had bussed fighters into Iraq, but they were beaten back by coalition forces, and he commented that there was "no question" that members of Saddam's regime had fled to Syria.[18] Even Colin Powell's normally more moderate State Department view had hardened—in an interview with the BBC he said that

Syria has been a concern for a long period of time. We have designated Syria for years as a state that sponsors terrorism. Now that the regime is gone in Baghdad, we hope that Syria will understand there is an opportunity for a better way for them if they would stop supporting terrorist activities and make sure they are not a source of weapons of mass destruction . . . for terrorist organizations or anyone else.[19]

Israeli Foreign Minister Silvan Shalom chimed in by saying terror organizations acting from within Syria "must be stopped. We know what kind of role Syria is taking in letting terror organizations increase their activities, but unfortunately they're not doing anything to prevent it from stopping. More than that, they are encouraging all of this."[20] Syrian ambassador to the United States Dr. Imad Moustapha, who at the time was deputy chief of mission, appeared on "Meet the Press" countering the claims of U.S. officials, saying they were only intended to shift attention away from the chaos in Iraq, and he referred to two articles in the *Washington Times* saying that General Richard Myers, chairman of the Joint Chiefs of Staff, said he had never seen movement of weapons of mass destruction from Iraq to Syria or in the other direction, and that Syria had been cooperating with the CIA in combating terrorism.[21]

A high-level American diplomat in Syria at the time of the war in Iraq suggests that yes, indeed, Syria was sending materiel to Iraq, but that Bashar did not authorize it; if anything, he was looking the other way. Some of Bashar's inner circle, probably in the military-security apparatus, made a "killing" with contraband shipped to Iraq, particularly a cousin of Bashar's in the republican guard, Dhu Himma al-Shalish, who has been described as highly corrupt and heavily involved in smuggling items in and out of Iraq.[22] Bashar apparently knows in general terms that this stuff was going on, but it is not regime policy. This is in accord with what others have said, i.e. that corruption in Syria, while less widespread than in the past, seems to be more blatant and concentrated in the hands of a few regime stalwarts and Asad relatives. Syrian experts have stated that the illicit contraband trade with Syria is something Bashar's father would not have permitted, because it would have run against his national security policy. According to some regime insiders, Bashar apparently was quite frustrated over all of this, that in a sense he *had* to cast a blind eye toward these activities. This clearly indicates that he has yet to develop the power base and legitimacy that his father enjoyed that would have allowed him to act more forcefully in this regard; his apologists say that he has been in office for only about five years amid tumultuous regional conditions, but his detractors say that this is a prime example of either his weakness or his deviousness. Bashar's supporters have said that he has yet to experience the stable regional and domestic environment that would enable him to nudge aside corrupt relatives, regime stalwarts, and fellow Alawites on whom he now reluctantly has to depend in such dire circumstances. Sources in Damascus at the time claimed that both sons of Saddam Hussein, Uday and Qusay, made their way to Syria after the war but were forced out of the country and back into Iraq at Bashar's insistence when U.S. pressure mounted amid the stark fact that American tanks were only about 150 miles from Damascus. If true, this indicates that Bashar does have a measure of authority to act on issues that are of immediate importance. It seems as though Bashar has to pick and choose when and where he will engage in forceful leadership and when and where he feels compelled to relent to powerful elements in the regime. It is a careful balancing act at the moment, one that has to be played on multiple fronts: Lebanon, Israel, and the United States.

Colin Powell visited Damascus in May 2003 and had a heart-to-heart discussion with Bashar regarding the continued porous border with Iraq as well as the closing down of the offices of Hamas, Palestinian Islamic Jihad, and the PFLP-GC in Syria. Bashar seemed to offer a level of compliance, stating that Syria was trying the best it could; but in June, Powell said that Syria had only taken limited steps to shut down the offices, describing Syrian overall efforts as "totally inadequate."[23] The fact that Colin Powell was the one saying these things had to make the Syrian regime stand up and take notice that the U.S.-Syrian relationship had clearly shifted. The Syrian response regarding infiltration into Iraq is that the border is too long (400 miles) to control tightly, and the regime often refers to the difficulties that U.S. authorities have in controlling its own border with Mexico. Considering Syrian limitations militarily in equipment, skilled personnel, and funding, this is anything but an outlandish rationalization on the part of Damascus, one that has been consistently articulated by the Syrians, most recently in Bashar's March 5, 2005, speech to the National Assembly. As Bashar told me in May 2005, "even if we had soldiers every ten miles, people could get through the borders, slipping through the gaps or even through bribing some of the soldiers."[24] U.S. officials believe, however, that even with this, the Syrians were less than enthusiastic in going the extra mile to secure the border for at least a year after the war ended. At the very least, tacit support for the Iraqi resistance was popular in the Arab street.

Fortunately from the point of view of Damascus, the Americans began to get bogged down in Iraq. U.S. forces were generally not welcomed with open arms, especially as basic infrastructure needs were not met in the expected manner; security and stability deteriorated in most parts of the country, and Iraqi exiles tended to dominate the local American-controlled political structure to the exclusion of indigenous elements. The premature disbanding of the Iraqi army and the de-Baathification process added to the ranks of the angry and disaffected, who over the course of time seemed to team up with an amalgam of former members of the Sunni ruling clique under Saddam and foreign jihadists exploiting the chaotic opportunities to attack the United States. They rallied more disillusioned youth throughout the Muslim world to their cause, as well as Iraqi nationalists who would oppose an occupation force of any size, shape, or color. Bashar could take a deep sigh of relief. As long as the United States was ensconced in the deepening quagmire in Iraq, the less enthusiasm and ability it would have to widen the neo-conservative agenda toward Syria. Bashar tried to walk a fine line: he wanted the Bush doctrine to fail in Iraq but he could not be seen to be actively promoting its failure by openly assisting the Iraqis—to be blunt, he did not want to anger the United States too much. On the other hand, he also wanted to send a distinct message to Washington that Syria could do to the United States in Iraq something similar to what it had done to U.S. forces in Lebanon in the 1980s. In that case, the conflict ended with the ignominious departure of American troops in early 1984 amid a broken down and divided country left open to Syrian designs. He at least had to have plausible deniability, however, which was a given since there was not much he could have done at the time anyhow to crack down on elements in Syria that were close to the regime. From the point of view of Washington, however, this meant one of two things: either Bashar was a conniving despot trying to manipulate the situation at the cost of American lives, or he was powerless to comply with American demands.

In essence, since Bashar was not yet able to crack down on the porous Syrian border or those elements linked with the regime behind the exchanges and associations with Iraqi insurgents, he would have to mold the existing situation in a way that might provide him with some leverage *vis-à-vis* the Bush administration, especially as the latter, in a presidential election year, was desperately searching for ways to stem the insurgency in Iraq and reduce American casualties. In return for more cooperation in Iraq, maybe the United States would again acquiesce in Syria's presence in Lebanon and intercede to restart negotiations with the Israelis. If this is in fact what Bashar was doing, it was a dangerous game to play, particularly with a U.S. administration that was less than amiably disposed toward him and his regime and more at the ready to utilize military force to achieve political aims. Maybe, then, Bashar was not the naïve, untested, and inexperienced young president some in the United States were making him out to be; maybe he was, as his father was wont to do, utilizing all of his assets in a critical situation to survive. Not that every step of the way was carefully choreographed—far from it; but the analytical side of this young man, the aspect of his being that led him to pursue and love ophthalmology, where one diagnoses and treats all of the varied, complicated parts of the whole toward a successful resolution, was becoming more and more apparent.

There is little doubt the Syrians were trying to complicate things for the United States in Iraq, inconspicuous as their actions were. It must be said, nonetheless, that even if Syria was the most compliant, helpful country on the planet for the United States, the situation in Iraq would not have been appreciably different.[25] In other words, Syrian influence on the situation in Iraq was marginal, but from the point of view of Damascus, that slim margin might have been the difference between regime survival and joining Saddam and his cohorts in the ash-heap of history. By the spring/summer of 2004, then, Syria could be more cooperative, even in the face of the implementation of the Syrian Accountability Act in May. By then it was in Syria's interests to have a stable Iraq next door. It was also in its interests to position itself as a friendly neighbor, the better to establish (or reestablish) the economic and business links it had begun to construct in the late 1990s as well as to form a working relationship at the political level. Damascus still wants the United States presence in Iraq to be minimized, but it also does not want Iraq to break apart into its constituent parts. This would not be an unlikely occurrence in the least considering the fact that Iraq was stitched together to begin with by the British after World War I, made up as it was of a largely Sunni Kurdish north centered around Kirkuk and Mosul, a Sunni Arab center based in Baghdad, and a Shiite Arab south based around Basra and the Shiite religious centers of Najaf and Karbala. Syria has its own ethnic and religious cleavages, and having one state—Lebanon—violently break down into its own constituent parts for almost a generation was proof positive that it did not want to see the same thing happen on its eastern border. In addition, the break-up of Iraq could potentially arouse minorities in Syria to agitate for outright independence, a possibility brought home by the Kurdish nationalist riots in eastern Syria in March 2004, certainly motivated by the enhanced autonomy of the Kurds in Iraq. Interestingly, the government-controlled Syrian media even denounced

Western plans floating around calling for a confederated Iraq as designs to undermine Arab unity—it should remain whole with a viable and strong central government.[26]

Syria and the New Iraq

Bashar repeatedly declared his commitment to a sovereign and stable Iraq. For example, on an official visit to Kuwait, Bashar pointed out that a Radio Damascus portrayal of the Iraqi interim government as a "US puppet" did not reflect the official position of his government.[27] The culmination of this rapprochement between Syria and Iraq occurred on July 26, 2004, when Iraq's Interim Prime Minister Iyad Allawi paid a visit to Damascus and met with Bashar. There he secured promises of cooperation on security issues as well as ways to improve economic contacts. Allawi stated that "it is clear that our visit here is the beginning of a bright chapter in relations between our two brotherly peoples. We are opening a new page with Syria"—which is eerily reminiscent of Syria's claims of "turning a new leaf" with Iraq soon after Bashar came to power.[28] Syrian and Iraqi officials after the visit announced that diplomatic relations, broken in 1980 with Syria's backing of Iran in the Iran–Iraq war, would soon be restored. Asad and Allawi agreed to form a committee to improve security along their common border, and the Iraqi prime minister stated that "he provided valuable information to our Syrian brothers about militants misusing the Syrian hospitality to bring chaos to Iraq."[29] An agreement was also reached in principle regarding the estimated $500 million to $1 billion of frozen Iraqi assets in Syrian banks since the fall of Saddam— Syria stated that it would return the money to Iraq when there is a legitimate Iraqi government. On this point, the United States has also been pressuring Damascus.

The developing Syrian-Iraqi-American dynamic came to a head during the successful attempt by Damascus to extend pro-Syrian Lebanese President Emile Lahoud's term, contrary to constitutional mandate, by three years. This was a mistake by Bashar, one that even a number of high-level Syrian officials have admitted to. Bashar and his foreign-policy advisers seem to have seriously misjudged the regional and international outcry over the incident. Even France, the European country with whom Syria enjoys the closest ties and a country that had been at odds with Washington over the war in Iraq, cosponsored UN Security Council Resolution 1559 passed on September 2, condemning the actions and calling upon "all remaining foreign forces to withdraw from Lebanon" and for the "extension of the control of the Government of Lebanon over all Lebanese territory." Clearly Bashar did not want the issue of Lebanon to be placed on the agenda of the United Nations Security Council, with a resolution passed, and with an associated mechanism to periodically check and report on Syrian compliance with the resolution. UN Secretary-General Kofi Annan reported on October 1 that Syria had not complied with the resolution. Again, they underestimated the staying power and lingering ideological influence of the neo-conservatives and the right-wing Christian evangelicals on the Bush administration. The emerging debacle in Iraq had not discredited them as much as many people had thought, and the Lahoud affair gave them fodder to bash Syria on a silver platter, resuscitating the momentum that anti-Syrian forces in Washington had with the passage and implementation of the Syrian Accountability Act. One of the chief proponents of the act, Representative Ileana Ros-Lehtinen (R-FL), said in late October that she was confident the Bush administration would support a request she made with Representative Eliot Engel (D-NY and one of the sponsors of the Syrian Accountability Act) to freeze the assets of Lebanese officials with close ties to Syria who "have flagrantly and unabashedly cooperated with the Syrian regime in maintaining its control over Lebanon."[30]

During this foreign policy fiasco, Bashar realized his mistake and may have learned from it. He began to listen to some different voices in the foreign-policymaking apparatus that were in no uncertain terms informing him of the repercussions of the error. This may or may not signal a change in foreign policy direction in the near future—time will tell. But for now Bashar was forced to cash in his chips. All of a sudden he indicated a more assertive willingness to cooperate with the Bush administration on the issue that was important only a few months ahead of the election: sealing off the Syrian-Iraqi border.

In September 2004, Assistant Secretary of State for Near East Affairs William Burns met with Bashar in Damascus, and, importantly, he brought with him some non-neo-conservative officials from the Pentagon to seriously discuss the border situation and the means with which to improve it. Deputy Secretary of State Richard Armitage soon followed the path to Damascus. Both were pleased with the talks and indicated progress had been made. State Department spokesman Richard Boucher stated that

> the Syrians did agree to take specific actions in coordination with Iraqi and multinational forces. These steps are designed to close Syria's border to individuals seeking to foment violence and destabilize Iraq. It is essential now that these steps be translated into action on the ground, and we will measure the Syrian commitment to the stability of Iraq by the concrete steps that it takes.[31]

Bashar had told Burns in their meeting that Damascus attached "great importance" to helping the Iraqi people restore their stability and preserve their
national unity.[32]

As mentioned previously, Colin Powell subsequently met with Farouk al-
Sharaa at the UN General Assembly meeting later in the month, whereupon
he stated that he sensed "a new attitude from the Syrians."[33] Reportedly
President Bashar sent a short personal note hand-delivered to President Bush
at this time, conveying positive words regarding further cooperation between
the two countries. From most accounts since this series of meetings and discussions in September, Syria has, indeed, been trying much harder to seal the
border and cooperate with American forces.[34] Syria took steps to enhance
its border guard as well as rebuild dunes and fences marking off the border
crossings that had fallen into disrepair.

Damascus has repeatedly challenged the Bush administration to produce
evidence of Syrian complicity in allowing foreign fighters into Iraq, but it has
received none officially. Bashar informed a U.S. delegation that met with him
in May 2004 that "We have asked the Americans to give us one name, one
passport. So far, we haven't received anything. We are waiting for evidence."[35]
According to Theodore Kattouf, former U.S. ambassador to Syria (September
5, 2001–August 23, 2003), the United States should have engaged Syria at a
military-to-military level even before the war, so that Syria would be well
aware of U.S. capabilities and how they had improved since the 1991 Gulf war.
This also would have established a pattern of interaction and cooperation at
the military level that would have proved invaluable during and after the war.
Apparently the military brass at the Pentagon supported this. However, the
civilian leadership at the Pentagon killed the idea—for ideological reasons the
United States wasted a year and a half of occupation of Iraq without engaging
the Syrians.[36]

It is interesting to note President Bashar's rather prescient take on the
course of the war in Iraq, again suggesting that he has a much better grasp of
regional affairs than popularly perceived. Although exaggerating the numbers
for effect, as early as October 2002 he was saying:

> You cannot change the regime without killing millions of Iraqis. Our con-
> cern is about entering the unknown. Even the United States does not know
> how a war in Iraq is going to end. There is no justification for a U.S. war on
> Iraq, it would kill millions of people and plunge the whole Middle East into
> uncertainty . . . the political effects are impossible to predict. I believe this
> kind of division would affect the whole region. . . . The whole region has
> similar religious and ethnic divisions.[37]

Dr. Imad Moustapha recounts the following:

> We told them [U.S. officials] everything regarding WMD in Iraq, the sup-
> posed tie with al-Qaida, etc., and our analysis was there at every meeting
> and it is in the minutes of every meeting, that their analysis of the situation
> was far from reality, that if they invade Iraq they will end up in a messy sit-
> uation, they will inflame Iraq and the region. And you see this today. At the
> time they were so scornful of our analysis, they felt we were just bullshit-
> ting. Every single thing we told them before they invaded has become a
> reality. Bashar said this to me a month ago—he said, you know how we
> always thought things would be the way they are now in Iraq? But he was
> still astonished at how accurate our analysis was of the situation. We told
> them, don't believe those who are misleading you, but they did not heed
> our advice; on the contrary, they accused us of misleading *them*.[38]

On Syria's cooperation with the United States on the border issues since
September 2004, Ambassador Imad states that

> Sometimes we do things we are not very happy about, but we need to do
> them because we need to be wise. And we need to keep channels open with
> this administration. They keep sending us messages on how important it is
> for Syria to cooperate with the new Iraqi government, and we do this not
> because the administration asked us to do this, but because our strategy is
> if Allawi claims it is a sovereign government, we say, "why not?" We will
> help them become a sovereign government. We do not believe he has a sov-
> ereign government, but we do not say this. What we say is that we believe
> you and we will help you become more and more sovereign, and this is our
> political objective today in Syria. And this is what the Americans want, so
> in a way this has made the bitterness to our opposition to the occupation
> of Iraq recede somewhat.[39]

This cooperative attitude extended to Syria's participation in an international conference in Sharm al-Shaykh, Egypt, on November 22 and 23, 2004,
to discuss a number of issues related to Iraq's future. The meeting brought
together the foreign ministers of Iraq's neighbors (including Farouk al-
Sharaa), the Group of Eight industrialized countries, China, the European
Union, the United Nations, and the Arab League. It represented the first real
attempt to coordinate international policy on Iraq since the overthrow of
Saddam Hussein. Iraq's foreign minister, Hoshyar Zebari, believed the meeting was designed to reassure Iran and Syria that U.S. forces in Iraq had "no

hidden agenda to attack neighbors," indicating that "cooperation on Iraq may not be sustainable without a broader and friendlier dialogue between these two governments and Washington."[40] The fact that Syria and Iran were included, with Colin Powell meeting with both the Syrian and (informally) the Iranian foreign ministers, was a very positive sign for Damascus. It indicated that Washington needed assistance *vis-à-vis* Iraq. The meeting also provided a forum for the Arab participants to reiterate to the rest of the world that progress in Iraq must also be matched with progress on the Palestinian-Israeli situation, especially with a possible window of opportunity in the wake of the death of Yasser Arafat.

There were again reports, however, in December 2004 from U.S. military intelligence officials that the Iraqi insurgency was being directed to a greater degree from Syria than previously recognized. Former loyalists of Saddam Hussein were reported to have found sanctuary in Syria and be channeling money raised in Europe and in the Middle East and other support to the insurgents.[41] General George Casey, the U.S. commander in Iraq, accused Damascus of harboring senior Baath party officials who were "operating out of Syria with impunity and providing direction for and financing the insurgency. That needs to stop."[42] In early January 2005 the Bush administration reportedly was considering imposing new sanctions on Syria to prod it to crack down on elements providing financial and logistical support for Iraq insurgents.[43] U.S. officials, including a "stern warning" from Deputy Secretary of State Richard Armitage in an early January visit to Damascus, reasserted the claim that the Syrian government was not doing enough against a network of Iraqis that included several close relatives of Saddam Hussein as well as his former number-two man Izzat Ibrahim, who officials purport has frequently traveled back and forth between Syria and Iraq.[44]

The episode with Saddam's half brother, Sabawi Ibrahim al-Hassan al-Tikriti (discussed briefly in Chapter Six) is interesting in this regard. According to a number of sources, including Bashar al-Asad, when Assistant Secretary of State William Burns and officials from the CIA and Pentagon met with the Syrian president in September 2004, Burns handed Bashar a list of eight names the United States believed to be leading Iraqi insurgents in Syria—the Bush administration wanted them turned over to U.S. and/or Iraqi authorities in order to see if Syria would match words with deeds. According to Bashar as well as the Syrian ambassador to the United States, Imad Moustapha (who was present at the meeting), Burns remarked that it was a positive discussion, but that there were powerful enemies of Syria in Washington and even in the U.S. delegation in Damascus at that time who wanted nothing more than to prove that Syria was not cooperating. Syrian officials agreed that they should not give these "enemies" any excuse to sanction more aggressive action; therefore, Syria would cooperate regarding the list. There appeared to be some consternation in Washington by December when there had been no action on the list, especially with the January 30 election in Iraq looming—the Bush administration wanted to reap the benefits of capturing leading insurgents to use as propaganda ahead of the election. Despite the "stern warning" delivered by Armitage on his visit to Damascus in early January 2005, Bashar described the meeting with the State Department's number two as very positive. Apparently a decision on Syria in the State Department was close to being made, especially with the new secretary of state, Condoleeza Rice, soon to take office: either Syria was going to be cooperative or not, and if it was not, then the U.S. line would get significantly tougher toward Damascus. Bashar mentioned that Syria had already made the decision to support the Iraqi elections since it was in their national interest to do so, and had set up polling booths for Iraqis in Syria and was allowing them to campaign openly for candidates.

However, he told Armitage that U.S. intelligence regarding the list of eight was faulty. According to Syrian sources, of the eight on the list, two had lived in Syria for thirty years, were in their seventies, powerless and had actually opposed Saddam Hussein, as most Iraqis in Syria. Another had already been apprehended in Jordan, one had been declared dead in Iraq, two other names the Syrians had never heard of and didn't know if they were in Syria or not, and one was in Yemen. The only one on the list that was known to be in Syria and was tied to the insurgency was Sabawi. Armitage informed Bashar that the United States needed a "scalp," i.e. Syria had to physically turn in Sabawi. According to Bashar, the U.S. felt that Syria did not act fast enough in apprehending Sabawi, thus reinforcing views in the Bush administration that Syria would not cooperate. Eventually the tribe that was hiding Sabawi sold him and over twenty of his cohorts to the regime but this took time, and it was not until late February that he and his supporters were turned over to Iraqi authorities. It also took time because Bashar did not want to inflame opinion in Syria or in Iraq against Damascus by doing something that would be unpopular on the Arab street. The delay, however, proved critical, for in the interim the Hariri assassination occurred, adding more fuel to the growing frustration in Washington over Syria. The turnover of Sabawi now seemed to be a Syrian concession following the fallout from the Hariri assassination rather than part of any budding U.S.-Syrian intelligence cooperation *vis-à-vis* Iraqi insurgents. Damascus received no credit; the tide had already turned against Syria in the Bush administration, exemplified by President Bush's inclusion of Syria in his State of the Union address, an attack that was replicated in speeches by other administration officials in the months to come.[45] The confusion in Damascus during this period was personified in the letter from the State Department to the Syrian regime explaining why it was recalling its ambassador to Syria following the Hariri assassination. While the world saw it as the U.S. response to the killing, according to Bashar, the letter did not even mention Hariri—it was totally about Syria's inability to deliver Sabawi on time.

While not accusing the Syrian government of directly aiding Iraqi insurgents and acknowledging that the anti-American insurgency would "continue to thrive" without assistance from Syria, U.S. officials were pondering the application of sanctions beyond that which had already been implemented by the Syrian Accountability Act, particularly in the financial arena under the purview of the Department of Treasury, aimed at alleged money-laundering activities by the Commercial Bank of Syria regarding illegal Iraqi funds diverted from the UN oil-for-food program.[46] Then Iraqi President Ghazi al-Yawar and Jordan's King Abdullah both expressed concerns about Syria's role in interviews to the *Washington Post*, Yawar commenting that "there are people in Syria who are bad guys, who are fugitives of the law and who are Saddam remnants who are trying to bring the vicious dictatorship of Saddam back. . . . They are not minding their business or living a private life. They are . . . disturbing or undermining our political process."[47] Only a month and a half ahead of the important elections in Iraq on January 30, 2005, to select a constituent assembly tasked to write a new Iraqi constitution, it seemed that Washington again was applying pressure on Damascus to do its utmost to dampen an insurgency that threatened the legitimacy of the election process. Official estimates put the number of Iraqis in Syria at 45,000, while unofficially the number is inflated up to 1 million. One must remember, however, that while "Iraqi Baathists in Syria" has become a provocative phrase, many if not most of these Iraqi Baathists opposed the regime of Saddam Hussein—that is the main reason they are in Syria in the first place, i.e. they had fled or were exiled from Iraq and were, indeed, more often than not working with Syrian intelligence to undermine Saddam (which is also why, as Bashar indicated, albeit *ex post facto*, Syria could have provided a great deal of accurate information to U.S. sources prior to the Iraq war). Having said this, even though many of these Iraqi Baathists are anti-Saddam, almost all of them sympathize with and have supported the Iraqi insurgency out of kinship and nationalistic feeling. However, they have done so on an individual and ad hoc basis, as many have acknowledged that the regime in Damascus has clamped down on efforts inside Syria to recruit Iraqi insurgents and discouraged public demonstrations of sympathy for those fighting against U.S. forces in Iraq, although some suggest this has been done more as an eye toward controlling the flow rather than actually stopping it.[48]

In addition, new PLO chairman Mahmoud Abbas visited Damascus in early December seeking Syrian reassurances that the country would not interfere in the January 9, 2005, election to choose a replacement for Palestinian Authority President Yasser Arafat. With the potential of a new round of Palestinian-Israeli negotiations leaving Damascus out in the cold (after all, Bush did state in December that "Asad needs to wait: first peace between Israel and Palestine, and then we'll see what to do with Syria"), Syrian officials were trying to reiterate that there should be coordination between the Palestinians and the Syrians, including linking the Palestinian issue to Syria's position in Lebanon.[49] In fact, the rumored possible air strikes against Syria floating about in Washington circles by mid-January may have been as much an attempt to intimidate Damascus into ceasing its support for Palestinian attacks in Israel during a delicate time following the election of Mahmoud Abbas as an attempt to warn Damascus to do more to stop the insurgents prior to the January 30 election in Iraq.

In response to U.S. accusations, Foreign Minister Farouk al-Sharaa stated that "Syria is interested in Iraq's future and security because it is part of Syria's security and what some media is saying of misinformation is fiction and baseless."[50] He later stated in an interview with CNN on January 24 that if anti-American insurgents "cross any bordering state to Iraq, it is against the will of the government of Syria . . . we are not friendly even with them because this is not the right way to help the Iraqis."[51] Added to this, Syrians point to King Abdullah of Jordan's so-called "Crescent of Shiism" speech, in which he posited that Syria was indeed working to stabilize the situation in Iraq because the anticipated Shiite victory at the polls on January 30 would create a Shiite crescent from Iraq to Syria and Lebanon (remembering that the Alawites are a schismatic Shiite sect). It is true that the United States did not intend for this to happen at the beginning of the Iraq war, but now it has settled on this as the only viable outcome in Iraq, ergo Syrian and American interests coincide in this respect—or so goes the Jordanian monarch's theory.

While Washington seems to be intent on ratcheting up the pressure on Syria, if not isolating the country altogether, Damascus seeks to utilize any leverage it might have as something it could offer the United States to push Washington to persuade Israel that restarting negotiations on the Golan Heights is in everyone's best interests. As long as Bashar can receive this type of quid pro quo, he can move on the Iraqi front and those elements in and outside the regime that have been facilitating cross-border activity. The dual messages being sent to Damascus in early December 2004 on both the Iraqi and Palestinian fronts reinforce Syria's potential centrality to overall Middle East stability, but they also have the potential of placing Syria in the cross hairs of Washington (and Israel) if Bashar is not careful. Where there is opportunity, there is also danger. Bashar cannot be seen making concessions without something tangible in return, and so far Washington has been offering lots of sticks but very few carrots. But the back and forth emanations and lack of policy coherence from Washington regarding Syria have been tremendously confusing to Damascus. The ambiguous policy of the Bush administration was captured in Powell's summation of his meeting with Sharaa at the November conference: "The Syrians have taken some steps recently [on Iraq] but we think there is a lot more they can do."[52] The American-Syrian "dance" on Iraq is likely to continue in the foreseeable future as long as the insurgency remains potent and/or the Israeli-Syrian track lies fallow. The ambiguity, however, in U.S. policy toward Syria has lessened in the aftermath of the Hariri assassination. Unfortunately for Damascus, it is not in the direction it had wanted and hoped for. Indeed, it has reached the point that a *Washington Post* article in June 2005 on U.S. plans to halt the spread of WMD, in which a Syrian goverment research facility was named by the Bush administration as a culprit, commented that, "With the naming of a Syrian facility, Damascus, which is suspected of providing cover for insurgents in Iraq and targeting political foes in Lebanon, could take the place once reserved for Iraq alongside North Korea and Iran as members of what Bush referred to as an 'axis of evil.'"[53]

Chapter 9

"The raw material is the brain"

The covered suq in Aleppo is one of the great sites to visit in Syria. Across from the majestic Mamluk citadel perched at the center of town, the suq evokes memories of centuries gone by. The hawking by the workers in the stores, the smell of spices, fruits, nuts, and fresh vegetables permeate the narrow corridors. The antiques, both genuine and campy, are available to gaze upon and purchase after a heavy dose of bargaining, as are the everyday products of life that interest only the locals. One day in 1998, Bashar visited the covered suq. He was in Aleppo to attend a conference sponsored by the Syrian Computer Society. He entered the suq, as is his way, with only his driver and one bodyguard. In a Middle Eastern suq, word travels fast about potential customers, whether it is a big spender or a dignitary. Soon enough, news got around that the son of the president was mulling about the suq, and it did not take long for a crowd of people to surround him, pressing against one another just to catch a glimpse of the man who would be president.

To escape the growing mass of people, Bashar randomly slipped into a small shop just to catch his breath. To say the least, the family running the shop was shocked and delighted that fortune had bestowed upon them such an honor. The son of the owner of the shop got out a napkin to wipe away the sweat beading down Bashar's face—the suq can be an awfully hot, stagnant place in normal circumstances; in a crowd it can be positively boiling. The son was about to press the napkin to Bashar's brow, when, all of sudden, Bashar noticed what was going on and exclaimed, "No, I will do it myself—we are about the same age." Thanking him for his kindness, Bashar asked the son if he needed anything, if he could be of any assistance to his family. The son said that all he wanted was to learn how to use a computer—as with most Syrians, they could not even afford to have one to begin with.

The next day Bashar gave instructions to the head of the Syrian Computer Society in Aleppo, Dr. Ghias Barakat, at the time chair of the English language department at the University of Aleppo who would become a member of the

Baath party Regional Command in charge of higher education policy, to make sure this person received the computer and printer Bashar was arranging to give the family. Ghias delivered the computer equipment in person, and the son cried when he received it. The son came to see Ghias the next day to again offer effusive thanks, but he also said that he did not know what to do with the equipment or how to set it up. So Ghias arranged to have the computer set up in the shop—on top of the computer the son placed a picture of Bashar alongside the Syrian flag. The next day, the son called Ghias saying he did not know how to operate the computer and asked if he could receive some guidance. Ghias then registered him for free in a computer course at the University of Aleppo.[1]

This story reflects Bashar in many ways. It is not a case of him grandstanding nor is it an isolated incident. Bashar has been the type of person who has wanted to help people his entire life, not only because he can be a compassionate man, but also because he knows he has the means to do so. It is also a story reflective of Syria. The country is similar to the son in the store in the suq. It wants to get better, to modernize. But it does not yet really know how. You can import all of the trappings of modernization and the façade of progress, but unless the people themselves have the mindset, philosophy, and skill to utilize and sustain it, the country will remain in a stagnant economic, cultural, and political condition. As Bashar commented to me: "The Arabs have achieved nothing, and they are behind. All they have is their history. Look at India, China, even Brazil. It is more than just having a computer. We need much more than that. We need to know how to creatively use them."[2]

Changing the Way Syrians Think

There are many who believe that Bashar is devoid of a vision for his country, that he does not have a serious plan to improve the economic and political environment through change. Without this vision, Syria will just muddle along, taking a step here and there in terms of progress—oftentimes associated with two steps backward—but implementing nothing in the systemic fashion necessary to really improve conditions in the country. A leading critic of the regime, Ammar Abd al-Hamid, an impressive writer and social analyst, wrote the following:

> This is the story of a little regime that thought it could—that is, deal with a changing world using the same old set of worn-out ploys and policies and actually get away with it. This is also the story of a regime which is beginning to realize, perhaps a little too late, that it actually couldn't—and therefore engaging in a furtive and desperate attempt at reinventing itself.[3]

In a speech to the Brookings Institution in Washington, DC, commenting on Bashar, Ammar also said:

> The President lacks a reformist vision. Because of this he focuses his energies on maintaining consensus among competing interests within the regime. But the regime is composed of many semi-autonomous institutions and the absence of a strong central authority has encouraged fragmentation within the system and the independence of local actors. For example, smuggling is rife because local authorities keep borders relatively porous in an effort to secure financial rewards. . . . The problem is further compounded by the government's failure to recruit new voices. There exists a pressing need for a new vision yet the current officials are unlikely to provide the leadership necessary for such a comprehensive change.[4]

Maybe it is just wishful thinking for a country that has so much potential yet is still so far from reaching it, but there are still those, including myself, who firmly believe that under the leadership of Bashar al-Asad, this could be the "little regime" that can. As opposed to almost everyone who has not had the opportunity to spend a good bit of time with him as well as those who just outright condemn the regime and/or are disappointed in it, I believe that while Bashar may not be a visionary per se—not yet, at least—he does indeed have a vision for the future of his country. What Bashar is attempting to do is nothing less than change Syria's operational philosophy, to restructure the Syrian mindset in business, politics, and culture. Education and human resource development are perhaps his two overarching goals at the moment, as he tries to create a critical mass of the skilled that will pay dividends down the road—what he wants is a society where everyone will know how to set up a computer, turn it on, and operate it. Unfortunately, this type of change is incremental and barely perceptible to the outside observer, thus lending credence to claims that he has yet to really achieve anything (or even try to do so). Maybe this is all Bashar could do up to this point—peck away at the edges, plan for the long term. He does not yet have the support base to implement anything but incremental change, as the "status quo beneficiaries" still are able to resist, if not block, dramatic reform measures.[5] This is where there is a disconnect that is continuing to retard his efforts: the gap between vision and implementation. As Bashar commented, "We have lots of ideas, but we do not know how to implement them. We issue laws, but we do not implement them. I issue a decree and the government should implement it, but now I have to follow up on everything all the time."[6] According to an International Crisis Group report in February 2004 that was based on Damascus University research, there have been over 1,900 decrees, laws, and orders signed by Bashar since 2000, yet only a handful have been implemented.[7] The regime has hired an American consulting firm to help restructure the government to make it more efficient, including the institution of the presidency. As some have stated, Syria has a presidency without presidential institutions. Bashar agreed with this, saying, "that's true, because in the past in Syria the president only attended to politics, especially foreign policy, and was not involved in internal issues such as the economy. I am the first one to be involved in that, so I need more of a structure, and we really need it now because we have never had these many changes before."[8] One of the changes a number of Syrian officials would like to see is for Bashar to have a regular set of advisers with whom he can discuss various important issues and to acquaint himself with the pros and cons of a particular problem or policy initiative. Too often he hears someone representing one side, and then he later holds a meeting with someone advocating an alternative point of view, rather than have a robust discussion with both perspectives being articulated at the same time in more of a debate format. The implication is that Bashar is sometimes swayed by the last person with whom he meets or by someone who is close to and has influence with him. He has to be careful, however, not to implement change that will seriously disrupt Syrian society and/or sacrifice depth of reform for expediency. One senses a race against time for Bashar because the honeymoon with the Syrian public for the sake of continuity and stability upon the death of his father is wearing thin—for some, indeed, it has already worn out. People want to see tangible progress, but as Bashar told me, you cannot drive an old, broken-down car very fast.

But first things first: the country has to go to class before it can collectively move to the next level, and it is in educational reform where Bashar has exerted the most effort to date, and with good reason. As Ammar Abd al-Hamid explained, "the indigenous resources in Syria are not good. There is not enough skill in Syria to bring about change—there is an intellectual deficit."[9] Of course, the Arab Human Development Report (AHDR) issued originally in 2002 under the auspices of the UN Development Programme found, *inter alia*, this "knowledge" deficit to be widespread in the Arab world.[10] When I asked about this, Bashar robustly agreed with the AHDR and admitted that it held especially true in Syria. In fact, this is why the Ministry of Expatriates in Syria has such a large portfolio these days—they need to bring back to the country all of those doctors, engineers, and other creative minds who were educated in the West and then decided to stay there. This is also why, to his credit, Bashar, much more so than his father did, has brought in assistance from the outside to help reform various aspects of society, such as British advisers in the banking industry and French advisers in the judiciary branch.

One of the mantras emanating from the regime has been what Bashar has called the "golden triangle." He wants to clean up the country, which is rife with corruption, nepotism, and incompetence, and so he has been emphasizing three things in terms of the hiring of staff in all areas of society: integrity/honesty, merit, and experience. Bashar wants people in the various ministries who will implement his vision, and, maybe most importantly, he needs people in the Baath party leadership who want reform instead of stifling it. His vision regarding education in the country is not only to modernize it but also to make it more independent, efficient, and self-sustaining, as well as less corrupt. Of course, all of this takes time, especially considering, as has been already emphasized, the ossified, corrupt, inefficient, and dilapidated condition of things he inherited, including the moribund educational system. As Bashar said on one occasion in an interview with Reuters, "Having a vision does not mean you can accomplish it within a day or a year . . . we have a long way to go and a lot of work to do. We are definitely moving forward. Not fast, but with the necessary speed."[11]

Typical of the inadequate coverage of events in Syria and of Bashar's efforts was the reporting in Israel and the West regarding a decision taken in May 2003 by the Syrian Ministry of Education to change the color of school uniforms at the elementary and high-school-equivalent level. Students were to shed their military-style look for that which more resembles what students wear in parochial schools in the United States. The Israeli daily, *Haaretz*, in what appeared to me to be sarcastic tone, wrote:

> An incredible revolution is taking place in Syria. Last week the Syrian Education Ministry was ordered to change the elementary school uniform from khaki to other colors, mainly dark and light blue. This instruction has already been subject to "profound" commentaries, suggesting the first signs of a ripening liberalization in Syria. "Inside sources" reported that the Syrian administration is even considering canceling the military training lessons in elementary schools. Colin Powell, who visited Damascus on Friday, must have been deeply impressed by the upheaval there.[12]

Newspaper reports and commentaries in the United States on the same subject tended to echo these sentiments, reflecting the fact that most people simply do not understand what is going on in Syria. It is also emblematic of politically conformist coverage in the U.S. rotating around accepted convention. The fact of the matter is that, as the *Washington Post* adroitly recognized, what is going on in Syria "is part of an effort to reverse the long tradition of militarism in their society."[13] It is something much more profound than a simple exchange of one fashion design for another. It is an attempt to alter a mentality, deeply embedded in Syrian society, namely the antagonistic attitude that supported and was exploited by the Syrian regime under Hafiz al-Asad *vis-à-vis* Israel, the United States, and anyone else who was considered the enemy.

Reforming the education system is clearly a priority in Syria, and Bashar knows there needs to be a great deal of development. He told me, "We developed in stages: in the 1970s, we had to make horizontal extension to make many more people educated, even just to read, but sometimes when you expand horizontally you lose quality. We extended education to the populace but we lost quality. Now we are in the process of improving vertically." He told me of the necessity of having competent people in the Ministry of Education, and he discussed how important it is to develop teachers and then construct a program of education. For that purpose a group of Syrians visited Europe and the United States to collect information in order to put a plan together:

> You have to have teachers who are specialized for certain age groups and are properly qualified with a diploma. Then we have to teach the student how to analyze and how to extract information and not for the teacher to just provide you with the information. Also, we need to teach people how to work as a team. A one-man show will not work, and it is not very well organized. How to organize, how to analyze, and how to create are important for the students to learn.[14]

I chatted extensively at the Baath party headquarters in Damascus with Dr. Ghias Barakat, at the time a member of the Baath Regional Command. He is one of the guiding forces in the reform of education in Syria, especially at university level. In his office, Dr. Ghias showed me the higher-education committee report that outlines the recommendations by the Baath party Regional Command for reform of the higher education system. It is a very thick document—a comprehensive review that we surveyed practically line by line. The plan emphasizes the encouragement of research as one of the main objectives of higher education, calling for the "modification of these laws and systems so that they assure they be updated to recent development and changes in science and technology in the world."[15] According to the Arab Human Development Report Index published in 2002 by the UN Development Programme, as a percentage of the GDP, Syria spent only 0.2 percent on research and development expenditure, compared with 6.3 percent for Jordan.[16] The Baath committee report recommended that the higher education system be "decentralized," that the "universities should enjoy more autonomy," and that the "faculties and departments should be given more of a role and more authority." It warned that textbooks should not be the only source of information, calling on universities to add reference materials, databases, and other compendiums of information to diversify the sources available to students. In fact, it bluntly stated that the existing textbooks, particularly in the sciences, are outdated, calling for new ones that do not "restrict the students."[17]

The committee report also advocates a "reconsideration of admission policy" in universities. Admission was free and practically guaranteed, but now universities should "associate such policy with development plans and societal and market needs, and take into account the capacity [student capacity] of faculties and departments. Criteria for admission should not be restricted to grades obtained at the baccalaureate [high school] level." The report calls for additional admission criteria such as placement tests, interviews, recommendations, and the examination of the scores of students in specific subjects rather than just a consideration of their overall grades. Dr. Hani Murtada, Syria's minister of higher education, who is one of a number of cabinet ministers who are not members of the Baath party, stated that one goal of the new admissions policy is to reduce the preferential treatment accorded Baath party members. Traditionally, 25 percent of university admissions were reserved for Baath party cadres whose test scores did not meet university standards. Murtada would like to cut this down to ten percent over the next year and eliminate the quota altogether soon after that.[18]

Educational reform requires money, however, a perpetual problem in developing countries that have over the decades tended to redirect capital toward more immediate, grandiose projects rather than investing in the long term. This is especially the case in socialist and/or state capitalist countries who as part of the social compact with their respective populations— intended in part to funnel off potential discontent—have provided free education filling their universities beyond the brim with students without the commensurate government investment, most of the latter earmarked toward heavy industry and manufacturing projects designed to raise employment levels and move traditional agrarian societies to an industrial footing. Unfortunately, in almost every instance, including in Syria, this import-substituting industrialization did not work, leading to a suffocating public sector, foreign exchange problems, rising unemployment and underemployment, inefficient industries, and usually a hefty external debt.[19] As the committee report recognizes, "the budget is barely enough to develop universities, and the universities do not have the right to generate income, therefore they rely completely on what the government provides."

According to the UN Human Development Report, the expenditure on education in Syria stood at an average of 11.1 percent of total government expenditure during the years 1999 to 2001, while it was at 17.3 percent in 1990, a 35 percent drop in ten years. The spending as a percentage of GDP has remained stable, which means that a significant rise in total government spending has occurred but with very little if any of these funds redirected toward education. A clear demonstration of this "misappropriation" of budget allocation was detailed in the World Health Organization's *World Health Report 2000*, in which it was stated that the southeast Asian country of Burma spent over 200 percent more on military expenditure than on health and education combined. The only countries with a worse ratio at the time were Iraq and Syria.[20] Bashar is attempting to correct this trend without gutting politically sensitive and sacrosanct government expenditures; perhaps the oil pipeline deal with Iraq, whether or not it was an illegal contravention of international sanctions, can be seen more clearly in this light. The university system in Syria—which has until recently been comprised of four state universities (University of Damascus, University of Aleppo, al-Baath University in Homs, and Tishreen University in Latakia), together totaling over 225,000 students and an array of vocational institutions—receives only 3 percent of the national budget. They keep asking for more, but it is not allocated; therefore, the system has to find ways to create local income for universities so that they can generate some funds on their own. As long as there is still an official state of war with Israel, 130,000 or so Americans troops next door in Iraq, and a top-heavy military-security apparatus, there is not much left in the national budget to be allocated to more productive enterprises.

To address this funding problem, the committee report urged an increase in the higher education budget, but also recommended the following:

1) Make the university system more "self-financing."
2) Transform the universities into productive institutions and launch programs that deal with in-service training programs for public and private sector entities.
3) Reconsider the policy of free education, especially for those who fail— possibly reward only those with good grades with free education.
4) Allow the state universities to accept Arab and other foreign students by charging fees. There are now about 9,000 foreign students studying at Syria's state universities, by far most of them from other Arab countries.
5) Increase fees for dormitories (currently about 25 Syrian pounds per month, which at current exchange rates is about 50 U.S. cents). Annual fees

to universities are currently $10 per year; the government is trying to raise this to $20 per year. This is not much, but it is a small step toward eventually charging tuition even at the state universities.

6) Encourage private enterprises to provide scholarships for students and/or to university programs.

7) Change the laws of finance in the government to allow universities to benefit from the money universities generate themselves.

One of the ways the government is trying to maintain its educational reach to the public while raising funds for the system itself—or at least making certain programs self-sustaining—is by the establishment of what are called Open Learning Centers (OLC) attached to the universities and vocational institutions. These are akin to Continuing Education programs in the United States, mostly held on college campuses but drawing a diverse crowd of students as well as adults. There are currently about 40,000 students in the Open Learning Centers in Syria. The classes are mostly held on weekends and in the evenings, but the difference is that the students must pay to attend these classes. Although new laws have been passed to double their monthly salaries, the traditionally low-salaried university professors in Syria actually can make more money by teaching in the Open Learning Centers than in their regular university position. As such, many are using these opportunities to supplement their relatively meager incomes. The most popular class at these centers by far is English. I visited one OLC English class on a weekend visiting al-Baath University in Homs, and there were at least 300 students in the class, with many sitting in the aisles and on the floor at the back and along the sides of the theater-style lecture hall.[21]

Most important in terms of providing a higher-quality education, and one of Bashar's major accomplishments to date, has been the creation of four private universities in Syria. They are housed in temporary buildings in the towns in which they are located, and none are in major cities, the idea being to extend educational opportunities into the rural areas. There are plans for about ten to fifteen more private universities. The cost is about $3,000 per student, and the universities vary in size; the one at Kalamoun, for instance, located between Damascus and Homs, has about 1,500 students. Private industrial interests and corporations build the universities, using the shareholder methodology to provide the initial investment; for instance, a friend of mine bought $500 of shares in Kalamoun University, and he estimates that in about three years his investment may be worth $5,000. The private universities apparently have considerable autonomy, and they can draw on staff from the state universities, who are allowed to teach at both for the time being. Dr.

Yasser Hourieh, the president of al-Baath University, believes that the private universities will create competition for staff and students and will force the state universities to improve—one hopes that this will indeed be the case.

There is an air of excitement in the field of education in Syria. As Dr. Yasser stated, "President Bashar has pumped new blood into the veins of the country. The country is no longer monotone, it is multicolor." The president has thrown his weight behind the reforms, and he is personally interested in their progress. And, as opposed to other areas of reform in the country, there doesn't seem to be any resistance from an "old guard" or other status quo elements in Syrian society. The tangible improvements in education are a hint of what could happen in Syria if everyone gets on the same page and when the full authority of the president is brought to bear. Not surprisingly, considering Bashar's background, the number of computers at all institutions of learning has increased exponentially. Just at al-Baath University in the five years that Bashar has been in office, the number of computers has increased from 40 to 1,400. This is even more than at many American colleges, but Syrian officials are quick to point out that they have to have that many because, unlike American students, the vast majority of Syrian students cannot afford to have a computer at home—they have to use those that are on campus. In addition, Bashar initiated the process that led to the establishment of the Syrian Virtual University located in the Ministry of Higher Education building in Damascus. It is a distance learning program that allows students to enroll in U.S. and other foreign universities without leaving the country.

Real progress is being made in Syria in education, contrary to what is popularly portrayed, and it is primarily due to Bashar's leadership and vision in this area. As Dr. Ghias Barakat stated, "Without President Bashar we could not even think of these reforms because he is supporting them and following up on them."[22] So it goes beyond the military uniforms; indeed, the regime wants to replace entirely the military training subject that students at the high school and university levels engage in one day per week.[23] In its place, Bashar would rather the students take computer science, music, language, art, etc. The regime wants to demilitarize the universities, and although this was announced soon after Saddam Hussein fell from power in April 2003, I saw in the committee report that this idea had been germinating for at least two years prior to the war. It might be said that the war in Iraq spurred the regime in Damascus to accelerate this change for cosmetic purposes, but it just reflects a systemic shift in philosophy in the educational system in Syria. Bashar also eliminated the requirement that students be members of the Baath party in order to participate in campus politics, dropping the "national culture" classes at university level which, as Joshua Landis points out, "formed the backbone of Baathi indoctrination for university students."[24] This is an attempt by Bashar to broaden the foundation of politics and education beyond the monopolistic grasp of the Baath party, and, again, in a way that will have more long-term rather than immediate results.

The bottom line is to make the university system work for the betterment of the country, particularly the economy. Bashar sees an intimate link between economic reform and transformation of the Syrian educational system. He wants institutions of higher learning to offer programs in banking, finance, and other subjects that will help Syria's economy as well as its efforts to integrate itself into the global market and become a part of the globalization process rather than watching it from the sidelines. The educational system must serve society's needs and the needs of the individual rather than exist as an autonomic right of passage.

Syria's Economic Development

While Bashar has made some inroads educationally in Syria, politically there has been very limited progress. Barring his premature removal from power by internal or external means, the economy is what will determine the long-term success or failure of Bashar's tenure. Here, thus far, progress has been a mixed bag at best and disappointing at worst. The problem is that Bashar cannot afford for much longer a disappointing economic performance. Economic reforms at both the micro and macro levels are desperately needed; otherwise, the country will just muddle along as it has been, from one crisis to another, vainly hoping that it can leverage these crises into economic gain to sustain the country—and the regime—for a little while longer, much as Hafiz al-Asad's timely participation in the 1991 Gulf war literally kept the economy afloat for another decade from Arab Gulf largesse and enhanced commercial interaction with the West. But those days have largely receded from view, particularly with American economic sanctions imposed on the country.

At worst, the country could implode, with regime instability leading to a potential civil war among Syria's varied ethnicities and religious sects, with radical Islamist groups waiting in the wings to assert themselves as the political, social, and economic environment deteriorates. Despite the effectiveness of Hafiz al-Asad's ruthless actions at Hama in 1982, this is not as far-fetched as it would seem, even in a country as staunchly secular as Syria, at least at the official level. The anger fueled by the war in Iraq and its aftermath, the continuing Israeli-Palestinian conflict, and the slow pace of internal reform have aroused an Islamic revival of sorts; reflecting trends throughout the Arab Middle East, more people are attending the mosque, more women are donning the veil, more religious leaders are advocating jihad and resistance, and even moderate Islamists are advocating an Islamic democracy modeled after that which exists currently in Turkey.[25] As one Syrian analyst commented, "There is very obviously a more populist militant Islam growing in Syria. You can never know whether this energy is going to be turned against the regime or the Americans. For the moment, events in the region and the humiliation felt by people mean that the anger is turned at the Americans."[26] Another commentator, from Aleppo, which has turned into a hotbed for a more virulent, *salafist* brand of Islamic militancy in Syria, said,

> The regime has propped up benign Islamists it keeps under its control for two reasons. One is to silence internal demands for reform and justify the continued clampdown because of the threat of Islamists as well as outside threats, such as from the United States. Syria also wants to show the world, including the US, that if the current regime crumbles, it will be replaced by those Islamists.[27]

The regime may be correct, and this may in part account for the delicate balancing act in its stance toward Iraq and Israel *vis-à-vis* its relations with the United States. Everyone is clear in Syrian officialdom that economic reform is necessary. It is no longer a question of if, but when. This does not mean, however, that everyone agrees on the methodology or the pace of reform, for the status quo interests remain a heavy anchor on the regime.

Bashar's inauguration speech certainly indicated that the economy was the immediate priority—as well it should be. In the speech, Bashar mentioned that the "other domains" in society "did not keep up with the excellent political performance," a clear reference to the less than satisfactory state of the economy. He recalls that Syria's infrastructure was largely built up in the 1970s and 1980s, and with it were created many opportunities in the public sector, accounting for approximately 20 percent of the workforce. This was of necessity and was "a temporary good, but you cannot build an economy in this way. In the 1990s we started thinking about supporting the private sector, but with the changes in the world [a reference to globalization], we are stumbling. We tried to develop but we have some bad ideas."[28] Syria has economic potential, and it has a long history of being a center of trade in the region that goes back centuries. Can Bashar revitalize it?

Until the second half of the nineteenth century, Syria's economy had long been a largely self-sufficient agrarian and trade-based one.[29] The opening of the Suez Canal in 1869, as well as the continuing economic problems of the Ottoman Empire by the 1870s (climaxing with its bankruptcy in 1875), forced a downturn in the Syrian economy for the remainder of the century and into the early twentieth century.[30] Generally speaking, Syrians are extremely adaptable to changing conditions, and they are resourceful in finding new markets and adopting new techniques when necessary. This did not, however, overcome the general economic malaise in Syria caused by World War I. A pattern of dependence upon Europe emerged in which the rate of economic growth was, for the most part, determined by outside forces. This development only accelerated and deepened with the imposition of the French mandate after the war.

As such, as early as World War I, there existed a strong feeling among high-placed Syrians that more state intervention was necessary in order for economic prosperity to return to Syria. As Roger Owen noted:

> By 1914 there was fairly general agreement in such circles that political weakness was partly the result of over-dependence on agriculture (to the exclusion of industry) and on foreign financial institutions, and that the only satisfactory way ahead was to use the state apparatus to intervene more directly in pursuit of a more national economic policy.[31]

Because of the mandate system, when the British and the French seemed just to trade places with the Ottomans with respect to economic decision-making, Syrians would have to wait until after World War II before they could actually begin to chart a new economic course and promote the state apparatus to a dominant position.[32] This, however, did not preclude change from occurring in other spheres. The older generation of Syrian leaders, primarily the landed aristocratic families of Damascus and Aleppo, who had held the predominant administrative positions—and thus political power—under both the Ottomans and the French, had been largely discredited by World War II in the eyes of the younger generation of Syrians. These younger activists had become politically aware during the mandate period and saw their elders as corrupt and failing to deliver on their promise of real independence. The older generation of leaders were also seen to have been co-opted by the French and led the nation economically toward what was termed capitalist exhaustion.

What was rejected by this new generation of leaders, symbolized by such movements formed in the inter-war years as the Baath party in Syria and the Free Officers Movement in Egypt, was not only the *anciens régimes* in and of themselves, but also their ideologies based on such western European imports as liberal constitutionalism and free-market capitalism. As someone once remarked, the leaders of the *anciens régimes* grew up quoting Voltaire, Locke, and Mill while their sons and daughters quoted Marx and Lenin (as well as

Hegel and Nietzsche on the other end of the political spectrum until fascism became discredited with the fall of Nazi Germany). In a way, the Arab world is still searching for ideological constructs that will establish stable, relatively free political systems that are characterized by good governance and economic well-being. In the wake of the failure of socialist and capitalist paradigms (which were imperfectly applied) have risen alternative ideologies to fill the void, particularly that of Islamic extremism.

As mentioned earlier in the book, the final straw for the *anciens régimes* throughout much of the Arab world was the humiliating defeat that led to the creation of the state of Israel in 1948. Within ten years of this epic event, all of the primary Arab combatants' regimes had been overthrown by movements professing a vehemently anti-imperialist, anti-Israeli, and Arab socialist doctrine. It was this wave that Hafiz al-Asad rode into the heart of Syrian politics in the 1950s and 1960s. As Charles Issawi wrote in the early 1960s:

> In the last forty years, and more particularly in the last ten, three main shifts of power have taken place in the Middle East: from foreigners to nationals; from the landed interest to the industrial, financial, commercial and managerial interests; and from the private sector to the state.[33]

It was, of course, a well-intentioned process aimed at redistributing wealth and political power more equitably, ending reliance on outside powers, eliminating corruption, and restoring justice. As pointed out above, the path of state capitalism was chosen by a number of countries in the developing world. One of the first official acts of these new regimes after they came to power was land reform in order to undercut the influence and wealth of the landed aristocracy.[34] As part of their social contract with the people, these regimes promised to establish adequate safety nets, provide employment, education, and social services, and ensure political and economic equality.

As typically happened in many countries, Syria instead developed a bloated and inefficient public sector that has for over four decades provided the support base for the ruling regime. In the process, it has established a classic "Bonapartist" state, where economic policy has been driven by regime survival, especially in a regional environment that was anything but a benevolent capitalist world order. As time went on, the wealth funneled to the state as the capital accumulator became the source of patronage in erecting a pervasive clientelist network, primarily in the military, bureaucracy, and other elements of society tied to the state apparatus.

Because of this dominant public sector tied into the political apparatus, when the Syrian economy faced crisis after crisis in the 1980s and into the

1990s, Hafiz al-Asad perforce embarked on what has been called a program of selective liberalization.[35] It had to be "selective" because of the following dilemma: if Asad (father and son) were to liberalize too much and/or too quickly, it could undermine the public sector patronage system that has maintained the regime in power. Some contend that Syria's selective liberalization has been as much directed by a desire to broaden the regime's support base during a time of change as by the intrinsic need to improve its economic situation in general; therefore, significant elements of the bourgeoisie have been brought—some would say forced—de facto and de jure into a coalition of sorts with the state.[36] This has led to enhanced access to political power and more corruption in the private sector, with lucrative results. On the other hand, it may have, as one scholar put it, "amalgamated" these societal elements together behind the regime, and it has not led to an acquisition of political power by the private sector.[37] Indeed, as Ghassan Salame wrote, this state of affairs can be described as "bourgeoisies leaving politics to their masters who secure the stability these bourgeoisies need to enrich themselves."[38]

Hafiz al-Asad provided that stability, something his predecessors were unable to do. He tried to insulate the public sector as much as possible from the effects of incremental liberalization, but ultimately it, too, has been adversely affected. There has been a decrease in real wages from inflation due to currency devaluation, reduction of subsidies, and some privatization. Under Bashar, however, the salaries of public sector employees has been increased in an attempt to keep pace. This explains the "zigzag" approach that Hafiz took toward economic reform. It also explains the regime's schizophrenia at times, when outdated repressive laws, despite the fact that they are all but ignored by both the populace and the government, were still kept officially on the books just in case they were needed for regime self-interest. Arbitrariness was thus used by Hafiz as a method of control (the 1986 foreign currency law, ostensibly to crack down on black market foreign currency exchanges, is a case in point). Furthermore, there is no outside party looking over the shoulder of the regime and pressuring it to accelerate the reform process; indeed, for better or worse, Syria is remarkably independent of any external interference in its economic decision-making. This is the way that Bashar's father wanted it, for economic decisions were based not on economic rationale alone, but also on political motives related to regime survival and regional standing.

The IMF and the World Bank do not, at least on the surface, integrate these political motives into their structural adjustment plans. This independent posture on the part of the Syrian regime does place it out on the proverbial limb at times, since there is no one else to blame for a period of economic lethargy. It is, however, a willing trade-off for maintaining what Volker Perthes calls economic "ad-hocism" and for avoiding the perception of being beholden to outside interests, a charge that has been particularly damaging to, among others, the Sadat and Mubarak regimes in Egypt.[39]

In addition to the continuing burden of an overly dominant public sector, there are a number of other problems inhibiting economic growth in Syria: a very small and restricted private banking system and no stock market to organize capital; an inadequate regulatory regime and insufficient transparency related to a corrupt and politicized judiciary that is anything but independent—this is a major impediment to attracting foreign investment; a private sector that may be too fragmented to lead the way in capital accumulation or to attain sufficient political power in order to accelerate reform; rampant corruption, especially the ubiquitous necessity of *wasta* or intermediaries (sometimes called the "five-percenters"), who in connivance with government officials have established proscribed entrances into the Syrian economy that require further investment of time, money, and energy on the part of foreign companies; and the absence of a tradition of large-scale domestic capital investment, or as Raymond Hinnebusch noted, "to become too big is to invite trouble from the government," as well as intervention by the powerful labor union (a strong remnant of the socialist compact), which have led to a proliferation of small-scale enterprises and investment in non-productive areas, such as commerce instead of manufacturing.[40]

Furthermore, economic growth has been hindered over the years by a widespread lack of professionalism within many government ministries, which have generally been unaccustomed to providing the data and services commonly expected by leading multinational corporations. There is outdated technology and techniques that make equipment congruency with Western firms difficult. There exists an overall hesitancy to enact policies that could lead to unregulated foreign competition.[41] As latecomers, it is believed that Syrian firms would be at a disadvantage in such a competitive climate and that the petit bourgeoisie (such as the son in the Aleppan suq) in particular could be overwhelmed by the multinationals.[42] This could then force important sectors in Syria to seek alternative leadership because the social contract made with the people by the state capitalist regime when it came to power would be broken, and there would be no legitimizing ideology that could soften the inevitable inequities and economic dislocation brought about by serious market-oriented reform.[43] Finally, Syria's annual population-growth rate is one of the highest in the region, about 2.5–3 percent. As such, Syria's population is in danger of outpacing the economy, if it hasn't already, with an estimated three hundred thousand young Syrians entering the labor market every year—with all of the ensuing negative economic, political, and social repercussions.

Syria seems to be well along the path of what has been called "second-rate modernization," a process that can actually retard economic growth by replacing traditional crafts and occupations, which do provide added value, with menial production-line jobs, thus perpetually placing the economy at a comparative disadvantage to the West.[44] There are those, however, who suggest that emerging-market countries such as Syria could essentially skip altogether the industrial/manufacturing state of economic development and move from a pre-industrial directly to a service-oriented economy, which has been a trend within the developing economies—see, for instance, India with computer services. If Syria's tourism market ever reaches its full potential, dependent primarily on a peace agreement with Israel, this could be a viable alternative. Although a very long way from doing so, Bashar believes that Syria can develop a niche industry that could find a lucrative market in Europe, the United States, and/or East Asia, possibly in some aspect of the computer industry. In his view, it will be a product of the mind rather than labor, which is one of the reasons why he accords such a high priority to improving the education system in Syria. As he stated, with "computer programming you don't need raw materials, the raw material is the brain."[45]

Syria's selective liberalization in the 1990s encountered some success, mostly buoyed by the economic windfall of grants and investment from Arab Gulf states, particularly Saudi Arabia and Kuwait. The latter, of course, were grateful for Syria's participation in the Gulf war coalition in 1991; affirming this, the Gulf Cooperation Council states (Saudi Arabia, Kuwait, United Arab Emirates, Qatar, Bahrain, and Oman) along with Syria and Egypt formed later in 1991 what came to be called the Damascus Declaration, or GCC plus two, a strategic alliance of sorts after the Gulf war that cemented the new direction of the Syrian regime. Domestically, Investment Law no. 10 (May 1991) set the standard for Syria's opening up to outside investment. This law offers the same incentives to local and foreign investors, meaning that companies that obtain licenses receive duty-free privileges for the import of capital goods and materials necessary for a project. At the time, it was hailed as an important step in the economic liberalization of Syria, and it was; however, it is a positive step only if followed up with other necessary reforms, and to date that has not really happened, especially as the business environment in Syria became typically captive to the deteriorating situation in the Arab-Israeli arena during the Netanyahu years and, of course, after the unraveling of the Syrian-Israeli peace talks in April 2000. Indeed, Syria will probably never reach its economic potential until peace with Israel is consummated, and for this very reason there are many, if not a majority of Syrians, who want peace with Israel and good relations with the United States: it makes good business sense. But business and politics in Syria, domestically, regionally, and internationally, are intimately intertwined, and under the current state of affairs in Syria, one will not go that far ahead of the other.

Regarding Investment Law no. 10, Bashar, in a clear demonstration of his understanding of Syrian economic woes, said the following:

> This was one of those things that was well intended, but it has lots of deficiencies and lacked proper implementation. It needed a better vision. We had more corruption in the 1990s. We did not change the administration; we had a very underdeveloped administration [government or bureaucracy], and we still have it. Without proper administration you will not have a good economy. Mainly it is the things we did *not* do: we did not foresee an economy, we did not see where the world is going, and we did not see that we were isolated, that we should be a part of the world. The private sector should be more independent, so it should take part in the burden of the state. The population is growing fast and the state cannot employ everyone. *We* can spend less money and develop more opportunities for the private sector. But that happens when you activate the private sector. You need new administration and new laws.[46]

Bashar's Economic and Political Strategies

I asked Bashar about his overall economic strategy. He said the following:

> Our strategy is to move from ideology to facts and figures, and we have succeeded in that to a great extent. We are no longer sticking to outdated terminology, we are coining our own terms, we are defining what socialism is, and we are refusing to let socialism define us. So our strategy is to have more job opportunities and to raise the living standards. But we still need to maintain the role of the state in order to achieve social justice and equity and to support the private sector. We need strategies that support both the public and private sectors. We have made mistakes in the process [in the past]. Now we have started to learn more from the experience of the developed countries. So we have free examples; in fact . . . we had a conference in Syria about banking, mainly by the British, because we have not had private banking for more than forty years. This is something completely new to us. So it is important for us to contact your institutions and to have the vision, we need a vision, a panoramic vision, to see in all directions very precisely so that we know where to go. We don't have the time, so we need help."[47]

Syria, in fact, could be in the early stages of having a conversation with itself over the shape and direction of the country, and the status of the Baath party has become a focus of this self-examination. It is clear that from the beginning Bashar wanted the Baath party, which has been a kind of shadow government operating behind the regime, to be less intrusive in the everyday affairs of state and Syrian life in general. He would like to see it become more of an advisory body rather than one that interferes with the government and dictates policy; instead of choosing people for this or that position, it should just recommend candidates, or even stay out of the process altogether and concern itself more with supervising the operational aspects of the state. New faces have been brought into the Baath party Regional Command. Although most have been lifelong party cadres, they do share Bashar's vision of reform and modernization; in this sense, they may be more technocrat than true reformist. But the party is still dominated by the status quo beneficiaries. As such, it will more easily be molded to fit Bashar's plans on an incremental basis rather than by being changed dramatically—and certainly it will not be eliminated at any time in the near future. Bashar has implemented some administrative reform, particularly new procedures for hiring in the bureaucracy that will compel ministries to be more efficient, open, and less obstructionist. In many ways it is not the so-called old guard that is retarding Bashar's reform efforts as much as the lower echelons of the bureaucracy who know only one way to perform their tasks. They are stubbornly resistant to change.[48]

Ambassador Imad Moustapha, commenting on the levels of corruption, incompetence, and entrenchment at the middle and lower levels of the bureaucracy, said the following:

> Theoretically it is possible [to remove them], but there are too many of them, and, of course, you don't want to risk social upheaval. In many ways it is not their fault; they are the result of that system [of the past], no one ever told them that they should continuously educate themselves or that they would be benchmarked or evaluated in their performance. If someone told them this today, they would not even understand what they are talking about. This is what President Bashar is attempting to do today, to emphasize efficiency, work ethic, integrity, and higher standards of performance—these are really the main obstacles to his reforms."[49]

Dr. Bouthaina Shaaban agrees with the ambassador, but she also pins some of the blame for the obstacles to reform a little higher:

I think there is a conflict between the people who have the vision to go with what Bashar demands and others who I think do not understand how to do it or have the energy to do it, and therefore they would rather stay where they are and stick to their position—they become complacent, and use this as a justification not to do the work. I believe this is as much inefficiency as an unwillingness to do things. Bashar is doing something very important: he is bringing people in to change things from within, who can restructure institutions and ministries from the inside even if the head [of a particular ministry] is not moving along with them. He is trying to put people everywhere who can go with his vision, who can carry forward his projects, even if it is little by little. Whenever he sees someone who may fit somewhere he interferes to put him there. This might take a little bit longer to translate into reality, to be visible to the Western world, but I think it is laying down a more solid base first. The problem is that we do not have strict procedures that apply to everyone. We have not developed enough our institutions, so if you have an active minister who is doing really well, he is blessed, he does not have a problem, but if you have a lazy one, there is no one who tells him, "you have to do this and that." I think in the last two years I have seen an immense change in this regard. When I was at the foreign ministry, I recruited about 70 people who took about a year of interview after interview, and we had strict instructions from Bashar that you don't listen to anyone, you don't talk to anyone, you pick people based on their merits, and it is so wonderful. I have 30 people like this now in my own ministry, and they are into IT [information technology], languages, so it is a development that enables me to do my job well. He is looking for people to fit the team.[50]

Over time, Bashar wants the public and private sectors to be more of a meritocracy than a nepotistic oligarchy. This is the ultimate goal of the "golden triangle." I asked him if he considered himself a socialist, to which he responded:

This is a term that used to mean a certain thing. But now there are new developments in the party, trying to make a new Baath party—an evolution. We discuss all the time, what is socialism? A few months ago we had the first private banks, and we just opened the first private universities. We have made changes in the media, the first private [-ly owned] magazine, and we are going to have FM [radio] stations. We do not only have one expression in the party. Everything can lead to prosperity and to a better life and mean more jobs and better income and social justice—this is socialism. We are not ready for privatization; we have private and public sectors and mixed sector enterprises.

Prosperity is the goal, and it doesn't matter what type of ideology it is. We are not doing privatization now not because of ideological reasons, but because it would throw people out of their jobs, and right now we need more jobs. That's how I consider myself a socialist.[51]

Bashar is certainly less doctrinaire when speaking of socialism. Essentially he is saying that whatever works in terms of creating economic prosperity he will try, as long as it does not disrupt societal well-being too much and, of course, maintains the stability of the regime. In an interview on the subject of "reexamining" the Baath party, Syrian Vice President Abd al-Halim Khaddam said the following:

A need is arising for reexamination and development in order to allow Syria to continue in its path of awakening. . . . Ideology is connected to fate and identity, and expresses the party's main principles. The way of thought, on the other hand, is the fruit of logic, and its goal is to meet the demands of reality. After the Baath party obtained the leadership of Syria in 1963, and primarily after February 1966 [after an intra-Baath coup that brought Salah Jadid to power as well as Hafiz al-Asad], the prevailing perception was that the party alone would engage in leading Syria's political enterprise and in developing the country. This is because it was perceived as a revolutionary party, which led to the party's standing alone in the political arena. This, however, had disadvantages that affected the people and the society.

He added:

There have been some mistaken activities that were unconnected to the policy of the party and the country, but were caused by human error, by security conditions forced upon the country in order to ensure the security of society and its sons, or by weakness of the supervisory and monitoring apparatus. It is natural for the reexamination to include the meaning of civil rights based freedom for freedom of thought, expression, and participation in political activity, as long as this does not conflict with the freedom of others and with the good of society.[52]

He went on to echo what President Bashar stated in his inaugural address regarding how democracy has to be country-specific, based on one's own unique history and tradition. Even though many of the right things are being said, they are qualified, but at least they are being discussed openly, which is quite an improvement from the recent past.

On top of these comments by the vice president, however, came the promotion of Mehdi Dakhlallah to the position of minister of information in the October 2004 shake-up of the cabinet. He had been the editor of the Baath party newspaper. In a series of editorials in the newspaper in the year after the fall of Saddam Hussein, he severely criticized the party, arguing that it is too big (there are about two million Baath party members), too meddlesome, and too far removed from its founding principles. He laments that young people have joined the party just to receive preferential treatment in getting good jobs and in university admissions. He calls on the party to become smaller, more principled, more democratic, and less intrusive in government. These are almost shocking statements, coming as they are from the editor of the Baath party's media instrument. The fact that he was brought into the cabinet *after* writing these sobering editorials I think says a great deal about Bashar's predilections. Dakhlallah wrote that "the Baath party is not going to change the world. Right now we are fighting to separate the party from government. This is an essential step in changing and developing this country."[53]

Even though he is the secretary-general of the Baath party, Bashar has selected over a quarter of his cabinet from outside the ranks of the party, and key posts in foreign countries, such as the Syrian ambassadors to the United States and Great Britain, are not held by party members. He is also trying to reduce the party's presence in the military by enforcing for the first time regulations on mandatory retirement age. Whereas in the past, under his father, military commanders kept their positions for twenty to thirty years, under Bashar they are being rotated and retired much more frequently. There is also some discussion that he may push to remove the article in the Syrian constitution that emphatically states that the party has "the leading role in society and in the state."[54] As Waddah Abdrabbo, editor of *The Economist*, comments, "The end result will be to get the Baath party out of the government and, particularly, out of making economic policy. These people know that change is coming. They can fight it for a year or two, but in the end they will not be able to do anything about it."[55] Bashar certainly hopes so. Maybe with the mandatory retirements, cabinet and Baath party Regional Command shake-ups, as well as strategic replacement Bashar can wait out enough of the status quo beneficiaries to create a critical mass supporting change in the important organs of the state. There are many, however, who doubt Bashar's ability to succeed in spite of the party. As one Syrian student commented, "This party has been around for more than forty years, and it's done nothing for us. This president is a good one, and I respect him. But he can do nothing against these people because they run everything."[56] Commenting on the resiliency of the so-called "old guard" or status quo beneficiaries in and outside of the party, reformist critic Ammar Abd al-Hamid wrote the following:

> This attempt at maintaining the appearances of openness, though mostly designed for the benefit of external observers, is, nonetheless, meant for internal consumption as well, and not only with regard to opposition members, but also the reform-minded elements within the regime itself. In other words, and in the aftermath of the retirement of Syria's longtime Minister of Defense, Mustafa Tlas, and the enforcement, by presidential decree, of the compulsory retirement age in the ranks of the military, many high ranking figures in the regime are now trying to *reposition* themselves so as to avoid being purged, no matter how benignly, or having their powers curbed.[57]

However, if Bashar can succeed in reforming Syria, the positive repercussions could be felt beyond the confines of the country itself, so the path that Bashar is beginning to chart could be immensely important for the region and ultimately for U.S. interests. As Rami Khouri opined in the *Jordan Times*:

> Transition in Damascus from a governance system that has not changed significantly in three decades to a more open meritocracy will impact on the region in several important ways. It would unlock Syria's huge human and economic promise; spur Lebanon's enormous creative and productive potential; reduce tensions between the US and many in the region; rationalize relations with the two important non-Arab neighbors of Turkey and Iran; promote the likelihood of a just bilateral peace accord with Israel, within the context of a comprehensive Arab-Israeli settlement; immeasurably spur economic, cultural, political and labour links between the Gulf states and the Levant; and open the door for a serious advance in Europe-Arab relations in all fields."[58]

Khouri recognizes the tremendous obstacles to this transition in Syria. The country has been surrounded by change at the domestic, regional, and international levels, with which it has had to deal under trying circumstances amid a changeover in power from father to son. He wrote that Syria

> is just now coming to grips with the challenges and changes that have forced themselves on the rest of the world: how to adjust to a post-cold war world in which a nation's importance and power reflect its economic vibrancy, governance quality, global trade linkages, and technological

prowess, rather than its ideological purity, military expenditures, interventionist penchants, or proximity to one of the two former superpowers. Iraq remains the glaring example of what Syria does not want to become.[59]

Bashar admits that he is definitely emphasizing economic over political reform first; to him, feeding the population and creating jobs are the more immediate needs. Syria, like many developing countries, envies China's economic progress, and wants to emulate the Chinese model of economic growth. In the same interview given by Abd al-Halim Khaddam mentioned above, the Syrian vice president said:

> When we see that the income is insufficient, there is a need to seek solutions that will provide income, as China has done. . . . Comparing Israel's per capita income to Syria's is worrying, and this will not be resolved except by a new vision and by giving a new revolutionary meaning to socialism, as has been done by other countries such as China or Vietnam.[60]

What the regimes in many developing countries want to replicate most, however, is not so much the economic reform plans in and of themselves, but the *implementation* of these plans. It is generally seen that implementing these plans in a successful manner necessitates a strong central government to, in essence, force-feed the required reforms on the populace as a whole. Regardless of the efficacy of such an approach—essentially perestroika without glasnost—it also fits tidily with any tendencies among regime stalwarts and established interests to want to remain in power and maintain the political status quo that is associated with it. As with Vladimir Putin in Russia, however, Bashar has to be careful not to subdue all of the forces, such as the media and independent business, who can discipline the state toward public sector reform. In Russia, far from reforming the secret police and the state monopoly companies, Putin, whom Bashar greatly admires, has made them the basis of his regime. Will Bashar ultimately do the same thing? The China model is all well and good if implemented wisely with true economic reform as the goal, not as a convenient methodology to avoid political reform and taking on the status quo beneficiaries.[61] Even though the China model is talked about repeatedly by Syrian officials and in the media, Bashar had some interesting comments when I asked him if he liked the Chinese approach:

> Not to follow, you cannot follow anyone. The role you choose must be your own. It is a good model for China and it is a successful model, but it is a

contradictory idea that you can have economic development without political development. The good thing about China is that it reached the limits of its development with stability—we cannot economically develop without stability, and I think this is universal. So everything leads from stability, first you have stability and then you can make economic, social, and political development and progress. . . . If the people need food, it doesn't matter what anyone writes on political theories. But it doesn't mean you should do the economic development and then wait for the rest. I am talking about which one you push more or concentrate on. But it doesn't mean you should do one without the other—you should do all of them together. Politics affects the economy, and the economy affects society and vice-versa; it is like a triangle, it is like a table—you need all of the legs.[62]

Again, the emphasis is on stability, which has been the sine qua non of the Asad lineage after so much instability in Syria prior to Hafiz coming to power in 1970. It is a difficult and delicate balancing act that will no doubt prolong some of the repressive characteristics of the regime, especially if the regional environment remains threatening. This is what faces most of the socialist and pseudo-socialist regimes that have hung on to power in Third World countries across the globe since the 1960s, i.e. deep, systemic economic reform is necessary, but the regimes usually do not survive the assertive implementation of such reform because typically the economies dip downward before sustained improvement is experienced, and/or political change, often brought about by such measures, sweeps away the *anciens régimes*, sometimes violently. So how to do this, survive, and generate an era of national prosperity is the question for which there is no easy answer. But almost every Syrian, old guard and new, realizes that systemic economic reform is absolutely necessary, and the government cannot continue the zigzag approach of Bashar's father—there needs to be sustained change. Economic growth in Syria for 2003 was approximately 3 percent, which is too low to create enough jobs for a growing population, especially among 15- to 24-year-olds (in fact, 60 percent of the country's population is below the age of 25), where unemployment is estimated at about 30 percent. Countrywide, unemployment is estimated at between 20 percent and 25 percent, although it could be higher and rise even further.[63] If this were to continue unabated, it would be a recipe for social unrest, led especially by growing Islamic extremism in the country—with the repressive apparatus of the state, if this unrest occurs, things could get very ugly, and Bashar would be faced with some incalculably tough decisions.

In addition, the country still owes at least $12 billion to Russia in Soviet-era debt, a figure Syria is trying to reduce if not wipe off the board completely, arguing that the debt ceased to exist when the Soviet Union ceased to exist. But since Syrian armed forces still depend to a considerable degree on Russian military equipment, Damascus cannot just walk away from the debt. The GDP per capita in Syria is less than $1,200, which places the country at the bottom end of the lower-middle income level.[64] The average mid-level civil servant earns only about $160 per month, despite recent raises in public sector salaries.[65] The Milken Institute in Santa Monica, California, compared in 2000 a host of Middle Eastern countries in terms of the degree to which their capital markets foster entrepreneurial capitalism. The countries examined were Morocco, Tunisia, Egypt, Israel, Lebanon, Jordan, Syria, and Turkey. Syria ranked last (Israel, Lebanon, and Tunisia, respectively, were at the top), being the only one without a stock exchange and having the lowest per capita income in the group.[66]

The endemic corruption in Syria is also a problem, and Bashar understands this. As in most countries where the public sector plays a dominant role in the economy, the opportunities for corruption are rampant. The Transparency International Corruption Perceptions Index of 2003 gave Syria a 3.4 score on a 10-point scale, which is very low, ranking sixty-six among all the countries examined—slightly above Egypt at seventy (3.3) and Lebanon at seventy-eight (3.0), but below Jordan, which received a score of 4.6. In its examination of the Middle East and North Africa, the 2003 Global Corruption Report stated the following: "Corruption continued to thrive in virtually all domains of economic, administrative, and political activity across the region." One of the key factors contributing to this trend, the report contends, is "the prevalence of authoritarian rule in the region" which "constitutes a major hindrance to transparency and accountability at both state and private sector levels. State budgets are insufficiently itemized to permit close scrutiny, while important state revenues are managed in extra-budgetary funds or parallel institutions that allow for discretionary spending."[67] For the most part, this certainly applies to Syria.

The report goes on to comment that

Television dramas, pulp fiction and cartoon books increasingly feature corrupt officials frustrating the everyday life of the main characters. A sitcom aired on Syrian state television during Ramadan [the Muslim holy month of fasting], *Maraya Hakaya* (Mirrors of Tales), revolved around a senior official and his cronies and satirized nepotism. Such populist forms of expression suggest that "culturist" accounts of corruption—explanations that hinge on the prejudice that corruption is rooted in "Arab culture" or the regime's mentality—do not hold water.[68]

President Bashar al-Asad needs to utilize this leverage at the populist level to continue his anti-corruption campaigns in a more systemic fashion.[69] As one high-level Syrian official told me, "One criticism of Bashar is that instead of replacing old guard and corrupt people he is just bringing in new people and trying to ignore corrupt ones, with the hope that they will just wither away. Bashar would be *so* popular in Syria if he got rid of corrupt ones immediately, but this is difficult, and it is a dilemma he faces." He is known to be a man of great personal integrity, much as his father was, but he cannot in perpetuity accept the trade-off of loyalty from his senior officials for selective corruption. This is, of course, easier said than done, especially as he has yet to secure his own unquestionable legitimacy and support base that would allow him to adopt tougher measures.

Some progress in reforming the economy is being made. In 2004 the first three private banks were issued licenses by the Syrian government, a step considered essential to the modernization of the state-dominated economy. This is a step that Bashar proposed three years ago, and he has been criticized because it has taken this long for the private banks to appear on the scene, with many suggesting that this was an example of the half-heartedness of his reform efforts. If anything, Bashar's mistake was to make the public announcement for the establishment of private banks too early, raising expectations before the regime understood all of the obstacles it had to overcome and how long it would take to actually do it. Asma al-Asad, the president's Syrian wife, who is an ex-banker and worked on Wall Street in New York with J. P. Morgan, had some interesting comments on the subject of private banks:

> We have not had private banks in Syria for fifty years. Our public banks are not functioning even to the standards of public banks anywhere else. People here who work in banking work from 8:00 to 2:00, but banking is now a twenty-four-hour process. We have staff who do not speak English, who do not have computers. So we are on a very, very basic level, and unfortunately the higher you go the worse it gets, and people want banking reform and the law was changed and we now have private banks. Well why did it take so long for the first banks to be established? We had no idea how to do this. In London you have the Bank of England, in the US you have the Fed, the monetary agency that is responsible for safeguarding and monitoring all the banks in the country—who is going to play that role here? We don't have the experience, and a lot of our bankers are coming in from the outside; our minister of economy [Ghassan al-Rifai, who received his Ph.D. from Sussex University in Britain] is ex-World Bank and spent twenty years

in Washington. Because we don't have the internal experience and we don't have the internal knowledge, you need to get it from somewhere. And we are using a lot of help from the British in the banking sector because we cannot do it alone, and we acknowledge that we cannot do it alone.[70]

Syria has also introduced measures to further modernize the financial sector as a whole: letting Syrians hold foreign currency, unifying the exchange rate, and allowing interbank lending, although it must be with the permission of the central bank. Western diplomats contend that Syria must lift foreign-exchange restrictions and introduce monetary and financial instruments such as treasury bills to facilitate interbank lending.[71] There remain the perennial plans to launch Syria's first stock exchange, but this has yet to materialize. In the wake of the Syrian Accountability Act, the country has also improved its economic relationship with the European Union, which has always been by far its largest trading partner. Syria is a member of the EU's Euro-Mediterranean Partnership, a trade, aid, and cultural pact that includes a political and security dialogue. As one European Commission spokesman commented, "It's quite clear that the EU has a policy of engagement with Syria. We believe this agreement would be a very good instrument to promote political and economic reform."[72] On May 27, 2004, the EU announced an agreement on a "landmark trade accord" with Syria, ending months of haggling over a clause about weapons of mass destruction. It stipulates that Syria must implement all international non-proliferation accords, cooperate on countering the proliferation of WMD, and set up effective controls for the export, transit, and end-use of WMD-related goods and technologies. The accord would be suspended if Syria failed to abide by these measures.[73] Before implementation, however, it must be approved unanimously by the EU's twenty-five member nations, a process that could still take some time.[74] But Syria is attempting to find ways around the Syrian Accountability Act while adopting reforms in a measured way that will change the country at the practical level of economy and administration as well as shift the operational philosophy of the country.

In the wake of the withdrawal from Lebanon, many Syrians looked with guarded optimism to the Baath Party Congress meeting held in June 2005 as a forum in which Bashar would announce far-reaching changes. This is the first such congregation since the one that consecrated his presidential nomination just after his father died in June 2000. Many were hoping that Bashar would use the occasion, so soon after the exit from Lebanon, to, indeed, take Syria in a new direction rather than retrench into further isolation. The announced reforms were more or less as expected depending upon one's viewpoint. In his March speech to parliament, Bashar promised a "great leap forward" at the Baath meeting. Those who were disappointed by the Baath congress decried it as a "great leap sideways." The opposition to the regime within Syria, however, is divided and relatively weak, and, in any event, many realize they need to calibrate carefully their efforts in an attempt to compel the regime to undertake reform seriously yet not play into the hands of the United States, which would result in the removal of the regime followed by utter chaos, not unlike that which now exists in Iraq. This is also something about which other Arab states are concerned, and, as such, have been imploring Washington to lighten up on Syria. All agree that the real test will be the extent to which the reforms are actually applied. Were they mere words, symbolic gestures intended to ease the internal and external pressure and criticism, or are they the starting gun for an era of real, in-depth reform?

Bashar announced that Syria was working to transform itself into a market economy. Although Syria has taken steps in this direction for at least fifteen years, the public embrace of a market-oriented approach certainly marks an important ideological shift away from the public-sector-dominated economy born out of socialist doctrine. Still, Bashar mentioned that economic change must be gradual so as not to be too disruptive or counter-productive. In addition, the Baath parties in other Arab countries are no longer going to be controlled from Syria; in effect, the National Command of the Baath party was abolished. Again, while Baath party membership in most Arab countries is paltry, it does indicate, albeit maybe thirty years too late, an abandonment of the pan-Arabism that was so imbued in Baath party ideology, and as such, it may be an indication that Syria will now concentrate more on its own domestic health than traditional pan-Arab causes and issues. There were also concessions announced regarding citizenship for stateless Kurds, although there still exist broad differences in the numbers offered by the government and by Kurdish groups. This came on the heels of earlier prudent moves by the government establishing Kurdish liaison councils as well as allowing for more Kurdish cultural autonomy. Despite these moves, about 50,000 Kurds demonstrated in early June in Qamishli, the main, mostly Kurdish town in northeast Syria, to protest about the death of six Kurds at the hands of the police over the preceding 15 months, including the popular reformist preacher, Shaykh Mashuq Khaznawi. The congress also produced more amnesties for political prisoners as well as a suspension of Law 49, a 25-year-old decree that stipulated the death penalty for membership in the outlawed Muslim Brotherhood.

Emerging out of the congress meeting as well was talk of eliminating the dreaded Supreme State Security Courts, and although there was discussion regarding the long-standing and related emergency law, this will likely continue to exist as long as the country feels threatened. Most importantly on the surface, the Baath party agreed to begin a national dialogue to discuss a new party law that would allow parties that are outside of the National Progressive Front to organize and occupy seats in parliament. This is only an embryonic idea at the moment that will require discussion for at least a year before actual laws are constructed and implemented. Of course, there is a great deal of skepticism regarding this announcement, with the belief that the dialogue will either not be sincerely held or fade away without any government action taken in the end. One Syrian dissident called the moves, "the modernization of authoritarianism."[75] Even with a new party law, Bashar does not envision the abolishment any time soon of article eight of the constitution, which sanctifies the Baath party as the ruling organ of the state, nor when his term is up in two years will he do what Mubarak did in Egypt: allow multiple candidates in the presidential election—Bashar feels it is too soon to do this by 2007, but he mentioned it is certainly a possibility after his second term.[76] The Syrian president sees the Baath as the only organization capable of maintaining the secular orientation of the country in the face of an Islamist resurgence. The regime also will not allow the formation of parties based on religious or ethnic (particularly Kurdish) affiliation, ones that might be susceptible of working against what Syrian officials call "the unity of the state." In what many see as an attempt to consolidate Bashar's power, 16 of the 21 members of the regional command were sacked at the meeting and the command reduced to 15. For sure, Bashar has tightened his grip on power in the face of the enhanced pressure on the regime. But is this a leap toward Bonapartism, much as his father reacted to external and internal pressure in the 1970s and 1980s, or is this an attempt to acquire the necessary support base to implement his vision of reform?

Bashar has to be farsighted, yet he also needs to tread delicately in the area of political reform. Excluding Islamists from forming parties based on the experience with the MB a quarter century ago (a fear shared in many Western circles) could be a mistake that might actually backfire, leading to a heightened level of Islamic radicalism. As the well-known Egyptian sociologist, Saad al-Din Ibrahim, wrote:

> Westerners should not be dismayed at the thought of allowing religious parties a role . . . for one thing, as citizens, Islamists are entitled to the same basic rights as others. . . . Islamists tend to be fairly well organized and popular. Yes, some have created armed wings to their movements, ostensibly to resist foreign occupation (Hezbollah in Lebanon, Islamic Jihad in Palestine) or in response to authoritarian regimes. But in all cases, a moderate, less-violent Islamist core exists. Excluding the religious parties from

the political mainstream risks giving the upper hand to the armed factions at the expense of their more moderate centers. Where Islamist groups are denied access to political space, their cause takes on an aura of mythical martyrdom, and their abstract calls for a return to Islamic principles of governance are not put to the test.[77]

Bashar should learn from the examples provided by Jordan, Turkey, and even Morocco, in which Islamist parties were integrated into the system through elections, turning out to be much more pragmatic than many had anticipated. He should also avoid the Algerian example, where in 1992 Islamist groups were allowed to run for parliament, but when they were perched to become the largest political bloc, the military intervened, negating the election results yet launching a bloody, decade-long civil war that cost some 150,000 lives. In addition to the continuing battle of confronting bureaucratic inertia, ultimately, it is the monopoly of power that the Alawites have in Syria that Bashar will have to address. This will not be easy, for he was primarily brought in as his father's successor first and foremost to maintain Alawite supremacy in the governing structures of the state, particularly in the military-security apparatus. In other words, true democratic reform would inevitably lead to the dissipation of Alawite control and status. But this is where Bashar and many of the leading Alawite figures must look around them and understand and digest evolving historical trends. Minority-rule is becoming anachronistic, and it more often than not comes to a violent end. In Lebanon it took a destructive fifteen-year civil war to finally dislodge the political stranglehold of Maronite Christians. In Iraq, it took a U.S.-led invasion to forcibly remove the minority Sunni regime of Saddam Hussein. Alawite hegemony in Syria *will* end. But will it end relatively peacefully or with a sudden bang? Bashar needs to see this and emerge above and beyond the constraints of Alawite manipulation. He can still do this because he, himself, is very popular in the country and the Alawites, for the most part, have not so alienated themselves from and repressed the population that they need to fear wholesale retribution of the type that many in Saddam's regime feared after its removal. To see that a group's long-term survival may depend on short-term concessions and relinquishment of power is much easier said than done. It will definitely require the energetic and forceful leadership of Bashar al-Asad.

The solution may ultimately be not to tune up the engine of the old, broken-down car or replace some parts here and there that will keep the wreck running. Bashar may well have to get a new car.

Chapter 10

The Man

The Presidential Building in the Rowda district of Damascus, where Bashar spends most of his working hours, was purchased by the government in 1972.[1] It was his father's main office and is located near his home in the Malki district. It is a very modest three-story building that looks more like his old home in the Seven Lakes area than the office of a president. The interior is nothing spectacular, even though it did receive a bit of a furniture facelift to replace the virtually rotting sofas, chairs, and tables that his father had. It has also been technologically updated to meet the minimum standards of globalization, whereby the leader of a country has to know what is going on all over the world and be able to communicate with leaders of other countries at a moment's notice. His father had barely a fax machine in the building.

In the reception room of the building where Bashar conducts his meetings with guests there is a large painting that dominates the side-wall. It is a classic portrait of Salah al-Din al-Ayyubi (Saladin) on his horse. Although of Kurdish origin, Saladin is a hero to many in the Arab world for his exploits against the Crusaders in the twelfth century, particularly the victory at the Battle of Hattin and the subsequent recapture of Jerusalem. Sometimes Bashar's father was known as the new "Saladin" in Syria, and the painting was placed on the wall during his father's tenure in power. But his father probably liked the painting because it reminded him of a powerful and popular figure in Middle Eastern history, something that he had himself striven to be, at least in his own country. Hafiz al-Asad was, indeed, powerful, and he was popular at a certain level in Syria, although there were probably more people who respected or feared him than liked him. The connotations deriving from Saladin's success against the Crusaders, who were from the Christian West, and the "liberation" of Jerusalem when compared with the cold war struggle against Western interests and Hafiz' lifelong confrontation with Israel probably also appealed to him, lending more power to the painting than meets the eye; of course, Saladin has represented this type of heroic resistance to scores of Middle East figures throughout the ages.

I suspect Bashar likes the painting and kept it hanging on the wall for an additional reason. H. A. R. Gibb, one of the leading Middle East scholars of the twentieth century, composed an interesting essay entitled, "The Achievement of Saladin." In it he wrote the following explanation of why Saladin was so successful in his day and commanded such great loyalty from his troops:

> Himself [Saladin] neither warrior nor governor by training or inclination, it was he who inspired and gathered round himself all the elements and forces making for the unity of Islam against the invaders. And this he did, not so much by the example of his personal courage and resolution—which were undeniable—as by his unselfishness, his humility and generosity, his moral vindication of Islam against both its enemies and its professed adherents. He was no simpleton, but for all that an utterly simple and transparently honest man. He baffled his enemies, internal and external, because they expected to find him animated by the same motives as they were, and playing the political game as they played it. Guileless himself, he never expected and seldom understood guile in others—a weakness of which his own family and others sometimes took advantage, but only (as a general rule) to come up at the end against his single-minded devotion, which nobody and nothing could bend, to the service of his ideals.[2]

The Anti-Dictator

Bashar is basically a principled man. He is very unassuming, his laugh that of an innocent young man. His voice is not the commanding type, yet what he has to say holds your attention because of his appealing sincerity. *He* even asked *me* after our first session if I was free the next day at 11:00 a.m. for another session—and if I could not make it then, would I be available at another time! This is the president of a country saying this to someone whose main reason for being in the country was to interview *him*. His personality, on the surface, has not yet been tarnished by power and position, but this has always been his way. He is, at heart, an honest and sincere man. Does this mean he won't bend the truth for what he perceives to be in his country's national interests, such as the opening of the oil pipeline to Iraq? No, he is now, after all, a politician and the leader of a country, so these redirections come with the territory. I believe he is essentially a morally sound individual, someone who has the best of intentions even if clumsily pursued at times. People who meet him usually come away struck by three things: his politeness, his humility, and his simplicity. When characterizing Bashar as a simple man, I mean this as a compliment. This is not a spoiled brat in any sense of the term; this is not a man who has been corroded by privilege, power, greed, ambition, or money. His ophthalmology supervisor when he was studying in London, Mr. Ed Schulenberg, recounted a story to me. While in London, Bashar purchased his first car. It was a BMW 318. This is a nice car, but not the type one would expect the son of a president to drive. Yet this car gave him great pleasure, and he would talk about it frequently and want to drive around in it whenever he could. Schulenberg was touched by the "excitement of a young chap getting his first car," especially as this "young chap" was by then twenty-seven years old.[3]

Bashar seems quite sincere when he talks about his mission, his vision, and what he wants for the country. Again, the major problem for Syria is not that the president does not know what needs to be done—it is rather that he needs to achieve it in a reasonable amount of time and in a way that is sustainable rather than expedient. I truly believe that Bashar is attempting to set an entirely new tone for the country, and it starts at the top, although he probably needs to articulate his vision more clearly and specifically. As one of his friends told me, Bashar could eliminate almost anyone in the country, but he chooses not to operate in that fashion. He sees himself as the compassionate healer, not the political assassin. The thuggish behavior that is so commonplace in the region and was associated with his father is not in Bashar's character—he and many others see this not as a weakness but as a strength. Like Saladin, Bashar wants his moral character, his integrity, the sincerity of his cause, and his humble simplicity to be the guiding lights that generate loyalty, effort, and hope among the Syrian populace.

There are many who would immediately scoff at this. It is not hard to find people in Lebanon, Israel, or the United States—and even in Syria itself—who do not see much difference between father and son. They contend that Bashar is simply a less overt but equally malevolent version of his father. For the most part, these are also people who have not met him or had the opportunity to sit down and speak with him—or even worse, have based their opinions of him on what has filtered down about him through the media, which is almost always a negative characterization. On the other side of the spectrum there are those who would agree with my characterization, but they also see him as too naïve and weak to succeed—these are, indeed, often people who have had the opportunity to meet with him only briefly. They are always impressed with his politeness; "he is such a sweet and gentle person" emerges as a common observation, but it is almost always followed in the same breath with something like, "but he is not tough enough to get it done," or "he is too nice a guy to counter the old guard." They may be right. In the end history will tell. But let me add this: after witnessing a murderous thug such as Saddam Hussein as well as a slew of other unsavory characters in modern Middle Eastern history, is it not refreshing that we are complaining about someone being "too nice" or having too much integrity? While maybe impractical in the end, is it not a good thing that we are implicitly criticizing a leader of a country in a part of the world that has known little but despotic authoritarianism because he may not have what it takes in terms of ruthlessness to lead Syria? We cannot have it both ways. Perhaps Bashar will succeed in spite of his gentleness and compassion. Maybe his "political" bedside manner will set a new standard of leadership in Syria, if not in the Arab world as a whole.

Contrary to popular perception, Bashar has made some tough decisions, indicating that when necessary he may have what it takes to lead in Syria while not departing from the standards he has set for himself and his country. For instance, he has markedly improved relations with his northern neighbor, Turkey, in a way that his father never would have—and against the advice of a number of regime figures. Bashar visited Ankara and actually acknowledged the fact that what in Syria is known as "Alexandretta" is now an integral part of Turkey (called "Hatay" by the Turks). This has been extremely important to Damascus in its attempts to prevent total isolation from its neighbors and as a possible conduit to the United States. The thawing of relations was crowned by the first state visit by a Syrian leader when Bashar came to Ankara and Istanbul in January 2004.[4] Bashar has also been more forthcoming regarding resuming negotiations with the Israelis than his father had been; indeed, after meeting with the Syrian president in November 2004, UN Middle East envoy Terje Roed-Larsen informed the press that "President Asad had reiterated to me today that he has an outstretched hand to his Israeli counterparts and that he is willing to go to the table without conditions."[5] In addition, Bashar continues to shake up his cabinet, such as in October 2004 when he sacked eight cabinet ministers, including the minister of the interior (essentially a head of internal security in the country). It is this cabinet shuffle that brought Baath party critic Mehdi Dakhlallah to the post of minister of information.[6] As Syrian expert Joshua Landis comments:

> His father held fast to the same group of people for 30 years. He valued stability above all else. He proved this by staying extraordinarily loyal to his original friends who helped him to power. He stuck by them and they by him. This policy was good for Syria in its day. Everyone wanted stability after so many decades of political turbulence. Syria was known as the banana republic of the Middle East in the 1960s. Many Syrians welcomed the change of reputation. But the cost was that Hafiz al-Asad produced a culture of caution, procrastination and extreme conservatism in Syrian

politics and among bureaucrats. Bashar knows he must break Syria's culture of caution and prevarication.[7]

This is the legacy Bashar has been up against—a culture of caution; a populace that wants change, realizes that it is necessary, yet is suspicious of it. And there is one other element that does not receive any attention as an obstacle to Bashar's efforts at reform, yet I believe it is a difficult issue for him. For Bashar to openly embrace reform by criticizing the policies of the past means he must attack his father. This is not some royal family where the kids are sent to prep schools and educated abroad for significant stretches of their lives, where they hardly ever see their father or, even worse, have to make an appointment to see him. The Asad family was a very close-knit one in which the father and mother were engaged in their children's lives. Even though Hafiz was a workaholic, he made sure he spent time with his children, and his children respected him and knew and understood that he loved them. Close observers point to the unbearable grief Hafiz endured when Basil died, and the fact that in many ways he was never the same again. You can see the love and respect Bashar has for his father and mother when he talks about his upbringing. More important, you can see it when he talks about his own family, his wife and his three children, about how he is trying to re-create the "normal" family atmosphere that his own parents had fostered. I can only imagine how uncomfortable it must be for Bashar to implement reform in a very public way. To do so inevitably means he must draw unfavorable comparisons with the past. In this respect, maybe his delicate criticism of some of Syria's policies of the past three decades, especially in the economic sphere, is as far as he is prepared to go for the moment. This is a psychological legacy that Bashar must overcome if he is to succeed.

Perhaps, then, in order to finally cross the Rubicon of change in Syria, Bashar needs to let his father go. Indeed, quite possibly the entire country needs to let Hafiz al-Asad go. This is easier said than done, because the shadow he cast was a long one—but it is time to move on. This does not mean tearing down statues and excising the name of Hafiz al-Asad from every book; but it *does* mean that, while acknowledging his important place in Syrian history and his contributions to the country, his time and way of doing things are over. Bashar has conceded this to a certain degree, especially in eschewing the personality cult status that gathered around his father; indeed, Bashar has ordered his and his father's and brother's ubiquitous portraits be taken down everywhere except in government facilities.[8] But the reform he is seeking to implement will not happen in an effective way until he completely escapes from the shadow of his father along with those elements in the regime who only see their future in the legacy of the past.

In fact, if President George W. Bush and President Bashar al-Asad were ever to meet in person, they would find that they have a lot in common. They could instantly compare their similar situations upon coming to office. Both have, to a greater or lesser degree, emerged from the shadows cast by their fathers—although I think it is safe to say that Hafiz al-Asad's shadow upon Syria is quite a bit longer than George H. W. Bush's upon the United States. In so doing, born by the circumstances of their time, both men have adopted policies and visions that are quite different from those which their fathers espoused and applied. Whether politically for or against Bush, most would agree that he is the type of person with whom Americans feel as though they could easily go down to the local cafe and have a nice chat. This is one of the hallmarks of Bush's popularity among certain segments of the population in the United States. One acquires a similar feeling upon meeting and speaking with Bashar—this is someone with whom you could really have a gregarious discussion over dinner and who would be a very loyal and devoted friend. Yet despite this outward façade of simplicity, both men have a steely resolve and determination boiling underneath to succeed in making their respective visions a reality. The personalities are similar, the visions on certain issues, however, inescapably clash.

Father to Son

Bashar is Hafiz al-Asad's son, and there is no getting around that. The "sons of the father" phenomenon is not unique to Syria and there is a new generation of leaders in the Arab world. The transition of power from father to son has gone smoothly in recent years in Jordan, Morocco, Bahrain, the United Arab Emirates, and Qatar. However, these are all monarchies where family succession is expected. Syria was the first Arab country to experience this type of succession in a self-professed republic. There are other potential "republican monarchies" on the horizon in the Arab world who have been closely observing the course of events in Syria: Egyptian President Husni Mubarak and his son Gamal; Yemeni President Ahmed Ali Abdullah Saleh and his son Ahmed; Muammar al-Qadhdhafi in Libya and his sons Saif al-Islam and Saadi; and, of course, until April 2003, Saddam Hussein and his sons, Uday and Qusay, in Iraq.[9] As William Quandt noted, "It's bizarre that in a whole series of countries that are nominally republics there's an expectation that the leadership will go from father to son. It shows how weak the political institutions are in those countries and how personalized politics is."[10]

For better or worse, there are aspects of Hafiz' personality that Bashar has inherited. He is very reflective, much as his father was. Also like his father,

Bashar likes to have a good bit of personal time to focus intensely on certain issues without distraction. He actively seeks this free time, often between meetings in his office, when he is engaged in sports, such as cycling, or when he is driving—in fact, he keeps a recorder with him wherever he goes to verbally jot down this or that thought that might arise while he is doing something else. At this point in his tenure, Bashar consults with his ministers more than his father did. Although not institutionalized in a functional manner, Bashar tries to elicit the full spectrum of opinions from his ministers and advisers before making important decisions: "I don't think it is a good thing to have one opinion. You need to have different opinions so I can see different parts of the problem. Teamwork to me is important—I like a lot of advice and opinions."[11] As such, as mentioned previously, Bashar is much more willing than his father was to bring in expertise from abroad to help modernize the country, whereas Hafiz, according to Dr. Bouthaina Shaaban, "was always looking inside. Bashar is more relaxed in dealing with embassies and foreign leaders and peoples, and he acts like it."[12]

Foreign Minister Farouk al-Sharaa, who has served under both, says that father and son share many of the same habits, appearance, and style. He contends that Bashar is actually more direct, less cautious, and less suspicious about others.[13] Importantly, he recognizes that they each are products of different times, circumstances, and origins. Whereas Hafiz was from humble beginnings as the son of a *fellah* (peasant), Bashar is the son of a president and, as such, even though he was not earmarked for a political career, is more comfortable or natural with the position because he has been living with it in one form or another throughout his life. In addition, Hafiz was in many ways a product of the cold war, whereas Bashar is emblematic of the technological age. Bashar tends to be more open and less sensitive to criticism, whereas his father paid much more attention to such attacks and as a result veered toward a more isolated and protective posture. On this subject, the foreign minister (pleasantly) commented that it would be interesting to go back to when Hafiz was Bashar's age as president to compare. Many bemoan Bashar's apparent inexperience, but as Farouk al-Sharaa points out, this is something one gains over the course of time—Hafiz was very experienced by the time he passed away, primarily because he had lived seventy years and often learned the hard way.

Bashar has three young children: two boys, Hafiz and Kareem born in December 2001 and December 2004 respectively, and a daughter, Zein, the name in Arabic meaning "something that is beautiful," who was born in October 2003. He is very much the family man, making sure that he sees his children at least once every day. Other than being president, he tries to live as normal a life as possible. Although his family does not want, they live modestly compared to the families of other world leaders and even those of other leading figures in Syria. Bashar is a father who is, as his wife mentioned, "on-board." He changes diapers, gets up in the middle of the night to calm a crying child, and is otherwise engaged in the lives of his children. During the entire first year of Hafiz's life, Bashar did not once miss giving him his daily bath. Both parents are keen to bring the children with them to work instead of hiring a full-time nanny. When they cannot be with their children, Bashar's mother, who lives in a similar three-story building next door to their home, will look after them. The family lives on the third floor of their middle-class-looking Damascene abode, while one of Bashar's brothers, Maher, lives on the second floor—the first floor is used for storage.

Ten years his junior, Asma Akhras officially married Bashar al-Asad in January 2001. She is a very impressive person. From a prominent Sunni Arab family in Homs, she was born and spent most of her young life in London, regularly visiting Syria during the summer holidays. Her family had known the Asads while growing up, although she did not know Bashar during this time because they were in different age groups and thus involved in different activities with different sets of friends. Her father, a renowned cardiologist, and her mother, a semi-retired Syrian diplomat, both found their way to London after their respective studies in medicine and law, got married, and have lived there ever since—going on thirty-four years now. They were adamant that Asma not forget her Syrian origins, and she learned Arabic and was immersed in Arab culture as much as possible. She feels completely comfortable returning to Syria to live. She graduated from King's College London in 1997, majoring in computer science, although her heart was telling her to pursue a career in business. After traveling to various locales the world over for about a year after college, she followed her heart's desire to Wall Street in New York, whereupon she worked in hedge-fund management and then investment banking for J. P. Morgan—she was the youngest investment banker in the company. She absolutely loved her time in New York, although she admits that it is quite different from the rest of the United States.[14]

One of the things that attracted Asma to Bashar was that he always tries to see the best in any situation. To him, anything can be solved, and that means he is completely open and willing to see every perspective and consider every opinion. She likes the fact that he is always thinking and that he wants to know what every Syrian is thinking. When they are riding together in a car Bashar will often see people in a variety of typical, daily postures on the side of the road or on the sidewalk, and he will wonder aloud what each of them is thinking, what each of them wants or needs. She is very private about how the two met and progressed toward marriage. Understandably, given the fact that they are under constant scrutiny, she wants that part of their life to remain theirs and no one else's—at least they have one thing in life that is theirs and theirs alone. She is very active in Syria in NGOs, something she brought with her from her involvement in NGOs in Britain while attending college. She is a workaholic, much like her husband, and she certainly seems to share her husband's calling to do everything in his power to make Syria a better place for their children and their grandchildren. Bashar and Asma al-Asad are the best interlocutors for Syria, and they should be out and about more in the Western media selling their positions and their country.

Asma is so articulate (and she has a classic English accent to boot), she is beautiful, and she is as sharp as her father and as diplomatic as her mother. A la Queen Nur (Noor), the wife of the late King Hussein, and Queen Rania, the wife of Hussein's son Abdullah, the current King of Jordan, she should be placed out in front for all to see and hear to show the world that Syria may not be what it is often portrayed to be in the West. Similarly, Bashar should be out there front and center, not only giving interviews to the *New York Times*, but also to *60 Minutes* and other prime-time news programs. He needs to have a conversation with America because in lieu of this the floor is being monopolized by groups that want nothing but the negative side of Syria to be publicized. Bashar has gone back and forth on this over the past few years. Consenting to do the interview with the *New York Times* in November 2003 was a step in the right direction. Allowing someone such as myself access to him in order to write this book was also the right thing to do, but he needs to do much more. When I spoke with him in May 2005, he seemed to be almost convinced that he should appear on one of the major American television news programs, but he still harbored some doubts. It is hoped that, by the time this book comes out, Americans will have had the opportunity to see another side of Bashar that is much more accurate than the "evil eye doctor" portrayal. The Syrians have traditionally been awful at public diplomacy. Hafiz al-Asad probably did not even know what the term meant—he was at worst completely uninterested in it and too suspicious of it at best. Bashar has done a better job of this, at least domestically, as his sudden jaunts amid very little fanfare to local cafes and restaurants have already won him a great deal of popularity from a people unaccustomed to seeing a human side to their leaders.[15] But as one prominent Syrian put it to me: "It is like being a defense lawyer in front of a jury; one has to make a convincing case even if the defendant is not guilty—Syria has not done this."[16]

Bashar is, as mentioned, a sports enthusiast. He is also an avid photographer, always interested in finding out and obtaining the latest technology in photography. As well as liking music by Phil Collins, he enjoys Kenny G., Vangelis, Yanni, some classical pieces, and 1970s Arab music. He loves classic rock, including the Beatles, Supertramp, and the Eagles, and he has every album by the Electric Light Orchestra. As far as films go, he is drawn more toward historical films and documentaries, and he does not watch much television even if he has the time to do so. As his wife does, he loves to travel, his favorite countries to visit being Italy and Morocco because of the mixture of history and art within a modern setting.

Religion seems to be a sensitive topic in any society these days; however, in a country that is officially secular (and socialist at that), led by a president from an obscure Islamic sect, it is even more delicate. I asked him if he considered himself an Alawite or a Muslim, to which he responded, "If God wanted sects he would have sent sects and not one religion." Asked if he considered himself a devout Muslim, he replied, "Being good is the most important thing, and doing good things, not only praying and performing rituals. I am devoted because I want to be a good person—this is more important." On his opinion of the role of religion in society, he said, "A secular society does not mean not being devoted to a religion. It means to accept the other regardless of religion. Religion is personal and not related to the government. Everyone is equal, and everyone can have their own rituals, churches, and synagogues."[17]

In my last moments interviewing Bashar in May 2004, I asked him what his major accomplishments have been since becoming president. He paused thoughtfully for a while, and then he laughingly told me that he usually only talks about what he has *not* achieved! To his credit, he said he really had not achieved anything yet. This is quite modest given the fact that he has established private banks, private universities, and reformed the administrative structure to a noticeable degree—which is, again, especially impressive considering the failing system he inherited. It also tells me that he has his eyes on the bigger picture, the long-term goals that have to do with changing the operational philosophy of Syrian society. In this some progress has been made, but as he says, they have a long way to go:

> We have made steps slowly because we moved from a direction in the late 1980s and 1990s to another direction. We need lots of things. In the past we never thought about it, like planning, marketing, etc.; we need a different mentality to join the outside world, the new economy, new administration, new international relations—we don't have this, we never cared. So it is not easy. You can't just say I have an idea and I am going to achieve it. Achieving this depends not on what you thought but on what you have, so we have

started to bring a new mentality to the government and society—this is the most important thing.[18]

Asked if he liked being president, he commented:

> I don't feel it. I don't feel myself being president. I feel myself as Bashar. I haven't changed, nothing has changed—as I told you last time the things I used to think about I still think about. But you like it only when you do something to make Syrians happy. That's when you like yourself as president, when you enjoy being president. But this is a very short time because most of the time I deal with problems and complaints. So you feel a responsibility. I enjoy helping my country because ever since I was young, people would always ask me for help—I see the same environment now but on a more expanded level.[19]

With this heavy responsibility and the challenges that lie ahead, I asked him how long he wanted to be president. He said, "Till I have nothing left to give . . . or [with laughter] they do not want me anymore."[20] Unfortunately for Bashar, if it transpires that "they" do not want him anymore, the lack of real democratic institutions in Syria almost preordains that his removal will be unpleasant. And then there is the question of exactly who "they" are. Could it be a galvanized civil society movement? Islamic militants? Opposition groups in and outside the country supported by external powers—a kind of Syrian "Iraqi National Congress"? Most likely it will be the status quo beneficiaries who believe that the temporary turmoil created by his removal from power will be offset by the longer-term maintenance of their political, social, and economic positions. Too much pressure from civil society activists elicits a forceful response by the status quo elements, as it already has with the Damascus winter. Pressure from the outside, from Israel and the United States, tends to galvanize a status quo reaction.

The status quo beneficiaries, however, may have overstepped their bounds, particularly with the Emile Lahoud affair and possibly even the related assassination of Rafiq Hariri. Were these anachronistic thuggish attempts at reining in Bashar or desperate efforts by regime stalwarts who saw the writing on the wall? While one hopes it is the latter, it is still too difficult to discern. Either creates a dangerous situation for Bashar domestically, especially as external pressure generally fails to recognize what is very much an internal struggle for the heart and soul of Syria, which may consolidate a wide array of regime elements trying to survive first and foremost rather than exploit divisions among them. The many paths are all fraught with landmines, and Bashar must navigate these very carefully. In a way, it may turn out that factions inside the regimes in Damascus and Washington may ultimately determine the disposition of U.S.-Syrian relations, and with this, the future of Bashar al-Asad. There is one problem, however: the legacy of Hafiz al-Asad's Syria established the foundation for unrestrained actions by those who feel their positions are threatened, an environment that, quite possibly, led to the assassination of Hariri. These ill-considered, brutish efforts only feed into the neo-conservative agenda in Washington, unwittingly accelerating a vicious circle in U.S.-Syrian relations that could lead to military action. As one newspaper editorial warily observed:

> Damascus has singularly failed to understand how profoundly intolerant of gangsterism and terrorist tactics international opinion has become since 9/11. Nor has it ever really grasped how much Lebanon has moved on since the sectarian bloodletting of the 1975–1990 civil war Syria helped bring to an end. Shielded by supine and sycophantic political clients, inebriated by lucrative racketeering and the impunity of an occupying power and ever ready to slip back in to the culture of the car bomb and proxy war, Syria and its local agents are hated across the mosaic of Lebanon's religious sects.[21]

This is the old way. Bashar needs to lead Syria in a new direction, away from his father's dictatorship and his cronies.

Not a Lion

In the first chapter I compared Bashar with the character of Michael Corleone from the Godfather movies—the reluctant, unexpected mafia don and the reluctant, unexpected president, both attaining their positions after their elder brothers were killed. Michael fully established his authority by sweeping away the deadwood, the obstacles in his path, so that he could attempt to implement his vision of making the Corleone family business legitimate. Many inside and outside Syria are wishing Bashar would do the same thing. Take command—finally confront the deadwood in Syria and cast them aside. But Bashar must also be careful. Michael Corleone *became* his father—and in an even more sinister form; indeed, the very act of violently clearing the decks of his enemies launched him along a trajectory from which he never recovered. The family business did not become legitimate.

Bashar cannot become a modern reincarnation of his father. If he does, he would indeed become the new lion of Damascus, but this is exactly what Syria does not need in the current climate and in its present economic straits. I do not think Bashar wants or intends to become a modernized version of Hafiz al-Asad. It is a slow, uphill battle to make the "family business" legitimate in Syria, the successful outcome of which is anything but assured. One must remember that Bashar's father embarked on a new path, the Corrective Movement, soon after coming to power, yet the regime, primarily its Alawite-dominated military-security apparatus, ultimately became Bonapartist. They were and still are primarily interested in regime maintenance. Syria, indeed, is, as some have said, a dictatorship without a dictator. This is not necessarily bad. If true change is to occur in Syria, the country must have a strong leader but not a dictator who would ultimately reinforce the dictatorship. Will the shell of the dictatorship molded by his father, the repressive and controlling institutions of the state, transform Bashar into a reluctant dictator? Or will Bashar, the president of Syria, eliminate the institutional basis of Syrian dictatorship and its deleterious trappings?

Bashar *can* stay true to his vision of Syria, of an economically reformed country, one that can begin to compete in the international market, one that is less isolated, and one that can eventually implement democratic reform. He has an almost ascetic quality to him that reminds me of Dr. Muhammad Musaddiq in Iran in the early 1950s. He was a reformer, actually a liberal con-stitutionalist, who was someone the United States should have embraced. Ultimately cold war strategic considerations trumped Wilsonian leanings as one of the groups the popularly elected prime minister of Iran aligned him-self with happened to be communist, so the CIA overthrew him in 1953. It was considered a stunning success at the time; however, considering the fact that it returned to power an ambitious, paranoid, megalomaniac known as Muhammad Reza Pahlavi, the Shah of Iran, whose repressive policies eventu-ally led to the Iranian revolution in 1979, one wonders in retrospect how "successful" the coup really was.[22]

Just because a person is not an avowed ally of the United States does not mean that that person should be removed. The post-Westphalian era has been marked by nation-states competing, often violently, with each other for resources, territory, or even prestige. The post-9/11 threats to international stability seem not to emerge from other states per se, but from inside other states, more particularly *failed* states, such as was the case in Afghanistan with the ruling Taliban regime and its association with al-Qaida. The Bush doctrine was designed to deal with this new type of threat through preventive war and pre-emptive action if necessary. It would seem to me, then, that the optimum way to really prevent threats from within states from emerging is to actually prevent states from failing. Perhaps Washington should embrace benevolent vision and good governance before instantaneous democracies.

Some may say that a successful political and economic transition must be based on institutions rather than individuals in order to succeed over the long haul, but the problem is that in order to erect these institutions one must first have a critical mass of people in leadership positions who are willing to do so. Bashar is one of these people. Thomas Friedman wrote in one of his *New York Times* editorials about Malcolm Gladwell's book *The Tipping Point*. In the book, as Friedman describes, Gladwell writes about how changes in behavior and perception can reach a critical mass and then suddenly create a whole new reality. The withdrawal from Lebanon was cathartic, and created a tipping point for Syria; maybe the Baath party congress a couple of months later will come to represent another one. Bashar has been trying for five years to create a critical mass in the regime as well as in the country as a whole toward adopting his economic and administrative reforms. Possibly the one will reinforce the other, allowing Bashar to finally tip the scales in his favor. But as Friedman wisely noted, "In the Middle East playground . . . tipping points are sometimes more like teeter-totters: one moment you're riding high and the next minute you're slammed to the ground."[23] Bashar must recognize this "tipping point" and position Syria in a new direction internally and externally. He has the opportunity to be at the vanguard of change in the Arab world—to be out in front of it rather than caught in its wake and to establish a template for a new type of leader in the region. He has the intellect, the drive, the energy, and the ideas, but these require implementation. There is still much to be done.

To many it may seem anathema to support in any way, shape, or form someone named Asad, but this attitude emerges from a combination of misperception, deception, and reality. Bashar is his father in some ways, but in many ways he is not. And Syria is certainly not Iraq. In my opinion, Bashar's intellect sometimes gets in the way of his boldness; just like an eye doctor, he attempts to manipulate parts of the whole in a strategic chess game rather than develop and articulate a bold strategy and then implement it. At the risk of sounding trite, he needs some of George W. Bush in him in this regard. Sometimes Bashar also retreats under the cover of Arab-Israeli typology, producing some rather unfortunate comments on the subject at times; he, himself, must emerge from this tendency. But he is a child of this conflict and approaches the situation from a completely different perspective and experience from us, so we need to inspect the entire package and not just isolated, convenient moments that can easily be disparaged. As such, Bashar al-Asad, in my strong opinion, is someone with whom we should be engaged, someone whom we should be helping to make sure Syria does not implode. He is really the only one in Syria who could achieve this. However, because of the significant obstacles that remain in Syria itself, he still may not succeed, but he most definitely won't if the United States maintains an antagonistic, if not militaristic, attitude without any avenues for positive reinforcement.

Former State Department official Richard Haas, commenting on Hafiz al-Asad upon the Syrian president's death, said, "He missed out on globalization, missed out on democratization, and he missed out on peace."[24] Bashar understands this, and he is trying to play catch-up in a domestic and regional environment that habitually inhibits one's ability to do so. Bashar is, indeed, the hope—and the promise of a better future. He has initiated and implemented some policies very intelligently in Syria in terms of trying to lay a strong educational foundation and wean the country from the "old way" of thinking and doing things. He has made mistakes, which he readily admits. But he does not want someone years down the road to say something similar about his presidency, and they won't if he grabs and fulfills his own legacy—if he is allowed to do so.

Appendix

United Nations Security Council

Resolution 1559 (2004)

Adopted by the Security Council at its 5028th meeting, on September 2, 2004

The Security Council,

Recalling all its previous resolutions on Lebanon, in particular resolutions 425 (1978) and 426 (1978) of 19 March 1978, resolution 520 (1982) of 17 September 1982, and resolution 1553 (2004) of 29 July 2004 as well as the statements of its President on the situation in Lebanon, in particular the statement of 18 June 2000 (S/PRST/2000/21),

Reiterating its strong support for the territorial integrity, sovereignty and political independence of Lebanon within its internationally recognized borders,

Noting the determination of Lebanon to ensure the withdrawal of all non-Lebanese forces from Lebanon,

Gravely concerned at the continued presence of armed militias in Lebanon, which prevent the Lebanese Government from exercising its full sovereignty over all Lebanese territory,

Reaffirming the importance of the extension of the control of the Government of Lebanon over all Lebanese territory,

Mindful of the upcoming Lebanese presidential elections and underlining the importance of free and fair elections according to Lebanese constitutional rules devised without foreign interference or influence.

1. *Reaffirms* its call for the strict respect of the sovereignty, territorial integrity, unity, and political independence of Lebanon under the sole and exclusive authority of the Government of Lebanon throughout Lebanon;
2. *Calls upon* all remaining foreign forces to withdraw from Lebanon;
3. *Calls for* the disbanding and disarmament of all Lebanese and non-Lebanese militias;
4. *Supports* the extension of the control of the Government of Lebanon over all Lebanese territory;
5. *Declares* its support for a free and fair electoral process in Lebanon's upcoming presidential election conducted according to Lebanese constitutional rules devised without foreign interference or influence;
6. *Calls upon* all parties concerned to cooperate fully and urgently with the Security Council for the full implementation of this and all relevant resolutions concerning the restoration of the territorial integrity, full sovereignty, and political independence of Lebanon;
7. *Requests* that the Secretary-General report to the Security Council within thirty days of the implementation by the parties of this resolution and decides to remain actively seized of the matter.

Notes

Preface

1. These figures are drawn from the 2004 CIA World Factbook–Syria, *www.cia.gov/cia/publications/factbook/print/sy.html*, and the August 2004 U.S. Department of State "Background Note" on Syria, August 2004, *www.state.gov/r/pa/ei/bgn/3580.htm*.
2. David W. Lesch, "Syria," in *Countries at the Crossroads: A Survey of Democratic Governance*, Sarah Repucci and Christopher Walker, eds. (New York: Rowman & Littlefield, 2005), pp. 533–550.

Chapter 2

1. Patrick Seale, *Asad of Syria: The Struggle for the Middle East* (London: I. B. Tauris, 1988), pp. 5–7.
2. For an excellent detailed analysis of Syria under the French mandate, see Philip S. Khoury, *Syria and the French Mandate: The Politics of Arab Nationalism, 1920–1945* (Princeton: Princeton University Press, 1987).
3. On the growth of Baath influence, especially in the foreign policy arena, see David W. Lesch, *Syria and the United States: Eisenhower's Cold War in the Middle East* (Boulder: Westview Press, 1992).
4. Patrick Seale, *The Struggle for Syria: A Study of Post-War Arab Politics 1945–1958* (New Haven: Yale University Press, 1986), pp. 148–158; for a discussion of the position of the Baath in relation to communism, see Salah al-Din Bitar and Michel Aflaq, *Al-Ba`th wa al-hizb al-shuyu`i* [The Baath and the Communist Party] (Damascus, 1944).
5. Indeed, so suspect was Syria's performance in the war that there were accusations in the Arab world, particularly from Transjordan (modern day Jordan), of Syrian betrayal. For an excellent essay on Syrian intervention in the war, see Joshua Landis, "Syria and the Palestine War: Fighting King `Abdullah's Greater Syria Plan," in Eugene L. Rogan and Avi Shlaim (eds.), *The War for Palestine: Rewriting the History of 1948* (Cambridge: Cambridge University Press, 2001).
6. He does the stationary bike, normal bicycling, as well as off-road cycling, especially on Friday mornings when the streets are relatively empty. He pulls his hat down so no one recognizes him, but the fact that he is followed by security guards in cars—they do not want to bike with him!—is a dead giveaway. He used to cycle some fifty kilometers in a day when he was younger; today he does about ten.
7. Today the division is as follows: sub-elementary, ages three to five; basic, ages six to thirteen; and secondary, ages fourteen to eighteen.
8. Ammar Abd al-Hamid, a prominent reformist critic of the regime, informed me that he had been at Le Frère along with the Syrian president, and he recalls that Bashar's

bodyguards were less conspicuous than those of all the other sons and daughters of the elite who attended the school. Interview with author, Washington, DC, October 1, 2004.

9. *Weekly Telegraph*, www.telegraph.co.uk, January 24, 2003.
10. Interview in Damascus, May 27, 2004.
11. Ibid.
12. Interestingly, Asma al-Asad tends to eschew the title of "first lady," preferring to be called simply Mrs. al-Asad. In her mind at least, the first lady of Syria is still Anisa al-Asad, who commands a tremendous amount of respect in the country.

Chapter 3

1. In actuality, today the occupied Golan Heights comprises about 1,150 square kilometers, since Israel returned about 100 square kilometers as a result of the 1974 Israeli-Syrian disengagement agreement following the 1973 Arab-Israeli war. For this and other important geographic and political facts regarding the Golan Heights, see the excellent piece by Muhammad Muslih, *Golan: The Road to Occupation* (Washington, DC: Institute for Palestine Studies, 2000).
2. As of August 2004 they were from Austria, Canada, Japan, Nepal, Poland, and the Slovak Republic.
3. The Druze (Druse) are an offshoot from Ismaili or Sevener Shiite Islam that developed during the Fatimid empire in Egypt in the eleventh and twelfth centuries. The Fatimid empire, which controlled most of the Levant during its time in power, was officially an Ismaili state, although they did not force this interpretation of Shiite Islam upon the population. The Caliph al-Hakim, a somewhat eccentric Fatimid ruler, is the central figure in the Druze split with mainstream Ismaili Islam; a disciple of his by the name of al-Darazi (Druze) propagated this new interpretation in what is now Syria and Lebanon, where most of the Druze population lives in the Middle East today. Not unlike the Alawites, it is a secretive sect, whose doctrine is a blend of pre-existing traditions that in many ways is quite different from those of Sunni and Shiite Islam.
4. Nasser's actions consisted of mobilizing his troops and demonstrably marching them into the Sinai Peninsula, arranging for the evacuation of the United Nations Emergency Forces (UNEF) that had been stationed in the Sinai since the 1956 Suez war, and announcing the blockade of the Gulf of Aqaba to Israeli shipping, an act that Israel considered a *casus belli*.
5. In particular, there was concern that the Rogers Initiative could lead to the implementation of the aborted Rogers Plan that was floated about and essentially abandoned in December 1969; it was based on what could be described as a rather pro-Arab interpretation of UN Security Council Resolution 242—even so, 242 did not mention the Palestinians by name, and it was vociferously opposed by both the PLO and by Israel, the latter doing everything it could (and succeeding) to undermine the Rogers Plan.
6. Steven Heydemann, "The Political Logic of Economic Rationality: Selective Stabilization in Syria," in Henri Barkey (ed.), *The Politics of Economic Reform in the Middle East* (New York: St Martin's Press, 1992), p. 32.
7. Robert O. Freedman, *Soviet Foreign Policy Toward the Middle East Since 1970* (New York: Praeger, 1982), p. 102.
8. Galia Golan, *Yom Kippur and After* (Cambridge: Cambridge University Press, 1977), p. 30. When Asad was defense minister under Salah Jadid in the late 1960s, there was a disagreement between the two over how close to draw to the Soviet Union. Asad favored a more limited relationship, enabling Syria to adopt a more independent posture. The Soviets actually supported Jadid in his struggles against Asad, something I am sure Asad did not forget. Even though Iraq and Egypt each signed a Treaty of

Friendship and Cooperation with the USSR in 1972 and 1971 respectively, Syria resisted doing so until 1980, when its strategic position in the Middle East was quite different and more desperate following the 1979 Egyptian-Israeli peace treaty.

9. The war is variously called the Yom Kippur war, since it occurred during this Jewish religious holiday, and the Ramadan war, since it also occurred during this Muslim holy month of fasting.

10. In reality, the Arab members of OPEC were involved in the strategic plans regarding an oil embargo primarily to prevent a U.S. ally and OPEC member, such as Iran, from divulging the operations and to better ensure unity of purpose.

11. Nadav Safran, *Israel, the Embattled Ally* (Cambridge, MA: Harvard University Press, 1982), p. 278.

12. In fact, Asad was informed of the exact timing of the attack personally by Egyptian Minister of War Ahmad Ismail on a visit to Damascus on October 3, 1973, which prompted Syrian anger over the short notice given. Mohammed Heikal, *The Road to Ramadan* (New York: Quadrangle, 1975), p. 244.

13. Patrick Seale, *Asad of Syria: The Struggle for the Middle East* (London: I. B. Tauris, 1988), p. 211.

14. Ibid., p. 244.

15. Interview with Bashar, Damascus, May 31, 2004.

16. *Tishreen,* May 23, 1991, as quoted in Eyal Zisser, *Asad's Legacy: Syria in Transition* (New York: New York University Press, 2001), p. 129.

17. Zisser, p. 131.

18. Charles D. Smith, *Palestine and the Arab-Israeli Conflict* (New York: Bedford/St. Martin's Press, 2001), p. 354.

19. Also, Saddam Hussein, long the strongman in Iraq, officially became president in July 1979. He immediately convened a Baath party regional congress meeting, at which scores of high-level Iraqis were openly accused of plotting against the regime. They were removed from the proceedings and many were summarily executed. The Iraqis quietly accused Syria of backing the plotters, although a majority of the accused were Shiite, long suspected by the Sunni Arab ruling clique as something of a fifth column within the country. The incident contributed to the souring of Iraqi-Syrian relations, thus making any real possibility of union even more remote. David W. Lesch, "Flanks, Balances, and Withdrawals: Syrian Policy in the Middle East Since the 1979 Egyptian-Israeli Treaty," in Robert O. Freedman (ed.), *The Middle East Enters the Twenty-first Century* (Gainesville: University Press of Florida, 2002), p. 200, n. 4.

20. David W. Lesch, "History and Political Culture in Syria: Obstacles to Integration in the Global Economy After the Gulf War," in Moshe Maoz, Joseph Ginat, and Onn Winckler (eds.), *Modern Syria: From Ottoman Rule to Pivotal Role in the Middle East* (Brighton: Sussex Academic Press, 1999), pp. 57–78.

21. Joshua Landis, *Syria Comment, www.syriacomment.com,* September 12, 2004.

22. Ibid.

23. Zisser, p. 143.

24. Seale, *Asad of Syria,* p. 421.

25. Ibid., p. 319

26. The Defense Companies were reduced from 55,000 to 20,000 personnel. Ibid., pp. 427–433. In addition, also aiding Hafiz's cause was the fact that the Soviets were putting pressure on Rifaat to stand down, telling him he did not have support.

27. Seale, *Asad of Syria,* p. 440.

28. Quoted in Moshe Maoz, "Changes in Syria's Regional Strategic Position vis-à-vis Israel," in *Modern Syria: From Ottoman Rule to Pivotal Role in the Middle East,* edited by Moshe Maoz, Joseph Ginat, and Onn Winckler (Brighton: Sussex Academic Press, 1999), p. 266. For a brief, though illuminating, treatment of the transformation of Soviet policy toward the Middle East under Gorbachev, see Georgiy Mirsky, "The

Soviet Perception of the U.S. Threat," in David W. Lesch (ed.), *The Middle East and the United States: A Historical and Political Reassessment,* 3rd edition (Boulder: Westview Press, 2003), pp. 397–405.

29. Quoted in Maoz, "Changes," p. 267.
30. It is commonly accepted that in return for its participation, Syria received tacit recognition by the United States of its dominant role in Lebanon. Iraq's preoccupation also allowed Syria to push out Iraqi-backed factions in Lebanon that had been resisting Syrian control. Syria's position in Lebanon was cemented with its Brotherhood treaty with the regime in Beirut in May 1991, only a few months after the conclusion of the Gulf war and concurrent with the Damascus Declaration, which aligned Syria and Egypt with the Gulf Cooperation Council states in a quasi-defense arrangement to broaden security in the post-Gulf-war environment in the Middle East.
31. The separate talks between Israel and the Arab participants following the plenary session at Madrid was a concession to Israel, particularly its hardline Likud prime minister, Yitzhak Shamir. Israel traditionally looked askance at peace talks held within the environment of international conferences with multiple participants, including the United States and the United Nations, because it believed this would bring undue pressure on Tel Aviv to make concessions it might not necessarily make in a bilateral setting. In one-on-one negotiations with an Arab state, Israel has much more leverage and flexibility. On the other hand, the Arab states typically have wanted peace talks in an international conference setting in order to enhance their collective bargaining power, especially if the superpowers and the United Nations are present. The Madrid process was ostensibly a mixture of the two positions, although weighted more toward Israeli concerns.
32. Israeli leaders, both Likud and Labor, believed that the two-track approach gave them some leverage to play off one against the other, but they also felt that they could not "overload" the Israeli public by pursuing both actively at the same time, i.e. it was thought that it would take a while for the Israeli public to digest the concessions made on one front before attending to the other—they could not occur simultaneously. Typically when one track bogged down for whatever reason, both Israel and the United States tended to shift more attention to the other. See in particular the following books by key participants in the peace process, which describe the intricate and delicate negotiations on both tracks: Dennis Ross, *The Missing Peace: The Inside Story of the Fight for Middle East Peace* (New York: Farrar, Straus, & Giroux, 2004); Uri Savir, *The Process: 1,100 Days That Changed the Middle East* (New York: Random House, 1998); and Itamar Rabinovitch, *The Brink of Peace* (Princeton: Princeton University Press, 1998). Ross was President Clinton's chief Middle East negotiator, while Rabinovitch and Savir were lead Israeli negotiators on the Israeli-Syrian track at various points in the 1990s. Of course, what is needed to complete the record is a similar work from someone on the Syrian side of the negotiations.

Chapter 4

1. In fact, Bashir successfully convinced a number of his own friends who had received advanced degrees in the West to return home to Syria—the home country needed them more than ever before.
2. This and subsequent information regarding Bashar's experience at the Western Eye Hospital is gleaned from my interview with Mr. Ed Schulenberg in London, November 12, 2004.
3. Eyal Zisser, *Asad's Legacy: Syria in Transition* (New York: New York University Press, 2001), p. 160.

4. A less flattering picture of Rajiv Gandhi is painted by Manas History and Politics website from UCLA. On Rajiv it states:

> He was not a man of any unusual academic achievements or other distinctions, and appears to have had few ambitions until the death of his brother Sanjay in 1980. The following year, his mother, Prime Minister Indira Gandhi, appears to have induced Rajiv, an airline pilot, to enter politics. After her assassination in 1984, Rajiv succeeded her as head of the Congress party, and was sworn in as Prime Minister of India. Rajiv, rather keen on preparing India for the twenty-first century, collected his buddies and cronies around him, and sought to increase Indian investments in modern technology. His "vision" of India, insofar as he had one, was that of a technocrat, and his policies did little to eradicate or diminish poverty and the vast inequities of power and wealth which are to be found in Indian society. Like his mother, he could not contain the political problems afflicting India, and found refuge in international entanglements and commitments. *www.sscent.ucla.edu/southasia/History/Independent/Rajiv.html.*

Rajiv was, himself, assassinated in a bomb explosion in 1991 while campaigning in an attempt to regain office. There are obvious parallels to Bashar at the beginning of Rajiv's career in politics; it is to be hoped that this is where the similarities, according to this one assessment of Rajiv, end.

5. Bashar had an interesting story of a presentation that was made to the SCS in 1994 at which the importance of the Internet was emphasized. At the meeting, on what was quite possibly the first official Internet link in Syria, the group got onto the Internet and linked to the White House website!

6. Zisser, pp. 162–163.

7. Quoted in Zisser, p. 163.

8. "Bashar's Challenges: The Establishment and its Discontents," *The Estimate*, vol. xii, no. 12, June 16, 2000, *www.theestimate.com/public/061600b.html.*

9. Ibid.

10. Christopher Hemmer, "Syria Under Bashar al-Asad: Clinging to His Roots," in *Know Thy Enemy: Profiles of Adversary Leaders and Their Strategic Cultures*, Barry R. Schneider and Jerrold M. Post, (eds.), July 2003, 2nd edition, *www.au.af.mil/au/awc/awcgate/cpc-pubs/ know_thy_enemy/*, p. 229.

11. Martha Brill Olcott, "Uzbekistan," paper delivered at a conference at Harvard University's Kennedy School of Government, "Winning the Prize for Repression: Who are the Real Rogue States?" October 14–16, 2004.

12. Of course, as Saladin was born in Tikrit, the hometown of Saddam Hussein, the Iraqi dictator frequently viewed himself as one of his successors.

13. Michael C. Hudson, "Witness to the Power Transition in Syria," *CSAS News*, September 2000, p. 8.

14. Rifaat announced from his villa in Marbella, Spain, over his son's (Sumer al-Asad) satellite television channel, Arab News Network (ANN), that he would seek to challenge Bashar for the presidency. The Spanish government, with whom Bashar has enjoyed very cordial relations (particularly with the ascension to power of a socialist-leaning government following the Madrid terrorist bombing in March 2004), informed Rifaat that it would not tolerate him seeking to overthrow the Syrian government from Spanish soil. ("Bashar's Challenges: The Establishment and its Discontents," *The Estimate*, vol. xii, no. 12, June 16, 2000, *www.theestimate.com/public/061600b.html*)

15. Scott Peterson, "The Grooming of Syria's Bashar al-Assad," *The Christian Science Monitor*, June 13, 2000.

16. Quoted in the *Financial Times*, July 8/9, 2000.

17. Michael C. Hudson, "Witness to the Power Transition in Syria," *CSAS News*, September 2000, p. 8.

Chapter 5

1. *Middle East Intelligence Bulletin* (MEIB), vol. ii, no. 7, August 5, 2000.
2. Christopher Hemmer, "Syria Under Bashar al-Asad: Clinging to His Roots," in *Know Thy Enemy: Profiles of Adversary Leaders and Their Strategic Cultures*, Barry R. Schneider and Jerrold M. Post (eds.), July 2003, 2nd edition, *www.au.af.mil/au/awc/ awcgate/cpc-pubs/ know_thy_enemy/*.
3. There was also a period of relative political liberalization in China in 1977–1978 that was termed the "Beijing spring."
4. Middle East Watch, *Syria Unmasked: The Suppression of Human Rights by the Asad Regime* (New Haven and London: Yale University Press, 1991), p. 146.
5. Congressional Research Service, "Syria: U.S. Relations and Bilateral Issues," *Issue Brief for Congress*, November 15, 2002, p. 10.
6. Ibid.
7. *Amnesty International Report 2001.*
8. Ibid.
9. *Jordan Times*, July 21, 2004.
10. *Syria Comment, www.syriacomment.com*, August 11, 2004; interestingly, at a conference (October 14–16, 2004) at Harvard University's Kennedy School of Government entitled "Winning the Prize for Repression: Who are the Real Rogue States?" sponsored by the World Peace Foundation at which this author participated, it was generally agreed that Syria was in a totally different class than the likes of Iraq under Saddam Hussein, North Korea, Burma, Uzbekistan, Turkmenistan, etc.; as one participant noted, Syria was "rogue-lite" when compared to some of these significantly more repressive and roguish regimes.
11. Congressional Research Service, pp. 10–11.
12. Alan George, *Syria: Neither Bread nor Freedom* (London: Zed Books, 2003), p. 33. This book is a highly critical assessment of Bashar al-Asad's regime in its first two years in power, essentially arguing that Syria has not changed its colors since the son succeeded the father. While accurate on many counts, I find the overall criticism to be a bit harsh and one-sided, but it does give voice to the civil society activists in and outside Syria, and as such makes us privy to alternative views about the regime and the direction in which Syria is heading.
13. George, p. 35.
14. Ibid., pp. 35–36.
15. Ibid.
16. Ibid., p. 37.
17. Ibid., p. 40.
18. Ibid., p. 44. On the "Damascus spring," see also an excellent essay by Najib Ghadbian, "The New Asad: Dynamics of Continuity and Change in Syria," *Middle East Journal*, vol. lv, no. 4 (Autumn 2001), pp. 624–641.
19. *Baltimore Sun*, May 14, 2004.
20. Ibid. The Syrian regime blames the attack on Islamic extremists. Others are not quite so sure, and there remains a good deal of mystery surrounding the motivation behind the attacks and the perpetrators themselves. Some foreign officials in Damascus claim it was simply a weapons-smuggling operation that accidentally ran across some police, while others suggest that, although unlikely, it also may have been a prelude to a move against Bashar.
21. George, p. 42.

22. Interview with the author, Damascus, Syria, June 1, 2004.
23. Bashar believes that eventually Syria can offer what India now does, computer skills and technology. Obviously Bashar has a predilection toward this arena, but he feels that, through education—with the educational reforms he is now implementing—combined with the traditional entrepreneurial skills of Syrians, his country can indeed become a player in the global market in this industry area.
24. Quoted in George, p. 49. George also notes that in late January, the Syrian minister of information Adnan Omran addressed a group of journalists in Damascus basically foreshadowing Bashar's interview in February, commenting on how civil society groups are often backed by foreign embassies, in essence calling them spies. He pointed out the parallel at the time with the case of Saad al-Din Ibrahim, a professor of sociology in Cairo, who was arrested along similar lines—for receiving money from foreign entities—and his civil society organization was closed down. Omran further stated that "any talk that undermines the unity of society is a threat to society as a whole." George, p. 48.
25. See in particular Patrick Seale's classic work, *The Struggle for Syria: A Study of Post-War Arab Politics 1945–1958* (New Haven and London: Yale University Press, 1986); also see David W. Lesch, *Syria and the United States: Eisenhower's Cold War in the Middle East* (Boulder: Westview Press, 1992).
26. CPJ, "Middle East and North Africa: Attacks on the Press 2003," *www.cpj.org/attacks03/mideast03/syria.html.*
27. *Baltimore Sun,* May 14, 2004.
28. Ibid.
29. Ghadbian, p. 638.
30. *www.latimes.com,* February 20, 2003. His newspaper, however, was in a constant struggle with the government since its opening in early 2001; it finally shut down publication in April 2003, resumed it again in July, but soon thereafter the government canceled the paper's license, saying it had violated the country's press law by not publishing for three consecutive months. CPJ, "Middle East and North Africa: Attacks on the Press 2003," *www.cpj.org/attacks03/mideast03/syria.html.*
31. *www.alertnet.org/thenews/newsdesk/NU548121.htm.*
32. Interview with the author, Washington, DC, July 17, 2004.
33. *New York Times,* December 1, 2003.

Chapter 6

1. This is a reference to the 1982 incident in Hama, Syria, where the Asad regime crushed a serious Islamist rebellion led by the Muslim Brethren. Testimony from "Syria: Peace Partner or Rogue Regime?" Hearing before the Committee on International Relations, House of Representatives, 104th Congress, Second Session, July 25, 1996.
2. "U.S. Policy Toward Syria and the Syrian Accountability Act," Hearing before the subcommittee on the Middle East and South Asia of the Committee on International Relations, House of Representatives, 107th Congress, Second Session on H.R. 4483, September 18, 2002.
3. "Syria: Implications for U.S. Security and Regional Stability," Hearing before the subcommittee on the Middle East and Central Asia of the Committee on International Relations, House of Representatives, 108th Congress, First Session, September 16, 2003.
4. Congressional Research Service, "Syria: U.S. Relations and Bilateral Issues," *Issue Brief for Congress,* November 15, 2002, p. 9.
5. Christopher Hemmer, "Syria Under Bashar al-Asad: Clinging to His Roots," in *Know Thy Enemy: Profiles of Adversary Leaders and Their Strategic Cultures,* Barry R. Schneider and Jerrold M. Post (eds.), July 2003, 2nd edition, *www.au.af.mil/au/awc/awcgate/cpc-pubs/know_thy_enemy/,* p. 238.

6. See in particular the article written by James Risen and Time Weiner, "C.I.A. Is Said to Have Sought Help from Syria," in *New York Times*, October 30, 2001. A high-level U.S. official informed me that this article is "right on the mark."

7. Congressional Research Service, p. 9.

8. Quoted in Hemmer, pp. 234–235.

9. The U.S. Senate passed the act in November 2003 by a vote of 89 to 4; in October the House had passed it by a vote of 398 to 4. The act was signed into law by President Bush on December 12, 2003. Officially it is termed the Syrian Accountability and Lebanese Sovereignty Restoration Act of 2003, sometimes known by the acronym SALSA. It directs the president to block the export to Syria of items on the U.S. Munitions List or Commerce Control List of dual-use items. In addition, it calls on Syria "To halt Syrian support for terrorism, end its occupation of Lebanon, stop its development of weapons of mass destruction, cease its illegal importation of Iraqi oil and illegal shipments of weapons and other military items to Iraq, and by so doing hold Syria accountable for the serious international security problems it has caused in the Middle East, and for other purposes." It recommends reducing diplomatic contacts, the banning of U.S exports to Syria except for food and medicine, prohibition of U.S. businesses from investing or operating in Syria, the banning of Syrian aircraft from operating in the United States, freezing of Syrian assets in the United States; and the blocking of property transactions in which the government of Syria has an interest or is subject to U.S. jurisdiction. The bill only recommends that the executive branch enact at least two of these recommended sanctions, and it does permit the president to waive the sanctions if it is determined that they would harm U.S. national security. In May 2004, Bush activated the sanctions on Syrian use of U.S. airspace and on U.S. businesses trading in Syria. Both or these are mostly symbolic, considering the fact that there were no Syrian carriers in the U.S. to begin with and that trade between the two countries was minimal—less than $300 million in exports and less than $200 million in imports in 2002.

10. Michael Klare, *Rogue States and Nuclear Outlaws: America's Search for a New Foreign Policy* (New York, 1995), p. 25. Or as Secretary of Defense Les Aspin stated in 1993 in an analysis of what constituted a rogue state, they were states with "rogue *leaders* set on regional domination through military aggression while simultaneously pursuing nuclear, biological, and chemical weapons capabilities." Quoted in Klare, p. 131.

11. This was in combination with the 1976 Export Arms Control Act. The Export Administration Act "sought to limit the military capability of a foreign state to sponsor international terrorism." Some of the exports subject to national security controls are dual-use items that can be used for military as well as non-military purposes. There is also the Foreign Assistance Act, which prohibits U.S. financial aid to any country designated by the State Department as a state-sponsor of terrorism.

12. U.S. Department of State, "Address by President Reagan Before the American Bar Association," *Current Policy*, no. 721 (July 8, 1985).

13. Anthony Lake, "Confronting Backlash States," *Foreign Affairs*, vol. lxxiii, no. 2 (March/April 1994).

14. For instance, the 1996 Anti-Terrorism Act allowed financial dealings in Syria as long as the transactions were not related to (or potentially related to) acts of terrorism.

15. Anthony Lake, *Conceptualizing U.S. Strategy in the Middle East* (Washington, DC: Washington Institute for Near East Policy, 1994), p. 35

16. *New York Times*, June 11, 2000.

17. James Zogby, "Why Congress is Out of Control," *Washington Watch*, August 11, 1997.

18. It is also not a surprise that an anti-Syrian chorus started to rise at this time because of the general breakdown of the Madrid and Oslo processes following the election of Netanyahu in May 1996, which itself was enhanced by the Hamas and Islamic Jihad suicide bombings in Israel the preceding February and March, followed by interim Prime Minister Shimon Peres' Grapes of Wrath military action in Lebanon in April.

This was a proxy blow against Syria, which houses political offices of both Islamic Jihad and Hamas in Damascus. Syria's failure to condemn the bombings explicitly greatly angered Tel Aviv.

19. Lebanon Study Group Report, "Ending Syria's Occupation of Lebanon: The U.S. Role," *www.meforum.org/research/lsg.html.*

20. They, too, have formed an alliance of sorts with the pro-Israeli lobby in Washington as well as with certain Christian evangelical groups who form a bedrock of support for the administration of George W. Bush. Christian Lebanese learned what other groups and countries (especially Turkey) have learned in Washington, i.e. if you adopt a more pro-Israeli line you can then count on the hefty support of the Israeli lobby on issues on your particular agenda—and in this administration the support of the evangelical right as well, which almost single-handedly has put the lamentable Darfur situation in the Sudan on the political map.

21. In fact, until recently, evolving Israeli–Turkish military cooperation over the past decade was seen in Damascus as a pincer movement designed to isolate and pressure Syria.

22. David Gardner, "Last Fling of the Party People," *Financial Times*, February 5–6, 2005.

23. *www.latimes.com*, February 20, 2005.

24. Ibid.

25. *www.state.gov/r/pa/ei/bgn/3580pf.htm*, p. 10.

26. AP Report, San Antonio Express-News, October 27, 2004.

27. Zeev Schiff, "Yaalon Challenges the Politicians," *Haaretz*, August 16, 2004. Schiff writes:

> When Syrian President Bashar Assad reiterated in January [2004] that he was willing to resume negotiations with Israel, Foreign Minister Silvan Shalom approached Prime Minister Ariel Sharon and recommended not rejecting Assad's proposal. Sharon's response was: Is the price clear to you? He wants the Golan Heights and I am not willing. The IDF agreed with Shalom. So did Chief of Staff Moshe Yaalon, as did head of Military Intelligence Aharon Zeevi-Farkash. Both of them doubted Assad's offer was serious. They knew the Iranians were pressuring him not to hold talks with Israel. But the IDF top brass believed that if it became clear Assad meant what he said, that would be good. And if the whole thing was only a gimmick to remove American pressure, well, it would be good to reveal the gimmick for what it was. The IDF holds the opinion—also found in the recently published memoirs of former U.S. President Bill Clinton and of U.S. special Middle East envoy Dennis Ross—that Israel is at fault for the failure of the talks with the Syrians at Sheperdstown, West Virginia, in January 2000, and that at the time it would have been possible to reach an agreement with Hafez Assad, the father of the current president.

28. Ross Leonard Fisher, "There's Something About Syria: US foreign policy toward Syria during the Clinton and George W. Bush administrations, 1994–2004" (thesis, University of Otago, Dunedin, New Zealand, 2004). In Fisher's excellent work, he points (p. 105) to an essay by Linda Frum as emblematic of the neo-conservative view toward Syria, "After Taliban? Tell Iraq, Iran, Syria: You're Next," *Chicago Sun-Times*, October 21, 2001.

29. Appearance on *Face the Nation*, February 11, 2001, as quoted in Ross Leonard Fisher, p. 95.

30. *New York Times*, April 15, 2003. After this, it was open season on Syria. In June 2003, Undersecretary of State John Bolton placed Syria on a "second tier axis of evil" along with Cuba and Libya. Syria was termed by administration figures as a member of the "junior varsity of evil," the "ladies' auxiliary of the axis of evil," and an "axis of evil aspirant." Quoted in Fisher, pp. 122–123. What is interesting is that there still remained

some wiggle room for Syria if it started to "behave" correctly in the eyes of Washington—after all, wasn't Libya rehabilitated when its leader Muammar al-Qadhdhafi revealed and then renounced his WMD?

31. Interview with author, Washington, DC, July 27, 2004.
32. For instance, Deputy Secretary of Defense Paul Wolfowitz, identified as one of the leading ideologues of the neo-conservative movement, stated in April 2003 during the war in Iraq that "there's got to be a change in Syria," adding that its government was "a strange regime, one of extreme ruthlessness." Former CIA director James Woolsey, a neo-conservative closely associated with Richard Perle and Wolfowitz, said on television that the war on terrorism should be seen as World War IV and should include as targets the "fascists of Iraq and Syria." Jim Lobe, "Foreign Policy in Focus Commentary," Global Affairs Commentary, October 14, 2003, *www.fpif.org/commentary/2003/0310syria_body.html.*
33. Interview with the author, Washington, DC, July 17, 2004.
34. Interview with the author, Damascus, Syria, June 3, 2004.
35. See June 26, 2005, *Washington Post* article detailing how Canada assisted the United States in 2002 utilizing "extraordinary renditions" to transfer terrorist suspects to Syria for more vigorous interrogation.
36. As has most of Europe. Even José Maria Aznar, former Spanish prime minister and one of the few Europeans who supported the U.S. war in Iraq and joined the coalition, expressed concerns over Washington's increasingly belligerent attitude toward Syria. Stressing his "very warm" contacts with Bashar, Aznar declared, "Syria is and will remain a friend of Spain and will not be the target of any military action." *Financial Times,* April 16, 2003.
37. *Financial Times,* May 6, 2004.
38. *Financial Times,* July 27, 2004.
39. See Anthony H. Cordesman, *Syria and Weapons of Mass Destruction* (Washington, DC: Center for Strategic and International Studies, 2000). When I asked Bashar what his reaction is to those who accuse Syria of having WMD, he stated,

> That's a very simple question. If we want to have it, we are not going to use it against Turkey, Iran, Iraq, or Lebanon—it would be against Israel, this is the only war we have. But how can we use them practically? If we want to use it to kill Israelis, how many Palestinians are we going to kill as well? So, practically, we cannot use them, while Israel can kill only Arabs. You cannot use them. Besides, the most successful experience against Israel was Hizbollah [guerilla warfare]. WMD is not to be used—it is a political deterrent. Maybe not everything you announce in politics . . . but I mean generally sometimes you have things you have and sometimes you announce things you don't have—for political purposes. You may have or you don't have.

Interview with the author, Damascus, May 31, 2004.
40. Recognizing that he probably overplayed his hand, Bashar al-Asad met with U.S. Assistant Secretary of State William Burns to assure him that Syria did not intend to stay in Lebanon forever. Syrian sources said that an imminent withdrawal was not being considered at that moment, but added that "if and when a pullout takes place, it will not be the result of agreeing to demands but rather the result of consultations and agreements between Syrian and Lebanese leaders." While in Damascus, the U.S. and Syria did agree to set up a joint security mechanism to coordinate activities on the Iraqi-Syrian border. *Haaretz,* September 9, 2004.
41. For a wonderful essay outlining the view of U.S. customs and values from the outside, see Kishore Mahbubani, "The Dangers of Decadence: What the Rest Can Teach the West," *Foreign Affairs,* September/October 1993, pp. 10–14.
42. Interview with the author, Washington, DC, July 27, 2004.

43. Interview with the author, Damascus, Syria, June 3, 2004.
44. Interview with the author, Damascus, Syria, May 31, 2004.
45. *Daily Star* (Beirut), May 26, 2004.
46. "U.S. Policy Toward Syria and the Syrian Accountability Act," Hearing before the sub-committee on the Middle East and South Asia of the Committee on International Relations, House of Representatives, 107th Congress, Second Session on H. R. 4483, September 18, 2002.
47. Jim Lobe, "Hariri Killing Sure to Bolster U.S. Hawks," in *Washington Report on Middle East Affairs*, April 2005, vol. xxiv, no. 3, p. 12.
48. *Jordan Times*, February 9, 2005.
49. See *Financial Times*, January 18, 2005, and January 21, 2005. The *FT* report states that, in a "recent interview," Bush stated that in order to understand his foreign policy one must read Natan Sharansky's *The Case for Democracy*, a book to which Rice also referred in her confirmation hearings. Sharansky is a leading Russian hardline Likud member in Israel, and Rice commented that

> the world should really apply what Natan Sharansky called the town square test . . . if a person cannot walk into the middle of the town square and express his or her views without fear of arrest, imprisonment and physical harm, then that person is living in a fear society. And we cannot rest until every person living in a fear society has finally won their freedom.

Quoted in ibid.
50. For a vivid description of the explosion zone and its immediate aftermath, see Robert Fisk, "The Killing of Mr. Lebanon," in *Washington Report on Middle East Affairs*, April 2005, vol. xxiv, no. 3, pp. 10–12.
51. Hariri spent about 20 years in Saudi Arabia from the mid-1960s to the mid-1980s, where he made a fortune in construction that *Forbes* estimated to be at $3.8 billion by 2003, making that year's World's Richest People list. He was also the biggest share-holder in Solidere, the joint-stock company that was by far the key player in the reconstruction of central Beirut following Lebanon's 15-year civil war.
52. A videotape was delivered to al-Jazeera, the independent Arab news agency, on the night of the bombing. In it, a young Palestinian man by the name of Ahmad Abu Adas said he was a member of a previously unknown Islamic militant group calling itself "Victory and Jihad in Greater Syria," and carried out the attack for Hariri's ties with Saudi Arabia.
53. *www.latimes.com*, February 16, 2005.
54. AP Report, *San Antonio Express-News*, February 17, 2005.
55. *Baltimore Sun*, February 15, 2005.
56. *www.cnn.com*, February 15, 2005.
57. Ibid.
58. Reuters report, *www.yahoo.com/news*, February 28, 2005.
59. *New York Times*, February 15, 2005.
60. For some other interesting—and ironic—inconsistencies in the U.S. position *vis-à-vis* Lebanon and Syria, see Stephen Zunes, "Implications of the Harriri Assassination," *www.fpif.org/papers/0502harriri.html*, March 2, 2005. Zunes points to the fact that UNSC Resolution 1559 "builds upon" UNSC Resolution 520, adopted in 1982 in the midst of the Israeli invasion of Lebanon. It, too, called for the withdrawal of foreign forces from Lebanon; however, little if any pressure from the United States was placed at the time on Israel to withdraw its troops.
61. Interview with author, Damascus, May 3, 2005. It appears, however, in the aftermath of the Syrian withdrawal from Lebanon that Paris has been trying to mend relations with Damascus, openly opposing the idea of regime change.

62. According to sources in Hariri's camp, the former Lebanese prime minister was directly threatened by Bashar al-Asad in a meeting with the Syrian president in Damascus a few days before he resigned. One aide to Hariri claimed that a gun was put to Hariri's head. Bashar al-Asad vehemently and somewhat laughingly dismissed this in my interview with him on May 3, 2005. He called the accusation "ridiculous." Bashar did admit asking Hariri if he was "with us or against us" on the Lahoud extension, only because Damascus needed to know who was on its side in the looming confrontation with the United Nations. Having come to know Bashar as I do, a threat posed in the manner put forth by the Hariri camp would be totally out of character for the Syrian president. Not that it would be impossible, but I have a hard time believing Bashar would ever act in this fashion toward anyone, much less a well-respected and powerful politician and businessman.
63. Quoted in the *Financial Times*, February 15, 2005.
64. Quoted in Lobe, "Hariri Killing Sure to Bolster U.S. Hawks."
65. Interview with author, Damascus, May 3, 2005. There is also a video from a security camera of a bank near the site of the explosion that shows a slow-moving pick-up truck passing by just before Hariri's convoy entered the area, although the actual explosion occurred just around the corner outside of the camera's range.
66. *New York Times*, March 25, 2005.
67. Quoted in Reuters, *www.yahoo.com/news*, February 28, 2005.
68. Quoted in Reuters, *www.yahoo.com/news*, March 1, 2005.
69. Hassan M. Fattah, "Syria Under Pressure: Worse Trouble May Lie Ahead," *New York Times*, March 3, 2005.
70. *www.cnn.com*, April 25, 2005.
71. *www.haaretz.com*, March 1, 2005.
72. AP report, "Israel Blames Syria for Suicide Bombing," *www.yahoo.com/news*, February 26, 2005.
73. *www.baltimoresun.com*, February 28, 2005.
74. AP report, "U.S.: Terrorists in Syria Bombed Tel Aviv," *www.yahoo.com/news*, March 2, 2005.
75. AP report, "Bush Demands That Syria Leave Lebanon," *www.yahoo.com/news*, March 2, 2005.
76. "Is an Arab Mediator Possible?" *www.haaretz.com*, February 9, 2005.
77. C-SPAN 2 broadcast, Middle East summit, Sharm al-Shaykh, Egypt, February 8, 2005. Also see *Financial Times*, February 9, 2005.
78. "Egypt, Saudi Arabia Press Syria on Withdrawal," *www.baltimoresun.com*, March 2, 2005.
79. "Syria Seen Rallying Arab Help over Tension," *www.turkishdailynews.com.tr*, March 2, 2005.
80. *Financial Times*, March 4, 2005.
81. For an English translation of the text of the speech, see the Syrian Arab News Agency website, *www.sana.org/english/Archives/Sunday/MainSun.htm*.
82. *www.aljazeera.net*, March 5, 2005.
83. *www.cnn.com*, March 5, 2005.
84. AP Report, *www.yahoo.com/news*, March 5, 2005.
85. *www.cnn.com*, March 5, 2005.
86. BBC news, *http://newsvote.bbc.co.uk*, March 7, 2005.
87. *www.syriacomment.com*, March 6, 2005.
88. *New York Times*, March 10, 2005.
89. As some have noted, however, Hizbollah may have damaged its image somewhat in Lebanon by appearing to be too much of a supplicant of Syria. Hizbollah has generally popularized itself in the country generating the image of a non-partisan resistance group, the only one that ever successfully forced Israel to retreat. This could be why

Hizbollah supporters in the demonstration chanted pro-Syrian and pro-Asad slogans yet carried Lebanese flags—this captures the dilemma Hizbollah could be facing.

90. *www.washingtonpost.com*, March 11, 2005.

91. Ibid. It appears, however, that following the Syrian withdrawal, Arab countries were trying to shore-up their relations with Damascus. Both Saudi Crown Prince Abdullah and Jordan's King Abdullah made brief visits to Damascus in the first week of May 2005 to meet with Bashar, assuring him that they do not support U.S. attempts to isolate Syria or effect regime change.

92. *Financial Times*, March 2, 2005.

93. For two different opinions on the probability of an Islamist Syria should the regime fall, see Michael Jacobson, "An Islamist Syria Is Not Very Probable," in *Daily Star* (Beirut), April 29, 2005; and Lucy Ashton, "Syrian Repression Drives Opposition into the Arms of the Islamists," in *Financial Times*, May 6, 2005.

Chapter 7

1. Joshua Landis, "Syria and the Palestine War: Fighting King Abdullah's Greater Syria Plan," in Eugene L. Rogan and Avi Shlaim (eds.), *The War for Palestine: Rewriting the History of 1948* (Cambridge: Cambridge University Press, 2001), pp. 178–205.

2. Dennis Ross, *The Missing Peace: The Inside Story of the Fight for Middle East Peace* (New York: Farrar, Straus, and Giroux, 2004), pp. 48–49.

3. The Syrian delegation also negotiated with the Lebanese, clearly cementing the ties between Syria and Lebanon with regard to a settlement with Israel.

4. Ross, p. 111.

5. As was pointed out in negotiations in late 1999 when Ehud Barak was the Israeli prime minister, the shoreline of the Sea of Galilee had actually receded significantly since the 1967 Arab-Israeli war, thus offering the possibility of Syria getting the June 4 line and Israel keeping the Syrians away from the shoreline. See Ross, p. 574.

6. Ross, p. 525.

7. Ibid., p. 112.

8. In a way, this was one of the reasons for Pakistani support for the Taliban regime in Afghanistan, i.e. it provided Islamabad with strategic depth in case of the real possibility of war with its arch-rival, India.

9. Ross, p. 523.

10. Quoted in Patrick Seale and Linda Butler, "Assad's Regional Strategy and the Challenge from Netanyahu," *Journal of Palestine Studies*, vol. xxvi, no. 1 (Fall 1996), pp. 36–37.

11. Quoted in Raymond Hinnebusch, "Does Syria Want Peace: Syrian Policy in the Syrian-Israeli Negotiations," *Journal of Palestine Studies* vol. xxvi, no. 1 (Fall 1996), pp. 44–45. Asad was quoted in *al-Ahram* (Egypt) in December 1995 as saying that Shimon Peres' vision of a Middle East common market was ultimately an attempt to "eliminate the concept of Arabism, and by extension the Arabs . . . our inner feeling of being a nation, and our national and social identity." Quoted in Seale and Butler, p. 36.

12. Ross, p. 517.

13. Ross, p. 569. On Syria's flexibility, see Ross, pp. 555–565. For instance, the Syrians agreed for the first time to an American presence at an early-warning station in Mount Hermon for five years after the Israeli withdrawal, which had been a major hurdle up to that point (p. 555). Along these lines, Ross also states the following:

> Amnon Shahak [former deputy chief of staff of the IDF; minister of tourism under Barak who was involved in the Syrian track] was to tell me in the summer of 2002 that the Middle East changed the day in Shepherdstown when, unbeknownst to us, Barak received the results of a poll that made doing the deal with Syria more prob-

lematic than he had thought. It was at that time that Barak decided to hold fast in Shepherdstown regardless of the Syrian moves. It was then that a deal was probably lost—and with it a chance for Israel to withdraw from Lebanon as part of a deal, not as if under the pressure and threats of Hizbollah.

Ross, p. 589.

14. As Ross observed, at a critical point in the run-up to Shepherdstown in the fall of 1999, "President Clinton nodded his assent to my suggestion, but he was quick to tell me he did not mind taking a risk if a deal was possible. He felt the bigger risk would be to lose any chance of doing an Israeli-Syrian agreement." Ross, p. 532.

15. Jeremy Pressman argues in a review of Ross' book that it appears that the offer the United States presented to Syria in Geneva was a withdrawal to the June 4 line in name only, since the map Ross was showing the Syrians moved the June 4 line even further back to the east of the 1923 line. According to this argument, perhaps the United States and Israel were trying to get Syria to agree to the demarcation, calling it the June 4 line while knowing that it probably was not. If this is true, then it follows that Barak probably in the end did not agree to withdraw to a June 4 border that was more in line with Syria's idea of where it was (or that of Frederic Hof, who has done research on where exactly the June 4, 1967, Syrian-Israeli border was located). As such, it is little wonder that Asad "cried foul," leading to the failure of the summit. See Jeremy Pressman, "Lost Opportunities," *Boston Review*, December 2004/January 2005, pp. 44–45.

16. Ross, p. 589. In my interview with Bashar on May 27, 2004, I asked him about his understanding of what happened at Geneva, and he said the following:

> Last time my father met with Clinton in April 2000, Clinton called my father, and [Saudi Crown] Prince Abdullah was involved. There were good relations between my father and Clinton. My father asked Clinton what he wanted to discuss, why a summit, as my father did not think it was appropriate. But then Clinton called him to meet with him because he was on his way back from Asia, Pakistan I think, and he stopped in Oman, then he went on to Geneva. He called my father and told him he was on his way to Geneva and that he would like to meet there because he had good news, that Barak accepted the June 4th line. However, at Geneva my father was told that Barak accepted to withdraw from 95 percent of the land, so my father was angry and he wanted to leave. He was surprised and Clinton was surprised; Clinton was surprised he refused, so somebody told him that we would accept this offer. When he stopped in Oman, Clinton met with some Omani officials along with [U.S. national security adviser] Sandy Berger and [U.S. ambassador to Syria] Chris Ross— they told Clinton at the time that since my father is sick he wants to have a peace before he dies so that he can help his son be president (which is opposite to what we have said, that I did not know I was going to be president) so he [Hafiz] will accept anything. And they hinted to Clinton that they had asked my father and that he had said OK. So Clinton presumed that my father had agreed to the proposal. What happened was that Barak was a little bit weak in Israel, and he wanted to play two cards, one for peace and one not for peace. For those who want peace he would tell the world he is a peacemaker, for the extremists in Israel he would say he would take peace but not give all the land back, so this is how it failed. It was not Clinton's fault or the Syrians, but then the Israelis then said my father was not interested in peace. In this way Barak could say my father only wanted peace on his conditions, and therefore the Arabs are responsible [for the breakdown].

17. The Shebaa Farms is an area measuring about 25 square kilometers and consists of fourteen farms located just south of Shebaa, a Lebanese village on the western slope of Mt. Hermon astride the borders of Syria, Lebanon, and Israel. When Israel withdrew

in May 2000, it did not do so from the Shebaa Farms, which it claims was part of the Golan Heights taken from Syria in 1967 and thus is subject to negotiations with Syria. Lebanon, particularly Hizbollah, and Syria claim that it is a part of Lebanon, and as such Israel has not fully withdrawn from the country. Since the withdrawal, Hizbollah has carried out periodic attacks against Israeli positions in the Shebaa Farms area, although it has been relatively quiescent of late. The United Nations officially verified on June 16, 2000, that Israel had completely withdrawn from Lebanon in accordance with UN Security Council Resolution 425 passed in 1978 after Israeli forces moved into Lebanon and established the cordon sanitaire along the border. Resolution 425 called on Israel to "withdraw forthwith its forces from all Lebanese territory," and to monitor and confirm the withdrawal of Israeli forces, it established the UN Interim Force in Lebanon (UNIFIL). The Israelis believe Syria has manufactured the Shebaa Farms case to maintain at least some level of Israeli–Lebanese friction that legitimated Syria's military position in Lebanon as well as retain at least a tad of negotiating quid pro quo with Israel over the Golan. According to this view, tension with Israel over the Shebaa Farms helped Damascus drown out the increasing rancor in Lebanon, especially within the Lebanese Christian community, calling on a Syrian withdrawal from the country, agitation that became more assertive and open when Bashar took power.

18. For full text of speech, see the Syrian Arab News Agency (SANA) translation at the following website: *www.sana.org/english/reports/Documents/syria.htm.*

19. I told Bashar that one of the worst things to happen when he became president was the tidbit of news floated in the Western media that he liked Phil Collins music. Immediately in the West, this created an unwarranted image of Bashar and heightened expectations for his presidency. He laughed in response and agreed with me, but he said he really does like his music as well as other Western musical artists and groups.

20. SANA, October 21, 2000, *www.sana.org/english/reports/Documents/president_ assad1.htm.*

21. Ibid.

22. SANA, November 12, 2000, *www.sana.org/english/reports/Documents/speech_by1.htm.*

23. Interview with the author, Damascus, May 27, 2004. The exact words he said to the pope were the following: "They [Israelis] are trying to kill all of the principles of the monotheistic religions with the mentality as the betrayal of Jesus." *Al-sharq al-awsat* (London), May 6, 2001.

24. *www.freelebanon.org/articles/a130.htm.* In response, Foreign Minister Farouk al-Sharaa stated that "if Israel tries to change the old rules of the game, as it has been claimed in a number of newspapers, then we are preparing the rules with which we want to play this game. . . . Israel cannot unilaterally determine the rules of the game." Quoted on the same website.

25. For instance, in answering questions from reporters at a news conference with British Prime Minister Tony Blair after his summit meeting with the Syrian president in Damascus in October 2001, Bashar stated that "The Syrian condemnation [of 9/11] doesn't come from what happened *on* 9/11, but as a result of other factors, including Syria's deep-rooted principles and recalling what Syria had suffered from terrorism in the 1970s." He also stated at the news conference that "we stand by the international coalition to combat terrorism; we, however, did not say that we stand by any international coalition to wage war. We stand against wars, which always have adverse and negative consequences for our people. We, in Syria, believe that war doesn't combat terrorism," while urging that terrorism be combated through "political and cultural means, security cooperation and information." SANA, October 31, 2001, *www.sana.org/ english/reports/Assad-Blair/president_assad_held_talks_with_.htm.*

26. In particular, see the essay in the *New York Times,* October 30, 2001, on Syrian–U.S. intelligence cooperation. I was informed by a high-level U.S. source that this article is extremely accurate.

27. As one high-ranking Lebanese internal security officer is reported to have said, "The Americans would rather deal with the Syrians. They're serious, they deliver what they

promise and they control the Lebanese Army." February 7, 2002, *www.msnbc.com/news/696569.asp?0cb=-317482.*

28. Ivo Daalder and James Lindsay, "The Bush Revolution: The Remaking of America's Foreign Policy," paper delivered at "The George W. Bush Presidency: An Early Assessment," conference at the Woodrow Wilson School of Public and International Affairs, Princeton University, April 2003.

29. For a text of the Saudi peace initiative, see *www.msnbc.com/news/730829.asp?cp1=1.* Regarding Syria, the plan calls for "full Israeli withdrawal from all the territories occupied since 1967, including the Syrian Golan Heights to the lines of June 4, 1967 as well as the remaining occupied Lebanese territories in the south of Lebanon." The fact that this clause had to stipulate that "full Israeli withdrawal" also included the Golan Heights and Lebanon indicates how much the focus of peace in the Arab-Israeli arena had veered toward the Palestinian track and away from the Israeli one since mid-2000.

30. In actuality, however, the development of trade and cultural contacts between Egypt and Israel has been very slow since the peace treaty; indeed, it was only in December 2004 that Egypt and Israel for the first time finally reached an agreement that allows Egyptian industry to sell products using Israeli parts duty free in the United States, by establishing seven industrial zones in Cairo, Alexandria, and Port Said in Egypt. Although Washington held up the agreement for several months, these joint industrial zones could replicate the Golan Heights pending an Israeli-Syrian accord, an arrangement similar to that which already exists between Jordan and Israel following their peace agreement in 1994. Given this slow development in Egyptian-Israeli relations, Syrians do not see any hurry in "normalizing" relations with Israel. On the other hand, one of the reasons Egyptian-Israeli relations remained cold on many fronts was the antagonisms regarding the Palestinian situation and the fact that for years Egypt was the only Arab country to have signed along the dotted line with Israel—all of this could be significantly abated if a Syrian-Israeli treaty is consummated, thus opening up the possibility of a more rapid development of normalization of relations.

31. SANA, March 27, 2002, *www.sana.org/english/reports/Assad-Beirut%20speech/Assad-Speech-Beirut27-3.htm.*

32. SANA, October 18, 2002, *www.sana/org/english/reports/Assad-Reuters18-10-02/president_assad.htm.*

33. *www.haaretz.com,* June 10, 2003.

34. Quoted in ibid.

35. *Washington Post,* October 6, 2003.

36. Bashar acknowledges that Palestinian organizations have "second-level" officials in Damascus, but no organizational capacity. He also stated that these officials are probably in touch with the Palestinian leadership in the Occupied Territories, but that he cannot stop them from doing that. He said, "We can't just throw [those who are here] into the sea, and I told [Colin] Powell this. There is a lot of support from Syrians for the Palestinians. And every month millions of Syrian lira go to Palestinians who have lost their homes, etc., and this is the right of the Syrians to do this." Interview with the author, Damascus, May 31, 2004.

37. *New York Times,* December 1, 2003. As Bashar told me, "if we start from the beginning it will take another fourteen years with more killing and blood." Interview with the author, May 27, 2004.

38. *New York Times,* December 1, 2003.

39. *Financial Times,* January 10–11, 2004.

40. Ibid.

41. Ibid.

42. Interestingly, at Pope John Paul II's funeral in April 2005, Bashar and President Katsav exchanged a handshake that was widely reported in the press. Bashar informed me, however, that the handshake was part of the Catholic mass ritual of exchanging a "sign

of peace" through a handshake. Katsav happened to be sitting in front of Bashar, and he turned around to shake Bashar's hand. Even so, Katsav had to know that Bashar was sitting behind him, and he could have easily not turned around. The position of president in Israel, however, is largely ceremonial, with little influence on actual policy.

43. Interview with the author, May 27, 2004. On this subject, Syrian ambassador to the United States, Dr. Imad Moustapha, said the following:

> Two signals came. Sharon said he was not interested. It was done by Katsav at the media level. Since coming into this position [as ambassador] I have dealt with this question many times, and I have repeatedly said that Syria is committed to peace with Israel, but it is the other party that is not. I would usually be politely denied or not so politely denied because the view here [in the United States] is that Israel wants peace and its neighbors, including Syria, are rejectionists. We have gone a little way in changing this perception. First there was the *New York Times* interview [with Bashar]. But Sharon was explicit. Now we have [former U.S. secretary of state in the Clinton administration] Madeline Albright's memoirs, but not enough people paid attention to hers, that Israel was the obstacle, and then [George H. W. Bush and Clinton Middle East envoy] Dennis Ross' book came out and is explicit in saying that Israel was responsible for the collapse of the Syrian–Israeli talks, and now Clinton's book also says this. Bashar is committed to peace with Israel, but it takes two to tango. I don't think Israel wants peace with it neighbors. But we were always portrayed as the party who did not want peace. When we engaged in the process, they backed off. The Israelis capably marketed their own version, but I think this has changed under Bashar.

Interview with the author, Washington, DC, July 27, 2004.

44. *Jordan Times*, July 10, 2004. It was also reported in this source that in talks with Egyptian President Husni Mubarak, Bashar and Mubarak urged the "quartet" to include Syria and Lebanon in its Middle East peace efforts.
45. Turkish Daily News, July 12, 2004, *www.turkishdailynews.com/FrTDN/latest/for.htm.*
46. For instance, see essay by Uri Bar-Yosef, "A Most Preventable War," September 29, 2004, *www.haaretz.com.*
47. *www.haaretz.com,* October 7, 2004. When I asked Bashar whether or not he would accept the return of the Golan Heights before a Palestinian settlement, he said,

> This is a very important question because, of course, we cannot say no, but does that solve the entire problem? That's why we always ask for a comprehensive peace; of course we say that we want our land, but if you do not solve the Palestinian situation with Syria and Lebanon at the same time you will still have conflict. What are you going to do with the five hundred thousand Palestinian [refugees] in Syria and the same number in Lebanon, and about four million in other Arab countries? What of those who still have hope? Through peace talks they can go back, not all of them, but they can go back, not to Israel but to Palestine because they would have relatives there. If they lose hope, if they see the Syrians going ahead, if there is agreement on the Syrian track, maybe the Palestinian track will be lost forever.

Interview with the author, Damascus, May 27, 2004.

48. AP report, *San Antonio Express-News,* January 9, 2005.
49. *www.haaretz.com,* October 10, 2004.
50. Ibid.
51. *www.haaretz.com,* October 19, 2004.
52. Quoted in *Syria Comment,* September 22, 2004, *www.syriacomment.com.*

53. Yezid Sayigh, "Palestinians Must Go to the Polls," *Financial Times*, November 22, 2004.
54. Robert O. Freedman, "Should Israel Begin Peace Talks with Syria?" unpublished essay, December 13, 2004.
55. Ibid.
56. Interview with the author, Damascus, May 3, 2005.
57. On Syria's actions to expel Palestinian militants and shut down the offices of militant groups in Damascus, see, "Syria: Killing of Hamas Man in Damascus Terror Act," *www.haaretz.com*, September 27, 2004; and "Analysis: Amos Harel on an Embarrassment for Damascus," *www.haaretz.com*, September 27, 2004. Reportedly, the head of the political wing of Hamas, Khalid Mashal, left Damascus in August—in the wake of Israeli assassinations of Hamas leaders in the Occupied Territories, Mashal had by default risen to the top of the Hamas political ladder.
58. *www.baltimoresun.com*, September 1, 2004.
59. *www.cnn.com*, September 26, 2004.
60. Ibid.
61. *www.haaretz.com*, September 27, 2004.
62. *Financial Times*, September 27, 2004.
63. After snubbing him the previous year, Colin Powell met with Syrian Foreign Minister Farouk al-Sharaa at the United Nations General Assembly gathering in September, describing the get together as a "good, open, and candid meeting," and he praised Syria for its support on patching up its porous border with Iraq as well as its redeployment of some four thousand to five thousand troops in Lebanon. *www.washingtontimes.com*, October 2, 2004.
64. *www.haaretz.com*, January 24, 2005.
65. *Jordan Times*, January 25, 2005.
66. Ibid.
67. For more on the "cooling" of Russian-Israeli relations in 2004 and in early 2005, see, Robert O. Freedman, "Russia and Israel: The Relationship Cools," in *Oxford Analytica*, January 2005. There were reports out of Moscow prior to Bashar's state visit that Russia was preparing to send new missiles (ground-to-ground Iskanders and surface-to-air Igla Sa-18 missiles) to Syria. Russian officials denied the reports, but Israelis were concerned that these missiles could find their way to Hizbollah and/or Palestinian militant groups. At the summit, Bashar also denied the reports about the missiles, and after pressure from both Washington and Tel Aviv, it seems as if the purported sale has been held up for the time being. See *Jordan Times*, January 25, 2005. The missile sale again surfaced in April 2005 upon Russian President Vladimir Putin's visit to Egypt, Israel, and Syria. At this time, Russia apparently agreed to sell anti-aircraft missiles to Syria, emphasizing the defensive nature of the weaponry.
68. Television interview on "Good Morning America," May 8, 2005.

Chapter 8

1. On Nasser's machinations *vis-à-vis* Syria during the 1957 American-Syrian crisis, see David W. Lesch, "Gamal Abd al-Nasser and an Example of Diplomatic Acumen," *Middle Eastern Studies*, vol. xxxi, no. 3 (Summer 1996), pp. 87–108.
2. See Malcolm H. Kerr, *The Arab Cold War: Gamal Abd al-Nasir and His Rivals, 1958–1970* (London: Oxford University Press, 1971).
3. Bashar in interview with the author, May 31, 2004.
4. In addition, Saddam spearheaded a so-called Pan-Arab Charter in early 1979, mapping out his vision of Iraqi leadership of a new era in the Arab world, again indicating his intention to fill the void. The fact that the Shah of Iran was also finally ousted by February 1979 with the culmination of the Iranian revolution offered Saddam the

opportunity to, in essence, kill two birds with one stone, i.e. fill the vacuum of power in the Persian Gulf arena as well as the inter-Arab arena.

5. Interview with the author, May 31, 2004.
6. *Middle East Intelligence Bulletin* (MEIB), vol. iii, no. 3, March 1, 2001.
7. SANA, January 31, 2002, as quoted in MEIB, vol. iii, no. 3, March 1, 2001.
8. "Syrian Priorities in Iraq: Pursuing Opportunities, Hedging against Risks," *ISS Strategic Comments*, vol. x, issue 7, September 2004, *www.iiss.org/stratcom*.
9. Interview with the author, May 31, 2004.
10. Middle East Media Research Institute (MEMRI), May 2001.
11. On October 8, 2001, the United Nations General Assembly elected Syria to a non-permanent seat on the UN Security Council. The fact that the United States did not lobby against the choice of Syria was a clear indication in the immediate aftermath of 9/11 that Washington was courting the Arab world in the new war against terror and the war in Afghanistan. Syria also voted in favor of UN Security Council Resolutions 1483 and 1511 following the war that formally lifted the UN sanctions on Iraq and approved the transfer of power to an interim Iraqi government.
12. With the lethal insurgency mounting in the months and years following the entry of U.S. troops into Baghdad in April 2003, many prefer to refer to the Iraq war of March–April 2003 as simply the first phase of the conflict, one that is still ongoing as of this writing.
13. *www.cnn.com*, April 14, 2003.
14. Ibid.
15. *New York Times*, April 26, 2005.
16. *www.cnn.com*, April 14, 2003.
17. Ibid.
18. Ibid.
19. Ibid.
20. Ibid.
21. Ibid.
22. MEIB detailed copies of documents seized at one of Saddam's military procurement companies obtained by two *Los Angeles Times* reporters:

> Files from the Baghdad office of Al-Bashair Trading company show that a Syrian company, SES International Corp., signed more than 50 contracts to supply arms and equipment worth tens of millions of dollars to Iraq's military prior to the war. The general manager of SES, Asef Isa Shaleesh [Shalish], is a first cousin of Assad, and one of its major shareholders, Maj. Gen. Dhu Himma Shaleesh, is a relative of Assad who heads an elite presidential security corps.

"Assad's Desperate Diplomacy," *MEIB*, vol. vi, no. 1, January 2004. *MEIB* is published by the United States Committee for a Free Lebanon and the Middle East Forum, both of which, as mentioned in an earlier chapter, have been committed to removing Syria from Lebanon and have adopted a harsh attitude toward Bashar al-Asad; their reporting is certainly tendentious on occasion, but a number of their analyses and surveys are reliable to at least a warranted degree, especially those written by Gary C. Gambill.
23. "Near Iraq, Syria Reportedly Still Quietly Backs Militants," *www.latimes.com*, August 12, 2003. The Syrians have asked the Americans why when these same Islamic Jihad and Hamas leaders visit countries such as Egypt or Qatar, the United States does not complain to these Arab states, who also happen to be allies of Washington. Apparently, the Syrians have agreed to have these individuals spend more and more time in other Arab countries and less in Syria, to the point where they are only really making brief visits to Syria. According to Syrian sources, the State Department seemed to go along with this, at least until the shift in U.S. policy by February 2005 following the Hariri assassination.

24 Interview with author, Damascus, May 3, 2005.

25. A *New York Times* article, commenting on the Syrian–Iraqi border situation, stated that "Western diplomats characterize insurgents who pass through here as a contributing but not essential factor to the resistance in Iraq. They also dismiss accusations about serious weaponry flowing across or Iraq's deposed Baathist leadership huddling here." The article quotes a senior Western diplomat as saying, "I don't see the insurgency being masterminded from Syria." *NYT*, October 26, 2004.

26. *ISS Strategic Comments*, vol. x, issue 7, September 2004.

27. Ibid.

28. *Financial Times*, July 27, 2004.

29. Ibid.

30. AP Report, *San Antonio Express-News*, October 27, 2004.

31. *www.haaretz.com*, September 30, 2004.

32. Ibid.

33. Ibid.

34. For example, while not a ringing endorsement, Lt. General Lance Smith, deputy commander of the U.S. Central Command, stated that Syria was now providing more cooperation than in the past. *Financial Times*, November 19, 2004.

35. *Baltimore Sun*, May 14, 2004.

36. Author's interview with Ambassador Theodore (Ted) Kattouf, October 26, 2004. According to former CIA Syrian expert Martha Kessler, Syria offered to station U.S. forces in the country before the invasion of Iraq in March 2003, an offer that was rebuffed.

37. SANA, October 18, 2002, *www.sana.org/english/reports/Assad-Reuters18–10–02/president_assad.htm*.

38. Interview with the author, July 27, 2004.

39. Ibid.

40. *Financial Times*, November 24, 2004.

41. *www.msnbc.msn.com/1d/6674025/print/1/displaymode/1098/*, December 8, 2004.

42. *Financial Times*, December 18, 2004.

43. *New York Times*, January 5, 2005.

44. In a television interview in Egypt following his visit with Bashar, Armitage, in my opinion, reinforced the lack of hard U.S. evidence:

> Mr. Elsetouchi (interviewer): But what the Syrians are saying is that you don't have enough evidence or you don't provide them with accurate information. So what's your response?
> Armitage: We had that discussion. In some cases, they're right. In some cases, we don't have exact locations. But our view is that they know these people, they've known them from the previous regime, and with a good effort, they can find them. And we're counting on Syria to help bring these fellows to justice and to stop their activities.
> Elsetouchi: Is what you're saying now is that they know where they are and they know them, but they allow them to operate from Syria?
> Armitage: Yes. I don't know that they know where each and every one are, but in general, they know where the foreign regime elements are, and they have to crack down on them. We're expecting them to do this and we're counting on them to do this, and we'll see if they do. (Quoted in *www.syriacomment.com*, January 12, 2005.)

45. As late as May 2005, U.S. pressure on Syria continued. In the immediate aftermath of Operation Matador, a U.S. military campaign in the western portion of the al-Anbar province in Iraq along the Syria border, Secretary of State Rice stated upon a visit to Baghdad that, "We're going to go back and look again at what the neighbors can do—

particularly the Syrians—to stop support for these foreign terrorists who we believe are gathering on Syrian soil and coming across. Their unwillingness to deal with the crossings of their border into Iraq is frustrating the will of the Iraqi people and killing innocent Iraqis. The Syrians have managed to get themselves in a situation of standing in the way of the progress of people in the Middle East and I would think that wouldn't be a very comfortable place for a Syrian regime to be." *www.yahoo.com*, May 16, 2005.

46. *New York Times*, January 5, 2005.
47. *www.msnbc.msn.com/1d/6674025/print/1/displaymode/1098/*, December 8, 2004.
48. *Financial Times*, December 18, 2004.
49. *Financial Times*, December 8, 2004.
50. Quoted from a report by Joshua Landis in Damascus, *www.syriacomment.com*, January 12, 2005.
51. *www.haaretz.com*, January 24, 2005.
52. *Financial Times*, November 24, 2004.
53. *Washington Post*, June 27, 2005.

Chapter 9

1. This story was recounted to me by Dr. Ghias Barakat, May 25, 2004.
2. Interview with the author, Damascus, May 3, 2005.
3. Ammar Abdulhamid, "Syria—the Regime That Couldn't," *Financial Times*, October 8, 2004.
4. Policy Forum hosted by the Saban Center for Middle East Policy, "The Internal Dynamics of Syrian Politics," Ammar Abdulhamid, July 20, 2004, *www.brook.edu/fp/saban/events/abdulhamid20040720.htm*. Author's interview with Ammar Abdulhamid, Washington, DC, October 1, 2004.
5. My thanks to Ammar Abdulhamid for providing me with this term. Regarding the anachronistic Syrian mindset, one high-level Syrian official recounted the following observation to me:

> Regarding our elections, when I came back to Syria [after having spent some time in the West] I saw our election process for the first time and I was amazed. We have citizens not asking what your views or policies are, they are not asking anything of the candidates, but they are just giving their vote either "because he is a religious leader or a businessman and he has been able to give me 'x' amount of money," or "because I have been told to do it because that's what my mother did or my father did." They are not voting on judgment. On the other side you have people running for parliament who are not saying what their policies are or what their stances are because nobody is asking. We want democracy but we need to know what it means. It's not just voting, it is knowing where your vote went and what it does and that you are putting someone in a position and you have to answer to me. And that sense does not yet exist. I saw it [lack of political sense] in the street when people were gathering around candidates, and it was like a social gathering; I was amazed, really amazed, and it shows how far we need to go to reach some sort of democracy.

Interview with the author, Damascus, May–June 2004.
6. Interview with the author, Damascus, May 3, 2005.
7. *Emerging Syria 2005* (London: Oxford Business Group, 2005), p. 14.
8. Interview with the author, Damascus, May 3, 2005.
9. Interview with the author, Washington, DC, October 1, 2004. Ammar comments that countries such as Jordan and Morocco have fared better than Syria, because since they are monarchies, the elite knew that their own children would be the next generation of

leaders, so they sent them to the top universities in Europe and in the United States for education and training. Again, even though Bashar was studying in the West per se, he was only in London in a highly specific capacity for about a year and a half.

10. The report also found two other "deficits" to be severely hampering development in the Arab world: freedom and womanpower, the latter of which Syria scores fairly high on when compared with other Arab states, and on the former it scores fairly low.

11. SANA, October 18, 2002, *www.sana.org/english/reports/Assad-Reuters18–10–02/president_ assad.htm.*

12. *Haaretz,* May 4, 2003.

13. *Washington Post,* May 12, 2003.

14. Interview with the author, May 26, 2004.

15. The text of the document was translated verbally to me by Dr. Ghias Barakat. I saw portions of the document in Arabic and could see that his translations, at least on those items, were indeed accurate.

16. *Syria Report,* October 12, 2004, *www.syria-report.com/various_news/news328.htm.* The number of researchers per million people in the period 1990–2001 in Syria was 29, whereas in Egypt it was 493, Iran 590, and Jordan 1,948. The UN Human Development Report Index ranks Syria at 106 in overall development for 2003 out of 177 countries, which is a four-place improvement from the previous year. By comparison, Lebanon ranked 80, Jordan 90, and Egypt 120.

17. Ghias, who received his Ph.D. from the University of Texas, added that the current texts at the universities in Syria are in many cases really only at the high-school level compared to those at institutions in the West.

18. *Washington Post,* September 25, 2004.

19. The universities in Damascus and Aleppo each have upwards of sixty thousand to eighty thousand students, while al-Baath University, the smallest of the four, has approximately forty thousand students. An example of how this affects educational efficiency can be seen in the case of President Bashar's translator, Dr. Nayef al-Yasin, who is also a professor of English literature at the University of Damascus. He alone has over one thousand students in each of his classes, and by decree the examinations were required to be multiple-choice because the individual professors obviously did not have enough time to grade one thousand essay exams periodically; unfortunately, multiple-choice exams are not conducive to learning English literature. The universities are attempting to change this decree, although they still do not know how to deal with the overwhelming number of students.

20. *www.Asiaobserver.com/Burma/Burma-background-health.htm.*

21. My thanks to my friend and colleague Dr. Yasser Hourieh, president of al-Baath University, for giving me a thorough guided tour of the campus. In fact, the Ministry of Tourism is making efficient use of many of these English language students, having them translate tour guides into English as part of their curriculum.

22. Author's Interview with Dr. Ghias Barakat, Damascus, May 25, 2004.

23. Many students like the military training for its own sake—who doesn't want to learn how to fire a gun?! But, more importantly, it exempts them from six months of mandatory military training. The regime wants to limit the military training for students to the summer months only and not intertwine it with normal university operations.

24. Joshua Landis, "What Does the New Syrian Cabinet Portend?" *Syria Comment,* October 5, 2004.

25. *Financial Times,* May 11, 2004.

26. Samir al-Taqi, in ibid.

27. Abd al-Razzak Eid, in ibid. Also, see an excellent article by Scott Wilson of the *Washington Post,* "Religious Surge Alarms Secular Syrians," *www.washingtonpost.com,* January 23, 2005. Wilson describes how even Syrian Vice President Abd al-Halim Khaddam suggested that Arab nationalist parties, presumably including the Baath

party, should "harness Islamic beliefs" to improve their political standing with the population. He—and this line of thought—was severely criticized by Syrian intellectuals who do not want the government to dilute the secular nature of the state simply for political cover.

28. Author's interview with Bashar, May 27, 2004.

29. For a more detailed treatment, see David W. Lesch, "History and Political Culture in Syria: Obstacles to Integration in the Global Economy After the Gulf War," in Moshe Maoz, Joseph Ginat, and Onn Winckler (eds.), *Modern Syria: From Ottoman Rule to Pivotal Role in the Middle East* (Brighton: Sussex Academic Press, 1999), pp. 57–78.

30. For a discussion of the Syrian economy during this period, see Roger Owen, *The Middle East in the World Economy 1800–1914* (New York: Methuen, 1981), pp. 76–82, 153–179, and 244–272.

31. Owen, p. 293.

32. For more on this transition, see the classic work by Philip S. Khoury, *Syria and the French Mandate: The Politics of Arab Nationalism, 1920–1945* (Princeton: Princeton University Press, 1987). Indeed, it was worse under the French because of the lack of resources that the French had in the country (as compared with the Ottomans) to essentially buy political loyalty; the difference in cultural attitudes and practices from the Ottomans; and the French policy of divide and rule imported from the quite separate colonial experience of Morocco.

33. Charles Issawi, *The Economic History of the Middle East 1800–1914* (Chicago: University of Chicago Press, 1966), p. 505.

34. On this transformation, see Hanna Batatu, "Some Observations on the Social Roots of Syria's Ruling Military Group and the Causes of its Dominance," *Middle East Journal*, vol. xxxv (Summer 1981), pp. 331–344.

35. Steven Heydemann, "The Political Logic of Economic Rationality: Selective Liberalization in Syria," in Henri Barkey (ed.), *The Politics of Economic Reform in the Middle East* (New York: St Martin's Press, 1992), pp. 11–39.

36. Volker Perthes, *The Political Economy of Syria under Asad* (London: I. B. Tauris, 1995), p. 254. This is an outstanding study of Syria's political economy during the reign of Hafiz al-Asad.

37. Ibid.

38. Ghassan Salame, *al-Mujtama wa al-Dawla fi al-Mashriq al-Arabi* [Society and State in the Arab East] (Beirut, 1987), p. 206 (as quoted in Perthes, p. 254).

39. Perthes, p. 208.

40. Raymond A. Hinnebusch, "Syria," in Tim Niblock and Emma Murphy (eds.), *Economic and Political Liberalization in the Middle East* (London: British Academic Press, 1993), p. 194. As Hinnebusch explains, if a company becomes too large, it will be noticed by the government, which means that it could become subject to the arbitrary crackdowns against black market activities in foreign currency and goods in which virtually all Syrian companies engage (although there's less of the former activity, since the Syrian pound has been "stabilized" at about fifty pounds to the dollar since the mid-1990s). The flip side of this is that in order to avoid arbitrary crackdowns, government officials must be paid off, and a company then becomes subject to the whim of others. With regard to the strong labor union (the General Federation of Trade Unions, or GFTU), one of the significant hallmarks of the Baath party, so many benefits and services need to be paid according to union strictures that many entrepreneurs cannot afford to hire more than ten workers or so, which puts downward pressure on the size of private sector businesses and inhibits the formation of a large-scale manufacturing sector.

41. As president of Middle East International Business Associates, Inc., a consulting company I formed in the mid-1990s to facilitate business opportunities for American and European corporations in the Arab world, I experienced these things first hand on numerous occasions when bringing these companies, many of whom were Fortune

500 corporations, into Syria. For one example of just such an encounter, see David W. Lesch, "Is Syria Ready for Peace? Obstacles to Integration in the Global Economy," *Middle East Policy*, vol. vi, no. 3 (February 1999), pp. 93–111.

42. Miyoko Kuroda, "Economic Liberalization and the Suq in Syria," in Niblock and Murphy, pp. 204–205.
43. Hinnebusch, p. 178.
44. Rodney Wilson, *Economic Development in the Middle East* (London: Routledge, 1995), p. 49.
45. Interview with the author, May 27, 2004.
46. Ibid.
47. Ibid. I can personally attest to the progress that has been made in Syria over the past four years. In the late 1990s my company led a noted U.S. hotel group to Syria to investigate the possibility of building a chain of mid-level hotels. The Ministry of Tourism in Damascus was woefully unprepared in terms of providing us with the data we needed to make an informed decision, such as the numbers and specific characteristics of tourists that visit Syria or any sense of a five-year plan of development, etc. Frankly, it was embarrassing. Upon a recent visit to Syria, whereupon I met with the current Minister of Tourism, Dr. Saadallah Agha al-Kalaa (who was in the Syrian Computer Society with Bashar), the necessary information was at his fingertips, in an up-to-date database. He also, in accordance with Bashar's instructions in all the ministries, has restructured the ministry, creating a department specifically for training personnel in the necessary skills, such as engineering, construction, marketing, promotion, planning, and quality control, and he has brought in a number of professors from universities to train his staff. He has even begun to send tour guides for theatrical training and to take courses in history, politics, and economics, for they must not only be knowledgeable about the country, they must also entertain.
48. One high-level Syrian official gave me the following example:

> Today, if a doorman who has the keys to the building does not show up for work, it is quite likely the building will not be opened. Why? Because he took the keys home with him. Because he does not see the whole process, and that's why it is so difficult to reform here. It is not institutions, it is built on people, and unfortunately that's why you find such an older generation in the ministries because they are the only people who know how to do things—in the old way. And how do they do it—by experience. And sometimes maybe he even just stamps a passport, but he knows where to stamp it and when to stamp it, but this is information he is not giving anyone else because this is not how he was taught. We need to change that. There needs to be ownership of the institutions. It is a very difficult mindset to change.

Interview with the author, Damascus, May–June 2004.
49. Interview with the author, Washington, DC, July 27, 2004.
50. Interview with the author, Damascus, June 1, 2004. I can attest to at least one example of this personally. My escort from the office of protocol in the foreign ministry was an extremely sharp and capable young man, Adeeb, who spoke several languages and had traveled frequently with President Bashar outside the country. I visited Adeeb's wonderful family at their very humble abode in the city of Homs. He was definitely not from the privileged elite, the kind that usually staffed such high-profile positions. He had taken and obviously scored high on written exams and had several interviews at the foreign ministry before he was chosen and offered the position.
51. Interview with the author, May 26, 2004.
52. MEMRI, August 30, 2004. The interview appeared in the Syrian weekly *Abyadh wa Aswad* [Black and White], whose editor is the son of Syrian Minister of Defense Hassan Turkmani.

53. *Washington Post,* September 25, 2004.
54. Ibid.
55. Ibid.
56. Quoted in ibid.
57. Ammar Abdulhamid, "Syria: De-Baathification from the Top?" The author personally e-mailed this essay to me. It appears on the website of his organization, The Thawra [revolution] Project: *www.thawraproject.com.*
58. Rami G. Khouri, "Reform in Syria Can Reform the Entire Middle East," *Jordan Times,* August 6, 2003.
59. Ibid.
60. MEMRI, August 30, 2004.
61. See Anders Aslund, "Putin's Quest for Power is Harming Russia," *Financial Times,* August 24, 2004.
62. Interview with the author, May 26, 2004. In response to a question regarding privatization, Bashar said,

> We have seen prior experience in privatization in Egypt, and I studied this before I became president, and I also discussed this with a Japanese official because they had this experience in the past as well. I asked him [the Japanese official] how many years did the plan take, and he told me ten years [for this one particular privatization project]. I asked him what was the population at the beginning, and he said fifty million, and then I asked him what was the population at the end [of the ten year period], and he said it was the same number. But each year we have two to three hundred thousand new Syrians coming into the job market. They need jobs, but we do not have jobs, so I must first think about these two to three hundred thousand before I think about getting rid of some jobs through privatization. I have two problems, which is different from the experience you have in the West: the biggest problem is our [population-] growth rate, which is still high—it is better than before, but it is still high; then you need to solve the problem of the private and public sectors before talking about privatization.

63. *Jordan Times,* February 22, 2004.
64. Some sources even place per capita income at the lower figure of $1,000 and the growth rate at less than 3 percent. *Haaretz,* May 4, 2003; *www.arabdatanet.com* (the per capita estimate obtained from *The Economist* Foreign Intelligence Unit Country Report 2003); also see U.S. Department of State "Background Note" on Syria, August 2004, *www.state.gov/r/pa/ei/bgn/3580.htm.* The average per capita GDP in the Middle East and North Africa is $2,210. It is important to note, however, that the purchasing power parity (PPP) GDP per capita in Syria is estimated at $3,300 (2004 CIA World Factbook—Syria, *www.cia.gov/cia/publications/factbook/print/sy.html*). The PPP method involves the use of standardized international dollar price weights, which are applied to the final quantities of goods and services produced by a given country, i.e. its gross domestic product (GDP). This is the most accurate and true method of comparing GDPs. By comparison, the CIA World Factbook at PPP lists the estimated 2003 per capita GDP for the following countries: United States, $37,800 (second highest on the list after Luxemborg); Israel, $19,700; United Arab Emirates, $23,200 (the highest in the Arab world); Saudi Arabia, $11,800; Lebanon, $4,800; and Jordan, $4,300.
65. *www.baltimoresun.com/news/nationworld/balte.syria14may14,0,3564491.story?col.htm,* May 14, 2004.
66. Forbes Global, *www.forbes.com/forbesglobal/00/1002/03119084a/htm,* September 22, 2000.
67. 2003 Global Corruption Report, "Middle East and North Africa," p. 205.

68. Ibid., p. 212.
69. In response to my asking whether he thought he had the necessary support around him to implement his vision, Bashar said,

> That changes every day. It depends on the mood, depends on the vision of the people. The mood changes every day, every hour since I took over. I don't think people are with or against the president. I think they are with or against a decision or an issue. I cannot tell if I am popular or not, but my relations with the people are good, and the best indication is that I think they trust me. Over the last few years we say we are going to do this and do that but we couldn't, and some understand that we have objectives for subjective reasons—some understand this, and some do not.

Interview with the author, Damascus, May 26, 2004.
70. Interview with the author, Damascus, June 3, 2004.
71. *Jordan Times*, February 22, 2004.
72. BBC News, May 12, 2004, *http://news.bbc.co.uk/go/pr/fr//2/hi/middle_east/3708957.stm*.
73. *Financial Times*, May 28, 2004.
74. *Financial Times*, October 20, 2004.
75. *Washington Post*, May 18, 2005.
76. Interview with the author, Damascus, May 3, 2005.
77. *New York Times*, May 21, 2005. Commenting on the prevalence of authoritarian regimes in the Arab world, Jon Alterman stated that, "Governments monopolise the vast ground between the liberal left and religious right, leaving only the radical fringes out of their grasp." Jon Alterman, "Middle East Freedom Needs a True Shift to the Centre," *Financial Times*, March 29, 2005.

Chapter 10

1. The real "palace" is the ornate "People's Palace" which was built in the late 1980s and sits atop a hill overlooking Damascus. My second meeting with Bashar took place here. The winding road leading up to the palace is blocked off to all but official traffic. As I approached the finely manicured grounds in front of the palace and, even more so, when I entered the gargantuan entrance hallway periodically stepped toward the president's meeting room, all I could think of was the palace that housed the Wizard of Oz. It was a magnificent site, and I had a very difficult time maintaining a sense of decorum. Neither Hafiz al-Asad nor his son actually live in the palace—it was and is much too ostentatious for their tastes; however, it *is* where the president frequently holds special meetings with foreign guests.
2. Hamilton A. R. Gibb, "The Achievement of Saladin," in his *Studies on the Civilization of Islam* (Princeton: Princeton University Press, 1982), p. 99.
3. Interview with the author, London, November 12, 2004.
4. Interestingly, at the same time, Ankara has cooled what had been a solid strategic relationship with Israel. Turkey has publicly reprimanded Israeli actions in the Occupied Territories and has offered to mediate between Syria and Israel. In addition, Turkey refused to allow U.S. troops transit rights through its territory in the U.S.-led invasion of Iraq in 2003, a stance that endeared itself to Syrians. Since the Adana accord in 1998, the volume of trade between Syria and Turkey has doubled, now totaling some $1 billion annually, about 10 percent of all Syrian trade. *Emerging Syria 2005* (London: Oxford Business Group, 2005), p. 26.
5. AP report, *San Antonio Express-News*, November 25, 2004. The then new minister of information in Syria, Mehdi Dakhlallah, elaborated to the press that "Syria's known,

declared and permanent position is that Syria is ready to resume negotiations from the point they broke off [in 2000]." The Israeli foreign ministry response to these remarks was that they were "nothing new. The problem is not with Syrian words, it's Syrian activity. If Syria wants to be a partner in peace, we need to see a change in Syrian behavior. You can't on the one hand say you're interested in peace and at the same time have a partnership with a group like Hezbollah, which is antithetical to peace." Ibid.

6. Major General Ghazi al-Kanaan, the long-time head of Syrian intelligence in Lebanon, was appointed to the post of minister of the interior in a move that many observers suggest is a sign of Damascus returning to a more pragmatic foreign policy in the wake of the Emile Lahoud fiasco. Kanaan was given the post at the age of sixty-two, only months away from his mandatory military retirement age (*Jordan Times*, October 5, 2004). In addition, having waded through the complex, intricate politics of Lebanon for years, Kanaan seems to be well prepared to deal with opposition groups in Syria in a much more sophisticated fashion than did the typical *mukhabarat* intelligence heads during the Hafiz al-Asad era. In other words, some suggest that Kanaan will be able to distinguish between real threats to the regime and the civil society activists and reformers who would like to work with the regime to bring about change. Also, Kanaan apparently has had good relations with American officials, especially in the intelligence community, and he visited Washington on at least one occasion in February 1992. This may have been at the time a prelude to improving intelligence cooperation with the United States as well as coordinating at the intelligence and military levels joint efforts to better control the Iraq–Syria border. See Joshua Landis, "What Does the New Syrian Cabinet Portend?" *Syria Comment*, October 5, 2004, *www.syriacomment.com*. In addition to these two posts (minister of the interior and minister of information), the ministers of economy and trade, industry, health, justice, social affairs and labor, and religious endowments were changed.

7. Landis, "What Does the New Syrian Cabinet Portend?"

8. While the portraits are certainly much less present than they used to be, you still find a number of them outside government facilities as you drive around the country, a remnant of the outpouring of sentiment expressed through the hanging of these portraits everywhere—from being plastered on car windows to being displayed on walls of buildings—following the death of Basil in 1994.

9. Although it is interesting that in early December 2004 there was a peaceful demonstration of about a thousand people in Cairo holding up signs and wearing labels saying in Arabic, "enough." They were demonstrating against Egyptian President Husni Mubarak running for a fifth term as well as his son Gamal succeeding him. A "republican monarchy" may not yet be in store for Egypt or elsewhere in the Arab world, especially if there is a perception that Bashar "failed" in Syria.

10. *www.cnn.com/2000/WORLD/meast/06/12/mideast.sons.ap/index.html*, June 12, 2000.

11. Author's interview with Bashar, Damascus, May 26, 2004.

12. Interview with the author, Damascus, June 1, 2004.

13. A contention shared by several other people who knew both father and son.

14. Emphasizing this point, she mentioned that one time she and some friends drove out to Connecticut, and as they were leaving New York City they saw a sign saying "Welcome to the USA"—she immediately stopped, got out of the car, and had one of her friends take a picture of her with the sign!

15. Syrian Prime Minister Muhammad Naji Otri told me that other government ministers have taken notice of Bashar's more low-key appearance and style and are starting to do the same thing, many shedding themselves of the large entourage of bodyguards typically seen in the past accompanying the elite crowd. And some are even emulating Bashar's encouragement to have more direct contact with the Syrian people, thus going on their own sudden jaunts to cafes and restaurants. Interview with the author, Damascus, May 24, 2004.

16. Or as Syrian scholar Sami Moubayed adroitly wrote,

> The West does not understand Syria and Syria shows little effort towards expressing itself and portraying its correct image. For years, the Syrians have believed that they have a mission and a cause, and those who understand it are welcome to do so, while those who don't can live in their ignorance. For a long time public relations in Syria was lacking.

Sami Moubayed, "Dr. Jekyll and Mr. Hyde," *Perihelion Working Papers*, January 2003, *www.erpic.org/perihelion/wps/syria.htm*.

17. Interviews with the author, Damascus, May 26 and May 31, 2004.
18. Interview with the author, May 31, 2004.
19. Ibid.
20. Ibid.
21. *Financial Times*, March 2, 2005.
22. For an intelligent argument by a participant observer on why the United States and Britain were correct in overthrowing Musaddiq, see Sir Sam Falle, "The Musaddiq Era in Iran, 1951–1953: A Contemporary Diplomat's View," in David W. Lesch (ed.), *The Middle East and the United States: A Historical and Political Reassessment*, 3rd edition (Boulder, CO: Westview Press, 2003), pp. 78–86.
23. Thomas L. Friedman, "The Tipping Points," *New York Times*, February 27, 2005. As one Arab commentator wrote, "This is no longer a question of defining Syria's regional role by the old power politics. It is one of recreating from the inside outwards a Syrian political society and economy that can not only survive the geopolitical maelstrom around it, but actively and positively contribute to a restructuring of its neighborhood." Ghayth Armanazi, "Europe Can Help Syria Go Forward," *Financial Times*, April 19, 2005.
24. *Time*, vol. clv, no. 25 (June 19, 2000), p. 21.

Select Biblography

Antoun, Richard T. and Donald Quataert, eds. *Syria: Society, Culture, and Polity*. Albany: State University of New York Press, 1991.

Barkey, Henri, ed. *The Politics of Economic Reform in the Middle East*. New York: St. Martin's Press, 1992.

Batatu, Hanna. *Syria's Peasantry, the Descendants of Its Lesser Rural Notables, and Their Politics*. Princeton: Princeton University Press, 1999.

Clawson, Patrick. *Unaffordable Ambitions: Syria's Military Buildup and Economic Crisis*. Washington, DC: The Washington Institute for Near East Policy, 1989.

Cordesman, Anthony H. *Syria and Weapons of Mass Destruction*. Washington, DC: Center for Strategic and International Studies, 2000.

Devlin, John F. *The Ba`th Party: A History from Its Origins to 1966*. Stanford: Hoover Institution Press, 1976.

Devlin, John F. *Syria: Modern State in an Ancient Land*. London: C. Helm, 1983.

Drysdale, Alasdair and Raymond A. Hinnebusch. *Syria and the Middle East Peace Process*. New York: Council on Foreign Relations Press, 1992.

Ehteshami, Anoushiravan and Raymond A. Hinnebusch. *Syria and Iran*. London: Routledge, 1997.

Freedman, Robert O., ed. *The Middle East Enters the Twenty-first Century*. Gainesville: University Press of Florida, 2002.

Freedman, Robert O. *Soviet Foreign Policy Toward the Middle East Since 1970*. New York: Praeger, 1982.

Gelvin, James L. *Divided Loyalties: Nationalism and Mass Politics in Syria at the Close of Empire*. Berkeley: University of California Press, 1999.

George, Alan. *Syria: Neither Bread nor Freedom*. London: Zed Books, 2003.

Golan, Galia. *Yom Kippur and After*. Cambridge: Cambridge University Press, 1977.

Hannah, John P. *At Arms Length: Soviet-Syrian Relations in the Gorbachev Era*. Washington, DC: The Washington Institute for Near East Policy, 1989.

Harik, Judith Palmer. *Hezbollah: The Changing Face of Terrorism*. London: I. B. Tauris, 2004.

Hinnebusch, Raymond A. *Authoritarian Power and State Formation in Ba`thist Syria: Army, Party, and Peasant*. Boulder: Westview Press, 1990.

Hinnebusch, Raymond A. *Syria: Revolution from Above*. London: Routledge, 2001.

Hopwood, Derek. *Syria, 1945–1986: Politics and Society*. London: Unwin Hyman, 1988.

Kerr, Malcolm H. *The Arab Cold War: Gamal `Abd al-Nasir and His Rivals, 1958–1970*. London: Oxford University Press, 1971.

Khalidi, Walid. *Conflict and Violence in Lebanon: Confrontation in the Middle East*. Cambridge: Harvard University Center for International Affairs, 1984.

Khoury, Philip S. *Syria and the French Mandate: The Politics of Arab Nationalism, 1920–1945*. Princeton: Princeton University Press, 1987.

Kienle, Eberhard, ed. *Contemporary Syria: Liberalization between Cold War and Cold Peace.* London: British Academic Press, 1994.

Lesch, David W., ed. *The Middle East and the United States: A Historical and Political Reassessment,* 3rd edition. Boulder: Westview Press, 2003.

Lesch, David W. *Syria and the United States: Eisenhower's Cold War in the Middle East.* Boulder: Westview Press, 1992.

Lesch, David W. *1979: The Year That Shaped the Modern Middle East.* Boulder: Westview Press, 2001.

Leverett, Flynt. *Inheriting Syria: Bashar's Trial By Fire.* Washington, DC: Brookings Institution Press, 2005.

Malik, Habib C. *Between Damascus and Jerusalem: Lebanon and Middle East Peace.* Washington, DC: The Washington Institute for Near East Policy, 2000.

Maoz, Moshe. *Asad, the Sphinx of Damascus: A Political Biography.* London: Grove/Atlantic, 1990.

Maoz, Moshe. *Syria and Israel: From War to Peacemaking.* Oxford: Oxford University Press, 1995.

Maoz, Moshe, Joseph Ginat, and Onn Winckler, eds. *Modern Syria: From Ottoman Rule to Pivotal Role in the Middle East.* Brighton: Sussex Academic Press, 1999.

Muslih, Muhammad. *Golan: The Road to Occupation.* Washington, DC: Institute for Palestine Studies, 2000.

Niblock, Timothy and Emma Murphy, eds. *Economic and Political Liberalization in the Middle East.* London: British Academic Press, 1993.

Owen, Roger. *The Middle East in the World Economy 1800–1914.* New York: Methuen, 1981.

Perthes, Volker. *The Political Economy of Syria under Asad.* Oxford: I. B. Tauris, 1995.

Pipes, Daniel. *Greater Syria: The History of an Ambition.* Oxford: Oxford University Press, 1992.

Rabinovitch, Itamar. *The Brink of Peace.* Princeton: Princeton University Press, 1998.

Rabinovitch, Itamar. *Syria Under the Ba`th 1963–1966: The Army Party Symbiosis.* Tel Aviv: The Shiloah Center for Middle Eastern and African Studies, 1972.

Rabinovitch, Itamar. *The War for Lebanon: 1970–1985.* Ithaca: Cornell University Press, 1985.

Rogan, Eugene L. and Avi Shlaim, eds. *The War for Palestine: Rewriting the History of 1948.* Cambridge: Cambridge University Press, 2001.

Ross, Dennis. *The Missing Peace: The Inside Story of the Fight for Middle East Peace.* New York: Farrar, Straus, and Giroux, 2004.

Safran, Nadav. *Israel, the Embattled Ally.* Cambridge, MA: Harvard University Press, 1982.

Salibi, Kamal. *A House of Many Mansions: The History of Lebanon Reconsidered.* Berkeley: University of California Press, 1988.

Savir, Uri. *The Process: 1,100 Days That Changed the Middle East.* New York: Random House, 1998.

Seale, Patrick. *Asad of Syria: The Struggle for the Middle East.* London: I. B. Tauris, 1988.

Seale, Patrick. *The Struggle for Syria: A Study of Post-War Arab Politics 1945–1958.* New Haven: Yale University Press, 1986.

Smith, Charles D. *Palestine and the Arab-Israeli Conflict,* 5th edition. New York: Bedford/St. Martin's Press, 2004.

Tanter, Raymond. *Rogue Regimes: Terrorism and Proliferation.* New York: Palgrave Macmillan, 1999.

Torrey, Gordon H. *Syrian Politics and the Military 1945–1958.* Columbus: Ohio State University Press, 1964.

Van Dam, Nikolaos. *The Struggle for Power in Syria: Politics and Society under Asad and the Ba`th Party.* London: I. B. Tauris, 1996.

Van Dam, Nikolaos. *The Struggle for Power in Syria: Sectarianism, Regionalism and Tribalism in Politics, 1961–1978.* New York: St. Martin's Press, 1979.

Wedeen, Lisa. *Ambiguities of Domination: Politics, Rhetoric, and Symbols in Contemporary Syria.* Chicago: University of Chicago Press, 1999.

Wilson, Rodney. *Economic Development in the Middle East.* London: Routledge, 1995.

Winckler, Onn. *Demographic Developments and Population Policies in Ba`thist Syria.* Brighton: Sussex Academic Press, 1999.

Zisser, Eyal. *Asad's Legacy: Syria in Transition.* New York: New York University Press, 2001.

Index

Note: Arabic names with the prefix al- are indexed under the part of the name following al-. The index follows the author's transliteration style as explained in the note on page xiii.